FIELDING'S

The Great Sights of Europe

1 9 9 3

FIELDING'S ALPINE EUROPE 1993
FIELDING'S AUSTRALIA 1993
FIELDING'S BENELUX 1993
FIELDING'S BERMUDA AND THE BAHAMAS 1993
FIELDING'S BRAZIL 1993
FIELDING'S BRITAIN 1993
FIELDING'S BUDGET EUROPE 1993
FIELDING'S CARIBBEAN 1993
FIELDING'S EUROPE 1993
FIELDING'S FRANCE 1993
FIELDING'S HAWAII 1993
FIELDING'S ITALY 1993
FIELDING'S MEXICO 1993
FIELDING'S NEW ZEALAND 1993
FIELDING'S PEOPLE'S REPUBLIC OF CHINA 1993
FIELDING'S SCANDINAVIA 1993
FIELDING'S SELECTIVE SHOPPING GUIDE TO EUROPE 1993

FIELDING'S THE GREAT SIGHTS OF EUROPE
FIELDING'S WORLDWIDE CRUISES 6th revised edition
FIELDING'S ALASKA AND THE YUKON
FIELDING'S BUDGET ASIA Southeast Asia and the Far East
FIELDING'S CALIFORNIA
FIELDING'S FAMILY VACATIONS USA
FIELDING'S FAR EAST 2nd revised edition
FIELDING'S HAVENS AND HIDEAWAYS USA
FIELDING'S LEWIS AND CLARK TRAIL
FIELDING'S LITERARY AFRICA
FIELDING'S SPANISH TRAILS IN THE SOUTHWEST
FIELDING'S TRAVELER'S MEDICAL COMPANION

FIELDING'S

The Great Sights of Europe

① ⑨ ⑨ ③

by
PATRICIA **FOULKE**
and
ROBERT **FOULKE**

FIELDING TRAVEL BOOKS

℅ WILLIAM MORROW & COMPANY, INC.
1350 Avenue of Americas, New York, N.Y. 10019

ISBN: 0-688-09168-7

Printed in the United States of America
First Edition
1 2 3 4 5 6 7 8 9 10

Text design by Marsha Cohen/Parallelogram
All maps by Mark Stein Studios

CONTENTS

MAPS

INTRODUCTION

Why do you want to go to Europe? In an era of frequent travel for business or pleasure, when reaching most parts of Europe is remarkably fast and easy, you may answer this fundamental question rather casually. Perhaps you recall a teacher or friend who whetted your curiosity about a particular city or country, and you may have clipped articles from travel sections or watched documentaries on TV to broaden that interest. But, for all of us, at the heart of the urge to travel lies a fundamental desire for the freedom to move about the world as we choose, to explore the strange, the remote, and the ancient aspects of civilization, to learn more about past and present customs and attitudes of other peoples. The driving force is curiosity more than simple pleasure, which one can find easily enough at home.

Perhaps only those who have been deprived of the freedom to travel—two generations of East Europeans—can fully appreciate how central it is to fullness of living. But, fortunately, European borders are no longer the barriers they were just a few years ago. In Eastern Europe, particularly, elaborate border stations have been abandoned, bypassed, and sometimes obliterated as symbols of oppression. Fifty years of blockage has been removed from the arteries of old Europe, restoring freedom of movement to a continent racked by hot and cold wars. The rejoined halves of Berlin, now separated only by a patch of rubble rather than a wall, represent the new freedom to travel most clearly, but a host of other magnificent and historically important cities—Budapest, Prague, and Cracow among them—are more open to exploration than they have been since the early decades of this century. In the reopened eastern half of Europe you no longer need to join an officially sponsored tour or stick to a limited itinerary. As an independent traveler, you can manage your use of time and space less mechanically, even though you go to many of the same places and share many of the same experiences.

Now, for the first time in two generations, you can go where you will throughout Europe. Wherever you may be, you can succumb to the fascination of place and absorb sensations: listen to church bells or the human sounds of a village, the songs of strange birds, the cacophony of a market square, the voices of a choir reverberating in the nave of a cathedral, the cries of children playing familiar nursery-rhyme games in a foreign language; smell the incredible fishiness of an Italian harbor town, the perfume of wild flowers growing in a Swiss meadow, the fragrance of an English herb garden, the aroma of moussaka wafting from Greek tavernas, or the pine scents of a Bavarian forest. You may want

1

to taste many wonderful culinary treats; lick an Italian gelato on a hot day, try some "real ale" in Britain, or savor cloudberries in Scandinavia. Feel the soft, fine sand on a Mediterranean beach, the comfort of a light quilt or "puff" on a cold night, the roughness of cobblestones under your feet, the spray blown from the cold North Sea on your face, and the warmth of a pub fire. For seeing, you can choose from an immense variety of landscape and townscape in Europe—from Norwegian fjords to Riviera beaches, from the valley of the Loire to the Alps, from Greek islands to sprawling London—with the visual pleasures of scores of cathedrals, castles, and chateaux in between.

To plan a satisfying trip, you will have to be honest about your own life-style and travel expectations. Do you want to cover a lot of ground and many sights in a short time, or would you rather poke along slowly, and not miss anything? Are you set for a more rapid post-war American version of the grand tour of the Continent that was considered an essential part of the education of English gentlemen for several centuries (they usually spent several years at it), or would you prefer focusing on the customs, cuisine, and characteristics of a single region for two or three weeks? Answers to questions such as these will help you to establish the foundations for a trip—its pacing and geographical scope. You can build the superstructure of days and places upon them, deciding whether to visit three or four cities or to explore one and its environs in some detail.

Our own experience suggests that such decisions will change at various stages of life. We feel lucky to have had the opportunity to live in Europe many times over the past forty years—studying, researching, traveling, and writing. Our first trips were planned without experience but with unquenchable enthusiasm. Of course, we wanted to see and do everything! Gradually, we learned to plan reasonable days and made choices to explore some areas in depth and others as samplers. Then our children appeared, traveled, grew, and traveled some more; over the years their ages and interests encouraged us to seek a variety of experiences. Frequent travel also made us pragmatic about the effort involved; we built on lists and records from previous trips as a basis for realistic estimates of distance, cost, and time. Throughout these experiences we have learned that planning, like cooking, is a complicated art that cannot be reduced to simple recipes. Some plans need big holes in them so you can wander around, others require you to pace yourself through the marathon. Both kinds, and all variations in between, are equally valid as long as they meet your expectations.

What This Book Can Do For You

Guidebooks have many shapes and purposes, but they share a single antecedent. The original guidebooks replaced guides, who were variously well-informed, incompetent, energetic, lazy, trustworthy, and fraudulent—when they were available. With their Baedekers in hand, Victorian travelers could dispense with the troubles of obtaining and paying guides. Their guidebooks also provided a verbal map of both place and period, not only locating the principle sights of a city geographically but spinning backward in time to weave them into the continuous tapestry of human events. Temporal placements are just as important as spatial ones, and the two must be connected to form the complete picture that makes a visit memorable. Without a Beefeater at hand to make such connections, the Tower of London remains a more or less visually interesting jumble of gray stone towers, courtyards, and fortifications. A good guide—or guidebook—brings it to life again in your imagination.

This book focuses on the major cities that have built European culture in twenty-two countries because they are the most frequent destinations for travelers. Sometimes those cities are only starting points for tours in the surrounding countryside or mere way stations leading from the airport to the sea or mountains, but even travelers intent on other places usually spend some time in the city of entry or departure. We assume that our readers, unlike Victorian travelers, do not have unlimited time. The necessary compression of trips is not so recent as we sometimes imagine; in 1894, at the end of the Victorian era, Baedeker was proclaiming that one could get from London to Athens in a mere sixty hours. But you will probably have less time than you might have had setting out for Europe at the turn of the century, whether traveling on business, pleasure, or a combination of both. This book assumes that you have from a day to a week to see the sights of the city in which you find yourself. If only a day, you must choose carefully among the various suggestions listed under sightseeing, which might take three or four days at a leisurely pace. Since most travelers want to escape the city and explore the surrounding countryside, we include an inner layer of day trips to places easily reached and enjoyed from your base in the city. If you have the time, you will want to stretch farther, taking excursions to more remote but accessible places requiring a stay overnight.

Thus this book's design is like a compass rose. First we explore sightseeing within a city and then take you outside to visit sites all around the periphery. Next we also write about some excursions that you can enjoy if you are willing to move out farther and stay overnight in your destination area. Twenty-one countries offer choices you can't refuse. We have also prepared an accommodation section in the appendix—not a long list of addresses without annotation, but a short list of historical hotels, inns, castles, chateaux, and pensions with our comments based on a recent visit.

Whether you are savoring a trip in person, in memory, or as an armchair traveler, our aim is to paint visual images of places for you, to make historical figures come alive, to entertain you with stories, legends, and anecdotes, and to excite your curiosity about a chosen place.

TRAVEL TIPS....................................

No matter how much foreign travel satisfies your imagination, it also puts some demands on your time and energy. To reduce the stress and bother of making the necessary arrangements, we offer some practical suggestions in the sections that follow.

MONEY   Although getting money in Europe is easier than it used to be, there are still frustrating times when it can be downright difficult. We always cash enough money at the airport to pay for a taxi, tips, and a meal in the local destination currency. Once abroad it pays to have several sources of cash that you can count on when you need some in a hurry. Traveler's checks are safe and reliable and can be cashed almost everywhere. The bank rate is usually better than that in a hotel, but some hotels do not charge a fee as banks do. Sometimes convenience is worth more than searching for a bank in a strange place.

Credit cards provide the best bank rate on the day they are processed in the U.S., usually lower than the rate received when you change money abroad. When you use your credit card (valid with either Cirrus or Plus) in an Automatic Teller Machine abroad, you withdraw money from your bank account at home at the commercial rate, which is the best of all. Ask your local bank about a transaction fee and make sure you have a four-digit PIN number.

Some countries have strict regulations on their currency; they may prohibit removal of any leftover money when you leave the country. It is wise to keep receipts when changing money, since you may need to show them as you leave.

ACCOMMODATION   In addition to our brief, selected accommodation section in the appendix we suggest that you contact the national tourist office to ask for its accommodation list. Besides hotels, some of them have special programs for stays in farms, mountain huts, hostels, bed-and-breakfast homes, guest houses and National Trust properties. Then you can do some cross-checking with guidebooks, accommodation association books, hotel-chain lists, brochures, and friends.

Variety is the answer when you're looking for accommodation in Europe. Part of the fun of traveling is to find and savor a place to stay that is unlike your own home and location. We've enjoyed staying in bed-and-breakfasts, castles, historic inns, chateaux, monasteries, country houses, apartments, resorts, small hotels, and city hotels in convenient locations.

Should you make reservations before you go? Certainly the season has some bearing on that choice. In high season most visitors want to make all reservations in advance, at least for the first night or two. And some very popular spots are booked months in advance even during low season. Be sure to ask for a reply by airmail (sea mail can take four to six weeks) or make the reservation by fax. When a location is packed, it is comforting to have a written confirmation in your possession. You may choose to have a travel agent make the reservations for you, but many American travel agents have limited information, usually at the high end of the price range in a given area.

During the off season it is usually easy to find places, unless they are only open during the summer or other tourist season. On some of our trips we have enjoyed making a choice of where to stop late in the afternoon, nipping into several places to glimpse the interior, inquire about the rooms, and decide whether to stay; at other times this search has been a waste of time taken out of other activities we would rather have enjoyed. Some off-season travelers set up firm reservations for part of a trip, leaving holes for flexibility.

If you want to wait until you get there, the local tourist information office in the airport, train station, or town can help you find accommodation. Bed-and-breakfasts are available throughout Europe and those are found by looking for signs in front gardens or windows.

We list some sources of information for you:

The Landmark Trust, Shottesbrooke, Maidenhead, Berkshire LS6 3SW, Great Britain, tel. (0628) 82–5925; fax: (0628) 82–5417. The Landmark Trust is a charity that rescues historic buildings and renovates them for use as holiday homes. They include castles, towers, halls, cottages, chapels, mill houses, temples, libraries, schools, and a parsonage.

Interhome (in U.S.), 124 Little Falls Rd., Fairfield, NJ 07006, tel. (201) 882–6864; (in Britain), 383 Richmond Rd., Twickenham TW1 2EF, Britain, tel. (081) 891–1294. Ski chalets, apartments, and hotels available year-round. Enjoy the freedom of making your own meals when you want to. Retreat into your own nest after a day of hiking, sightseeing, or skiing. All apartments are fully equipped with cooking utensils and dishes.

Information about castle hotels can be found from:

Gast im Schloss, Postfach 120520, Mannheim, Germany 6800, tel.: (0621) 12–6620; fax: (0621) 12–66212; in U.S.: Jaques de Larsay, 1–800–366–1510.

Relais & Chateaux (in U.S.), 2400 Lazy Hollow, Suite 152D, Houston, Texas, 77063, tel. 800–743–8033; fax: (713) 783–0951; (in France), 9 Avenue Marceau, 75116 Paris, France, tel.: (1) 47–23–41–42; fax: (1) 47–23–38–99.

Romantik Hotels (in U.S.), 14180 Woodinville-Duvall Rd., Box 1278, Woodinville, WA 98072, tel. (800) 826–0015, information: (206) 486–4079; fax: (206) 481–4079. **DER Tours,** 11933 Wilshire Blvd., Los Angeles, CA 90025, tel. (800) 937–1234; fax: (213) 479–2239; (in Britain), **The Business Village,** Bromhill Rd., London SW 18 4JQ, tel.: (081) 187–5038/5039; fax: (081) 871–1210.

AIRLINES   For your convenience we have compiled a list of toll-free numbers of national airlines:

Austria: Austrian Airlines (800) 843–0002
Belgium: Sabena World Airlines (800) 955–2000
Czechoslovakia: Czechoslovak Airlines (800) 628–6107
Denmark, Sweden, Norway: SAS (800) 221–2350
Britain: British Airways (800) 247–9297
        Virgin Atlantic (800) 862–8621
Finland: Finnair (800) 950–5000
France: Air France (800) 237–2747
Germany: Lufthansa (800) 645–3880
Greece: Olympic (800) 223–1226

Hungary: Malev (800) 223–6884
Ireland: Aer Lingus (800) 223–6537
Italy: Alitalia (800) 223–5730
Luxembourg: Icelandair (800) 223–5500
Netherlands: KLM (800) 777–5553
     Martinair (800) FON–HOLLAND
Poland: LOT Polish Airlines (800) 223–0593
Portugal: TAP Portugal (800) 221–7370
Spain: Iberia (800) 772–4642
Switzerland: Swissair (800) 221–4750
Turkey: Turkish Airlines (800) 874–8875
Yugoslavia: JAT Yugoslavia Airlines (800) 752–6528
U.S. Airlines:
American (800) 433–7300
Delta (800) 241–4141
Continental (800) 231–0856
Northwest (800) 225–2525
TWA (800) 221–2000
USAir (800) 428–4322
United (800) 241–6522

PASSPORTS AND CUSTOMS Passports are available from passport agencies of the U.S. Department of State in large cities. Or call your local county office to ask for an application to be sent by mail. Each application requires two passport photographs ($2'' \times 2''$), proof of citizenship such as a birth certificate or most recent passport, and the current fee.

  For information on current customs regulations, write for *Customs Hints for Returning U.S. Residents,* available from the U.S. Government Printing Office, Washington, DC 20402. It's a good idea to bring sales slips along for previously purchased European cameras, watches, and jewelry to avoid paying duty again. As you travel save sales slips to help you fill out the customs form upon re-entry into the U.S.

INSURANCE Please check with your insurance agent before you go to be sure you are covered for theft, accident, or other problems. Resolve medical insurance coverage in advance as some policies will not cover people when outside of the country.

TELEPHONE Country codes are given in each chapter. If you are dialing from within a country, omit the "0" at the beginning of the regional or city code. Public telephones are usually cheaper than those in hotel rooms; check for surcharges levied by the hotel. In some countries you can purchase a telephone card, which avoids the hassle of producing change for calls.

TIME ZONES Greenwich Mean Time (GMT), which is five hours ahead of U.S. Eastern Standard Time, applies to Britain, Ireland, and Portugal. Central European Time is one hour ahead of GMT and six hours ahead of U.S. Eastern Standard Time is in effect for Austria, Belgium, Czechoslovakia, Denmark, France, Germany, Hungary, Italy, the Netherlands, Norway, Spain, Sweden, and Yugoslavia. Much of former Eastern Europe plus Finland, Greece, Turkey, and western Russia is two hours ahead of GMT.

PHOTOGRAPHY Increased security, which we applaud, also causes some problems for film. Photographers feel that repeated exposure to x-rays will harm the quality of photographs especially with fast film. In some airports the personnel will conduct a hand search of film although they all prefer not to do this. Other airports have signs indicating that everything must go through the X-ray equipment. After traveling with large quantities of film for our professional writing projects, we have ranged from insisting on hand search to giving up when we knew it was not possible.

PACKING After years of feeling burdened with our mound of luggage, we have discovered travel with only a carry-on bag. It works, and the relief is very welcome. In the old days we thought we had to have lots of clothing including a variety of shoes to choose from. We carried heavy and light garments to satisfy every possible sport and activity; somehow we didn't know about layering. Then, when we lived abroad on sabbatical leave with young children, we packed a couple of foot lockers with educational toys and books, plus clothing. Even the cost of sending them air freight didn't seem to cure us.

Now we can travel for a couple of months with a single carry-on bag each. We like soft-sided bags with several compartments. Ours have a thin section on the bottom where we place things we may not use often; they pack down into almost nothing and are out of the way. The center compartment contains a plastic shirt bag with "dress" blouses and scarves. Everything else is folded and stacked in two piles. The zipper on the top opens into a generous area to push plastic bags in a row filled with underwear, slippers, nightgown, and anything else that won't mind a wrinkle. We also use a plastic zipper sweater bag to hold all odd items so we can find them by just sliding out the bag. It starts out folded a couple of times and takes different shapes as needed.

The trick is to use a basic color such as black for slacks, skirts, and jackets and liven it up with shirts, blouses, and scarves. We layer when the weather turns cool. A quick wash every third day keeps us in clean clothes. And best of all, the bags are easy to carry. We sometimes bring a set of wheels for long airport corridors or carry bags with shoulder straps. (When additional books and papers accumulate, we each have two carry-ons and the wheels are welcome.)

An alphabetical list of possible clothing is useful—we photocopy the list, underline what we plan to take, and check it off when packed. After a trip we make notes on the packing list of items that could be omitted or add suggestions about what would be handy on the next trip. Our basic list follows:

Clothing: bathing suit, belt, blazer, blouse/shirt, winter boots, cap, coat, dress, gloves, hat—rain/sun, jacket—light/rain, jewelry, kerchief, nightgown/pajamas, purse—large/small/dress/extra coin, robe, scarves, shoes—dress/sport/walking, shorts, skirt, slacks, slippers, socks/hose, sweater—cardigan/pullover, ties, underwear.

Documents: camera receipts, checks, credit cards, passport, traveler's checks.

Miscellaneous: address list, basin stopper, calculator, camera/film/batteries, carry bag with zip top, clothesline, corkscrew, cups (collapsible or small plastic for water), electric-converter plugs, flashlight, glasses—reading/sun, hangers (inflatable or folding), insect lotion, laundry bag, locks for luggage, money belts, photos (extra passport-size), plastic bags, sewing kit, tissues, towelettes, travel clock, umbrella, washcloth, watch, wheels.

We keep a kit full of small-sized cosmetic and medical items always packed. Sometimes we carry an extra prescription bottle for each other in case of loss. A plastic box in the closet contains a variety of travel items (from the above list) to choose for each trip.

THEFT AND EMERGENCIES   In 40 years of travel we have never been "ripped off." However, one of us worries quite a bit and the other will use a money belt when cajoled. Our favorite devices are worn inside slacks or skirts, with a strap hooked over a belt or pinned to the inside. Some of our relatives have made small pockets with a zipper to be sewn or pinned inside clothing—they dreamed this up many years ago and it works. We like to wear one of each—one for credit cards and the key to luggage locks, the other for money; wallets and purses stay locked inside luggage in the hotel on some days.

We follow the general principle that the less we take the less there is to lose. To begin with, we use a different flat wallet for travel and leave most of our credit cards and miscellaneous wallet contents at home. We choose a couple of credit cards, carry a few personal checks without the checkbook as well as traveler's checks, and add local money. Then we photocopy all credit cards, airline tickets, passport inside cover and facing page, traveler's check numbers, camera receipts, and any other documents we might need if stolen. Copies can be spread around so that one can always be found. Don't forget to include the number to call in case your traveler's checks are missing. If you lose your passport, contact the nearest embassy or consulate (listed in country chapters).

Medical emergencies can happen, and if they do, often hotel personnel will recommend a doctor or hospital. The **International Association for Medical Assistance to Travelers** (IAMAT), 417 Center St., Lewiston, NY 14092–3633 offers a list of English-speaking doctors, a world immunization chart, and information on various other medical services. Also check with your credit card companies to find out their policy in regard to medical emergencies that require evacuation, which can be exhorbitantly expensive out-of-pocket. British citizens should check with the National Health Service to see which countries will provide reciprocal services for them.

Develop a Mediterranean Sense of Time

Europe offers travelers more opportunities than they can manage to take advantage of in many trips, much less one. With so much to choose from, remember to consider your body. A vacation is supposed to be pleasant and relaxing, providing memories for years to come. Plan ahead so you are still happy when you emerge from a museum or historic site. Sit down for a drink and relax while watching the local scene.

We lump these tricks for truly enjoying travel under the general idea of a Mediterranean sense of time because we were first exposed to it while living in southern Italy. There time flows with the needs of the human body and spirit, not with timetables and deadlines. If the weather or our mood changes, we alter our plans accordingly; as independent travelers we are not locked into someone else's schedule. So when friends ask us whether we don't get tired of so much travel, the answer is clearly no. When we travel, we take full possession of our freedom, and we do what we wish.

AUSTRIA

Currency unit • Austrian schilling, divided into groschen
Language • German
Time difference from USA • six hours later (Eastern Standard Time)
Telephone access codes • to USA 00 (from Linz) or 900 (from Vienna) or USADirect (022) 903–011; from USA: 43
National Tourist Offices • USA: Austrian National Tourist Office, 500 Fifth Ave., New York, NY 10110, tel.: (212) 944–6880; Austria: Vienna Tourist Board, Palais Grassalkovics, A-1025 Vienna, Austria, tel.: (011) 43–1 211140–0; Salzburg City Tourist Office, Auerspergstrasse 7, A-5024 Salzburg, Austria, tel.: (011) 43–662 80720; Innsbruck City Tourist Office, Burggraben 3, A-6020 Innsbruck, Austria, tel.: (011) 43–512 59850; Britain: Austrian National Tourist Office, 30 St. George St., London W1R OAL, tel.: (071) 629–0461
Airlines • Austrian Airlines: USA: (800) 843–0002; Britain: (071) 439–0741
Embassies • American Embassy: Boltmanngasse 16, A-1091 Vienna, Austria, tel.: (222) 3155–11; British Embassy, Jauresgasse 12, A-1030 Vienna, tel.: 756117/8

Austria held a mystique for me when I first visited as a student in 1952. The country was then occupied by four powers (Britain, France, America, and Russia) and our group was cautioned to be especially careful not to take photographs of Russian guards in Vienna. As the train stopped at the Austrian border, Russian guards got on and stalked through the cars. We felt very uncomfortable as they looked at each passport, sometimes joking that the photograph did not look like its owner. Our spirits lightened after we met a group of students who were our escorts for the Austrian part of the trip. One night another girl and I went with two handsome medical students through the Russian zone to a home where we had dinner, then danced and sang the evening away. We felt a little nervous as we passed through the Russian sector; our mothers would not have approved had they known what we were up to. Later visits with my husband have been more relaxed, but never quite as exciting as that first exposure to a beautiful and slightly dangerous world.

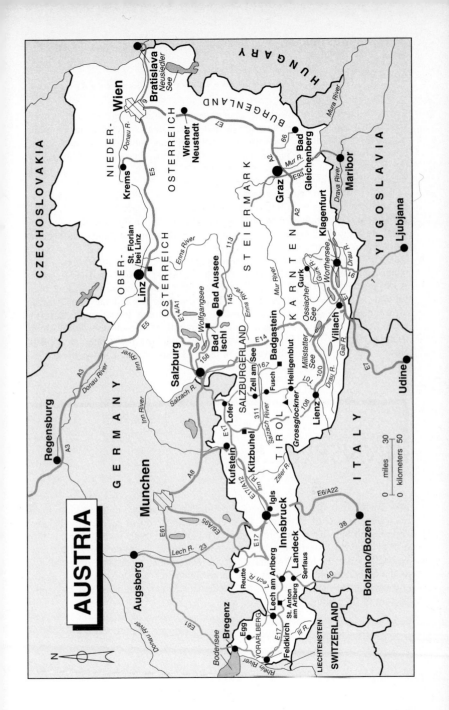

HISTORY..

Caves dating back to paleolithic days have given archaeologists reason to believe that people lived in the area at that time. Data collected from neolithic times, from 5000 B.C., point toward early people as hunters, fishermen, farmers and food gatherers. Saltmining was very important economically, including the oldest mine in Durnberg, near Hallein and Salzburg. The Celts controlled the salt trade during the last centuries B.C.

By 15 B.C. the Romans had arrived and put up Roman walls to keep out the barbarians, who were finally able to invade and conquer by 400 A.D. Attila the Hun was notorious for his cruelty and his power. In 788 Charlemagne arrived; this Frankish ruler was crowned by the Pope in 800, thus starting the Holy Roman Empire of the German Nation.

The House of Babenberg began its reign in 976 and continued until 1246, when the Habsburg dynasty took over. The Habsburgs lasted until 1918, when Austria was defeated in World War I. In 1919 the Republic of Austria was formed, with a new constitution in 1920 proclaiming it a federal state. Austria also joined the League of Nations in that year. Austrians fought in the German army during World War II and allied bombs inflicted much damage in cities such as Vienna. In 1945 Vienna was divided into the four zones mentioned earlier, but in 1955 the Belvedere or State Treaty restored independence to Austria and the occupying troops left.

INNSBRUCK

Few cities can match Innsbruck for sheer drama, whether you are looking up at the cross on top of Nordkette from city streets or down at the city below, compressed between mountain ranges. We have done both several times at the turn of the year. After a day of skiing and gazing at the mountain walls rising vertically from the town, we have felt the extraordinary peace of deep valleys as the bells rang in a new year once more. Innsbruck has drawn us back again and again to re-experience both the excitement of the mountains and the equilibrium of the valley.

HISTORY......................................

This natural trade-route crossing has been inhabited since the Bronze Age; Celts and Illyrians were followed by the Romans. In 1180 the Count of Andechs built a market town beside the bridge over the river, hence the name "Innspruke" or "Inn Bridge." By 1239 Innsbruck was founded as a town and in 1363 the Habsburgs moved in. Emperor Maximilian I developed the town into an administrative center and encouraged cultural expansion. He first married Maria of Burgundy, who was the daughter of Charles the Bold, and later Bianca Maria Sforza. The reign of Maria Theresia during the 18th century brought more splendor to Innsbruck. Tirol was given back from Bavaria to Austria in 1814 at the Congress of Vienna, and Innsbruck became its capital in 1849.

SIGHTSEEING................................

Part of the fun of being in Innsbruck is wandering around the well-preserved medieval old town with its narrow streets, tall slender houses, and onion domes. There are oriel windows and decorated doors to spot, and some of the buildings have arcaded fronts.

Maria Theresien Strasse is both a street and a square, called a "strassen-platz" or street-square. Views of the mountains rising steeply right from the town include that of the **Nordkette,** topped by snow at an altitude of 7657 feet. **St. Anne's Column** (*Annasaule*) stands in the middle of the street as a focal point for photographers, who can easily frame it with mountains. This monument standing next to the Rathaus was erected in 1706 to commemorate the welcome withdrawal of Bavarian troops on St. Anne's birthday. St. Anne and St. George are portrayed on the base and the Virgin stands on top of the column.

A narrow street, **Herzog Friedrich Strasse,** leads from the junction of Maria Theresien Strasse with **Marktgraben** and **Burggraben** (where the old wall and moat used to stand) right into the heart of the old town. It continues past #39 where Montaigne stayed in the **Golden Rose Inn** in 1580, #31, the **White Cross Inn** (*Weisses Kreuz*) where Mozart and his father lodged in 1769 and where we have chosen to stay on many visits, and #22, the **Trautsonhaus,** which dates to 1541.

At the north end of the street stands the famous **Golden Roof** (*Goldenes Dachl*), which was built in 1494 as part of the ducal palace. One legend claims that Friedrich the Penniless, Duke of Tyrol, was tired of innuendos about his poor financial status so had the roof covered with gold coins. It may be nearer to the truth that the Gothic oriel window and the 2657-tiled gilded roof were placed there in 1494 on the occasion of Maximilian I's marriage to Bianca

Maria Sforza. A frieze of coats of arms from Syria, Austria, Hungary, the Holy Roman Empire, Germany, Philip the Fair, and the Sforza family spans the balustrade on the first floor. The first floor balcony is ornately decorated with scenes of acrobatic dancing surrounding two central panels of Maximilian with his second wife, Bianca Maria Sforza, wearing an Italian headdress and his first wife, Maria, in her Burgundian headdress. A series of carved animals runs across the facade just below the roof. (The original carvings are now in the Tyrolean Museum for protection; they have been replaced by copies.) The royal family and the court often sat on the balcony below the golden roof to watch events in the square below.

In December, to complement the golden dazzle of the roof, a gigantic Christmas tree is lit in front. The end of the street looks like fairyland. It's one of those romantic experiences that we look forward to again and again on our winter visits.

Also in the building is the **Olympic Museum** (*Neuhof*) with exhibits of posters, badges, equipment, and uniforms. Olympic Winter Games films from 1964 and 1976 in Innsbruck are also there to view.

Helblinghaus, which is opposite the museum at #10, is a startlingly decorated building with a rococo facade. In the 18th century it was given a facelift with the addition of decorated window frames and pediment. The convex bowed windows were designed to provide more light inside because narrow streets tend to cut out the sunlight.

The fortified former **gate tower** at the end of Herzog Friedrich Strasse is called *Ottoburg*. This 1495 tower has four oriel windows.

The **Imperial Palace,** also called Court Castle (*Hofburg*), dates from the 14th century; it was expanded by Emperor Maximilian I, ravaged by both fire and earthquakes, and later rebuilt under Maria Theresia. Two domed towers stand on the north and south ends. The rococo facade is pale yellow with white trim. An ornate pediment tops the entrance. It was finished in time for the wedding of Maria Theresia's son Leopold, but the festivities were halted when Emperor Franz I died unexpectedly.

Inside, a wide stairway leads up to a reception hall that contains Habsburg portraits beginning with Charles V of Lorraine who lived in Hofburg. Another painting portrays Charles V receiving the keys of the town from Turkish chiefs.

The **Giants' Hall** is famous for its oversized men painted on the walls. Maria Theresia's husband, Emperor Franz I, reigns in the center painting. Maria Theresia and her son Emperor Joseph II flank Franz I. Portraits of all of her children, including Marie Antoinette, hang on the walls. The allegorical painting on the ceiling portrays the power of the Habsburg-Lorraine dynasty including the triumph of the rulers holding hands with Turks in chains below. The artist, Anton Maulpertsch, pictured himself pouring gold and silver coins onto a table.

The **Silver Chapel** contains a silver embossed Madonna and silver relief tablets on the altar. Ferdinand II of Tyrol lies in his tomb along with his reclining statue and Habsburg coats of arms in mosaic work. The cedarwood organ in the chapel is one of the oldest organs in German-speaking countries; it dates from the 16th century.

The **Court Church** (*Hofkirche*) was built by Ferdinand I as a memorial for his grandfather, Maximilian. His large black sarcophagus has a bronze figure of the Emperor created by Alexander Colin. Twenty-eight large bronze statues of ancestors and friends stand around the cenotaph. Statuettes of saints and 20 busts of Roman emperors are also there.

The **City Belfry Tower** (*Stadtturm*) is the place to go for a view of the city from a 16th-century dome. Its octagonal upper story is topped by turrets.

Hofgarten is a large park where concerts are held during the summer. Weeping willows frame lakes and provide shade for strollers.

St. James' Cathedral (*Dom zu St. Jakob*) is a baroque structure dating from the early 18th century. Inside, copies of frescoes by Cosmas Damian Asam (the originals were damaged in 1944) are displayed. The German Renaissance painter, Lucas Cranach the Elder, created the painting, *Our Lady of Succour,* over the altar. The tomb of Archduke Maximilian, a Grand Master of the Teutonic Order, was restored in 1950. St. George and his dragon are featured beside the praying archduke.

The **Museum of Tyrolean Folk Art** (*Tiroler Volkskunstmuseum*) houses exhibits of regional farm life including models of Tyrolean farmhouses. Tyrolese rooms exhibit styles from Gothic to rococo. The museum is famous for its collection of Tyrolean Christmas cribs and scenes. Costumes, musical instruments, furniture, and tools are also there.

The **Ferdinandeum Tyrolean State Museum** (*Tiroler Landesmuseum Ferdinandeum*), 15 Museumstrasse, is a historical museum of Tyrol. Collections include exhibits on the art of Tyrol as well as that of Dutch and Flemish masters. An altarpiece of 36 Limoges plaques by Pierre Raymond is a favorite. The carved originals from the Goldenes Dachl are also there. Artifacts from excavation of the Roman city of Virunum are on display.

The **Triumphal Arch** (*Triumphforte*) was built in 1765 for the marriage of Leopold II with the Infanta Maria Ludovica of Spain. Maria Theresia and Franz I were supposed to have passed under the arch but Franz died before the wedding festivities were finished. Therefore, one side presents wedding celebration and the other illustrates mourning.

DAY TRIPS FROM INNSBRUCK......................................

Mountain Destinations

Visitors to Innsbruck are sure to want to take the *funicular* up to **Hungerburg** for a bird's-eye view of the city as well as the Series and Nockspitze peaks. An aerial tram heads up from Hungerburg to Seegrube and Hafelekar, which are on the Nordkette. Or you can ascend to Patscherkofel, Seefelt, or Mutters. Skiers and hikers will want to try combinations in big doses or small.

Ambras Castle (*Schloss Ambras*) perches near Wilten overlooking the Inn Valley. Dating from the 11th century, the castle was a gift to Archduke Ferdinand II from his father in 1563. Ferdinand was an ardent art collector and his portraits are hung there. Collections of arms and armor are on display with jousting exhibits. The castle is in two groupings—the lower or entrance, and the upper, which is a former medieval fortress.

EXCURSIONS FROM INNSBRUCK.....................................

The Arlberg

The Arlberg area is known worldwide as the birthplace of modern alpine skiing and the source of the Arlberg technique, which dominated the sport for decades. A system of cable cars interlinks the villages of St. Anton, Zurs, and Lech, making the area ideal for skiers who want an extended system of runs from a single base, or for hikers and climbers in the summer. There is one run along a very spectacular gorge for half a mile. The open fields at very high altitude are almost completely above the tree line. We enjoyed beautiful spring skiing in bright sun (bring very dark glasses for the flat light). Our son attended ski school for a week in Lech when he was six years old. Although he was the only person who spoke English, he learned by imitation and at the end of the week wanted to "ski until our money runs out."

Riding the cable cars, including one that crosses between two peaks high above an intervening valley, can provide a day's entertainment in itself, as well as a moving platform for photographing a mountain panorama. The villages themselves are busy but pleasant, and they are surrounded by chalets scattered about the lower mountainsides that provide a perfect base for exploring the beauties of this whole region.

SALZBURG

For most visitors, Salzburg and music are inseparable. Mozart provided a cultural focus that still rings through the city in annual music festivals. Then Maria, from the *Sound of Music* reminds visitors that the surrounding hills are alive too.

HISTORY...

The visual image of the castle towering above the city is equally powerful for those who have climbed up inside its massive bastion walls to survey the city. Both the sounds and the sights of this beautiful city strike chords that reverberate in the imagination.

A settlement on the site of the present Salzburg dates back to Neolithic times when trade routes crossed there. Salt mines in nearby Hallein were in operation as early as 900 B.C. and the salt was sent out through Salzburg. Illyrians, then Celts, and finally Romans lived in the area; old Roman milestones are still visible along the Kuchl road. The Bavarians were in power during the 6th century. During the late 7th century, St. Rupert the Bishop arrived and founded the Benedictine Abbey of St. Peter as well as a nunnery in Nonnberg. Salzburg grew to become an archbishopric with power over the Bavarian dioceses. One of the largest cathedrals in the Kingdom of the Franks was built under St. Virgil. The town also grew through commercial enterprise, such as salt mining, hence the name Salzburg.

A fire in 1200 destroyed much of the city, which was rebuilt until another fire roared through town in 1598. Vincenzo Scamozzi was commissioned by the Prince Archbishop Wolf Dietrich von Raitenau to design a new city, in Italian style, with palaces, gardens, churches, fountains, and squares. Later, Wolf Dietrich was removed by the Pope because of his conflict with the Elector of Bavaria over salt rights. Dietrich died in 1617 at Hohensalzburg Castle, after being a prisoner for five years.

Leopold Mozart moved to Salzburg in 1737; he was a violinist and became court composer in 1757. Wolfgang Amadeus Mozart was born in 1756 in Salzburg and the city has not been the same since; the world focuses on music and Mozart in Salzburg. The Salzburg Festival is now held in a new theater designed by Clemens Holzmeister.

SIGHTSEEING..

Hohensalzburg Fortress (*Festung Hohensalzburg*), 34 Monchsberg, the largest completely preserved fortress in Central Europe, dates from 1077. It is a gigantic, crenellated, turreted, imposing structure usually seen from the town below. My first glimpse of the castle was in 1952 during a wild and dizzying Viennese Waltz in the Winkler Cafe, which has a perfect view both up to the fortress and down into the town.

Archbishop Leonhard von Keutschach remodeled and added to the complex in the early 1500's; his emblem, a turnip, can be spotted all over the castle. Prince Archbishop Max Gandolf Kuenburg finally finished construction in 1681.

Visitors can walk up or take the funicular to the castle. Inside, you can walk through the state apartments with decorated walls and coffered ceilings, the towers, and the dungeons. The **Golden Room** features a ceramic stove decorated with fruit and flowers and coats of arms dating from 1501.

The **Salzburg Bull** (*Salzburger Stier*) is a 1502 barrel organ, which is operated by hand. Every day the organ peals out the original 1502 chorale as well as the music of Mozart and Hayden. The **Rainer Museum** houses memorabilia from the Archduke Rainer's 59th Infantry Regiment, which guarded the castle from 1871 to 1918. **St. George's Chapel** contains a red marble monument to Archbishop Leonhard von Keutschach who died in 1519.

Nonnberg Convent (*Stift Nonnberg*), located to the east of the castle and down the mountain, is the Benedictine convent founded by St. Rupert. The Gothic church contains a gilded and carved altarpiece focusing on the Virgin and Child painted between St. Rupert and St. Virgil. Visitors may also remember that Maria von Trapp spent part of her life there.

The high dome of the Cathedral is visible below the castle. Mozart was baptized there in 1756. Over the years the style has changed from its original to late-Romanesque to baroque. Salzburg marble adorns the west front in between two symmetrical towers. Bronze doors were added in 1957 using the themes of faith, hope, and charity. The dome, which was damaged in World War II, was restored in 1959. Remains of the earlier cathedral, which went up in smoke in the 16th century, have been excavated.

St. Peter's Church (*Stiftskirche St. Peter*) was a Romanesque abbey and Benedictine monastery founded by St. Rupert in 696; it was renovated during the 17th and 18th centuries in baroque style. The tomb of St. Rupert stands in the third chapel; that of Mozart's sister Marianne ("Nannerl") von Berchtold zu Sonnenburg in the fourth chapel. Near the upper windows paintings portray the life of St. Rupert on the north side and that of St. Benedict on the south side. The nave vaulting contains frescoes representing St. Peter's life.

St. Peter's Churchyard (*Petersfriedhof*) is contained on three sides by wrought-iron arcades housing family tombs. Ancient Christian catacombs and St. Maximus's Chapel were found in the rock wall of the Monchsberg.

Franciscans' Church (*Franziskanerkirche*) dates from the 8th century. The

Romanesque nave shrouded in darkness contrasts with the brightly lit Gothic choir. Palm-topped columns support the star vaulting. Animals and leaves decorate the pillars. A marble altar standing behind the high altar came from the original cathedral.

The **Festival Theater** (*Festspielhaus*) stands on the site of the old **Court Stables** (*Hofmarstall*); three gateways are still there. This complex of auditoriums includes galleries and a large festival hall. The **Old House** (*Altes Haus*) and the **New House** (*Neues Haus*) have a foyer in between.

The **Residence of the Archbishops** (*Residenz*), 1 Residenzplatz, dates from 1120 with renovation in the early 1600's. The *Fountain of Hercules* in the main courtyard features horses, dolphins, and a triton with a conch shell. The state rooms have been renovated to Renaissance style of 1600; concerts are presented during the season. The *Residenzgalerie* contains 17th- and 18th-century works of art originating with the collections of the archbishops, the Czernin collection, and that of Schonborn-Buchheim.

Nearby, on the Residenzplatz, the **glockenspiel** plays melodies by Mozart on a 17th-century carillon. The *Salzburg Bull*, a 1502 organ, in the Hohensalzburg answers with its own melodies.

Mozart's Birthplace (*Mozart Geburtshaus*), 9 Getreidegasse, is the site of his birth in 1756. A museum contains his violin, paintings, original scores, letters, a clavichord of 1760, and a pianoforte of 1780. Nearby, Tanzmeistersaal was the home of the Mozart family from 1773–87. Chamber concerts are presented there during the summer.

Across the Salzach, **Mirabell Gardens** contain pools, statues, sculpture, and flowers. The 17th-century mansion built by Wolf Dietrich was ravaged by fire in 1818. The original staircase, complete with carved marble cherubims by Georg Raphael Donner, still stands. **Schloss Mirabell** is now the official residence of the burgomaster.

The **Mozarteum** was built in 1910 for the College of Music and the Performing Arts. The **Magic Flute House** (*Zauberflotenhauschen*) is where Mozart wrote *The Magic Flute* in 1791; it has been moved from the Nachmarkt in Vienna to the Mozarteum.

The **Marionette Theater** (*Marionettentheater*), Schwarzstrasse 24, next door was built by Anton Aicher in 1913 and is still operated by his descendents. Two-foot-high marionettes still entertain and take many curtain calls. Mozart operas are a specialty of the family.

DAY TRIPS FROM SALZBURG...............

Hellbrunn

Hellbrunn Palace was built for Prince Archbishop Markus Sittikus in 1612. Inside, the banquet hall is alive with trompe l'oeil painting. Outside, watch out for "surprises." As a visitor in 1952 I quickly learned to stand on a dry piece of ground while listening to the guide; the Archbishop had a bizarre sense of humor, which included drenching his guests with strategic sprays of water. The trick fountains spurt from unexpected places throughout the gardens. Guests seated on stone stools around a table were often startled by a gush of water rising from each stool; etiquette demanded that they remain seated, while being soaked, until the Archbishop chose to stand.

A **hunting lodge** (*Monatschlossl*) dating from 1615 contains the **Salzburg Folk Museum**. Behind the folk museum visitors can climb to the Watzmann-Aussicht for a view of the countryside. The **Stone Theater** (*Steinernes Theater*) is located in an abandoned quarry gorge nearby.

HALLEIN.......................................

Salt mines provide one of the main industries in the area. Salt pans evaporate brine and have done so there since Neolithic times. One of the highlights of a trip years ago was an excursion down into the Durrnberg Mines. Dressed in white outfits with white caps perched on our heads, we walked through underground galleries, floated on a raft through a salt lake, and slid down on toboggans to the depths below. To exit we all sat on a long wheeled cart and zipped out of the mine; the photo taken just as we emerged, still in our white suits, spurs an unforgettable memory.

VIENNA

Vienna (Wien) is a magic city for one half of this writing team. Not every young girl has the chance to celebrate her 21st birthday in Vienna, as I did. At 8 a.m. the owner of the hotel and two waitresses knocked on my door and presented me with a lovely bouquet of red roses. Our tour leaders, Happy (Fritz) and Traute, sent me a corsage of candies wrapped in cellophane standing on stems like flowers. My breakfast that morning was special—an egg, ham and pickles, and birthday cake—in contrast to our usual rolls and beverage. At lunch the waiter brought me a goblet of white wine and they all sang *Happy Birthday*. After dinner we danced the *Viennese Waltz* into the evening, so euphoria was with me all day. Later I served as a guide for my husband on his first trip to

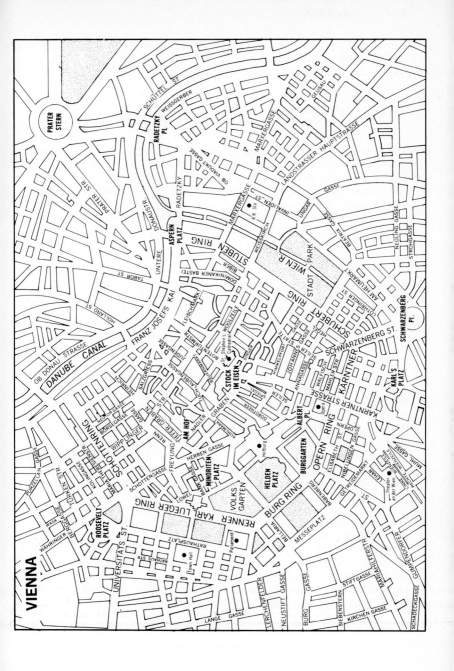

Vienna, and now we both sense the power and elegance of one of Europe's most beautiful cities.

HISTORY......................................

The Roman town of Vindobona dates from the 1st century A.D. when legionaries built a fortified settlement on the shores of the Danube. Emperor Marcus Aurelius defended Vindobona against invaders before his death in 180. The town was ravaged by fire in 395, abandoned by the Romans, and taken over by the Ostrogoths in the 5th century. By 881 the name had been changed to Weniam. Attila the Hun arrived in 453, but luckily perished before he could devastate Vienna. The city reeled under attacks by Goths, Franks, Bavarians, and Slavs for several hundred years.

During the Crusades Richard I of England was captured and the ransom paid for his release paid for the building of the walls of the city. The Holy Roman Emperor chose the Babenbergs as hereditary dukes of Austria in 1156. In 1221 the duke presented Vienna with a city charter, which is the oldest constitution for the city. The Babenberg duke was killed in battle with the Hungarians in 1246, leaving no male heir. In 1276 Rudolf I of Habsburg, who had been the Holy Roman Emperor since 1273, fought the king of Bohemia, Ottocar II, the man famous for grabbing the Babenberg lands. Ottocar was slain in battle in 1278. The Habsburgs ruled Vienna from 1278 until 1918.

Throughout their long reign the city prospered, in spite of many vicissitudes. In 1529 the Turks began to invade Vienna, trying repeatedly from nearby Hungary. In 1679 the black plague swept through Vienna. By 1740 Maria Theresia and her son Joseph II had developed many good programs of reform for Austria. Napoleon invaded Vienna in 1805 and stayed until his defeat in 1814. In 1809 he lived at Schonbrunn; in 1810 Napoleon married Maria Louise who was the daughter of Emperor Franz. The Congress of Vienna was in session from 1814 to 1815. During that time the map of Europe was reconstructed. After Emperor Franz I died in 1916 the Austro-Hungarian Monarchy disintegrated and in 1918 the republic of Austria was founded.

Adolf Hitler came to Vienna in 1938 and the city has never been the same. The Jewish citizens suffered unmercifully, leading some to flee the country and almost certain death.

In 1945 Vienna was placed under the supervision of the four Allied powers (America, Britain, France, and Russia); this was lifted in 1955, the Austrian State Treaty was signed, giving Austria neutrality and independence, and the forces withdrew. By 1952 the Cathedral had been partially restored and opened to the public again; the Opera House came to life in 1955.

Vienna has always been thought of as a city of music. The "Vienna School" of music included Mozart, who performed for the Empress Maria Theresia in

1762, Haydn, Beethoven, Dittersdorf, Schenk, Albrechtsberger, and Czerny. Aristocratic families had plenty of distinguished musicians to choose from for their balls.

SIGHTSEEING.....................................

The **Cathedral of St. Stephan** (*St. Stephansdom*), Stephansplatz, is the focal point of Vienna, right in the center of town. This Gothic structure is distinctive with its glazed tiled roof in almost a herringbone pattern. The **steeple** (*Steffl*) is 450 feet high and visitors can climb up to 315 feet for a view. We feel a special affinity for this cathedral as a silk print of it has hung in our home for forty years.

A smaller Romanesque church on the site was consecrated in 1147, destroyed by fire in 1193, and again in 1258. Part of the west front is original to the next church built there. The north tower was not finished but instead topped with a copper cupola in 1556. Visitors can ascend by a lift to the level of the bell for a view. In 1945 the cathedral burned and the **Pummerin** bell, or "boomer," in the north tower plummeted to the ground and broke into many pieces. Another bell took its place in 1952.

The **Giant's Door** (*Riesen Tor*) certainly looks big enough for a giant; it dates from the 13th century church. The **Heathen's Towers** (*Heidenturme*) also belonged to that structure. Before you enter, look outside to the right for a stone with a Roman inscription from 400 A.D. Here is proof that stones were taken for building purposes from ruins of the Roman legionary camp.

Inside, the nave contains a series of large pillars reaching up to the reticulated vaulted ceiling. The carved stone pulpit was created by Anton Pilgram in the 16th century; look under the ramp to see him holding his sculptor's tools, leaning out of a window with a twinkle in his eye. The sculptor must have had fun creating a number of little animals climbing up the railing—toads and lizards representing evil try to reach the priest, but he is protected by the little dog at the top.

Beyond the choir the **Virgin's Chapel** contains a gilded carved wooden altarpiece called the *Wiener Neustadt*. The Virgin and Child are framed by sculptured figures.

The red Salzburg marble tomb of Emperor Friedrich III stands in the **Apostles' Chapel**. Don't miss the procession of animals including apes, monkeys, boars, birds, and dogs crawling around his tomb, also to symbolize evil spirits. Good spirits, in the form of 12 mourning monks are there to protect him. A photograph of the top of the sarcophagus (which is too high to see) shows the emperor with his orb, scepter, five eagles, and the Austrian flag. The catacombs under the cathedral contain urns holding the organs of Austria's emperors.

The **Archbishop's Palace** (*Erzbischofliches Palais*) contains the cathedral and Diocesan museum. The museum includes Syrian glass bottles, illuminated manuscripts, portraits, reliquaries, sacred implements from the cathedral, and sculpture.

The **Imperial Palace** (*Hofburg*), 1 Michaelerplatz, which was once the Palace of the Habsburgs, dates from the 13th century when the Duke of Austria built a fort outside the walls of the town. Future sovereigns added wings, which accounts for the diversity of style in the Hofburg. Emperor Ferdinand I lived there from 1533 until his death.

The **Treasury** is where jewels of the Holy Roman Empire and the Austrian Imperial Throne are kept. The Imperial Crown of the Holy Roman Empire is set with a number of sapphires, rubies, emeralds, and pearls, with a red velvet covering and a cross on one side. The 1602 crown of the Austrian Empire, which was originally the family crown of the Habsburgs, is very ornate with a lily-like base, two semicircles resembling a mitre, and an arch.

We were impressed with a 3rd-century agate bowl in translucent blue and brown. It is thought to have been carved with diamonds in Constantinople. A collection of tabards for heralds includes the lion of Bohemia with a figure-of-eight or double crossed tail.

The cradle of Napoleon II in silver and gilt is decorated by a horn of plenty, angels, eagles, and a wreath of stars with an N in the center. A gold pitcher and basin set was used by the Habsburg family for christenings. Don't miss the 2680-karat emerald carved in Prague in 1661, a jewel of the Habsburgs. Coronation robes include an Islamic robe made in Sicily with many tiny pearls and cloisonne enamel decoration. A relic of the true cross with a nail hole, the Burgundian Treasure, and that of the Order of the Golden Fleece are also there.

The **Amalienhof** went up between 1575 and 1605 and the **Leopoldinischer Trakt** between 1660–69; those wings comprise the private rooms of Maria Theresia and are now the federal chancellor's residence and not open for viewing. The **Imperial Apartments** are open on the first floor of the chancellery wing and the Amalientrakt. Rooms are furnished lavishly with Aubusson and Flemish tapestry, crystal chandeliers, and period furniture. A Chinese clock is unusual with an animal stationed at each hour.

The **Court Library,** which is now the National Library, was finished in 1726. The **Neue Hofburg** houses several museums including the **Museum of Fine Art** (*Kunsthistorisches Museum*), Maria-Theresien Platz, which contains works by world masters including Dutch, Flemish, German, Venetian, and Florentine works. We were very impressed with a series of Titians including *Dance,* where Zeus's face is close to Danae (who later bore his son) in the guise of gold rain; Tintoretto's *Susanna in the Bath* and *Sebastiano Venier* with a battle at sea visible behind him; Reubens' *Medusa* complete with snakes and scorpions; and Bruegel's *Winter* and *Fight between Carnival and Lent.*

The **Ephesus Museum,** Heldenplatz, contains collections from that famous archaeological site in Turkey. The **Museum of Ethnography** houses Montezuma's exotic feather headdress. The **Portrait Collection** of the National Library completes the complex.

Also in the Hofburg, the entrance to the **Spanish Riding School** (*Spanische Reitschule*), Josefsplatz, where the famous Lipizzan horses perform, is just opposite the **Winter Riding School**. Visitors may watch training sessions on a first-come-first-served basis, or may write for tickets in advance.

The **Church of the Capuchin Friars** (*Kapuzinerkirche*), on Neue Markt, contains the **Imperial Burial Vault** underneath. All reigning Habsburgs who died from 1633 to 1916 lie there. (However, their hearts were placed in urns in the Church of the Augustinians.) Maria Theresia and her husband, Emperor Franz I, share a double casket. They recline raised on one elbow to face each other. A cherub holds a crown over their heads. A number of small sarcophagi contain their children who died young; we felt a twinge of sorrow as we lingered there. Isabella of Parma's sarcophagus hovers over a very tiny one containing her infant who died after living only a few days. Her other daughter, who died at age 7, is nearby.

The earliest coffins are that of Kauser Matthias, who died in 1619, and that of his wife Anna, who died in 1618. A row of black sarcophagi are decorated with skull and crossbones, animals such as lions symbolizing nobility, and eagles to bring the soul to heaven. The scenes on Kauser Karl VI, from 1740, show battle scenes with lions at the base and a mourning lady. His wife Elizabeth's tomb has a ship because she went to Barcelona, and a snake with its tail in its mouth in a circle representing eternity.

The last coffin is that of Empress Zita, widow of Emperor Karl I, who reigned from 1916–18. She died in 1989 and her permanent sarcophagus was installed the day before we visited in May 1991.

On Maria-Theresien Platz, two museums face each other in the same neo-Renaissance style. The **Natural History Museum** (*Naturhistorisches Museum*) houses prehistoric, geological, and botanical sections. The *Venus of Willendorf* from the Stone Age is a favorite. Skeletons and fossils are also on display. The **Museum of Fine Art** described earlier, is the other.

Prater is a large park, and was once a hunting reserve of the aristocracy. Emperor Josef II opened it to the public. The **Giant Wheel** (*Riesenrad*) is a landmark that can be seen from afar. Built by Walter Basset, the wheel was destroyed in 1945 but by 1946 it was whirling around again.

Belvedere Gardens were designed in 1693 by J. L. von Hildebrandt and redone in 1717 by Dominique Girard. Fountains and statues give life to the gardens. The 1721 Upper Belvedere structure once contained the Imperial picture gallery. Archduke Franz Ferdinand lived there from 1904 to 1914 (when he was assassinated at Sarajevo) and since 1924 it has again become the Austrian Gallery for 19th- and 20th-century art.

Take time to stroll down the hill through the gardens past Roman mythological and muse statues, flowers, fountains, and trees trimmed like cones and spheres. The second palace, **Lower Belvedere,** was once a summer residence.

It now contains the **Museum of Medieval Austrian Art** and the **Museum of Austrian Baroque Art**. A wooden statue shows St. Rochus revealing his wound from bubonic plague. Beside him stands a small dog who brought bread every day to keep him from starving.

A bronze bust of Maria Theresia and her husband Franz I precede a collection of the sculptor Franz-Xaver Messerschmidt created after he became insane. He "pulled faces" while standing in front of a mirror, sketched them, and sculpted grotesque faces. We were impressed with his earlier work—large lead statues of Maria Theresia and Franz I in their coronation robes. He was skillful in catching detail of garments, crown, hair, and face.

The **Gold Room** contains the *Apotheosis of Prince Eugene* in marble created by Balthazar Permoser. Look for the artist at the foot of the Prince.

The first building of **Schonbrunn Palace** was a hunting lodge, ravaged by the Turks in 1683. In 1695, Emperor Leopold I planned a palace for his son, Josef I. Maria Theresia used Schonbrunn as her summer residence. Her daughter, Marie Antoinette, who later became the Queen of France, lived there as a child.

Mozart first appeared at Schonbrunn before the Empress as a child prodigy at the age of six in the Hall of Mirrors. On that day, October 13, 1762, the royal family sat in the front row on golden chairs. Wolfgang and his sister Nannerl took turns playing and singing with echoes of "Bravo" in their ears. Then Emperor Franz stood and walked to the piano where he asked young Wolfgang to play a tune with one finger only, which he did. Finally, a black cloth was laid over the keys and he played without seeing them. After it was over he jumped into the Empress's lap and gave her a big kiss. It is also said that he offered to marry Marie Antoinette when he was older.

Napoleon lived in Schonbrunn from 1805 to 1809. In Napoleon's chamber stands the bed where his son, Napoleon II, died at age 21. The second Napoleon's death mask is there but his heart lies in a silver urn in St. Augustine Church. Karl I, who was the last Habsburg, signed his Abdication Act there in 1918.

The apartments are sumptuous with gilding including ivory and gold-tile stoves. Portraits of Maria Theresia's many children hang on the walls. Frescoes, crystal chandeliers, tapestries, and period furniture are all in place. In the guest wing, the **Blue Salon** has a magnificent Chinese tapestry. The **Napoleon Room** was his study, now hung with Brussels tapestry. The **Room of a Million** contains Persian miniatures on parchment. The **Imperial Coach Collection** contains 60 coaches and carriages including a gilded coronation coach.

The park surrounding Schonbrunn is one of the most elaborate in Europe. Light opera is presented in the Palace Theater during the summer. Formal gardens, where strollers wander amid arbors, grottoes, and fountains lead to the **Zoo** (*Tiergarten*), the **Palmery** (*Palmenhaus,*) and the **Pavilion** (*Gloriette*). The *Neptune Fountain* was created by Franz Anton Zauner in 1780. It is in motion with tritons (half man and half fish) and sea horses amid shells and marine life. Above the fountain lies the **Pavilion,** with a fine view of the gardens and palace

AUSTRIA · · 27

below and the city beyond. The climb is well worth the trouble, and you can wander down along a series of paths through the woods. Don't miss the "fake" Roman ruins. Maria Theresia was following the fashions of the times in 1778 when she commissioned a scene of crumbling arches, urns lying about, and headless statues in her garden.

DAY TRIPS FROM VIENNA ··················

Vienna Woods

Not many cities are so fortunate in their surroundings as Vienna, where one can live in the city and reach beautiful wooded hills in half an hour.

The **Vienna Woods** (*Wienerwald*) are popular for walks as well as drives through villages such as Perchtoldsdorf, Modling, the 1133 medieval cloister at Heiligenkreuz, and Gumpoldskirchen. Baden is the place to visit 15 sulfur thermal springs amid the ghosts of summer residents Schubert, Strauss, and Franz I. **Beethoven House** is renowned as the place where the composer wrote his Ninth Symphony.

Crown Prince Rudolf, the son of Emperor Franz Joseph, used Mayerling as his hunting retreat; a chapel remains. The prince shot his lover, Baronesse Vetsera, and then killed himself there in 1889.

Vineyards perched on steep slopes produce wine, and hiking paths wind through much of the woods. Try not to drive a car onto a wide, paved hiking path as we did up in the hills.

BELGIUM

Currency unit • Belgian franc (BF)
Languages • Flemish, French, Dutch, German
Time difference from USA • six hours later (Eastern Standard Time)
Telephone access codes • to USA 001, USADirect 110010; from USA 01132
National Tourist Offices • **USA:** Belgian National Tourist Office, 745 Fifth Ave., New York, NY 10151, tel. (212) 758–8130; **Brussels:** Town Hall, Grand Place, tel.: (02) 513–8940 or 61 Rue Marche aux Herbes, 1000 Brussels, tel.: (02) 512–3030 **Great Britain:** Belgian National Tourist Office, Premier House, 2 Gayton Rd., Harrow Middlesex HA1 2XU, tel.: (081) 861–3300
Airlines • **Sabena:** **USA:** (800) 541–4551 or (516) 466–6100; **Britain:** (081) 780–1444
Embassies • **American Embassy:** 27 Boulevard du Regent, B-1000 Brussels, tel.: (02) 513–3830; **British Embassy:** Brittania House, rue Joseph II 28, 1040 Brussels (02) 217–9000

Belgium is a country that many visitors pass through as they land on the ferry from England or enter from the Netherlands, Germany, or France. Most of them know only Brussels, Bruge, Ghent, and Antwerp. We found that we really didn't know the south at all as we set off on a tour to visit its many castles and gardens. Time seemed to stand still there; it's the perfect place to enjoy a relaxed, uncrowded pace for a few days—canoeing its many beautiful rivers, hiking wooded hillsides, or wandering through unspoiled villages.

HISTORY......................................

Julius Caesar ruled, from 57 to 50 B.C., this home of the Gallo-Celtic tribes, called Belgae. The Franks arrived to work as mercenaries for the Romans, but with their own chiefs. Chlodio, then Meroveus, Childeric, and finally Clovis, ruled one after the other. In 800 Charlemagne was crowned Emperor of the

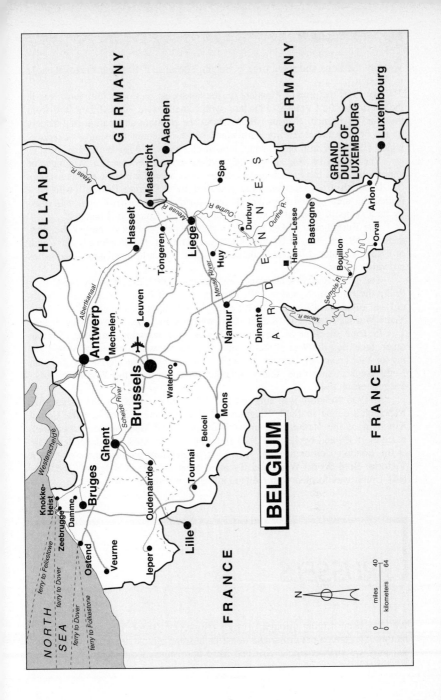

West by the Pope and spent time in Belgium because it was near his royal castle in Aachen.

By 1100 the area of Flanders (in the northwest section of Belgium) was in the control of the Counts of Flanders, who actually were granted their land from the Kind of France. Constant fights about the possible annexation of Flanders by the French included some particularly vicious encounters using *goedendags*, which are spiked iron balls swung around on chains to bash aggressors.

The Dukes of Brabant (in the northeastern area) were not in danger of annexation from the French and therefore were spared constant intrigue. Liege (in the southeastern section) was governed by a "Prince-Bishop" who controlled the area around the city. Hainaut (in the southwestern area) was ruled by the Counts of Hainaut, who were subject to the Counts of Flanders.

The Burgundian Dukes hatched a plan to gain control of part of Belgium and in 1369 the Duke of Burgundy married Margaret, the daughter of the Count of Flanders. Later, Margaret inherited Brabant, which her husband added to his growing empire.

The Holy Roman Emperors' reign began with Maximilian in 1494, then Philip the Handsome, and in 1506 Charles V inherited the title as a seven-year-old and ruled for 40 years. By 1555 religious conflict was rampant; the Thirty Years War lasted from 1618 until 1648, when the Peace of Munster was signed.

In 1667 the War of Devolution began, with wars erupting one after the other, including the War of the Spanish Succession, which ended with the signing of the Treaty of Utrecht in 1713. Belgium was considered the Austrian Netherlands at that time, and war broke out again with the War of Austrian Succession in 1744.

In 1795 Belgium was annexed to France and occupied by the Allies after Napoleon's defeat in 1814. Belgium and Holland were melded into the United Kingdom of the Netherlands under William I. The Belgian Revolution took place in 1830, and by January 1831 Belgium was declared an independent state at the London Conference; the first King of Belgium was an uncle of Queen Victoria. Both World War I and II caused great damage in Belgium. The Benelux Union was formed with Holland and Luxembourg in 1944.

BRUSSELS

We have been driving through Brussels (Bruxelles, Brussel) for over 30 years, finding it a convenient crossroads for trips heading almost anywhere in Europe. Recently we stopped for a visit and liked it so much we returned for another week. We are drawn time after time to the magnificent Grand' Place, especially when it is glowing with light at night, to the magnificent museums of ancient and modern art, and to a wealth of performances in opera, theater, and ballet. And like the hub of a wheel, the city is central for excursions out into the country in all directions—to medieval merchant cities like Antwerp, Ghent, and Bruges in the northern lowlands and to castles and dry river valleys in the southern highlands. And to the delight of those who like to stay in one place, you can live in Brussels and reach all the surrounding destinations on day trips.

HISTORY..

No one knows how early a town was established on Brussels' present site. Excavation has revealed evidence of Neolithic man, then Roman habitation. After the Romans left, the Gallo-Roman inhabitants found a safe refuge from the marauding Franks in the marshes of the Senne River. In 966 the name *Bruocsella,* which means ''a village of the marsh,'' was listed in a document by Emperor Ott I the Great. Charles of France built a castle on an island in the Senne River as well as a chapel in the village in 977. By 1100, the first fortified walls were built around Brussels; a second set was added in 1379. A new castle was built on Coudenberg Hill, now the location of the Place Royale.

The House of Leuven ruled the city during medieval times until Duchess Jeanne died in the early 1400's. Philip the Good, of the House of Burgundy, took charge in 1430. The wealthy Dukes of Burgundy poured money into Brussels and became patrons for many artisans. The Grand' Place developed in elegant style with the construction of the Town Hall, and wealthy guilds built houses along the square. Medieval festivities took place in the Grand' Place, complete with officials in colorful ceremonial garb and flags flying. Religious strife and squabbling for the next couple of hundred years included the bombing of the Grand' Place by Louis XIV's French troops led by Marshall de Villeroy in 1695. Furious inhabitants were determined to rebuild their square in grand baroque style—and they did.

The French Revolution and two world wars saw men from other countries marching and fighting in Belgium. When that dust cleared, another wave of construction began—as Brussels became the headquarters of the European Economic Community, the North Atlantic Treaty Organization, and other international organizations. Today, 25% of Brussels' inhabitants are foreign residents. Language is bilingual (French and Flemish) with a number of other languages as well. This international city has charm, elegance and flair.

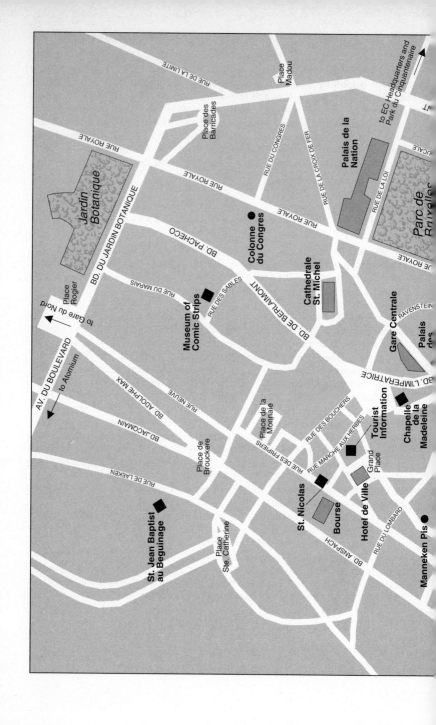

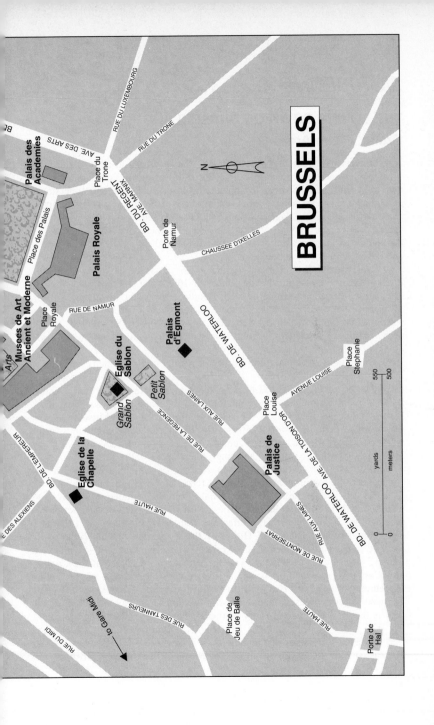

BRUSSELS

N

Palais des Académies

AVE. DES ARTS

RUE DU LUXEMBOURG

RUE DU TRONE

Place du Trone

BD. DU REGENT

AVE. MARNIX

Palais Royale

Place des Palais

Musees de Art Ancient et Moderne

Arts

Place Royale

RUE DE NAMUR

Porte de Namur

CHAUSSEE D'IXELLES

Eglise du Sablon

Grand Sablon

Petit Sablon

Palais d'Egmont

RUE DE LA REGENCE

RUE AUX LAINES

BD. DE WATERLOO

AVENUE LOUISE

Place Stephanie

Place Louise

Eglise de la Chapelle

BD. DE L'EMPEREUR

RUE HAUTE

Palais de Justice

AVE. DE LA TOISON D'OR

RUE DES ALEXIENS

RUE DE MONTSERRAT

RUE AUX LAINES

BD. DE WATERLOO

yards   550
meters   500

0   0

RUE DU MIDI

to Gare Midi

RUE DES TANNEURS

Place de Jeu de Balle

RUE HAUTE

Porte de Hal

SIGHTSEEING......................................

THE LOWER TOWN OF BRUSSELS
Grand' Place Area

Almost everyone heads first for the Grand' Place—unable to resist the dazzling ornate spires and step-roofed gilded gables of this medieval fairyland. You cannot see it from afar but need to approach from one of the cobblestone streets, emerging into a vast square, almost too heady to believe. A kaleidoscope of color swirls in waving flags, gilt facades, sweeping birds, flowers, wicker cafe chairs, and people moving about. Many writers, including Jean Cocteau, rate the square as the most beautiful in the world. And at night the lighted peaks and turrets lend a very romantic aura.

The **Town Hall** (*Hotel de Ville*) has a Gothic facade dating back to 1402; it managed to survive the bombardment in 1695. The figure of St. Michael, designed by Martin van Rode in 1465, stands on top of the tower, as if it were a weathervane. Above the main entrance stand statues of the five most revered patron saints: St. Michael, St. Sebastian, St. Christopher, St. George, and St. Gery. Statues of prominent local citizens depict 14th-century characters. Inside, 16th- to 18th-century Brussels tapestries (look for the "BB" or "Bruxella in Brabantia" logo) are hung with portraits of royalty and noblemen.

Directly opposite the Town Hall is the **Maison du Roi,** which was originally the *Broodhuis,* or Bread-house. Later, in the 16th century, the Duke of Brabant built a stone house there and changed the name to House of the King. It was rebuilt again in the 1870's and now houses the **City Museum** (*Musee Communal*) where the history of Brussels is displayed. Maps, engravings, paintings, retables, porcelain, pewter, lace, silver, sculpture, and tapestries are there. Most visitors want to see the amusing collection of 350 costumes sent from around the world to fit the little *Mannekin Pis* (see page 35, below). The first one was sent by Maximilian of Bavaria in 1698, later one by Louis XV in 1747.

The very ornate guild houses, in "Italo-Brabant" baroque style were completely rebuilt after the 1695 destruction. Moving in a clockwise direction one sees first #7 **House of the Haberdashers** with a statue on top of St. Nicolas, patron saint of merchants; #6 **House of the Boatmen** with the gable as the stern of a ship; #5 **House of the Archers** with a bas-relief of Romulus and Remus, Roman emperors and the Phoenix at the top; #4 **House of the Coopers and Carpenters,** which looks like a wooden chest; #3 **House of the Tallow Merchants;** #1 and #2 **House of the Bakers** with a bronze bust of St. Aubert. The next series of houses, located west of the Maison du Roi are not all guilds: #37 is the **House of the Hosiery Makers**. On the east side of the Maison du Roi #26 and #27 were once the **Houses of the Painters,** later sold; #24 and #25 belonged to **Houses of the Tailors,** with a statue of St. Boniface on top. The east side of the square belongs to the **House of the Dukes of Brabant** with busts of the dukes on the nineteen pillars. The **Brewery House** at #10 has a museum and a tasting room; #9 was once the **House of the Butchers;** and #8 contains a memorial to **Everard 't Serclaes,** leader of the guilds in the 14th century who was executed in the Square. It is said that anyone who touches Everard's arm will be happy for a year.

Nearby, at the corner of Rue de l'Etuve and Rue du Chene, stands the spouting *Manneken Pis.* This bronze statue was designed in 1619 by Jerome Duquesnoy. Some say that the model for this child was Julian, who put out the fire from an incendiary bomb in this way. He has been kidnapped several times over the years, in 1745 by the English, 1747 by the French, and in 1817 by a reprieved French convict.

The **Toone VII Theatre Museum,** located on Petite rue des Bouchers, offers performances as well as a museum. Marionettes who played the stage many years ago rest comfortably on display; who knows what they do at night after the doors are closed! The knight might decide to dance with a princess, or the deathly skeleton get into trouble with his scythe. The folklore of Brussels can be glimpsed here in paintings, posters, manuscripts, and carved wooden pieces of furniture.

The **Galeries Saint Hubert,** built in 1846, were the first arcades in Europe. The **Galerie de la Reine** and the **Galerie du Roi** are divided by the Rue des Bouchers. It is pleasant to window shop there in inclement weather as well as walk through on the way to another sight.

Place de Brouckere

Place de Brouckere, named after Charles de Brouckere who was burgomaster of Brussels 1848–1860, can be considered the modern center of the Lower Town. A mint provided the name for the Centre Monnaie, which now houses the post office, shops, city offices, a Metro station, and large underground car park. (Beware when parking in the car park on a weekend. We needed to catch an early morning ferry from Ostend which meant leaving Brussels before the car park opened. After neglecting to read the signs when we went in, we had a moment of panic until finding that it was necessary to place certain coins in the slot to release the gate and drive out.)

The **Theatre de la Monnaie** offers a full schedule of opera and ballet. In 1830, during a performance of Auber's *La Muette de Portici,* political unrest had reached fever pitch and the call "to arms" was shouted during the third act. Reportedly the entire audience responded with thunderous applause and rushed out to begin the Revolution. The oval ceiling has been painted with vivid colors, set off by a Venetian crystal chandelier weighing one and one-half tons. Burgundy velvet and gilt decorations make this concert hall warm and elegant.

The **Anspach Center,** located southwest of Centre Monnaie, contains the **Musec du Jouet,** a museum of toys dating from the mid-19th century. The **Musee de Cire** displays material portraying the history of Belgium from Julius

Caesar to the present day in wax. Life-size wax figures, dressed in period costume, are incorporated into 20 scenes, complete with background and sound.

On the other side of De Brouckere are two churches worth a visit. The **Church of Saint John the Baptist** in the Beguinage is on rue du Marronnier. Built in 17th-century Italo-Flemish baroque style, the facade is considered to be one of the most beautiful in Belgium. John I, Duke of Brabant, gave the Beguines permission to live in a community in 1250. The first name was Our Lady of the Vineyard. Their church was destroyed during the religious wars, then rebuilt in the 17th century. During the French Revolution the community of Beguines was disbanded and its possessions confiscated. The last Beguine of Brussels died in 1883. Inside, the wooden pulpit has a carved canopy of palm leaves and angels. The altar was sculpted in black and white marble by van Mons for the Beguinage in Kortenberg, then transferred here.

The **Church of St. Catherine** was built in the 19th century on the site of a 17th-century church. The belfry of the original church still stands as well as parts of the 12th-century town walls nearby. Inside, the church is a mixture of Renaissance and baroque. The collection of paintings is worth seeing.

THE UPPER TOWN
Royal Brussels and Parliament

The **Royal Palace** is open to the public for one month during the summer. The original building, ordered by the Dukes of Brabant, burned in 1731; another was built in the form of two pavilions that King William joined with a gallery in the early 1800's. Leopold II modified the palace in the early 1900's in Louis XVI style.

The **Small White Drawing Room** is ornate with gilt on columns, ceiling, sconces, armchairs, and mantlepiece. Crystal chandeliers hang from the ceiling and crystal sconces are spaced along the walls. The **Large White Drawing Room** has tapestries adorning the walls; a perfect spot in which to hold audiences with foreign statesmen. The **Empire Room** is a ballroom with a polished parquet floor. The **Throne Room** contains massive crystal chandeliers, red velvet draperies and chairs, and enormous square pillars. The **Great Gallery** features paintings in its arched ceiling, interspersed with hanging chandeliers.

The **Church of Saint Jacques sur Coudenberg** stands on the site of the original chapel built by Charles of France. This building, dating from 1776, was built in neo-classical style, with a hexagonal tower and dome added in 1849. The royal family attend church here.

Parc de Bruxelles (or Warande) is directly in front of the palace. Belgium became independent after a thousand years of foreign domination following a battle fought in this park. Dutch troops tried to win against Belgian patriots who rose up in 1830 and gained their freedom. Sculptures in the park include *Diana* by Gabriel Grupello.

THE UPPER TOWN OF BRUSSELS

Most of the art museums are located up on the hill, right next to the Royal Palace. The neo-classical building for the **Belgian Royal Museum of Fine Arts** was built in 1876 by the architect Balat. Four Corinthian granite columns soar into the air, topped by four figures symbolizing Painting, Sculpture, Architecture, and Music. The building is divided into two sections, one for ancient art and one for modern art. They are linked by escalators and passageways.

The **Musee d'Art Ancien** extends back beyond a large rectangular sculpture hall into three circuits identified by color. The blue route contains 15th- and 16th-century works, the brown houses 17th- and 18th-century works, and the yellow is for the 19th century. Favorites include: Hans Memling's *Martyrdom of St. Sebastian,* portraits of children including Anne of Austria holding a bird, and Cranach's *Adam and Eve* with Eve holding not one but two apples and wearing an innocent expression. The serpent poised in a tree is pointing to the apples.

The **Musee d'Art Moderne,** Place Royale 1, descends down into eight subterranean floors which are confusing to say the least. One has the sense of being lost much of the time down there, especially if trying to keep track of a slower companion.

SABLON AREA

The **Place du Grand Sablon** is popular for its antique shops; an antique and book market is held there on weekends. The **Church of Notre Dame du Sablon** (*Zavel Kerk*), dating from the 15th century has an exceptionally handsome choir. The **Guild of Crossbowmen** built a chapel on the site in 1304 and later a church. Legend relates that Beatrice Soetkens stole a statue of Our Lady from the Cathedral in Antwerp and came by boat into Brussels. The crossbowmen befriended her and kept the statue safe until it could be installed in the church. The statue was carried in a procession, now repeated every July as the Brussels' *Ommegang.* The church has five aisles and brilliant 14-meter-high stained-glass windows. Claude Bouton is depicted on his monument with part of his skeleton exposed.

The **Petit Sablon** (*Kleine Zavel*) gardens are encompassed by a wrought-iron railing decorated with 48 bronze statuettes symbolizing the Brussels Guilds. The statues in the center are those of Count Egmont and Count Horne who were formidable against Spanish domination in the 16th century.

The **Church of Notre Dame de la Chapelle** (*Kapellekerk*) contains the tombs of Peter Bruegel the Elder and the Spinola family. The original building was constructed as a chapel in 1134. Frans Anneessens, who was beheaded in the Grand Place in 1719 as a leader of the independence movement, is honored by a memorial in the large chapel. A carved oak pulpit portrays Elijah's flight into a cave to outwit Jezebel and an angel bringing him food.

St. Michael's Church and Place du Congres

Walk up to the Place du Congres for a sweeping view of the lower town. The pillar was constructed between 1850 and 1859 with King Leopold's statue at the top to commemorate the constitution installed by the National Congress of 1831. King Albert I presented a tomb for an unknown soldier there in 1922. Two bronze lions guard the tomb.

The **Cathedrale Saint Michel** (*Sainte Gudule*) is the national church of Belgium. St. Gudule was a young girl who journeyed across the marsh to pray even though the devil kept blowing out her candle. Her body was kept in the church from 1047 until it mysteriously disappeared during the 17th century. Philip the Good and Charles the Bold held ceremonies of the Order of the Golden Fleece in the church.

The architecture of the cathedral varies from early Gothic-Romanesque to late Gothic-baroque. Stained-glass windows were created by Barend van Orley. The neo-Gothic altar is made of gilded copper. The carved wooden pulpit was made by Hendrik Verbruggen in 1699 for a church in Louvain, later brought here. Chapelle du Saint Sacrement de Miracle is said to be where the Host was secreted away during troublesome religious times in the 16th century.

DAY TRIPS FROM BRUSSELS.................

ANTWERP

Antwerp belongs to Rubens; we couldn't wait to visit his home and imagine his life there. See if you can draw your eyes away from his in the self-portrait in his home, then savor his magnificent paintings in the cathedral. The wealth that supported Rubens and other painters grew from centuries of Antwerp's commercial success as one of Europe's principal trading centers, and you will see evidence of that old prosperity everywhere, but especially in the guildhalls surrounding the great market square and in warehouses around the harbor.

History

According to legend, the giant Druon Antigon insisted that every boatsman who passed his castle pay a toll; if he couldn't pay, his hand was cut off. A Roman warrior, Silvius Brabo, killed the giant and threw his hand in the river. Thankful, the local inhabitants called their town Antwerpen (hand werpen) which means "throw the hand." Other theories report that the name came from the derivation meaning "at the wharf."

Historians report that life existed there as early as the 2nd century. During the 9th century, Norsemen invaded; in 836 they destroyed the existing town and built a fortress. In 1406 Antwerp was united with Brabant under the House of Burgundy. Because the Bruges River silted up Antwerp became more powerful as a seagoing port. During the 16th century Antwerp was the economic center of Europe under Charles V. Prosperity was evident in trade and industry; many public buildings went up and Flemish culture expanded. In 1794 Napoleon began building docks and a naval dockyard to strengthen his position against the English across the Channel.

Sightseeing

Market Square (*Grote Markt*) is the center of Antwerp. The *Brabo Fountain* is huge and full of motion. Brabo stands on a tall tower high over rough rocks, poised over a fountain to throw the giant's hand into the river.

The **Town Hall,** dating from Antwerp's "golden age" in the 16th century, is the largest building on the square. A statue of the Virgin, patron saint of Antwerp, stands five stories up on the facade of this Renaissance building. Below her resides Philip II of Spain. The eagles on the roof stare in the direction of Aachen, which was the seat of the Holy Roman Empire, to which Antwerp belonged. During the Spanish turbulence in 1576, the Hall was burned on the inside but later rebuilt and decorated with paintings. The **Marriage Chamber** contains an old chimneypiece and lovely caryatids by Cornelis Floris. Another chimneypiece stands in the **Burgomaster's Room**.

Ornate guildhouses line the square; some of them are authentic, others are reconstructions. A number of the houses bear the symbol or trademark of their guild. Restaurants and cafes flourish on the ground floor of many of them.

The Gothic **Cathedral of Our Lady** (*Onze Lieve-Vrouw*), 21 Groenplaats, is the largest church in Belgium and Holland. It has seven naves and 125 pillars. One of five planned towers was completed after 200 years of work in the 16th century; it is 123 meters high. One of the "Seven Marvels" of Belgium is a mammoth triptych painting by Rubens—*Descent from the Cross*. The facial expressions convey compassion and love as Jesus is taken down from the cross. The colors were designed to fit the mood with brilliant light and deepening shadow. Some of his other work is also here: *Raising of the Cross* and *Ascension of Mary*.

The carillon contains 47 bronze bells; the heaviest and oldest bell, dating from 1459, is named Gabriel. The carillon's automatic mechanism looks like a large cylinder, called the drum, with many tiny slits. As the drum rotates, steel pins operate the bell-clappers. The carilloneur plays a keyboard with both hands and feet; the feet pound pedals with great force.

The **National Maritime Museum** (*Scheepvaartmuseum*), 1 Steenplein, is the oldest building in Antwerp, dating from the 12th century. The building itself is a prize; one wanders through a series of little rooms and up and down steep stairs. The museum is arranged in 12 sections ranging from the waterfront, inland navigation, fishing, shipbuilding, and the history of shipping. There are enough models, artifacts, and displays to keep visitors' attention for some time.

Displays focus on superstitions and taboos of sailors; tattooing, including women, around 1900; a "skin boat" called a coracle, figureheads, and a state barge for Napoleon's 1810 visit caught our eye. In the Council Chamber there are paintings of the waterfront in old Antwerp. A number of vessels are berthed just outside the Steen, including a barge, the *Lauranda,* where visitors can see how the bargee and his mate lived in years past.

When Peter Paul Rubens arrived in Antwerp to train at the Academy he had a large house built for himself at 9 Wapper. Now a museum, **Ruben's House** contains his paintings as well as those of others and furniture of the period. This house was a place where artists, noblemen, and royalty gathered. Long after Rubens' death the house fell into ruin, but it was fully restored and opened as a museum in 1946. The studio has an exceptionally high narrow doorway to accommodate large canvases as they were moved in and out. Rubens' *Adam and Eve* hangs beside the door. The dining room contains a self-portrait by Rubens, looking at the visitor with staring eyes. One of the pictures in the art gallery is Willem van Haecht's *The Gallery of Cornelis van der Geest,* which portrays a royal visit to the collection of one of Rubens' friends. Rubens died in the large bedroom upstairs. A crystal necklace belonging to his second wife, Helene, is on display as well as her portrait in the small bedroom. Rubens' name is inscribed on the chair he received as Dean of the Guild of St. Luke, found in the corner bedroom. His grandparents' portraits hang in the living room. Old prints provided authentic information for gardeners as the garden was designed in the Italian-Flemish style popular in Rubens' time.

The **Provincial Diamond Museum,** at 28-30 Jezusstraat, offers a look at one of Antwerp's most prosperous industries—diamond cutting. Displays explain how the diamonds are found, extracted, worked, and placed into jewelry. Diamond cutting in Antwerp dates back to 1483, if not before. Many of the documents detailing diamond cutting were destroyed during World War II but one remains with the date 1483.

WATERLOO

Waterloo, where Napoleon was defeated in 1815, contains a number of museums, dioramas, and exhibits of memorabilia. Visitors can climb 226 steps up to the top of the **Lion's Mount,** (*Butte du Lion*) created by many pails of earth carried up by Belgian housewives to commemorate the spot where Netherland's Prince of Orange was wounded. The lion on top was the work of J. F. Van Geel; it weighs 28 tons. The wraparound view of the vast battlefield is indeed panoramic. At the bottom of the hill there is a building containing a large "panorama" (*Braine l'Alleud*) of part of the battle painted by Louis Dumoulin. The **Duke of Wellington's museum** (*Musee Wellington*), located several miles away in Vieux-Genappe, has a new wing showing every stage of the battle. Another section contains local history, and a third area has a collection of memorabilia and pictures.

GENT

Children, and others, are fascinated by the story of the copper dragon of Gent (Ghent), perched on top of the Belfry. It's like looking for the Loch Ness Monster in Scotland to emerge—we waited and watched, wondering if the dragon was about to spout fire as he is said to have done in the past to commemorate great events in the life of the city. But the engineering of Gent's great bell tower is more than legendary, as is the bustling commercial activity that surrounds and penetrates the old city.

HISTORY.....................................

Gent, the capital of Flanders, is poised on a number of islands in the rivers Schelde and Leie. Also known as the "city of flowers," Gent blooms much of the year in city flower stands as well as just outside town where the nurseries flourish.

Dating from the 7th century when St. Amand established a monastery and church, Gent became a major commercial center larger than Paris during the 13th century. The economy focused on the cloth industry. During the next several hundred years Gent's rebellious citizens staged many revolts, leading to the imprisonment of Charles the Bold's daughter Mary. She was forced to sign the Great Privilege, which was in fact a liberal constitution. During the 16th century, the cloth industry folded and boatmen took over as the ruling guild with their export of grain along rivers and into France.

SIGHTSEEING.....................................

Visitors who enter the **Castle of the Counts** (*Gravensteen*), on St. Veerleplein, are treated to a harpist playing classical music. Melodies waft up the stairs and into the Countess's Room. Originally built in 868 by Count Baldwin I, the fortress was rebuilt by Philip of Alsace in 1840. Count Egmont, who is remembered in Goethe's play and Beethoven's overture to it, was imprisoned in Gravensteen during the 16th century. A number of rooms were used as prisons; those who would rather not view torture equipment should avoid the count's private quarters. The top of the tower is the place to go for views of the city and the surrounding countryside.

St. Bavo's Abbey (*St. Baafsabdij* or *St. Baaf's*), Gandastraat, houses a treasure by Jan Hubert Van Eyck, the *Adoration of the Mystic Lamb*. Facial expressions and brilliant colors depict the Mystic Lamb delivering the world from original sin. Surrounded by angels, apostles, patriarchs, prophets, and bishops the lamb seems to have everyone in control. The painting spreads to wings and also has an upper layer containing paintings of Christ, the Virgin, St. John the Baptist, Adam and Eve, and Cain and Abel. In 1566 the panels were hidden in the tower of the cathedral to save them from destruction by the iconoclasts' raids. Three years later they were taken to the Town Hall with plans to send them to Elizabeth I of England as a present. This almost-adventure was stopped by one of the families who commissioned and paid for the triptych. In 1794 agents arrived from Paris to take back treasures; they removed the four middle panels. In 1815 the peace treaty provided for the return of the four panels to Gent. However, when the bishop was away, some of the panels were sold to an art dealer in Brussels. Later they made their way to Berlin. During World War I the panels were hidden away, then returned to their home in Gent; during World War II they again roamed around Europe and were eventually brought back home.

The **rococo pulpit** is spectacular, with a pair of marble figures: Time sits on a stone block and leans against a tree stump, Truth has a dove behind her head and her foot on a globe. The branches of the tree hold up the pulpit and the canopy has a dove on the underneath side. A cherub is in the process of grabbing an apple from a coiling snake.

Monseigneur d'Allamont's tomb, in black and white marble, is startling, with a rakish skeleton sitting on the tomb talking to the bishop. Anthony Triest, who was bishop of Ghent from 1621 to 1657, reclines in marble on top of his tomb, leaning on one elbow.

The **Belfry and Cloth Hall** (*Belfort en Lakenhalle*) are Gothic structures dating from the 14th century. The Belfry was a symbol of power of the guilds; the bell of Roalant was used to call the citizens to arms. We were told that Roalant was the name of a man crossing the alps in battle, blowing his horn and fighting for the city. Visitors can take a lift to the top of the tower for a view of the city. Stop on each floor coming down to see the pullies, weights, and drum with pegs sticking out to trigger the chimes and 52 bells, and hear explanations of the entire process. The lowest room was where charters and documents were kept safe. Two doors guarded the room, each with three locks; keys were kept by several different guilds.

The Belfry is topped by a spire inhabited by a great, ferocious, gilded copper dragon; some say the dragon was brought from Constantinople during the Fourth Crusade. However, ancient city records state that the dragon was ordered and paid for by the city in 1377. Take your choice. In 1500 he belched fire for the baptism of Charles of Habsburg, the future Emperor Charles V.

Later, he spat fire in 1648, for the signature of the Treaty of Westphalia; in 1683, when the Turks were stopped in Vienna; in 1709 as a welcome to the Duke of Marlborough; and finally in 1819 for the visit of the Prince of Orange. He has been repaired a number of times including in 1689, when he received a new brass tongue and seven brass teeth. When the wooden superstructure of the belfry needed to be removed in 1839, the dragon lived at the University; in fact, he did not leave there until 1913, when he returned to his post.

The adjacent **Cloth Hall** was the site of medieval wool trading. Now a large model of Gent is on display there. An audiovisual entitled *Ghent and Charles V* is played for visitors.

The **town hall** (*Stadhuis*), Botermarkt, is a mixture of Renaissance and Gothic architecture. The Peace Treaty of Ghent was signed in 1576 by Protestants and Catholics there. An unusual ''maze'' painting hangs near the site of the treaty signing. The town hall is not open to visitors except during group visits arranged in writing at least three weeks in advance.

Near the town hall stand a number of guild houses, along the Korenlei and the Graslei banks of the Leie River. The best view of these houses, dating from the 12th to 17th centuries, is from the Korenlei side of the river. They range from Romanesque and Gothic to Renaissance styles. Beginning at the bridge, the houses start with the **House of the Free Boatmen,** belonging to one of the strongest guilds in town. The boatmen had the right to make sure all cargo was carried on their boats through Gent. The house, dating from 1355 but sold to the boatmen in 1530, is called *The Windlass*. There is a bas-relief of a ship over the door, handsome with three masts and high-backed stern. The **House of the Corn Measurers** dates from 1698; an earlier **Corn Measurers house** dating from 1435 is farther along the row. The very small building is the **House of the Receiver of the Staple,** which is a toll or customs house. The **Staple Warehouse,** a Romanesque hulk dating from the 13th century is one of the oldest buildings in the area. The first **Corn Measurers house** is next, then finally the **House of the Free Masons,** dating from the 16th century.

BRUGES

Bruges (Brugge) is one of the most romantic cities anywhere, because it is a living relic of its own heyday. With its cobbled streets and lacework of canals visitors feel transported back in time to medieval days. A canal trip gliding past gabled houses and under arched bridges or clopping along by carriage leaves lasting memories. Lights on the canals at night turn the city into fairyland.

Bruges is a walking town and there are photographic opportunities from every bridge and around every corner.

HISTORY....................................

The North Sea had worn away a channel into the land and by the 4th century, people settled beside the river Zwin, on the site of Bruges. In 862 Judith, the daughter of the French King Charles the Bald, was captured by Boudewijn to be his wife. King Charles sent his new son-in-law to Flanders to guard it from invading Norsemen who had earlier constructed a landing platform, called a *Bryggja,* so their ships could land. Boudewijn built a fortress there and by the 10th century a trading town had grown up around it. As the Zwin silted up, the port of Damme developed, with access to Bruges by a canal.

Bruges' "golden age" was at its peak in the 14th century with the powerful guilds prospering. During that century, Bruges also developed a luxurious court life after the marriage of Margaret of Male and Philip the Bold, during the Burgundian era. Decline set in around the 17th century and for a time Bruges lay dormant, perhaps thereby preserving its heritage. Travel writers, such as Georges Rodenbach who wrote *Bruges la Morte,* focused attention on Bruges. The city came back as a tourist center because time had stood still there.

SIGHTSEEING....................................

A boat trip through the canals in this "Venice of the North" is one of the best ways to begin a visit to Bruges. From the landing stage we floated past the Old Palace of Justice, under two bridges, beside houses built for the poor by the rich during the Middle Ages, the Rijksmidden School, the Old Burgher's house, a statue of the Flemish painter, Van Eyck, the old British Consulate dating from the 18th century that is now a school, a typical Flemish-style red brick house dating from 1675, the Cathedral, the Old Fish Market, some nesting swans, the Church of Our Lady, which contains a Michelangelo statue, lots of pansies in flower boxes, the Memling Museum, the Lake of Love, the home of Marguerita, former countess of Flanders, flowering trees over the canal, rose gardens, the smallest window in Bruges, and a view of the belfry. This kaleidoscopic view of Bruges provided just the background we needed to visit sites at leisure on foot.

The **Market Square** is the center of Bruges, flanked by 13th-century halls, the belfry, and the neo-Gothic Government Palace. The 260-foot-high belfry octagonal tower contains a museum of medieval treasures and forty-seven bells in the carillon. Anyone can climb up the 366 steps to the top of the tower for a view. Opposite the belfry stand the guild houses; the one with fishermen on the facade housed the fishsellers. The monument in the center of the square honors Jan Breydel, a butcher, and Pieter de Coninck, a weaver. They were staunch fighters for independence against the French.

The **Basilica of the Holy Blood** (*Heilig Bloedbasiliek*) dates from 1139, although the upper chapel was remodeled in the 15th century. A few drops of the blood of Christ were given to Count Ditrich (or Derrick) of Alsace during the Second Crusade; he gave the vial to the city of Bruges in 1150. The crystal vial was placed in a larger transparent cylinder sealed at both ends with a gold mounting and golden crowns decorated with jewels. Two golden angels, kneeling on one knee, hold the vial between them. A silver tabernacle on the altar holds the relic, which is the focus of special worship on Fridays; a priest, a policeman, and a member of the Confraternity of the Holy Blood guard the relic as people come up to kiss the glass vial. The relic is carried in the Procession of the Holy Blood on Ascension Day every May. Thousands line the streets during this procession in which the citizens of Bruges dress in costume, sing and portray Biblical events.

The **City Hall,** one of the oldest Gothic city halls in Benelux, dates from 1376. Inside, the wooden and polychromed vaulted ceiling is magnificent. A double row of six hanging arches flows toward representations of the New Testament. Mural paintings of Albert and Julien De Vriendt depict major events in Bruges' history.

The **Palace of Justice,** built during the 18th century, is on the site of the Palace of the Franc. The Alderman's Chamber contains oak carved scenes depicting the Emperor Charles with his parents and grandparents. A black fireplace is topped with four sculptures in white marble.

Religious persecution during the 16th century led to an influx of Catholic priests and nuns into the safety of Bruges. The 13th-century **Beguinage Church** (*Begijnhof*) founded for lay nuns by Margaret of Constantinople, is now a convent for Benedictine sisters. Small houses are laid out in a row beside tall trees on a green lawn; a haven of peace and quiet. When we were there, daffodils sprouted everywhere on the lawn. The first house in the row is now open as a museum with each room containing furniture of the period. A collection of old lace, a linen press used to iron wimpels, china, and cooking utensils are on display. The Beguinage Church is dedicated to St. Elisabeth who was the first patroness of the Beguinage. J. van Oost painted the portrait of her that hangs above the high altar.

The **Groeninge Museum,** Dijver Canal, built in 1930 on the site of the Augustin Monastery, contains a collection of Flemish Primitive, the Old Masters, and modern work. Painters include Jan van Eyck, Pieter Breughel, Hans Memling, Pieter Pourbus, Jacob van Oost, Gerard David, and Petrus Christus.

The **Memling Museum,** housed in the former Hospital of St. John, contains the major works of Hans Memling. His *Shrine of St. Ursula* is considered one of Belgium's leading places of interest. This ornate shrine is made of wood and looks just like a Gothic chapel. Sailing ships are filled with people on some of the side panels. *The Mystic Marriage of St. Catherine,* with the baby Jesus sitting on his mother's lap, shows the mystic ring being placed on St. Catherine's finger.

The **Folklore Museum** (*Museum Volkskunde*) offers one room after another displaying the life of Bruges in ages past. We had time to see costumes and samplers, lace-making spindles and equipment, a baby minder, a cradle, and a washer with a hand wringer. The kitchen has forms to make licorice, chocolate molds, and cookie molds. In the *apotheek* there is a scale to weigh poisons and a machine to distill water. The schoolroom contains an abacus, slates, and quill pens. We saw a cobblers shop and a hatter featuring top hats and fancy ladies' feathered hats; collections of coats of arms, pipes, canes, music boxes, candles, eyeglasses, and accordions. Again, we wished for more time to wander at leisure.

SOUTHERN BELGIUM'S CASTLES ....

Beloeil

Southwest of Brussels stands **Beloeil Castle,** which reminds us of a Loire chateau in its facade, elegant interior, and adjoining formal gardens. The Princes of Ligne have lived there since the 14th century and still do; family gifts from royalty through the ages are on display.

A small, wooden writing desk, with legs that unscrew for traveling, is in the drawing room. It was given by Frederic of Prussia to Prince Charles-Joseph de Ligne. In the Epinoy room three Brussels tapestries by Devos portray happy-faced people dancing during the harvest festival. A large carved and gilded boat-shaped bed is also there. The Amblise room contains a Louis XVI four-poster bed, also carved and gilded, that was made for Queen Marie-Antoinette of France. Also, there are four lacquer cupboards that are said to have belonged to Madame de Pompadour. A first floor gallery is full of family portraits and five blue Delft china pieces. The library contains 20,000 volumes dating from the 14th through the 19th centuries.

Gardens begin with geometrically planned beds near the chateau, a ''great lawn,'' where plays were performed years ago, a rose meadow containing the first Bengal roses brought into Belgium, lakes, ponds, and bridges.

A new outdoor area called **Minibel** presents many of Belgium's historical and architectural treasures—in 1/25th scale. Children can wander beside buildings in miniature, watch trains zooming around a track, and see Napoleon at Waterloo.

Annevoie

Annevoie, not far southwest of Namur, was once the property of the Counts of Montpellier. The castle is not open to the public, but you can visit the unusual gardens. A completely natural water system brings water from above into fountains and over waterfalls without the use of machinery. Statues, including a ferocious-looking boar, bring life to the manicured gardens. Some of the fountains look like umbrellas, others like fans, and some shoot over rocks bouncing down in rhythm.

Lavaux St. Anne

Lavaux St. Anne, located south of Dinant, was probably the first castle built in the area. Abandoned in 1750, it was restored beginning in 1934; during World War II it hid paintings by the masters. Today the castle is fully restored and includes a museum of rural life displaying plows, tools, and machines. The hunting museum contains memorabilia such as brass horns and hunting jackets, an antler chandelier, stuffed animal heads, and an extensive collection of bird species. The watchtower on the third floor was the place where boiling oil was dropped on intruders.

Spontin

The Chateau of Spontin lies east of Dinant, in the Bocq River Valley. The earliest known Lord of Spontin was Robert de Beaufort, who lived in the 13th century—originally the family owned all of the land from Namur to Luxembourg. There are secret passageways leading under the moat that emerge in the churchyard. The oldest part of the castle, the keep, contains a collection of medieval weapons and a coat of mail. Spontin is a river sanctuary for golden pheasant, ducks, geese, and kingfishers.

CZECHOSLOVAKIA

Currency unit • koruna (KCS)
Languages • Czech (Bohemia and Moravia), Slovak (Slovakia)
Time from USA • six hours later (Eastern Standard Time)
Telephone access codes • to USA: USADirect 00–420–0010; from USA: 42
National Tourist Offices • **USA:** CEDOK, 10 E. 40th St., New York, NY 10016, tel.: (212) 689–9720; **Prague:** CEDOK, Na Prikope 18, Prague 1, tel.: (42) 2–2127–111; **Britain:** CEDOK, 17/18 Old Bond St., London W1X 3DA, England, tel.: (071) 629–6058/9
Airlines • **Czechoslovak Airlines: US:** (800) 223–2365 or (800) 628–6107 or (212) 682–5833; **Britain:** (071) 255–1366/1898
Embassies • **American Embassy:** Trziste 15, 12548 Praha, Czechoslovakia, tel.: 53–6641/8; **British Embassy:** Thunovska Ulice, 14 Mala Strana 11800 Prague, tel.: 53–3347/8/9

There is a special delight in anticipating a first visit to a country one has admired from a distance since childhood. Underlying that anticipation and giving it edge is a question: Will the country satisfy expectations or prove them illusions?

When we arrived in Czechoslovakia, we found castles galore, enough to satisfy any romantic childhood dream. Many of them are out in the country, accessible by traveling a winding road through villages, perhaps by a stream, and finally coming to the first view of pinnacles and spires. Others are the focal points of cities. As we climbed the many steps up to the castle complex in Prague we paused by vendors set up along the side, noticed lovers walking hand-in-hand, children carrying musical instruments under their arms and a few elderly people resting. We were full of anticipation and were not disappointed at the top.

HISTORY..

The first inhabitants were probably the Celts, who stayed until Germanic tribes invaded in the 4th century. Western Slavs arrived in the 5th century and re-

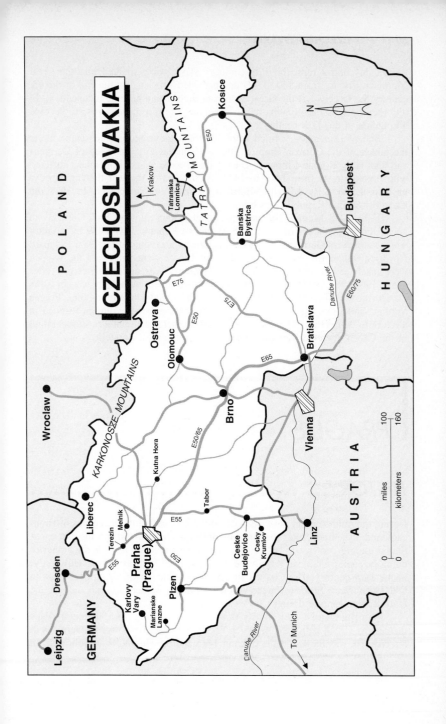

mained in control until the 10th century. Slavic tribes melded into the Great Moravian Empire from 830 to 907 and became Christian. By the end of the 9th century the Czechs left the Great Moravian Empire and became independent. In 995 they became the principality of Bohemia. The Czech body rose to become a kingdom in the 12th century.

John of Luxembourg ruled from 1310 and the kingdom then came under the power of the German Empire. His son, Charles IV, was King of Germans and also Holy Roman Emperor. During the Hussite Wars, Bohemians suffered with revolutionists from 1419 to 1434. At the end of the war the Jagiello dynasty took over. By 1526 the Habsburg dynasty was in power. In 1918 the Czechoslovakian Republic was born.

In the 1938 Munich Dictate France and Britain allowed Nazi Germany to annex the border areas of the Czechoslovakian Republic. By 1939 the country was occupied by Germany. In 1942 two Czechs assassinated the Nazi Reinhard Heydrich; all of the men in the village of Lidice were shot, and the women were taken to concentration camps. The country was under Soviet rule after May, 1945. By 1948 the National Front government was in place. In 1968 Soviet troops and tanks were back to occupy the country disrupting the "Prague Spring" and shocking the West. In 1989 the November Revolution resulted in a return to democracy. Now the Czechoslovak Socialist Republic is a federation of the Czech Socialist Republic and the Slovak Socialist Republic.

PRAGUE

HISTORY......................................

During the ninth century, two villages were inhabited below the castles of Hradcany and Vysehrad. Later the kings of Bohemia chose to occupy the castles. A Slavic trading center was active in 1000, with merchants from many countries doing business. Charles IV built the New Town, as well as Prague University, in the 14th century. His Charles Bridge joins Little Town (*Mala Strana*) with Old Town (*Stare Mesto*). Prague was the capital of western Europe and also the Holy Roman Empire during Charles IV's reign.

John Huss spoke vociferously from the pulpit during the 15th century—his theme was Czech nationalism, which finally removed the power of Germans in the city. He was burned at the stake in 1415 and the Hussite Wars followed. In

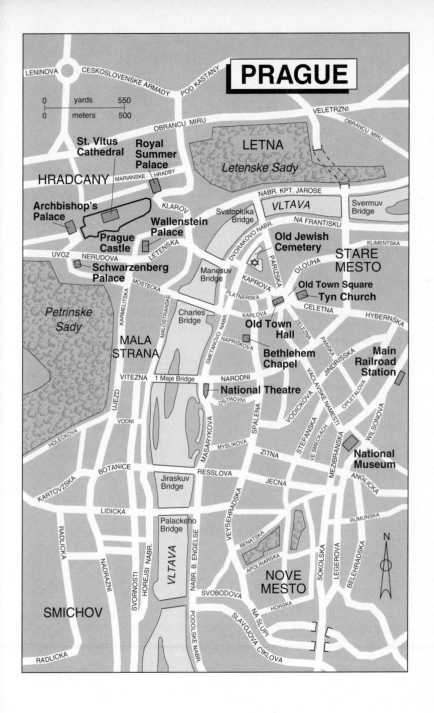

1419 the defenestration of councillors (throwing them out from the windows) of the New Town Hall took place.

After Ferdinand I and the Austrian Habsburg dynasty came to power in Prague in 1526 the Czechs resisted efforts to return to Catholicism and German rule. In 1618 two Czech citizens were thrown out of a window of Prague Castle by Austrians—which precipitated the Thirty Years' War. Since then Prague has been occupied by the Austro-Hungarian Empire, German troops, and finally the Soviets before achieving independence in 1989.

SIGHTSEEING.....................................

The **Moldau River** (*Vltava*) winds like an "s" curve through the city, dividing the **Little Quarter** (*Mala Strana*) and the **Old Town** (*Stare Mesto*). The **Charles Bridge** is one of the oldest stone bridges in Europe. It was built by Charles IV in 1357. Thirty statues stand along its length, enclosed by a Romanesque tower on one end and a Gothic tower on the other.

THE CASTLE DISTRICT

Prague Castle (*Hradcany*), entrance on Hradcanske Namesti, hovers over Mala Strana; it can be seen from all over town. Most of the battlements are gone as the Habsburgs built tall buildings with lots of windows where the walls once stood. The Czech government is ensconsed up there; it is also the official residence of the president. Wear comfortable shoes for the long walk up to the castle. Ancient streets require care in order to avoid a twisted ankle. The castle complex provides more than enough to see in several hours or days.

St. Vitus Cathedral stands as a Gothic monument. Dating from 1344, the building was finished in 1929. Emperor Charles IV is buried there, in company with King Wenceslas; look for the amethyst and jasper pieces imbedded in the walls of the Chapel of St. Wenceslas. Wall paintings describe the Passion cycle on the lower section and the legend of St. Wenceslas on the upper.

Bohemian kings lie in the crypt. The cathedral treasury contains the gold and silver collection as well as the Bohemian crown jewels. St. Wenceslas' 1346 crown sparkles with 20 sapphires, 25 emeralds, and 20 pearls—truly a dazzling display—however it is displayed only on special occasions after being opened by seven keys held by seven institutions. You can see copies of the crown, orb, scepter, and sword in the historical exposition of the **National Museum** (Lobkovicz Palace).

The **Old Royal Palace** contains **Vladislav Hall** dating from the 15th century. Coronations were held there as well as tournaments—an unusual ramp entrance allowed horsemen to enter so jousting could take place indoors. Today it is used for the election of the President of the Republic and other state functions. The **Bohemian Chancellery** is a large room with a Gothic vault and another handsome green tile stove—used for warmth as well as decoration. The Imperial Charter of Rudolph II is there, as well as a document of the Confederacy of the Estates from 1619—colorful with a pile of seals attached to the page. Don't miss the print of the "Second Defenestration" when Governors Jaroslav Borita of Martinice and Vilem Slavata of Chlum were tossed out of the window of the Chancellery in 1618. Hatred of the Catholic Spanish party led to the anti-Habsburg insurrection.

All Saints' Chapel (*Kapel Vsech Svatych*) was modeled after Sainte-Chapelle in Paris. We enjoyed the eye-level view of a cherub, swinging his arms and legs in vigor. The gold baroque altarpiece presents more angels. Relics of St. Procopius are enclosed in a tomb.

The **Old Diet** (*Stara Shamovna*) contains a gold throne with red velvet canopy and an embroidered emblem of Bohemia. Portraits on the walls focus on Habsburg rulers.

Don't miss walking upstairs to the **Office of the Land**. Rolls of property holdings are kept on shelves. Colorful shields decorate walls and ceiling and another green tile stove stands ready for warmth.

Sternberg Palace (*Sternbersky Palace*), Hradcanske Namesti 15, houses the National Gallery, which contains many the paintings of French Impressionists and other European masters as well as of modern Czechoslovakian work. Picasso, El Greco, Holbein, Tintoretto, Rubens, Rembrandt, and Bruegel are all represented there. We were especially entranced by the Cranach paintings, including *Judith and Holoferns;* Canaletto's *View of London and the Thames;* Ricci's *The Ascension of Mary;* Pieter Bruegel's *Senosec;* Peter Paul Rubens' *Hygieia* holding a snake; Rembrandt's *Ucenecv Pracovne;* Anthonus Van Dyck's *St. Bruno;* Agnolo Bronzino's *Eleanor of Toledo*, with brilliant royal blue and rose colors; and Hans Holbein's *Lady Elizabeth Vaux.*

On the next floor we admired Picasso's *Zena, Harlekyn, Toreador 1911,* and *Klarinet 1911;* Pierre Bonnard's *Rozhovor r Provenci;* Henri de Toulouse-Lautrec's *Moulin Rouge;* Vincent Van Gogh's *Zelene Zito;* Paul Gaugin's *Utek;* Camille Coro's *Fontainbleau.* Sculptures include Auguste Rodin's *Gustave Mahler* and Edgar Degas's *Tanecnice.*

In 1987 a historical exposition, *Monuments of Our National Past,* opened in Lobkovicz Palace. Nineteen rooms of exhibits trace the past from early times to 1848. From the top floor you can see ancient artifacts including iron pots, bowls, jewelry, papyrus, coins, and a helmet from 1000 A.D. A 1086 Kodex illustrated manuscript is there, also a 12th-century Prince's crown, copies of the Holy Roman Empire crown, orb, scepter, and sword. We were impressed with the most expensive piece in the building—an ivory madonna presented by a French king to Charles I. Don't miss the wooden painting of St. Jerome—unusual, as the painting continues onto the frame in 3-D style. A wooden Last Supper also has figures reaching out in 3 D. A 1548 baptismal font is made of tin with embossed decoration. A 1612 burial shield is rich with golden threads, two black bears also add life. Look up in several rooms to see painted wooden ceilings.

The next floor down contains long wooden stocks for prisoners, baroque musical instruments, and marionettes, among other things. A remarkable exhibit presents a 15th-century shield of King George plus modern sketches of his face as it may have been. Eight photos detail exhumation of his coffin, opening it, and experts working with his skeleton.

Gardens on the ramparts are a perfect place to relish the view of the city and the river. Lilacs are fragrant and glorious in the late spring.

The **Golden Lane** (*Zlata Ulicka*) consists of little houses built into the walls of the Castle in 1541 originally for guardsmen. Craftsmen and tradesmen lived there, as well as Franz Kafka, who lived at #24. The alchemists who lived there never did find out how to turn lead into gold, but Kafka succeeded in transmuting the terrors of the twentieth century into lasting literature.

The **Loretto Convent** (*Loretanske Namesti*) contains a replica of the Santa Casa from Loreta, Italy. Among other gold and jewels, the *Sun of Prague* (a Viennese work of 1699 called a monstrance) contains over 6000 diamonds. Loretto is thought to be a replica of the Virgin Mary's home. The carillon in the Loretto dates from 1694.

STARE MESTO (OLD TOWN)

Stare Mesto dates back to the 12th century. The **Powder Tower** is the place to climb for a look at the view. During the 18th century, gunpowder was stored there. In the Old Town Square the **clock** goes into action every hour with a skeleton, cock, the apostles, and Christ appearing. The skeleton, as death, actually strikes the hour. The astronomical part of the clock presents Prague as center of the universe. The outer black circle portrays the old Czech time in Gothic numerals and Roman numerals give hours today. Babylonian time is represented in Arabic numerals. The clock hand symbolizes the sun; the moon and the zodiac are also there. The calendarium is a circular plate divided into 365 days.

Next to the clock, the 1338 **Town Hall** (*Staromestske Radnice*) is the site of weddings and exhibitions. The oldest building of the Town Hall belonged to Wolflin of Kamen: the next oldest has a Renaissance window with the inscription *Praga caput regni* (Prague, the head of the kingdom). In this house the old council room has a panel beam ceiling, sculpture, gilded chairs, and emblems of the old town guilds.

A monument stands in the **Old Town Square** (*Staromestske Namesti*) commemorating the burning at the stake of John Huss. It was erected 500 years after his death in 1415. John Huss spoke from the pulpit of Bethlehem Church from 1402 until his death.

Tyn Church (*Tynsky Chram*), Staromestske Namesti, dates from the 14th century. The tomb-portrait of Tycho de Brahe, a famous Danish astronomer who painted in the court of Rudolf II from 1601, is there.

Charles University was founded in 1348 and the original building, the **Carolinium**, still stands at Zelezna 9. John Huss was rector of the University, and the institution became one of the centers of the Hussite revolutionary cause. The Carolinium was in the hands of the Jesuits from 1620. The **Tyl Theater,** Zelezna 11, should be open soon after restoration as part of the National Theater—Mozart's *Don Giovanni* was first performed there in 1787.

The **Jewish Quarter** dates back to the 10th century; the ghetto is among the oldest in Europe. The **Maisel Synagogue** displays Hanukkah menorah candlesticks, a collection of spice boxes, and Torah mantles. The **Jewish Cemetery** contains layers of graves on top of each other.

NOVE MESTO (NEW TOWN)

New Town is famous for its **Wenceslas Square** (*Vaclavske Namesti*), which is a wide attractive avenue. We were moved by the memorial from November 1989 to honor those who died during communist rule from 1948 to 1989. A cross with a barbed-wire wreath stands in front of jars of fresh flowers placed by families, each with a picture of a husband, father, or son. The equestrian statue of Wenceslas may be watching, according to legend, for the Czech time of greatest need when he will return.

The **National Museum** (*Narodni Museum*), Vaclavske Namesti 68, contains prehistoric, geological, numismatic, and zoological collections. A mammoth head leers from the wall on the top floor, accompanied by a bison skeleton and elephant skull with tusks. Paleolithic displays from 1,000,000–200,000 B.C. include tools, shells, and caves, continuing through the ages with refined flint tools, mammoth bones and tusks, bowls, and skeletons. A special exhibit caught our eye—copies of Mycenean gold including the (mistaken) mask of Agamemnon, bowls, swords, and daggers. Celt burial areas revealed necklaces with two knots, swords, bowls, and jewelry.

MALA STRANA (LITTLE QUARTER)

The **Charles Bridge,** built in 1357, is alive with statues from the 18th and 19th centuries. As visitors leave the bridge they can't help but notice the old homes, statuesque palaces, winding narrow streets, and charm of this area. Although the fire of 1541 destroyed much of the district, later palaces were built in Renaissance splendor.

The **Church of the Infant of Prague** (*Prazskeho Jezulatko*) or the **Church of Our Lady Victorious** (*Kostel Panny Marie Vitezne*), at Karmelitska 13, houses a wax figure of the baby Jesus. Polyxena Lobkowitz presented the figure in 1628; it is said to possess special power. The infant is dressed in a variety of costumes depending upon the Christian calendar.

You'll think you're in Paris as you see the **Petrin Tower** (*Petrinska Rozh-*

ledna), a 197-foot replica of the Eiffel Tower. Since 1891 this has been another place for a view of the city. The funicular station is near the First of May Bridge.

VYSEHRAD

Vysehrad is the original site of Prague; most of the castle was obliterated by the Hussites although some of the walls remain. Located several miles upstream from the city, the palace is accessible from the Gottwaldova metro stop. Visitors walk through the gates of the **Vysehrad Citadel** to the **Church of Saints Peter and Paul**. The **Rotunda of St. Martin** is also up there. The cemetery contains graves of Smetana, Dvorak, Bozena Nemcova, and Karel Capek. The new **Palace of Culture** contains concert halls and restaurants.

DAY TRIPS FROM PRAGUE ··················

Karlstejn Fortress

Emperor Charles IV built the castle to have a secure place to keep the Bohemian crown jewels. Located 28 km southwest of Prague, visitors approach along a river on winding roads alive with fruit trees. The castle stands on a ridge over the village. The Church of Our Lady contains medieval frescoes. Sparkling gems decorate the walls of the private chapel of the king. Inside the tower is the Chapel of the Holy Rood where the crown jewels were kept until 1420.

Konopiste

This medieval castle is located 45 km southeast of Prague. Archduke Ferdinand used this chateau as his hunting lodge until his assassination in 1914 in Sarajevo (a deed that contributed to the beginning of World War I). Inside there are collections of weapons and hunting trophies, sculpture and paintings.

Nelahozenes

Nelahozenes stands on the bank of the Vitava, 30 km from Prague. Antonin Dvorak was born near the castle in 1841; a museum in the house is devoted to him, as is another museum in Zlonice, which is 15 km away. The Central Bohemian Gallery of 20th-Century Art is contained in the castle. The Knights' Hall houses a collection of Renaissance art.

DENMARK

Currency unit • Danish krone (DKR)
Language • Danish
Time difference from USA • six hours later (Eastern Standard Time)
Telephone access codes • to USA 009 or USADirect 0430–0010; from USA: 45
National Tourist Offices • **USA:** The Danish Tourist Board, 655 Third Ave., 18th floor, New York, NY 10017, tel.: (212) 929–2333; **Denmark:** Danish Tourist Board, H.C. Andersens Blvd., Copenhagen, Denmark, tel.: (22)–33–11–13–25; **Britain:** Danish Tourist Board, Sceptre House, 169-173 Regent St., London W1R 8PY, tel.: (071) 734–2637/8
Airlines • **SAS: USA:** (800) 221–2350; **Britain:** (071) 734–4020
Embassies • **American Embassy:** Dag Hammarskjolds Alie 24, 2100 Copenhagen O, Denmark, tel.: (01) 42 31 44; **British Embassy:** 36-38-40 Kastelsveg DK 2100 Copenhagen, tel.: (01) 26 46 00

HISTORY......................................

Norsemen from Denmark sailed off to invade western Europe and the British Isles from the 8th century onward. Christianity arrived with the monk Ansgar in the 9th century. Harald Bluetooth was the first Christian king in the 10th century. Harald's son Sven took over England and his son, Canute, was in control of England, Denmark, and Norway from 1018 to 1035. In 1397 the Kalmar Union of Denmark, Sweden, and Norway was created under Queen Margrethe I and maintained through the reign of Christopher III until 1448. The monarchy was begun under Christian I who also reigned over Norway.

In 1849 Denmark became a constitutional monarchy with a parliament, the *Folketing,* which abolished the absolute rule of the monarch. Thorvald Stauning developed Denmark's first Social Democrat administration. Denmark joined NATO in 1949 and in 1972 joined the EEC as the only Nordic member. The ruling monarch, Queen Margrethe II, traces her family back to Gorm the Old, who was a Viking chieftain in 900 A.D.

Denmark is made up of about 500 islands. Tourists tend to visit some of the larger islands such as Zealand, Funen, and Jutland.

COPENHAGEN

Among the capitals of Europe, Copenhagen (Kobenhavn) may be the least pretentious, the one most committed to maintaining human scale to enhance the fun of daily living. The center is filled with walking streets, bits of waterfront, attractive squares, and, most of all, parks and gardens. Whenever we are in Copenhagen, we head for the waterfront park to gaze at the **Little Mermaid** again. It has nostalgic pull for us because the first time we saw it, many years ago, our children were three and six years of age and eager to gaze at her face— and her tail. Then we return to Tivoli Gardens for another batch of parental memories as we watch other children playing among wonders as ours once did. Where else does the joy of living get such priority, we ask ourselves, and vow to return once again.

HISTORY.....................................

The city was founded in 1167 when Bishop Absalon built his citadel there. Earlier known as Harbor or *Havn,* the name was changed to **Merchants' Harbor** (*Kopmannaehafn*). In 1443 the city became the capital of Denmark. King Christian IV, who reigned until 1648, is responsible for building many of the structures seen in town today. Copenhagen was invaded time and again by Britain, Sweden, and Germany, suffering occupation until 1945.

SIGHTSEEING.....................................

If you'd like to see where Bishop Absalon built the first fortress in Copenhagen, head for Christiansborg Palace. In 1158 Bishop Absalon galloped from Roskilde to choose this site for his castle. He knew he needed a place from which to control the entrance to the town and to send out ships to curtail approaching pirates. In 1249 a large fleet finally succeeded in invading the town and destroy-

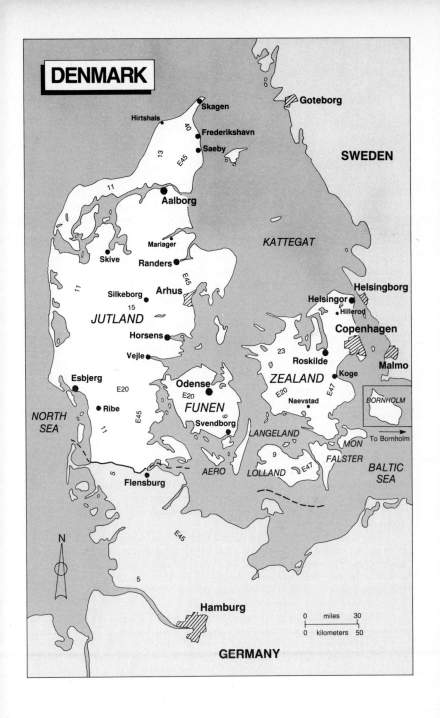

ing the castle. Ruins of Absalon's fortress lie underneath the present building and may be visited.

Bishop Absalon was also a scholar and a warrior, keen to outwit and vanquish pirates, among others. He would have been pleased to know that during World War II, explosives used by the resistance in their efforts to stop the Germans were hidden in his castle. It is said that in 1940, when supplies were running low, this hidden cache of explosives was used.

A poignant story is told about Leonora Christine, sister of King Frederik III, who was imprisoned in the palace by her brother. She and her husband, Corfitz Ulfeldt, had tried to oust Frederik from the throne and she ended up paying the price. She wrote *My Sorrow* in the Blue Tower and kept herself busy with embroidery and playing the piano. Leonora's nephew finally released her after 22 years.

Another palace built over the first for the royal family residence was destroyed by fire in 1794 and yet another palace burned in 1885. The present building was constructed in 1907, after 28 entries were submitted in competition—architect Thorvald Jorgensen won. It is hoped that this palace will not fall to fire—reinforced concrete with granite facing should protect it.

Visitors enter the palace and put slippers over their shoes in the **Giant Room**. Six limestone giants hold the ceiling up on the back of their necks and shoulders—they look pained, understandably. The entrance to the **State Apartments** is up the **King's Staircase,** white marble with 24-karat-gold decoration. The large red flag at the bottom of the stairway was given to Christian X in 1919. The 1738 tapestry portrays Christian VI receiving provincial officials in the first Christiansborg Palace.

Upstairs, the **Throne Room** contains two red velvet thrones against a red curtain with a pattern of three lions. The gray and white marble is from Greece. The wooden parquet floor reminds us of a grandmother's quilt in the star pattern. In 1972 the queen stood at this window as she prepared to assume her role as monarch at her father's death.

Christian IX's chamber is colorful with large paintings covering the walls including one of Christian X riding across the border to Southern Jutland in 1920. We were especially impressed with the large family portrait in the next room of Christian IX, his wife Louisa, three sons and three daughters with their spouses, and grandchildren.

The Royal New Year's ball is held in the **Great Banqueting Hall,** which is lit by six ornate Venetian-glass chandeliers. A sculpted ceiling is enhanced by frescoes. The room is also used for dinners when foreign heads of state visit.

The **Dining Hall** contains mahogany taken from the Queen's Staircase in the second palace. Look under the long table to see the original staircase bannister railings used in construction of the table.

Abildgard Hall takes its name from the painter Nicolai Abildgard, who painted 20 allegorial paintings. Only three survived the fire of 1794 and they were saved by being cut out of their frames and flung out of the window.

The **Queen's Library** dates from the middle of the 17th century. Books

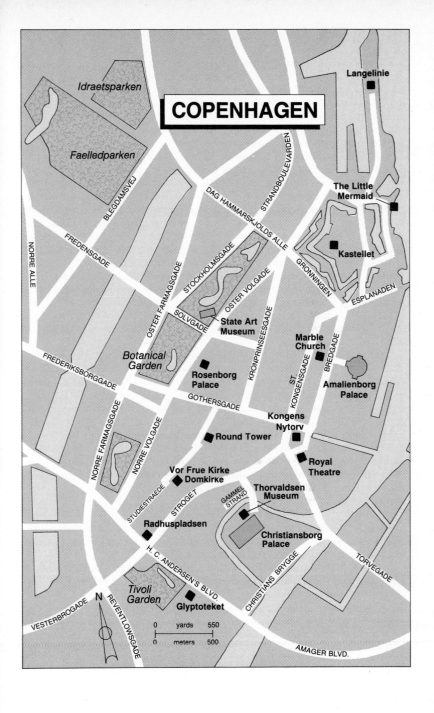

COPENHAGEN

Idraetsparken

Faelledparken

Langelinie

The Little Mermaid

Kastellet

STRANDBOULEVARDEN

DAG HAMMARSKJOLDS ALLE

BLEGDAMSVEJ

FREDENSGADE

NORRE ALLE

STOCKHOLMSGADE

OSTER FARMAGSGADE

SOLVGADE

OSTER VOLGADE

ESPLANADEN

GRONNINGEN

State Art Museum

Botanical Garden

FREDERIKSBORGGADE

Rosenborg Palace

KRONPRINSESSEGADE

Marble Church

BREDGADE

ST. KONGENSGADE

Amalienborg Palace

GOTHERSGADE

NORRE FARMAGSGADE

NORRE VOLGADE

Round Tower

Kongens Nytorv

Royal Theatre

Vor Frue Kirke Domkirke

STUDIESTRAEDE

STROGET

GAMMEL STRAND

Thorvaldsen Museum

Radhuspladsen

Christiansborg Palace

H. C. ANDERSEN'S BLVD.

CHRISTIANS BRYGGE

TORVEGADE

Tivoli Garden

Glyptoteket

VESTERBROGADE

REVENTLOWSGADE

N

AMAGER BLVD.

0   yards   550

0   meters   500

are housed behind glass in cases all around the room including on a balcony above, accessible by a small elevator. The fresco on the ceiling is called *Flying Storks* and was created by Johannes Larsen.

Alexander Hall takes its name from Bertel Thorvaldsen's frieze on three sides of the room. The story portrays Alexander's entry into Babylon. The 1884 fire damaged part, which looks white. Porcelain reliefs on the doors and panels are copies of Thorvaldsen's work.

Folketing, the Danish Parliament, meets in the southern part of Christiansborg Palace. The **Supreme Court** is housed in the northern section. Visitors can climb up several flights of steps (80 steps) to the gallery to observe the Lower House of Parliament. As in most other parliaments around the world, some people are usually listening to a speaker while others mill around. Each member has his or her own seat in the horseshoe-shaped series of desks. The rostrum was made from a thousand-year-old oak. The tapestry behind is wild—entitled *Like a Fleet Anxious to Weigh Anchor* and created by Berit Hjelholt.

Christian VII developed a theater in the southern wing in 1767, which is now the **Theater Museum** (*Teatermuseet*). The old court theater houses 2000 musical instruments, photographs, portraits of actors, and memorabilia from ballet, opera, and dramatic performances. Hans Christian Andersen had a part in the ballet *Armida* where he played a satyr. His name is on the 1821 program displayed in one of the glass cases. Ballet slippers and costumes belonging to Anna Pavlova are also there.

Thorvaldsens Museum (*Thorvaldsensmuseet*), 2 Porthusgade, contains works by the Danish sculptor and his contemporaries. Outside, the building is colorful with murals portraying events in his life. Bertel Thorvaldsen is buried in the courtyard garden among his statues. His private collection of Egyptian and Etruscan antiquities is also there. **Christ Hall** houses casts of marble models of the sculpture made for the Church of Our Lady, the Cathedral of Copenhagen. Christ is in the middle with 12 apostles around him.

The **Royal Library** (*Det Kongelige Bibliotek*), on Slotsholm, contains the most extensive collection of books and manuscripts in Denmark. Records of early Viking voyages to America and Greenland are there. The building is placed in an attractive garden. An **Arms Museum** (*Tojhuset*) adjacent to the library, contains weapons, uniforms, and armor in a long arched hall.

The **Stock Exchange** (*Borsen*) is well known for its soaring spire enhanced by the twisted tails of four dragons standing on their heads facing the four points of the compass. Christian IV gave the job of designing the building to Lorentz and Hans Steenwinkle, famous Renaissance architects.

The **National Museum** (*Nationalmuseet*), 12 Frederiksholms Kanal, has a vast collection of exhibits ranging from the Stone Age to the present day. The director of the museum in the mid-1850's, Christian Thomsen, devised the practice of separating prehistoric artifacts into categories beginning with the Stone Age, and followed by the Bronze Age and the Iron Age. His system was adopted by international archaeologists. Look for the **Hindsgav Dagger,** which was made of flint during the Stone Age. Rune stones, ships, and burial mound artifacts date from the Viking period. Traditionally, the body was accompanied into the grave with a jug of wine to ease its journey into heaven. Collections include coins, folklore, Viking ships, costumes, Danish pottery and silver, Viking helmets, and ancient wind instruments called lurs. The six-foot-long lures came from the Bronze Age; some were recently dug up in peat bogs where they were found to be well preserved.

On Hans Christian Andersens Boulevard at Dantes Plads stands a neo-Classical building containing the **New Carlsberg Sculpture Museum** (*Ny Carlsberg Glyptotek*). This museum houses the collection of Carl Jacobsen, who founded the Carlsberg breweries. Collections focus on Egypt, Greece, Italy, and the Near East. French impressionist paintings, Danish painting, and modern sculpture are on display. Rodin's *The Thinker* sits in the garden and Kaj Nielsen's *The Water Mother* is in a marble pool in the conservatory.

Tivoli Gardens were created after a Danish architect, George Carstensen, spent some time in 1822 mapping out the Royal Vauxhall Gardens in London. He had permission from King George IV to duplicate, in some respect, the Vauxhall Gardens, which closed during the middle of the 19th century. In the 1951 Festival of Britain, architects used Tivoli as a model for their new Festival Gardens in London's Battersea Park.

Floral displays include a riot of seasonal color interspersed with ponds, lighted trees, and tubes made of perspex that toss air bubbles up and up and up. Ducks swim placidly through the action. Lights at night reflect on the water and it all looks like fairyland. Fireworks are sometimes shot up as the park closes.

The first planetarium in Scandinavia has recently opened in Copenhagen. **Tycho Brahe Planetarium,** 10 Gammel Kongevej, was named for a 16th-century astronomer. Outside, the dazzling tubular glazed-tile structure has a slanted copper roof that certainly adds pizzazz to the waterfront. Architect Knud Munk designed the building. Inside, a new Zeiss optical projector uses computer-generated graphics to simulate space travel. Visitors can go on a cosmic voyage into space through the galaxies. A custom-built heliostat provides views of the sun.

The **Town Hall** (*Radhus* or *Radhuset*), Radhudspladsen, is a tall red brick building one can't miss. Look for the polar bears on the facade and edge of the roof. A statue of Hans Christian Andersen is nearby. From the tower, visitors can see not only Copenhagen but the sea and surrounding country. **Bishop Absalon's statue** sculpted by Bisson stands over the entrance to the building; as founder of the city, he is in a place of honor. A statue of *Two Lur Players* play their wind instruments for all time. Inside, the **World Clock** created by Jens Olsen is so accurate that it will lose only four seconds in the next 300 years. It reveals phases of the moon, positions of the stars, and eclipses.

The **Cathedral Church of Our Lady** (*Vor Frue Kirke*), 6 Norregade, has been rebuilt and restored several times since Bishop Absalon first built a chapel there during the 13th century. Moses and David stand in bronze at the entrance. Inside, Thorvaldsen's marble figures of Christ and the Apostles stand in glory. A kneeling angel holds a shell for the font.

The **Round Tower** (*Rundetarn*), Kobmagergade, was built by Christian IV in 1643 as an observatory. A spiral ramp winds up 117 feet to the top. In 1716 Peter the Great came to visit and drove his horse-drawn carriage up there. Changing exhibits are on view in the **Old Library,** which is halfway up the tower.

Rosenborg Palace (*Rosenborg Slot*) on Oster Voldgade, is a 17th-century palace built by Christian IV for his summer use. He helped plan the gardens, which are still called The King's Garden. **Hans Christian Andersen's statue,** holding a book and pointing with his finger as he tells a story, is well known to children.

The collection inside belongs to the royal family. The oldest piece is a silver gilt **Oldenburg Horn,** which was owned by Christian I. Some say that elves gave the horn to the king. The **Crown Jewels** include the queen's crown, which was made for Sophie Magdalene in 1773. Christian IV's gold crown has an open top and is set with diamonds, pearls, and enamels. The **Knights' Hall** contains an ivory coronation chair, which is held up by whale tusk columns and guarded by three silver lions. Twenty-five acres of botanical gardens lie across from the Palace.

Since 1794 four identical mansions called **Amalienborg** have been home to the royal family. When the queen is in residence, the guard changes every day at noon. Guards march from Rosenborg Palace to Amalienborg Square, wearing bearskins and dark blue tunics (red for dress occasions). Margrethe II and her family live in the building to the right after entering the square through the arches. The palace is not open to the public.

The **Royal Museum of Fine Arts** (*Statens Museum for Kunst*) on Solvgade, houses the National Gallery and includes Danish and European works of art. Among the European masters' works are Filippino Lippi's *The Meeting of Joachim and Anna Before the Golden Gate of Jerusalem* in rich royal blue and red; Titian's *Portrait of Giovanni Bellini;* Tintoretto's *Christ;* Francesco Guardi's *The Doge's State Barge on Ascension Day* with a parade of boats and flags flying; Alessandro Magnasco's *The Monks' Prayer by Sea;* Claude Lorrain's *Landscape;* Nicholas Poussin's *Jehovah Opens the Sea for Moses;* Cranach's *Melancholy, Portrait of a Young Woman, Venus with Cupid Stealing Honey,* and *Virgin and Child Adored by Infant St. John;* Adriaen Van de Venne's *How Well We Are Matched,* which is a hilarious painting of a skating owl couple in peasant dress; and Willem van de Velde's *Storm.*

Many visitors go first to see the **Little Mermaid** (*Lille Havfrue*) along the Langelinie Promenade. Edvard Eriksen was the sculptor of the mermaid. A ballerina with the Royal Ballet was the model, but Eriksen used his pregnant wife, with her full breasts, as the model for that aspect of her anatomy. Hans Christian Andersen's story has made her come alive for people the world over. We have enjoyed a picnic lunch on a bench near her, watching nannies wheeling baby carriages, businessmen strolling in three-piece suits, and tourists and everyone else walking along the half-mile promenade during the lunch hour. Nearby, the statue of a bear with two cubs stands beside the water.

The largest fountain in Copenhagen is the **Gefion Fountain** on Amalie-gade. The goddess Gefion turned her four sons into oxen so they could plow out enough land for the island of Zealand from Sweden in one night. They did!

DAY TRIPS FROM COPENHAGEN..............................

Lyngby

An **open-air museum** (*Frilandsmuseet*) is located at Lyngby near Sorgenfri station. Some of the houses were moved from other sections of Denmark; farms, country manors, and windmills are there to be enjoyed.

Klampenborg

Deer Park (*Dyrehaven*) is the place to walk through herds of tame deer, or take a hackney-coach ride through the park. Christian IV built his royal hunting lodge, Hermitage, in the middle of the park. Inside, he had a special table made that could be raised from and lowered into the floor below. The servants could then place food on the table, raise it, and not be hovering around in the dining room.

Rungstedlund

On May 15, 1991, the queen opened the **Karin Blixen Museum**. Baroness Blixen, who wrote under the pen name Isak Dinesen, was born there and also resided in the house after returning from Kenya in 1931 until her death in 1962. Blixen had spent 18 years in Africa. As we approached the house we enjoyed the sight of lavender flowers climbing up a trellis along one side of the building. The study contains her personal library, her own African paintings and her desk. The living room seems comfortable, with needlepoint pillows and soft sofas. Meryl Streep and Robert Redford starred in the movie version of her *Out of Africa*.

Humlebaeck

Louisiana Museum has been a favorite of ours since we first visited 30 years ago. Knud Jensen bought the dilapidated estate in 1955 just as he was about to sell his prosperous cheese business. He then set about developing galleries from the old main building which was built during the 1850's. The original owner was a nobleman who had three wives, all named Louise—hence the name. In 1958 Jorgen Bo and Vilhelm Wohlert created the additional modern building;

in 1966 another extension was added. Louisiana is not only popular with visitors but with the Danish who tend to bring their families on weekends and spend the day seeing the latest exhibitions and having a picnic.

Jensen's collection includes works by Danish painters prior to World War II, through representational art of the 60's, the abstract expressionists of Copenhagen, Brussels, and Amsterdam (known as the COBRA group), and into the present day. Thirteen sculptures by Alberto Giacometti, three reclining nudes by Henry Moore, and several pieces by Alexander Calder are there. Painters include Andy Warhol, Roy Lichtenstein, Morris Louis, Josef Albers, Yves Klein, and Ellsworth Kelly.

On our own last visit we enjoyed Scott Burton's *Lava Rock Chair;* Arthur Kopeke's *Landlept,* which features everyday items on his canvas—a shoe, a wheel, a glove, a cigarette box, a roller skate, a scooter and an old tea kettle; Francoise Morellet's *Sphere,* a hanging wire concoction; Alfred Jensen's *Squaring of the Numbers;* and outside, Alexander Calder's *Almost Snow Plough* and *Little Janey-Waney,* which is a large red three-legged piece with a mobile.

One of the most appealing aspects of Louisiana is the interplay between the works of art and the natural beauty outdoors. Large glass windows bring the two together, with gardens, trees, ponds, and views of the sea beyond interspersed with outdoor sculpture.

Helsingor

Immortalized by Shakespeare in *Hamlet,* **Kronborg Castle** is one place most visitors want to explore. In 1430 King Erik of Pomerania ordered a tax, called the Sound Duty, to be paid by all ships entering or leaving the Baltic. King Erik was King of Denmark, Norway, and Sweden and felt compelled to build fortresses on either side of the Sound in order to collect his tax as well as keep the peace. A tower named Karnan still stands from the original Helsingborg Castle.

The present castle was built by King Frederik II in 1574 and completed in 1585. A number of the old walls were used in construction of the new castle. In the north wing, a fragment of the original chapel contains a circular window with frescoes. Coats-of-arms of King Erik and Queen Philippa are still visible. After the Castle was completed, King Frederick ordered that the new name was to be Kronborg; anyone who called it by the old name had to pay the fine of a good bullock.

In 1629 a fire raged through Kronborg Castle, destroying all of the interior. Christian IV reconstructed the exterior and some of the interior before he died in 1648. In 1658 Swedish cannons laid seige and the castle was taken. Fortifications were added outside of the moat that cost money that might have been spent on restoration. The **Dark Gate,** an unusual S-shaped gate, was built during the reign of Frederik III to deter invaders.

Today the castle houses paintings, furniture, and tapestries, as well as stunning views of the sound from the windows. The **Queen's Apartment** contains paintings by Morten Stenvinkel, whose brother was commissioned by Christian IV to restore the castle after the fire. A winding stairway, which is hidden in the wall, leads up to a room where Caroline Mathilde, queen of Christian VII, was held prisoner because of her alleged relationship with the Prime Minister, Struense. The **King's Apartment** contains inlaid paintings on the ceiling done by Honthorst, a Dutch painter.

Forty-two tapestries were woven by Flemish weavers for the **Great Hall of the Knights**. Seven of them are still at Kronborg; they hang in a small dining room. The **chapel** survived the fire and still contains its oak pulpit and reredos carved by Thomas Frandsen from marble and alabaster. Weddings are held in the chapel.

During the 12th century a Danish historian, Saxo Grammaticus, related the story of Prince Amleth who was the son of a king in Jutland. Shakespeare used this legend for *Hamlet;* no one knows if he actually visited Kronborg Castle, although two of his friends, George Bryand and Thomas Pope, did visit in 1586. *Hamlet* was performed in 1816 at Kronborg, then again in 1837, 1916, and every year since 1937. Laurence Olivier played Hamlet and Vivien Leigh played Ophelia in 1937.

The legend of Holger Danske, who is said to be sleeping in the casements until he is roused to save Denmark from disaster, still fascinates visitors. As a hero he was renowned for his ability to get the better of anyone. His statue sits with folded arms and fierce expression in the upper casements near the Dark Gate.

The **Danish Maritime Museum** is housed in Kronborg Castle. Its purpose is to trace the history and development of Danish commerce and shipping through the ages. Prehistoric artifacts include a model of a Stone Age dug-out canoe; the original was discovered in Amosen. Another model, the *Hjortspring,* came from the Celtic Iron Age and the Nydam boat model dates from the Germanic Iron Age.

The Viking Age displays include two Kvalsund boats that portray the transition from the Nydam boat to Viking ships. The Oseberg ship from 800 A.D., a queen's burial ship, was uncovered in 1903; the Gokstad ship dating from 900 A.D. was a king's burial ship. Sections of the *Bayeux Tapestry* show scenes from William the Conqueror as he invaded England.

The Middle Ages are concerned with the voyages of discovery—Vasco da Gama, Magellan, Cabral, and Columbus. Denmark contributed as well, when Christian I sent Hans Pothorst and Didrik Pining to Greenland and Newfoundland.

The 16th century saw the development of nautical astronomy by Tycho Brahe on the island of Hven. Frederick II took a keen interest in his new maritime law which was in use by 1561.

Dutchman Jacob Admiral created the drawings of stranded ships hanging on the walls of the spiral staircase. Asiatic displays include Chinese clay figures from Canton, chinaware, models of Chinese junks, and paintings.

A model of Rasmus Moller's shipbuilding yard in Faborg during the 1870's gives a good picture of the scene in those days. Denmark was known for ship-building and there were shipyards all over the country.

Hillerod

Frederiksborg Castle is located on three islands in a lake; its Dutch-renaissance structure has soaring spires and turrets topped with golden balls, solid red brick walls with sandstone decoration, and a double moat. The **Neptune fountain** in the courtyard was created by Adriaen de Vries, a famous Czech craftsman. The original fountain stands in Stockholm; this is a copy.

Christian IV built Frederiksborg in 1602. A devastating fire roared through the palace in 1859 but it has been reconstructed to its original state. The **Museum of National History** has furnished the castle with antique furnishings, glassware, and paintings that portray the history of Denmark. The **Knights Room** contains a vaulted ceiling bearing the coats-of-arms of Christian IV and Queen Anna Catherine. Actual antlers protrude from stags painted on a frieze of the chase.

The **chapel** survived the fire and its two stories contain alabaster statues of the disciples. Jacob Moore, from Hamburg, designed the silver-and-ebony altar. Organ recitals are held there using the 1610 organ. The gallery is colorful, with many coats-of-arms of the Knights of the Order of the Elephant. The symbol of the elephant stands for wisdom and strength. Christian I started the order in 1462 and it is extended to important persons in Europe and the United States; Queen Elizabeth, Dwight Eisenhower, and Winston Churchill have all received the Order.

Roskilde

Roskilde was a royal residence beginning in the 10th century. By the Middle Ages it had become a well known religious center with 12 churches and eight convents.

Bishop Absalon was responsible for the construction of **Roskilde Cathedral** (*Roskilde Domkirke*) in 1170. Romanesque and Gothic styles blend in the pink brick cathedral. Members of the Danish royal family are buried there beginning with Harald Bluetooth in 987 (in an earlier structure on the site).

Visitors want to see the **500-year-old clock,** which houses little moving figures from its perch in the nave. Peer Dover strikes a bell with a hammer on the hour and Kirsten Kimer rings a bell on the quarter hour. After the hour has been struck the figure of St. George, with his sword in his hand, fights the dragon, who screams aloud.

The **chapel** of Christian IV holds a life-size bronze statue created by Thorvaldsen. A monument to Christian III is adorned with cherubs holding trumpets. The lovely alabaster statue of his wife, Margrethe, is a tribute to her beauty.

A granite pillar reminds many of us of the door frame at home that bears the marks of the top of our growing children's heads taken over the years. This pillar marks the height of many members of royal families in Europe and Asia. We were told that some of them had tall hats on when their measurements were taken—Peter the Great measured six feet ten inches!

The **Viking Ship Hall** (*Vikingeskibshallen*), Strandengen, contains the remains of five Viking ships from 1000 A.D. In 1962 frogmen went down to search for a ship and found not one but five from that period. The *Wasa* was raised from Stockholm harbor in 1961 with success; the same method was used in Roskilde. Over 50,000 artifacts were recovered from the ships, preserved in the museum. Now some of them are on display.

We found the display of ships against a backdrop of a wild sea tossing whitecaps perfect. One could imagine these ships trying to make headway, less easily than the rainbow-colored windsurfers on the real sea.

Fyn

Nyborg, on *Fyn* (Funen), will probably be the place where most visitors disembark from the Zealand ferry. During medieval days, Nyborg was the center of parliamentary Denmark; the oldest constitution in the country was signed there in 1282.

Nyborg Castle (*Nyborg Slot*) was built in 1170 and is one of the oldest royal castles in Scandinavia. The castle was built there to guard the Great Belt Strait from Wendish pirates. In 1658 the Swedes damaged the castle. To top it all, King Frederik IV removed bricks from its walls to use on his palace in Odense. Today the Great Hall has been renovated and the west wing survives.

Ladby

Ladby is north of Nyborg and worth a trip to see a 1100 year old 72-foot Viking ship. A Viking chief was interred in this ship along with his valuables, four hunting dogs, and 11 horses. The ship was discovered in 1935 by archaeologist Helweg Middelsen.

Odense

Odense is the place everyone wants to visit to see **Hans Christian Andersen's Hus,** 37-45 Hans Jensensstraede, birthplace of Hans Christian Andersen, who was born in 1805.The house contains letters, manuscripts, and illustrations of his stories. He received personally inscribed books, including *A Christmas Carol* from Charles Dickens. Jenny Lind, the famous Swedish singer, was very close to him and although they did not marry, they continued to carry on a personal correspondence. His trunk is in the house along with his hat, umbrella, and a rope he always carried when traveling, in case of fire.

His childhood home, **Hans Christian Andersen's Barndomstijem,** 3-5 Munkemollestraede, is a little half-timbered house where he lived until he was 14. The family was poor; his father was a shoemaker and they lived in a very small flat. Hans was not happy in school and quit at the age of eleven. At fourteen he went to Copenhagen to seek his fortune. He wrote stories by observing life around him and by making up scenes for his puppets.

St. Knud's Church (*Sankt Knuds Kirke*) houses the tomb of King Canute (Knud) the Holy, who was a nephew of an early Christian king, Canute the Great. Canute the Holy was killed on the steps of the high altar of St. Albani's Church in Odense and later canonized. St. Knud's Church was built as a memorial to him.

Inside, the gilded altar was designed by Claus Berg. Stained-glass windows serve as a colorful backdrop to the altar. The rococo pulpit is also gilded and has a spiral stairway with a silver rail. The **Chapel of the Counts of Ahlefeldt** carries the tale of a girl who "danced 'til she dropped." A daughter in the family loved to dance and at one ball danced with 12 knights in succession—until she collapsed and died while in the arms of the 12th knight.

Behind the church stands a statue of Andersen, created by Louis Hasselrils. He is immortalized for all time in the Fairy Tale Gardens in the city park.

Funen Village (*Den Fynske Landsby*) is an open-air museum just south of Odense. Farms, houses, mills, vicarage, smithy, and jail are all there. During the summer Hans Christian Andersen performances are given.

JUTLAND (JYLLAND)

Arhus

Arhus is Denmark's second largest city; it has been a religious center since the 10th century. The **Old Town** (*Den Gamle By*) is different from most open-air museums in that the buildings are not rural but represent town houses. The collection was designed to provide a glimpse into Danish urban culture dating back to the Renaissance. Besides town houses there is a brewery, saddler's workshop, tannery, post office, barber, printer, bookbinder, engraver, bakery, hatter, clockmaker, blacksmith, apothecary, fire station, woodcarver, cooper, sailmaker, weaving mill, theater, and windmill. Cobbled streets lead past a pump in the square, duck-inhabited water flows beside a water mill, and gardens are colorful all summer long.

Peter Holm began collecting buildings almost 70 years ago with his first— the **Mayor's House**. The mayor was also the grocer, and his half-timbered house contained a shop. One ceiling has a series of birds painted within squares. Decorated chests are standing in a row along a stone hall. The **Farmer's Room** was a waiting room where people who had traveled for a long time into town could have a lunch they brought with them or rest. The **Blue Chamber** shows Dutch influence with its decoration. The cane-panelled armchair probably came from the East Indies. A cabinet with tortoiseshell inlay is said to be Dutch. Don't miss the "giraffe" piano in the 1820 Parlor. A summer house stands in the garden of the Mayor's House.

Also in the museum, the **Historical Collection** is contained in four houses beginning with one dating from 1585. The houses display silver, porcelain, coins, period furniture, and ecclesiastical art. The **Textile Collection** houses looms, country costumes, and a history of urban costume from the middle of the 18th century.

Arhus Cathedral (*Domkirken*) is the longest church in Denmark at 101 yards. It was consecrated to St. Clement and the present church is the third on the site. A three-panelled altarpiece was carved by Bernt Notke in the 15th century. During the summer concerts are given on the 18th-century baroque organ.

The newest treasure in town is the **Town Hall,** which was built in 1941. Murals and lots of glass make the building a showplace. In front of the building stands Mogens Boggild's *Pig's Well,* which features a mother pig and her young.

The **Museum of Prehistory** (*Forhistoriskmuseet*) is located at the Moesgard Manor Farm. The manor house contains ethnographical and archaeological artifacts from the Stone Age, Bronze Age, Iron Age, and Viking Age. Many visitors want to see the Grauball Man, who was discovered in 1952 by men digging peat. Unhappily, his throat had been cut and his left leg broken. It is thought that he was involved in a ritual sacrifice. His hair turned red from the peat; skin, nails, and teeth are still remarkable intact. After being quiet under the peat for over a thousand years this nude man is now exposed to the stares of visitors.

The museum has managed to piece together fragments of bronze, clothing, chain mail, and leather. Runic stones, especially the popular troll's head used by the museum on their literature, are on display in one hall.

Ribe

Ribe is one of the oldest towns in Denmark and its houses have been preserved with care. The town was once a seaport until silt filled in the harbor; now it is four miles away. This medieval town was founded in 860.

The **Cathedral** (*Domkirke*) was constructed during the 12th century in late Romanesque and early Gothic styles. It stands on an earlier site of a wooden church built around 860. The present church is surrounded by green lawn interspersed with cobblestones; the building is on several different levels. The tower provides a fine view of the surrounding land; its bell tolled out storm warnings as well as other disasters. Some say that the devil used the "Cat Head Door," which features a lion's head sticking out his tongue, when he wanted to enter at night. Others say that the cat's head decoration over the door on the south side was put there by a merchant who was grateful to his cat for getting rid of the rats at home. A statue of Hans Tausen, Bishop of Ribe in 1542, stands outside. He was one of the proponents of Lutheranism in Denmark.

Inside, the painted organ has King David and his harp, accompanied by evangelists, at the top. King Christopher I lies in his tomb under the altar. Arnfast, who was the abbot of a monastery in Ryd, poisoned the King in 1259.

Look for a pillar under the pulpit, which still retains the marks of flood waters from 1634.

Over one-hundred houses still stand, tilting and sporting their half-timbering. They are protected by the National Trust. Storks nest on houses and on wooden platforms that have been especially placed so they will choose to build a nest there. (It is believed they will bring good luck.) A town crier goes on his rounds dressed in a long coat and a pointed hat, holding a lantern in one hand and a staff in the other. Besides reassuring village folk that all is well, the crier also sings some traditional songs.

ENGLAND AND WALES

Currency unit • British pound, divided into 100 pence
Language • English
Time difference from USA • five hours later (Eastern Standard Time)
Telephone access codes • to USA 010 or USAdirect 800 89–0011; from USA: 44
National Tourist Offices • **USA:** British Tourist Authority, 40 W. 57th St. New York, NY 10019, tel.: (212) 581–4700; **Great Britain:** British Travel Centre, 12 Regent St., London, SW1, tel.: (071) 730–3400 **Canada:** 94 Cumberland St., Suite 600, Toronto, Ontario M5R, tel.: (416) 925–6326
Airlines • **British Airways: USA:** (800) 247–9297; **Britain:** (081) 897–4000; **Virgin Atlantic: USA:** (800) 862–8621
Embassies • **American Embassy:** 24/31 Grosvenor Square, W., London 1A1AE, tel: (071) 499–9000

Those of us who are avid anglophiles have followed British royal lives for years, having none of our own to worry about. Many in the United States heard Elizabeth's coronation on the radio in 1953; we remember her clear, steady voice coming across the airwaves on that day. For the next occasion in 1960 we were living just outside of London and chose to drive in the day before Princess Margaret's wedding to photograph the flowers and decorations along the Mall and in the parks, then watched the ceremony on television. Again, we were living in England during Queen Elizabeth's Jubilee in 1977, which we watched on television after enjoying the decorations on homes and everywhere else imaginable. In the United States we got up in the middle of the night to see the ceremony of Prince Charles' marriage to Princess Diana on television. Since then we have kept up with births and marriages, absorbing each new development into our mental map that stretches back to the first monarchs of Britain. We always feel as if we're on familiar ground when we stroll down Birdcage Walk or Pall Mall, remembering how it looked for one of the royal events. Going to London is like coming home to the roots of our own culture.

HISTORY......................................

People were living in England during the Paleolithic period. A skull and flint tools found in Kent dated from that time. The Red Lady of Paviland was found in the Gower Peninsula of Wales and she dates back to 16,500 B.C. Both Stonehenge and Avebury stand as reminders of Stone Age dwellers. Neolithic men buried their dead with personal possessions that date their existence to between 4000–2000 B.C. The Celts arrived from 1000–500 B.C. and the Cymri tribes invaded during the Iron Age from 700 B.C. to 43 A.D., leaving castle ruins such as Old Sarum near Salisbury, Caer y Twr in Anglesey, Hambledon Hill in Dorset, and the Uffington "white horse" in Oxfordshire.

Roman invaders tried to curb the Celts, but their Gaius Julius Caesar appeared only briefly in 55 and 54 B.C. Emperor Claudius arrived after 41 A.D. and stayed for sixteen days. By 79 A.D. the Roman governor Agricola was moving north and reached Scotland. Hadrian's Wall was built in 122 from Tyne to Solway; sections still roll up and down the hills today. The Romans built roads and towns, complete with baths and villas.

The Dark Ages, after the Roman legions left, continued from the 4th century into the 5th and 6th, when Picts, Scots, Franks, Angles, Saxons, and Jutes invaded. Later Viking raiders arrived to plunder existing settlements. Seven kingdoms (Kent, Essex, Sussex, East Anglia, Mercia, Wessex, and Northumbria) were governed by a series of kings. By 925 King Athelstan of Wessex called himself "King of the English and Lord of the whole of Britain." In 1066 William the Conqueror arrived in Pevensey Bay to claim the throne.

By 1215 King John agreed to the Magna Carta, which laid out the terms of the feudal barons. The new government was designed to set a limit on the king's power. The charter was signed at Runnymede, near Windsor.

The royal line of succession dates back to the reign of Egbert who was king of the English in 827. The first king to be crowned in Westminster Abbey was William I (the Conqueror) in 1066, thus beginning the House of Normandy. King William is remembered for his Domesday Book. King Henry II, of the House of Plantagenet, was crowned in 1154. Henry appointed his friend, Thomas Becket, Archbishop of Canterbury, thinking he would then have more power over the church. However, Becket opposed the king's ideas and was eventually murdered in Canterbury Cathedral. The House of Lancaster came into power with Henry IV who was crowned king in 1399. He had forced King Richard II to abdicate, then imprisoned him first in the Tower and later in Pontefract Castle, where he died.

Edward IV, of the House of York, was crowned in 1461. Henry VII was crowned in 1485, the first of the House of Tudor. His son was the famous King Henry VIII who romped through six marriages, beheading two of his wives. James I, of the House of Stuart, was crowned King of Scots in 1567 and King of England in 1603. He was the son of Mary Queen of Scots. England was ruled by Oliver Cromwell and his army after the death of King Charles I in

1649. After Cromwell's death King Charles II, the rightful heir, was placed on the throne. George I, of the House of Hanover, was crowned in 1714.

Edward VII, of the House of Saxe-Coburg Gotha, was a man sixty years of age when he succeeded his mother, Queen Victoria, in 1902. The reign of the House of Windsor began with King George V in 1911. He brought England through World War I and was respected and loved by his people. King Edward VIII reigned for only eleven months, then renounced his throne to marry the woman he loved, Mrs. Wallis Simpson. George VI was crowned in 1937, with Queen Elizabeth, the Queen Mother, at his side. Queen Elizabeth II was crowned in 1953, following the death of her father.

LONDON

HISTORY....................................

There is some evidence that ships sailed in and out of the Thames as early as the 5th century B.C. Prehistoric flint workers discarded 600 flints for later centuries to discover. A hand-axe was uncovered on the site of Piccadilly Circus.

In 43 A.D. Roman invaders found that the gravel deposits along the Thames were perfect foundation for building a bridge (near the present London Bridge). In 60 A.D. Queen Boadicea attacked the resident Romans and burned their town. When the Romans were recalled home because of Germanic threats in 410 A.D. Londinium went into a decline. The Saxons brought it back as a healthy trading port, which lasted until the Vikings invaded in 836 A.D. The White Tower was finished as a defense against further invasion in 1097. London Bridge was built in stone by 1217; it was the only bridge across the Thames at that time.

London, unlike most other capital cities in Europe, developed in two distinct areas: the financial and mercantile center remained in the "City" along the bank of the Thames, while the Royal Palace, Westminster Abbey, and Westminster Hall moved several miles upstream.

Disaster struck London, probably the largest populated city in Europe in the 17th century, with the bubonic plague in 1665. The Great Fire erupted in 1666 and in four days destroyed churches, the cathedral, and almost all buildings and homes. The half-timbered buildings were replaced with brick, streets were widened, and market areas enlarged. London continued to be a leading power and proceeded to grow into a city of one million persons by 1801, when the first census was taken. Villages that once lay outside of London were now enclosed by the sprawling metropolis. World War II devastated London, but a number of the remnants of ancient times still remain.

SIGHTSEEING......................................

Although London is a huge sprawling city of seven million, it is possible to enjoy it in reasonable chunks. You can contain your exploration to a distinctive section and really get to know it. With a small area in mind you can choose to walk through historic buildings, loll in parks and feed the ducks, or take your time to explore museums. It's like going to a smorgasbord and sampling whatever appeals to you; get ready for several days of feasting. London in sections is manageable; if you can't see everything you would like—not to worry. That means planning another trip to London, which is not a bad thought.

Parliament and Westminster Abbey

Big Ben is heard chiming all over the world; its unmistakeable shape combined with parliament must be familiar to everyone. The clock is housed just below the gilded spire, which soars up 330 feet.

Big Ben's twin, the tower on the other end of Parliament, is named **Victoria Tower**. The Union Jack flies on top when Parliament is sitting. Dating back to 1078, **Westminster Hall** is the oldest part of the Houses of Parliament. The Hall has been used for trials, such as Thomas More's in 1535 and Charles I's in 1649. Sir Winston Churchill's body lay in state there in 1965.

Visitors to the **Houses of Parliament** enter from the **Old Palace Yard** and proceed to the **Queen's Robing Room,** decorated with an elaborate coffered ceiling, carvings portraying the Arthurian legends, a throne, and St. George and the Dragon on the fireplace.

The **Chamber of the House of Lords** contains the **Royal Throne** on a dais, with the padded **Woolsack** for the Lord Chancellor. The Woolsack, stuffed with wool, is symbolic as the source of wealth for England. Eighteen statues of barons who fought for the Magna Carta are flanked by stained-glass windows and frescoes. Red padded benches in tiers on each side match the red robes worn by peers.

The **House of Commons** contains the **Speaker's Chair** under an ornate canopy. There are two sides to the House: members go either to the "aye" side or the "nay" side, depending on their vote.

Outside, **Parliament Square** contains large trees, lawns, flowers, and statues. Winston Churchill stands with his cane, observing the goings on at Parliament. Richard Coeur de Lion rides on horseback with his sword raised high. Other statues include Benjamin Disraeli, Abraham Lincoln, and Sir Robert Peel.

Across the street from Westminster Hall stands the **Church of St. Mar-**

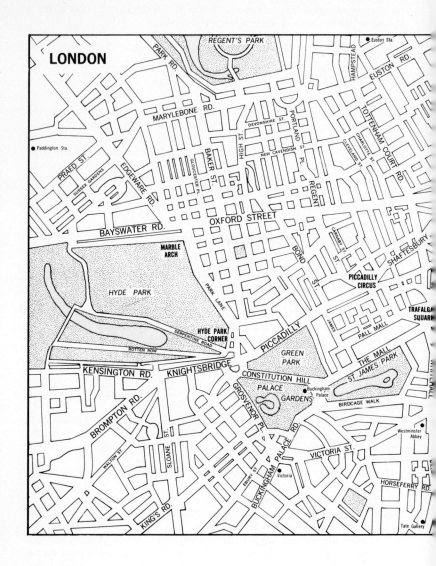

garet, the parish church of Westminster. Dating from 1189, it has been altered several times. Inside, the east window portrays the betrothal of Catherine of Aragon and Prince Arthur. Samuel Pepys was married there in 1655 and Winston Churchill in 1908. Sir Walter Raleigh is buried in the chancel.

Westminster Abbey's beginnings are shrouded in mystery; there is a legend that King Arthur and Queen Guinevere held court in the area. The foundation of a monastery or church dating from the early 7th century, during the time of Sebert, King of the East Saxons, has been found. The representation of Westminster on the Bayeux Tapestry tells us that it had a central tower and transepts and a lead roof. Bases of columns and a circular arc were found as well.

During the days of the monastery, only royalty and high ecclesiastics were buried there. Elizabeth I decreed that others could have the same privilege, and so noblemen chose to be buried there. In the 17th century, English poets became members of the nobility and could have memorials in Westminster, hence Poets' Corner. By the 18th century, other notable persons, such as Shakespeare, were either buried there or had monuments erected. Sixteen Waterford crystal chandeliers mark the 900th anniversary of Westminster, a gift from the Guinness family. A green marble slab is inscribed, "Remember Winston Churchill."

The **grave of the Unknown Warrior** contains the remains of someone whose body was brought from France on November 11, 1920. The inscription on the black Belgian marble slab reads: "They buried him among the Kings because he had done good toward God and toward his House."

Ahead, the nave altar and choir screen are brilliant with gilt and lacy arches over two niches. One contains a reclining Sir Isaac Newton, the philosopher and mathematician who developed the law of universal gravitation among other discoveries.

Coronations take place before the altar in the **Sanctuary.** The **Coronation Chair,** which waits in St. Edward's Chapel, is then moved to the Sanctuary. King Edward I ordered the chair to be made to enclose the **Stone of Scone** which he had brought home from Scotland in 1296. Legend reports that Jacob had placed his head on this very stone for his pillow at Bethel. The stone was taken to Egypt, Spain, Ireland and finally to Scotland. The painted wooden chair indeed contains the flat rectangular stone under the seat. It is guarded by four lions at the corners of the legs.

The **Cloisters** were destroyed in the Great Fire of 1298 and later rebuilt during the 13th century. The monks spent a great deal of time in these pleasant havens. Brass rubbing is available in the North Cloister; we suggest selecting a small brass that will fit in your suitcase and your home. We made the mistake of rubbing many over-six-foot brasses in various churches around Oxford which are still in our attic unframed.

Royal London

From Westminster Abbey it is a short stroll across Storey's Gate to Birdcage Walk which will take you to **Buckingham Palace.** We like to cross Birdcage Walk and head into St. James's Park for a leisurely break before reaching **The Mall** and turning left toward Buckingham Palace. Henry VIII declared this as the first park of the Court. During Tudor days, deer roamed in the park. Charles II constructed aviaries along Birdcage Walk. The lake in the center is attractive with waterfalls and fountains, and is a favorite with ducks and other wild fowl; the view of Buckingham Palace is unobstructed.

The view both ways down The Mall is pleasant with its row of plane trees; there are often decorations up on the street lights for one occasion or other. At one end stands the hefty **Admiralty Arch,** which cars drive under. At the other end sits the **Queen Victoria Memorial,** built in 1901 of white marble. A gilded bronze Victory reaches up on top; the thirteen-foot-high statue of Queen Victoria is seated on the east side. We remember driving around and around the memorial in 1960, waiting for the placard to appear on the palace gate announcing the birth of the Queen's baby.

Here is a good place to watch the Changing of the Guard at Buckingham Palace, which takes place every other day. The Brigade of Guards march from St. James's Palace to Buckingham Palace. A band accompanies the old guard and the new guard who touch left hands to signify the change of guard.

If the royal standard is flying, the queen is in residence. Buckingham Palace is not open to visitors, but the **Queen's Gallery,** on Buckingham Palace Road, is. During World War II, bombs destroyed a chapel in the south wing of the Palace; in 1961 the gallery was created on that site. Works of art from the royal family's private collection are changed twice a year.

The **Royal Mews,** along the same road, display royal carriages and cars. The **Gold State Coach,** dating from 1762, is still used by the Queen on state occasions, the **Glass Coach** takes royal brides and bridegrooms from Westminster Abbey, and the **Irish Coach** takes the Queen to the State Opening of Parliament.

Trafalgar Square

Charles I rides again on his bronze statue in the triangle between Whitehall and Trafalgar Square. Hubert Le Sueur's signature can be found on the left front foot.

Admiral Horatio Nelson's 145-foot-column rises from Trafalgar Square, as a tribute for his leadership and subsequent death in 1805 at the Battle of Trafalgar. The Admiral, cast in bronze three times his size at 17 feet, stands tall above the bronze lions guarding the bottom of the column. Trafalgar Square is always filled with pigeons, people feeding them from paper bags and others having lunch or sitting in the sun. Fountains spraying add life to an already lively scene.

St. Martin in the Fields stands on the northeastern corner of Trafalgar Square, no longer in the fields. It is the parish church of the royal family. The Pearly King and Queen ceremony is held here every year when people dress in costumes sporting many mother-of-pearl buttons.

The National Gallery and the National Portrait Gallery take up the entire "high" side of Trafalgar Square. The present gallery was completed in 1838, with several extensions including one in 1973. More than 2000 paintings are now housed in the Gallery.

Whitehall

The Horse Guards' forecourt, on the left heading down Whitehall, is the place to see another Changing of the Guard. Two guards are mounted on horseback, two more stand in the archway. In early June, on the Queen's Official Birthday (her actual birthday is in April; June usually provides better weather.) Trooping the Colour is held on the Parade Ground visible behind the clock-tower.

On the opposite side of the street stands the Banqueting House, a Palladian-style building designed by Inigo Jones in 1625 and the only remaining piece of the original Whitehall Palace. At the top of the steps a stone has been placed on the wall to mark the spot where Charles I walked to the scaffold for his beheading in 1649. Ironically, it was Charles I who ordered the ceiling paintings inside, and he is prominent in one: *Allegory of the Birth and Coronation of Charles I*.

Number 10 Downing Street, the official residence of the Prime Minister, might be roped off for security reasons when you visit London. Number 11 is the residence of the Chancellor of the Exchequer and Number 12 is the Government Party Whips' office.

A right turn onto King Charles Street will take you to the Cabinet War Rooms, the underground emergency operations center used during World War II. It was designed in 1938 to protect Winston Churchill, the War Cabinet and the chiefs of staff of Britain's armed forces against air attacks. Twenty-one rooms opened to the public in 1984.

If you have followed our route from the beginning at Parliament, you have just finished a triangular pattern encompassing some of the most important sites in London. We do not expect anyone to complete this route in a day—more likely several trips or a lifetime of travel to London.

Tower of London

William the Conqueror built an earth-and-timber castle in the southeast corner of the Roman city walls. He wanted to control the River Thames in case invaders should try to sneak up the river, as well as deter any possible revolt by the people in the city. In 1077 William built a large, 90-foot-high, Kentish limestone tower, called the White Tower, which was so called because at one time it was white-washed. The walls at the bottom are 15 feet thick and 11 feet at the top. Four turrets stand at the corners; one is rounded because it contains a circular staircase.

The castle-fortress was expanded with two additional fortified walls and a large moat. Henry III created a new castle inside the walls with the White Tower in the center. The entire complex covered 18 acres and was considered impregnable.

The **Tower Guard** is part of the same regiment guarding Buckingham Palace and St. James's Palace. Changing of the Guard takes place on Tower Green during the day. Visitors can apply in writing to witness the **Ceremony of the Keys,** which takes place every night—gates are locked and the keys given to the Resident Governor of the Tower. With floodlights on the towers it is an occasion to remember, and gives an eerie feeling when one remembers the past of this fortress.

Bloody Tower is directly across from Traitor's Gate; the Little Princes were murdered here. After their father, Edward IV, died in 1483, the little boys lived in the Tower, supposedly under the protection of their uncle, Richard, Duke of Gloucester. Although preparations were made for the older boy, Edward, to be crowned, Uncle Richard himself was crowned instead, as Richard III. No one knows if the bones of two boys, found near the White Tower in 1674 were theirs or not. The Earl of Northumberland shot himself in the Bloody Tower in 1585 and Sir Thomas Overbury was poisoned there.

The **Inner Ward** is a large area inside the **Outer Ward;** impregnable with its double protection from the outside. **Tower Green** is on our left as we climb the steps up to the scaffold site where so many were beheaded. Anne Boleyn was lodged in the Queen's House, also to the left, before her execution. Reportedly, her ghost appears below the window of her room.

Ravens are an important part of the Tower tradition. It is said that if ravens leave, the Tower will fall and the kingdom as well. Six ravens are in residence there; they live for about 25 years. Their cage is near Wakefield Tower.

The **Crown Jewels** are kept in the Waterloo Block building, with entrance near the Chapel Royal. Downstairs, in the basement, the lights are dim and one begins to walk around a circular showcase containing exquisite crown jewels displayed on deep velvet. Strict security is in order here, and visitors are told to keep moving slowly when viewing the inner sanctum of the most precious jewels. However, one can go around again and again to see everything in dazzling array. It may take a couple of revolutions to spot favorites such as the **Imperial State Crown,** which Queen Elizabeth wears for all state occasions. It has more than 2800 small diamonds and a number of old and historic gems including the **Second Star of Africa,** which weighs 317 carats. It is the second largest diamond in the world.

The **Crown of Queen Elizabeth,** the Queen Mother, contains the **Koh-i-noor** (Mountain of Light) diamond. Queen Victoria had a small four-ounce crown made for her to wear with a bun hair-style. She thought the Imperial State Crown was too large for her, as a short woman. There are two Prince of Wales Crowns, one from 1728 made for Prince Frederick Louis, son of King

George II, and another from 1901 which was made for Prince George, later King George V for the coronation of King Edward VII in 1902.

The **White Tower** houses a collection of arms and armor including weapons such as the crossbow, swords, and a pair of Monlong Pistols made in 1695 for William III. A reconstruction of a prison cell contains words inscribed on the walls by prisoners.

Outside again, **Tower Bridge** stands firm with twin Gothic towers and movable sections that part in the middle and loosen their jaws to let river traffic move through. The walkway was opened in 1982 after being closed since 1909; some thought it was a lair for villains and prostitutes. Inside the towers visitors can see the control cabin, steam pumping engines, and video displays.

We have always enjoyed a trip on the Thames; after a visit to the tower it is pleasant to put your feet up and cruise along the river to any number of stops upriver. One can plan to take the tube from, for example, Westminster one way to the Tower and cruise back or vice versa.

The City

The City of London consists of just one square mile extending from Aldgate in the east to the Royal Courts of Justice in the Strand in the west, and the Thames River in the south to City Road in the north. Dating back to Roman times when it was called Londinium, the City is the oldest part of London. However, the buildings have never been allowed to become old; frequent fires removed each generation of buildings and new ones were built.

The **Guildhall,** on King Street in the center of the City's municipal life, dates from 1411, although its facade has been changed in later years. The City's coat-of-arms, with the Cross of St. George and St. Paul's sword, is held up by winged griffins. The Great Hall is used for the Lord Mayor's Banquet in November, which is attended by the Cabinet and the Prime Minister, public meetings, and other events. There are replicas of large wooden figures of Gog and Magog, who were the mythical originators of prehistoric London. Their fierce eyes seem to glower at visitors and they are dressed in full battle regalia.

Most children have read the story of Dick Whittington and his cat. Dick, a poor boy, sold his cat to a king and queen in a foreign land to control the mice and rats in their castle. As a child he also had a premonition that he would be mayor of London and he was—not once but three times. Unlike the legend, the real Dick Whittington came from the family of a local squire in Gloucestershire, made his fortune, and then became Lord Mayor. His money went toward developments in the city such as constructing Greyfriars Library, the Guildhall Library, the foundation of a college, rebuilding Newgate Prison, and Leadenhall Market. An engraver portrayed him with his hand on a cat, hence the legend.

To the east of the Guildhall stands the **Bank of England** facing Threadneedle Street. Look for the pediment of the "Old Lady of Threadneedle Street." The Bank of England was incorporated in 1694.

The **Stock Exchange,** Bank, is housed in a new steel-and-glass building on Throgmorton Street. Visitors may watch the activity from the gallery and watch a film on the Exchange.

The **Royal Exchange,** Bank, is known for its 180-foot-tall tower and carillon, which rings out traditional English songs. The grasshopper on the gilded vane comes from the crest of the builder, Sir Thomas Gresham.

Mansion House is the official residence of the Lord Mayor. Inside, the **Egyptian Hall** is used for banquets and public meetings.

North of the Guildhall, in the midst of ruins of the old city wall, is the **Museum of London,** at the Barbican. Visitors can lose themselves for hours in this fascinating museum, and peer out of some of the windows to view the wall close up.

Royal Britain, on Aldersgate Street, an attraction that opened in 1988, portrays English history and pageantry, with particular focus on the royal family. Visitors walk through a series of corridors with displays beginning with the wild tribal lands of prehistoric times, the Roman invaders of the first century A.D., King Arthur and the Knights of the Round Table, coronations of all of the kings, Henry VIII, Mary, Queen of Scots, Queen Victoria's Diamond Jubilee, a film of *Henry V* starring Laurence Olivier, and ending with movies of the present royal family.

Just north of the Museum of London stands the sixty-acre **Barbican Arts and Conference Center**. Begun in 1962 on the site of a bombed-out area once containing a medieval stronghold, the Barbican buildings are modern blocks up to 18 stories with walkways in between. Over 6000 people live in apartments there. Visitors arrive at the Barbican to attend the Royal Shakespeare Theatre, the Pit Theatre, to visit the Barbican Art Gallery or to listen to a concert performed by the London Symphony Orchestra.

Part of the fun of strolling around in this area is the chance to church-hop; there is a church on almost every corner. The City contained 87 churches within the walls before the Great Fire; today there are 39 left, with nine towers of former churches still standing.

The most famous of all is **St. Paul's Cathedral,** Ludgate Hill, which survived wartime bombing when all around it fell. Londoners took heart when they saw its cross and dome rising above the flames of the December 29, 1940, bombing raid. A church has stood there since 604 A.D., although the first several were destroyed, the present building has been standing since its completion in 1708. Christopher Wren designed the new church, beginning work in June 1675. The facade contains two rows of double Corinthian columns: the lower has six pair, the upper has four. The pediment contains a relief of a phoenix and the Latin word *Resurgam* to signify the rebirth of the building. Standing at the top of Ludgate Hill, the cathedral is the largest in the City (and the second largest in the world after St. Peter's in Rome); its dome rises above most of the modern buildings around it to be a focus in the London skyline.

From the inside of the cathedral we see the third layer with its frescoed paintings encircled by the whispering gallery. It's true—one can stand on one side of the gallery, say a few words in a whisper and it can be heard all the way across the 107 feet of space in the other side of the gallery.

An effigy of John Donne, a poet, lawyer, and Dean of St. Paul's from 1621 to 1631, stands in the South Choir Aisle. Because he had secretly married the daughter of Sir Thomas Egerton, the furious father had him thrown in prison. Always witty, John Donne etched on his cell walls: "John Donne-Ann Donne-Undone."

The north aisle of the nave contains a memorial to the Duke of Wellington who is seen riding his horse on top of a tall arch. He is buried in the Crypt.

Admiral Horatio Nelson's tomb stands in the center beneath the dome. His remains were buried in a 16th-century marble sarcophagus that was originally designed for Cardinal Wolsey in 1524 by the sculptor Benedetto da Rovezzano; the original tomb was confiscated by Henry VIII and stored in Windsor Castle until Nelson died in 1805. His body was brought from Gibraltar to London preserved in a keg of spirits, then it lay in state in Greenwich, and finally went in funeral procession on the Thames to St. Paul's. His memorial stands upstairs in the main aisle of the transept; he holds a length of line beside an anchor.

St. Paul's has had royal associations for many years; not every event has been held in Westminster Abbey. The Royal Wedding of the Prince and Princess of Wales was held in St. Paul's in 1981. Earlier, in 1977, Queen Elizabeth came to St. Paul's to give thanks for her Silver Jubilee, as had Queen Victoria in 1897.

West of St. Paul's, just off Fleet Street on Gough Square, stands **Dr Samuel Johnson's House**. He wrote a definitive English Dictionary while living in this house. A first edition of the Dictionary is on display. Ye Olde Chesire Cheese, a well known tavern where Johnson used to drink, is just around the corner.

Still in the City, **Fleet Street,** which was named after the River Fleet, was once called "The Street of Ink" because a number of national newspapers had their offices there. Most of them have now moved to Docklands or other places. **Temple Bar,** as the western boundary of the City, is the place where Queen Elizabeth stops to receive and then return the Pearl Sword from the Lord Mayor when she enters the City.

Holborn

North of the Royal Courts of Justice stands **Lincoln's Inn,** another center of English law dating from the 14th century. The name Lincoln came from Henry de Lacy, the Earl of Lincoln, who was a legal adviser to Edward I.

Sir John Sloane's Museum, Lincoln's Inn Fields, once the architect's home, contains architectural drawings and models of Sloane's work as well as those of others, a collection of Greek, Roman and Egyptian artifacts and paintings by Reynolds, Canaletto, Turner, and Hogarth.

Not far to the northeast stands Charles Dickens's house at 48 Doughty

Street, where he lived from 1837 to 1839. His reputation reached its peak during that period. He wrote *Pickwick Papers, Oliver Twist, Nicholas Nickleby,* and began *Barnaby Rudge* there. His study contains the desk and chair used during his writing. Memorabilia in the house include his manuscripts, letters, first editions of his books, paintings and the family Bible.

Bloomsbury

Bloomsbury is an area visitors often choose to live in for a spell when doing research or teaching. London University now inhabits many of the 18th- and 19th-century terraced houses, and others have been joined as hotels. Walkers will see plaques on the walls with information on the famous people who once lived there. Virginia and Leonard Woolf, Clive and Vanessa Bell, Lytton Strachey, Charles Darwin, E.M. Forster, Duncan Grant, Maynard Keynes, Rupert Brooke, D.H. Lawrence, Bertrand Russell, and Charles Dickens all lived in the area.

The **British Museum,** on Great Russell Street, is very difficult to describe; as the repository for any category one could think of, it may be considered without rivalry anywhere in the world. From the Elgin Marbles to the Rosetta Stone, scholars and visitors will find a wealth of contents. The circular **Reading Room** may have moved by the time you visit. Scholars from all over the world have signed into its somber and hushed atmosphere to read books that are not easily available anywhere else.

Regent's Park and Area

Regent's Park, its 472 acres laid out by John Nash in the early 19th century, dates back to the 7th century, when the village of Tyburn belonged to the Abbey of Barking, a convent. Domesday Book describes Tyburn as a community of eight families who farmed the land within their 600 acres. A number of different families inherited the manorhouse over the years until the Dissolution of the Monasteries, when the king took the house and grounds for his private hunting lodge, and called it Marlebone Park. A ring mound was built around the land to keep poachers out and the deer in.

Today the park, fringed with the same terraced houses, contains open spaces, a romantic, serpentine lake with unusual angles and landscaping taking advantage of its curves, statues, shady trees, a rose garden, pond, open-air theater, and tennis courts. Londoners and visitors enjoy walking and playing in the park. An inner circle contains **Queen Mary's Garden;** the queen was very fond of roses and this garden maintains color during the warm months. The Royal Botanic Society maintained the garden from 1840 to 1932. Ornate gates lead into the garden and the mermaid fountain and lily-pond.

An iron bridge signals **Regent's Canal** underneath. In 1795 Paddington was linked to the Grand Union Canal, which continues up into the Midlands. This canal flows through Camden Town to King's Cross and emerges at Dockland. Long canal boats, colorfully painted, ply the water with tourists from

Little Venice or Camden Lock. Trips last about 1½ hours and there are several companies running them. You can also walk along the tow-path; you'll see a number of canal boats moored in Little Venice or along the way.

London Zoo, founded in 1826, is located at the northern end of the park. Sir Stamford Raffles founded the Zoological Society of London in 1826; in 1827 members were allowed inside a five-acre site, and by 1848 the public could enter for one shilling each. We know from personal experience with a three-year-old that the Children's Zoo is a big hit. Toddlers can move right in to pet baby animals, with parents watchful. The "Moonlight Hall" area contains nocturnal animals who are awake!

Back on the south side of Regent's Park again we can visit **Madame Tussaud's,** on Marylebone Road, which houses wax models of famous people from all over the world. Madame Tussaud began her career in Paris in the 18th century when she made wax figures for Louis XVI. During the Revolution, when in prison, she made models from the heads of guillotine victims. Now, these figures may be seen in the Chamber of Horrors.

The **Tableaux** contains the sleeping figure of Madame du Barry, mistress of King Louis XV of France. She is the earliest in the collection, modelled in 1765. Since 1837 a clockwork mechanism has made her breathe—startling to visitors.

The **London Planetarium,** next door to Madame Tussaud's, presents star shows every 40 minutes. In the evening the Planetarium offers shows using laser light choreographed to current rock and pop music.

Kensington

Queen Victoria ordained that Kensington be named a royal borough in 1901. With **Hyde Park** connected to **Kensington Gardens,** the area has been popular with the aristocracy for many years. During the 18th century, the park was the place to ride in fashionable carriages; today people ride horseback on **Rotten Row**. The **Serpentine** is often swarming with small boats on nice days. **Marble Arch,** built in 1827, looks like a Roman triumphal arch; it once stood near Buckingham Palace.

Kensington Palace was taken by William III in 1689 and ordained a royal residence. All reigning sovereigns lived there from 1689 to 1760. **Queen Victoria's Bedroom** is the room where Princess Victoria was awakened to learn that her uncle, William IV, had died and that she would be queen. To the left of the black marble fireplace stands the cradle each of her nine children slept in.

At the southern end of Kensington Gardens stands the **Albert Memorial,** designed to honor Queen Victoria's husband. His fourteen-foot-tall bronze statue sits in the middle surrounded by representations of poets, composers, artists and architects.

Across the street is the **Royal Albert Hall,** spectacular in red brick with an iron and glass dome. Concerts, ballet, conferences, meetings, and exhibitions are held there. A 150-ton organ, once the largest in the world, is inside.

Continue walking down Exhibition Road to the series of museums beginning with the **Science Museum,** which contains working exhibits with buttons to push and handles to turn. **Foucault's Pendulum** moves to show the rotation of the earth. The puffing billy, built in 1813, is the oldest locomotive anywhere. A **1392 clock** from Wells Cathedral is one of the oldest in the world.

The **Geological Museum,** on Exhibition Road, begins its tour with the Story of the Earth, which focuses on tectonic plates. The galaxy and planets are presented as a cyclorama; pushing a button will illustrate the birth and death of stars. A display of the inside of the earth in cross-section style leads into a map showing how volcanoes and earthquakes are attracted to edges of the plates in the Earth's crust. At the press of a button, a volcano will erupt, then an earthquake takes over.

The **Natural History Museum,** on Cromwell Road, houses vast collections of animals, insects, birds, fish, plants, minerals, and rocks. Charles Darwin's theory of natural selection is explained with a variety of exhibits and models. Fossils are presented within their geological timetable. The skeleton of a Tyrannosaurus is forty feet long. You can walk around a large model of a whale and another of a whale skeleton.

The **Victoria and Albert Museum,** South Kensington, dates back to the Great Exhibition of 1851 held in Hyde Park. Five thousand pounds was spent on buying objects of applied art from the Exhibition as the nucleus of the new museum which was opened in Marlborough House in 1852. In 1899 Queen Victoria laid the foundation stone for a new building and it was opened by King Edward VII in 1909.

The **"V & A"** is Britain's National Museum of Art and Design. Objects used in everyday life such as ceramics, glass, furniture, jewelry, metalwork, textiles, and dress show the development of the decorative arts all over the world.

Favorite items include the **Great Bed of Ware,** a large 1580 Elizabethan bed that will hold four persons; anyone who slept in the bed could carve his initials on it. Ben Jonson and Shakespeare have written about the Ware bed.

Other Sites to Visit in London

While we have tried to group London sites in pockets for convenient touring there are many, many outside of the natural geographical groupings. One of those is the **Tate Gallery,** right on the Thames at Millbank. The Tate opened in 1897 in its neoclassical building, and has expanded several times since then. The collection includes British works and a separate Modern Collection containing sculpture and painting by artists born after 1850.

DAY TRIPS FROM LONDON ....

The following day trips are all on the outskirts of London. While talking about each area in London, we grouped sightseeing activities for the convenience of pedestrians. Because London is so large and sprawling, some of the sights require a little more effort to reach, but each of them can be reached by tube, bus, or train.

EAST OF LONDON

Greenwich

Greenwich, located on the south bank of the River Thames, is just four miles downstream from Tower Bridge. In fact, one of the most interesting ways to get to Greenwich is to take the tube to Tower Hill, then follow signs to Docklands Light Railway, which opened in 1987 at Tower Gateway. The railway will take you over and through the new Docklands area to Island Gardens in 16 minutes. The gargantuan task of regenerating eight square miles of dockland into glass and steel office blocks and apartments will probably be in process for some time to come. You can watch the progress from the train as you glide over it. After leaving the train you will walk under the river through the Greenwich Foot Tunnel for about five minutes. Then take a Victorian lift up to ground level and you are in Greenwich. You can return the same way, take a boat, or hop on British Rail.

The *Cutty Sark* still stands tall in its cradle on the banks of the Thames. Built in 1869 as one of the last great sailing clippers carrying tea from China, she radiates the pride of her past. We return time and again to feel the warmth and relive her proud sailing days. She was the fastest ship afloat—with 32,000 square feet of canvas, she could make 363 miles in a day. Her name relates to the short chemise of Nannie, from Robert Burns's poem *Tam o'Shanter.* Her mainmast towers 152 feet and she is fully rigged as she used to be in the old days.

Below, cabins have been restored and are on view; a museum exhibit relates her story. The life of the sea sounds romantic, but it was not always secure—men had to move out on bouncing yards to furl sail and face shipwreck when tacking into an unknown harbor.

The *Gipsy Moth IV,* sailed by Sir Francis Chichester around the world single-handedly, stands nearby. She is dwarfed at 52 feet in length by the 224-foot *Cutty Sark.*

The **National Maritime Museum** contains artifacts and explanations of Britain's naval history. Standing as it does very near the River Thames's shore, with its green park extending behind it and up the hill, the lawn of the Museum seems a great place to view London without all of the hustle and bustle of a big city.

The **West Wing** has four floors of exhibits beginning with yachts and boats on the lower ground floor. We often like to begin a tour of a maritime museum with the earliest chronological displays. One can do that here in the archaeological gallery, which explores data from the Bronze Age to medieval times. Because early boats were made of organic materials such as bark, hides, reeds, and wood, most have completely disintegrated over time. Dugout canoes did survive and the museum has five plank boats and three logboats. Special processes are necessary to preserve such boats when they are exposed to air; they are sprayed with polyethylene glycol over a long period to prevent drying out.

Sailing ships are featured in the museum in model form, paintings, and displays. Beginning with square-rigged three-masted ships in the 15th century, to the unwieldly carrack with its high fore and after castles, the Spanish and Portuguese galleons, English galleons with lower fore and aftercastles, the addition of topgallant sails and spritsails, fore-and-aft triangular headsails and staysails—shipbuilders were constantly improving their vessels for better stability and speed.

Neptune Hall contains the riveted steel steampaddle tug *Reliant,* into which visitors can climb to explore the crew's quarters, the master's cabin, and the wheelhouse. The **Barge Hall** houses Queen Mary's shallop from 1689, handsome with its red stripe around the topsides and red cushions inside. It was used to ferry the monarch to the royal yacht or to a flagship. King George V and Queen Mary were the last to ride in it, during the Victory Pageant in 1919.

The **Old Royal Observatory,** its six buildings now part of the National Maritime Museum after its move to Herstmonceux Castle in Sussex in 1948, is still the place where Greenwich Mean Time is observed. Beginning with the 1767 publication of the *Nautical Almanack,* navigators charted their longitude in relation to the Greenwich meridian. A Meridian Conference was held in Washington in 1884 and the Greenwich meridian became the standard.

Flamsteed House is unmistakeable with the red ball on its top; the ball, since 1833, has been hoisted halfway up the mast at 12.55, to the top at 12.58 and is dropped at 13.00. In the courtyard beside Flamsteed House anyone can stand with a foot on each side of the brass line marking the Greenwich Meridian.

SOUTHWEST OF LONDON
Kew Gardens

Kew Gardens, or the Royal Botanic Gardens, had their start in 1759. The original nine-acre plot is now 300 acres. Each gardener added his expertise; one of them, Sir Joseph Banks, sailed with Captain Cook on his first around-the-world voyage, adding plants from Australia, the Pacific, and Africa.

The **Palm House,** designed by Decimus Burton in 1848, was made of glass and iron with curved roofs. Palms, tropical shrubs such as cocoa and bananas, and other tropical trees live in perfect conditions. Outside roses flourish in a formal garden amongst replicas of the "Queen's Beasts" designed for her 1953 coronation. A number of other greenhouses grow exotic plants.

In the gardens there is a ten-story-high pagoda that can be seen from afar. The Japanese gateway makes a nice photographic setting.

Hampton Court Palace

Cardinal Thomas Wolsey, Archbishop of York, was determined to build a house worthy of his status and wealth. In 1514 he ordered the best building materials from all over England, as well as France. He furnished it with tapestries, carpets, and furniture created by the best craftsmen. When it was ready, he moved in with his retinue; he conducted business and entertained lavishly. However, by 1525 Wolsey knew that it was prudent to give his sumptuous home to King Henry VIII who otherwise could have caused trouble for him. The mercurial king, did him in anyway after Wolsey was unable to secure Henry's divorce; Wolsey lost all of his possessions and died in 1530 on the brink of being tried for treason.

Henry VIII immediately set about making Hampton Court even grander than it had been in Wolsey's day. He touchingly entwined his initial with that of Anne Boleyn over gateways and on ceiling panels, then had her "A" removed after he ordered her beheaded. His next queen, Jane Seymour, died in childbirth at Hampton Court; her son, Edward VI, was christened in the Chapel Royal in 1537.

Elizabeth I, who reigned from 1558 to 1603, was not fond of Hampton Court, perhaps because she had almost died of smallpox there. James I spent Christmas, 1603, at Hampton Court. It is thought that Shakespeare performed in his play *Measure for Measure* during Christmas, 1604, in the palace.

In 1642, after Charles I tried to arrest five members of Parliament unsuccessfully, he fled to Hampton Court. But in 1645 the Parlimentarians confiscated Hampton Court and made Charles a prisoner there. Although he escaped to the Ilse of Wight, he was captured, returned to Hampton Court and imprisoned, tried, and executed at the Banqueting House in Whitehall in 1649.

Oliver Cromwell, the Lord Protector, spent weekends at Hampton Court while he was in power. With the return of Charles II, who spent three months in Hampton Court with his bride, Catherine of Braganza, the palace was once again under royal care.

During Queen Victoria's reign the palace and gardens were opened to the public beginning in 1838. A program of restoration was begun, which still continues today.

The **Great Hall,** with its ornate carved hammer-beam roof, still contains Henry's and Anne Boleyn's initials. A dais was placed at one end of the room for royalty and important guests; above is a fan-vaulted window.

The **Royal Chapel** has a timber vaulted ceiling, with glistening gilt on a blue background. The trompe l'oeil window was painted by Thornhill; Gibbons is responsible for the oak reredos. Both were commissioned by Wren during the period he was renovating for Queen Anne. Henry Purcell composed some of his best work for performances in the chapel.

Some say the **Haunted Gallery** is still visited by the ghost of Catherine Howard, who ran down the gallery in pursuit of her sentencer, King Henry, when he was at prayer in the Royal Chapel. Her screams did not influence his decision and she was beheaded.

The gardens are extensive, dating back to Wolsey's time, and developed further by succeeding generations. Lancelot "Capability" Brown was responsible for planning many of the gardens. He also planted the "great vine," which has grown at a spectacular rate, possibly by its roots having become involved with the palace sewer system.

The **Maze** originally came from Wren's designs for William and Mary. Hedges, now six feet tall, provide fun and challenge for visitors of all ages.

Royal Tennis Courts were originally built in 1530 by King Henry VIII. The courts are now used for Real Tennis (the Renaissance progenitor of the game we play today); many of the limited numbers of players left in the world have played on those courts.

EXCURSIONS FROM LONDON ....

If one visualizes a large circle outside of London, all of the following places can be reached on a long day trip or better yet, on a two- or three-day excursion. Bus tours from London reach all of them and return on the same day, but then we are leaving the driving to them. Depending upon road conditions, independent drivers can reach all of them in two or three hours. We have grouped several within the same area; if visiting more than one, we strongly suggest staying overnight.

We are organizing this section as if we were looking at a compass rose around London. That way your eye can move around in a clockwise fashion and the groupings will make sense. We will begin with Canterbury in the southeast corner and end with Cambridge in the northeast.

SOUTHWEST OF LONDON

Canterbury

Canterbury has been the religious center of Anglican Christianity since St. Augustine founded the Christian Church in 597. His church burned in 1067 and the present cathedral was begun in 1070.

Archbishop Thomas a Becket was murdered in 1170 by four knights who thought they were pleasing King Henry II. Becket and Henry, at one time allies, had clashed and the King was heard to complain "Who will deliver me from this turbulent priest?" Rome made Becket a martyr-saint and pilgrims began to journey to Canterbury to pray at the site in the northwest transept where Becket was killed, and also beside his tomb in the crypt. Their knees eventually wore depressions in the mosaic tiles of Trinity Chapel where they came to pay homage. In 1538 Henry VIII railed against Becket, denounced him for "treason, contumacy, and rebellion" and ordered his tomb opened and his remains scattered.

Canterbury Heritage Museum, on Stour Street, is housed in a medieval building on the riverbank. The museum presents Canterbury's past by a walk through time. Viking and Roman displays include artifacts from that era. A copy of Thomas a Becket's tomb is there.

Canterbury Pilgrim's Way on St. Margaret's Street, provides the chance to almost experience the sights, sounds and smells of Chaucer's *Canterbury Tales.* Homes, inns, and workshops feature both people and animals in their daily routine. Audiovisual equipment picks up voices to bring it all to life.

Dover

The "white cliffs of Dover" have long been thought of with nostalgia, even by those of us not born in Britain. I can remember my grandmother singing the popular World War I song. Curiously, the chalk cliffs are no longer white but a white mottled with green streaks of vegetation. They will still remain the symbol of the main gateway to and from the continent, at least until the "Chunnel" (Channel Tunnel) removes them from travelers' sight in a few years.

One of the newest developments in Dover, the Eurotunnel, is a link between England and France that will speed travel between the British Isles and the Continent, connecting them symbolically as well as physically. In December of 1990 we enjoyed all of the hoopla as a whiff of garlic finally came through the little opening from France. The French said, "You are no longer an island," and a sign on the English side noted, "Almost there—Allo! Allo!" Workmen shook hands through the tunnel and the deed was done.

The **Eurotunnel Exhibition Center** (St. Martin's Plain, Folkestone) has offered a museum of the project. We found it especially poignant to walk into a cave-like room over a rough floor laid with tracks, pass a cart loaded with stone, and peer over the shoulders of two figures with shovels—then hear the distant sound of digging by their fellow workmen. The ping of hammer on stone farther into the tunnel is unmistakable. Of course, the heroes of the battle were two white submarine-like boring machines that drove forward relentlessly like two battering rams.

Miniature models of the tourist shuttle wagons and freight shuttle wagons show double-deckers for cars in the form of a "rake" carrying 120 cars. Rakes of single deck wagons will carry 65 cars or 13 coaches and 26 cars. Passengers will remain in their vehicles during the trip. Video displays and games cover all aspects of tunnel travel.

Rye

Once a port, Rye had grown from a fishing village into a powerful trading center. The town also became a member of the confederation of the Cinque Ports. Its harbor silted up in the 16th century. But its past remains with part of a 14th-century wall, cobbled streets, and a number of lovely half-timbered houses.

St. Mary the Virgin Church dates from around 1150; it was built by local craftsmen who were supervised by master craftsmen from the Abbey of Fecamp in Normandy. In 1377 French invaders set fire to the church and carried off the bells. The next year Rye men went to France and recovered their bells. The clock was in place by 1561; it is unusual with two "quarter boys" to strike the quarter hours. The original pendulum was much longer and some say that children used to swing on it, throwing off the time.

The **Lamb House** site was originally owned by James Lamb who was a licensed vintner with his brewery in the garden. In 1726 a ship carrying George I beached itself during a storm on Camber Sands. James Lamb brought the king back to his home to spend the night. To add to the excitement Martha Lamb gave birth to a baby boy during that night. The king was godfather to the little boy.

In 1897 Henry James leased and then bought the house. James came to love Rye and once wrote *"Never* again will I leave it."* A German bomb fell on the Garden Room during World War II. We strolled through the garden and were delighted to find a "secret garden" arch on the west side and a grave marker for pets entitled "Tosca, Nick and Peter."

SOUTH OF LONDON
Brighton

Brighton was a fashionable seaside resort in the 18th century and it still has charm today. Once a little fishing village, the town became famous after Dr. Richard Russell from Lewes recommended that his patients try bathing in the sea. George IV came with his entourage and settled in to enjoy the social life as well as the sea. He also secretly married Maria Fitzherbert there in 1785.

The **Royal Pavilion** was built by John Nash between 1815 and 1822. The building is startling with its onion domes, minarets, peaks, and turrets, all put together with Eastern flair.

Inside, the pavilion contains Regency furniture, silver, porcelain, glass and gold plate, pagoda ornaments, bronze candelabra, clocks, and paintings. Queen Elizabeth II owns much of the interior furnishing and has loaned it to Brighton. The **Music Room** had been restored for the second time when we visited. During the horrendous wind storm of 1987 one of the three-ton minarets from the roof had fallen into the room producing a gaping hole.

Bogner Roman Villa

The Villa is located northwest of Brighton, six miles north of Arundel and northeast of Chichester. Mosaics in the villa date from the 4th century. The first mosaic to be uncovered was one surrounding a water basin of six dancing girls with flying veils. A Venus mosaic contains a bust of the goddess with a peacock-like bird on each side sitting on a green branch. A series of winged cupids seem to be playing as gladiators. *Winter* is the only surviving one of four in the seasons room. The head of Medusa is surrounded by snakes and a myriad of geometric patterns. Displays in the museum give a clear explanation of the process of mosaic work.

SOUTHWEST OF LONDON
Portsmouth

Portsmouth, nicknamed "Pompey," has been watching ships sail in and out since the 12th century. Today, the **Royal Dockyard** houses three restored ships, complete with fittings and their legends.

The *Mary Rose,* built in 1509, plunged to the bottom while battling a French fleet in 1545. Apparently she began to heel too much as the crew hoisted sails, water rushed in through open gun ports and she sank very quickly. The remains of 200 men were found trapped within the vessel. Most of them were in their late teens and early 20s, with a few in their 40s and a couple of boys.

She lay secure in the mud for four centuries before being raised in 1982. Although only the starboard side of the hull was recoverable, the men who died with her were still there, with their clothing, weapons, and possessions still in place.

Divers, led by Prince Charles, worked together to raise this historic ship. The salvage operation took place over a period of several years as they worked against time to save her from microorganisms and colonization of marine plants and animals. Visitors are allowed to walk on catwalks around the *Mary Rose* and to watch whatever restoration is in progress. It is like looking into a half-model.

The **HMS Victory** was ordered to be built the same year Horatio Nelson was born. They were joined when he, as an Admiral claimed her as his flagship in the Mediterranean. Britain was successful in her sea battle with both France and Spain during the Battle of Trafalgar, but Nelson lost his life in that battle on October 21, 1805. He was shot by a musketeer in the *Redoubtable* who was poised 50 feet up in the mizzentop. A handkerchief was placed over his face as he was carried below, so that his men would not recognize him and lose courage. As he lay on his pallet, knowing there was not much life left, he asked that a lock of his hair and his belongings be given to his mistress, Emma Hamilton.

Today the *Victory* stands in dry dock, handsome with fresh black and yellow topsides and red gunports. Everything is shipshape as visitors walk aboard. Cannons stand on rolling platforms along the main deck, silent but ready. She has 27 miles of standing and running rigging and her sails could cover four acres. She flies the flag of the Commander-in-Chief, Naval Home Command at the main top-gallant masthead, the White Ensign at the stern, and the Union Jack at the jackstaff.

The **Great Cabin,** where the officers and Admiral Nelson had their meals, is decorated as it was during the Battle of Trafalgar. Nelson had a day cabin, which contains a table and armchair. He also had a sleeping cabin; his cot hangs from a pole and the original was covered with draperies made by Lady Hamilton; the replicas there now were made by Queen Mary when the ship was refurbished in 1922. His wooden folding bed and a cabinet for his personal things are also on display.

The **HMS Warrior** arrived in Portsmouth in 1987 after being restored. She was first launched in 1860 and was claimed to be the fastest, largest, strongest, and best armed warship in the world. Her iron hull measures 418 feet in length. Using both sail and steam she took advantage of the best aspects of both. She kept the peace by keeping the enemy at bay. Other countries built similar ships, and as development moved ahead the *Warrior* became obsolete.

In 1968 the Duke of Edinburgh was involved in the Maritime Trust. The *Warrior* was restored in Hartlepool and a replica of her original 12-foot figurehead was placed on her bow in 1985.

Visitors today can sit at mess tables on the main deck and have a look at the crew's quarters as well as those of the captain and officers. The Penn twin-cylinder steam engine is demonstrated for visitors.

Fishbourne Roman Palace

Between Portsmouth and Chichester to the east stands the reconstruction of Fishbourne Roman Palace. The site was probably inhabited as early as 43 A.D. and the palace dates from 75 A.D. It is likely that Tiberius Claudius Cogidubnus, a native king who helped the Romans during their invasion, was the man who enjoyed life there.

The palace was unearthed beginning in 1960; mosaic floors are laid out for visitors who walk above them on walkways and ramps. Eight mosaics include cupid riding on a dolphin, winged sea panthers and sea horses, scallop shells, a Medusa head, geometric designs, and Solomon's knots. Because the bedding under the mosaics deteriorated over time each has been removed in sections and replaced on a stable base. A conservation display pictures the painstaking process by the use of gridlines and nylon mesh to keep the stones in place.

A GROUP OF CATHEDRALS AND ANCIENT SITES: STONEHENGE, OLD SARUM, SALISBURY, AND WINCHESTER

Winchester

Two of England's great cathedrals lie close together; one other, Wells, is farther west. Winchester was once the seat of Roman government, then Saxons, Danes, and Normans, until William the Conqueror set up his court in London. The cathedral, built from 1079, is one of the longest in Europe. Jane Austen and Izaak Walton are buried there, as well as some of England's kings including Ethelwulf, Egbert, Canute, and William II.

Winchester Castle has disappeared, but its Great Hall remains. King Arthur's "roundtable," actually dating only from the 14th century, is on display.

Salisbury

Salisbury, designed by Bishop Poore in the 13th century, has a Gothic cathedral with a soaring spire that is the tallest in England at 404 feet. The ancient clock mechanism dates from 1386 and is said to be the oldest in England. The Magna Carta is on display in the Chapter House.

Old Sarum

Two miles away stand the ruins of Old Sarum, dating back to the Iron Age. The Romans built a fortress there, and later a cathedral was constructed by Herman, the first bishop of Old Sarum. Because of friction between the inhabitants of the castle and the church, Bishop Poore asked Richard I for permission to build another church farther away, in Salisbury. The old cathedral was demolished and some of its stone taken to the new location. The approach to Old Sarum is bucolic, with cows grazing in fields of buttercups when we were there. Here's the place to let travel-weary children run off steam around the existing foundations. A dry moat encircles the foundations on a hill.

Stonehenge

Stonehenge, a grouping of prehistoric stones, has baffled men for years. No one really knows why they were erected in circular fashion. Modern Druids like to hold a midnight to sunrise vigil there on June 21 as part of a sun-worshipping rite. English newspapers carry stories prior to that date—will they be allowed to continue this practice or not?

Scholars, using the radio carbon process to date the stones, know that they have been standing since 2800 B.C. The outside boundary of Stonehenge consists of several concentric circles. Close to the road stands the Heel Stone, or

Friar's Heel, said to have been thrown by the Devil as he was working on Stonehenge. This stone weighs 35 tons and must have needed at least 250 men to move it.

Although there are 900 stone circles left in the British Isles, Stonehenge is unique because of its upright stones with stone lintels on top. Its stones are also larger than any of the others' and the shaping is more refined.

When we first visited Stonehenge in 1959 we were free to walk around and touch the stones. Today visitors cannot go anywhere near the stones and the place has become commercialized, which is a pity. It is still worth the trip to see Stonehenge but we suggest a visit to Avebury Ring (see below) where you can walk and touch at will.

WEST OF LONDON
Windsor

Windsor Castle is the closest of our excursion choices. Visitors may choose to continue on to Avebury Ring and Bath along the same motorway.

The Windsor area was inhabited by the Saxons who built a palace for their king two miles down the river. William the Conqueror used this palace until he decided to build a castle on the hill for better security. His castle was probably built of wood, now replaced with stone. Today it is one of the main residences of the royal family; the flag flying indicates that the queen is at home.

As visitors enter the Lower Ward, **St. George's Chapel** stands on the left. Built in the "perpendicular" form of late medieval English architecture, which focused on flying buttresses to hold the weight of the roof, thinner columns, and more glass—all give an illusion of light and space. The carved stalls in the choir pay homage to the Knights of the Garter, complete with each one's helmet, crest, and banner above the stall. Other carving in the choir tells the Gospel story, the legend of St. George, or satirical images such as a cat playing the organ.

Visitors of all ages are fascinated by the "smallness" of **Queen Mary's Doll House.** Each room with its tiny furnishings can be seen in microcosm—design, detail, and decoration are concentrated in a manageable whole. From the King's Bedroom, decorated in Chinese motif, to the elegant dining room, with silver, china, and glassware on the table, you can imagine life in the 1920s. Don't miss the doll's house in the day nursery, a gramophone that plays "God Save the King," and a theater set for "Peter Pan."

Avebury Ring

Wear comfortable walking shoes because the Avebury Circle area is extensive in a 28 acre landscape. The bucolic setting, with green grass setting off the circles of stones, is quiet and peaceful. The outer bank, surrounding the area is between 14 and 18 feet high. Two smaller stone circles lie inside.

The **Barber Stone** carries a story complete with a smiling skeleton. During the 14th century, a barber-surgeon came along as stones were being toppled over. Giving a hand, he was accidentally crushed when the stone fell. His pelvis was crushed, neck broken, and right foot wedged under the stone so his corpse could not be removed. His leather pouch contained three silver coins dating from 1320, his iron scissors and a lance lay beside him.

The **Devil's Chair** stands near the south entrance. It is said that if you sit in the chair you can see smoke emerging from the small hole above. Or you can run around the stone 100 times and listen for the voice of the devil.

There are several other prehistoric sites to visit in the area. **West Kennet Long Barrow,** dating from 3700 B.C. is accessible from a lay-by on the A4 at West Kennet. **Windmill Hill,** used as a settlement and ceremonial ring 3700–2500 B.C. is just north of Avebury. The **Sanctuary,** which dates from 2500 B.C., is near Overton Hill. Silbury Hill can be seen from almost anywhere as it towers over the landscape.

Bath

Prince Bladud, the leper father of Shakespeare's King Lear, discovered the hot springs of Bath when he lived in exile as a swineherd around 500 B.C. One can imagine his surprise as he rounded the hills at the top and stared down into a steaming center.

The Romans arrived in 43 A.D. and blessed the springs in honor of their goddess Minerva. They enclosed the King's Bath spring, built a temple to Sulis Minerva nearby, and a large pool complete with Turkish bath and sauna.

Later kings and queens began to come, attracting courtiers and the fashionable world as well. Beau Nash arrived on the scene and took over the job of controlling the behavior of visitors in town. He was firm but popular, so Bath gained a reputation for elegance and good order.

Although many people enjoyed coming to Bath for social life, others were sent by their physicians to be cured by the waters. Today visitors can join tours at the Roman Baths Museum. Water emerges into the King's Bath at the rate of a quarter of a million gallons a day, and the temperature remains at 46.5 C. Visitors can explore the Great Bath, a circular bath, and a system of heating the rooms; the hypocaust, a cavity underneath the floor where hot air circulated, looks like piles of bricks, which supported the floor. The bronze head of Minerva gleams in the museum; mosaics, stone monuments, coins, and votive offerings are on display.

NORTHWEST OF LONDON
Oxford

We'll always have a soft spot in our hearts for Oxford after living there for three months 25 years ago. Our children were small, and eagerly pulled us along on walks through college gardens to see deer, smell the flowers, and feed the hungry ducks. It's a different world when one leaves the bustle and noise of the business area by passing through college gates into the quiet of courtyards and gardens beyond. With the opportunities of those who come to work as well as sight see, we had plenty of time to savor spring blooms amid historic buildings as we met faculty, listened to lectures and concerts, and visited the libraries, galleries, and museums of this remarkably open university. (The Department of External Studies provides similar opportunities through conferences and courses for short-term visitors.)

Oxford University is the oldest university of English-speaking people. Scholars used to meet and talk there long before the university itself was founded. Friars came to Oxford beginning in 1221, and taught and housed students of religion. Each college selects and teaches its own students as a self-governing body. The students must then sit for a university examination and thereby receive their degrees. Favorite colleges to see include Christ Church, Magdalen, and Trinity.

One of **Christ Church's** famous sons was Lewis Carroll (the pseudonym for Charles Dodgson), who took Alice Liddell, the daughter of the Dean of Christ Church, and her sisters on a boat trip. He entertained them by making up a story, later called *Alice's Adventures in Wonderland*. The Great Hall contains a 20th-century ''Alice'' window.

Magdalen (pronounced ''Maudlin'') College has a bell tower that stands high as seen from the other side of the Cherwell across Magdalen Bridge. Octagonal turrets on each corner top the four stones. The pinnacles reach 145 feet in height. On May Day choristers climb to the top of the tower to sing hymns. This has been happening since 1504.

Trinity College was founded in 1554. Its 15th-century chapel, designed by Dean Aldrich of Christ Church (and perhaps Wren) dates from 1690. Statues on top of the chapel tower symbolize geometry, astronomy, theology, and medicine. The chapel was given by Dr. Bathurst, who was president of the college in the late 17th century. It is likely that the altarpiece was created by Grinling Gibbons.

Besides visiting the colleges, visitors enjoy ''punting'' on the river in flat-bottomed boats. College crews row, building up their stamina for ''Eights Week,'' which takes place in June.

The **Bodleian library** was restored after most of its books were destroyed during the reign of King Edward VI. Sir Thomas Bodley was the principle donor and the library was officially opened in 1603. The new Bodleian has 11 floors with a conveyor to carry books from one library building to the other. Bodley had arranged with the Stationers' Company that a copy of every book published should be sent to his library.

The **Ashmolean Museum** contains collections from all over the world; it was founded by Elias Ashmole in 1675. Begun with Greek artifacts known as the Arundel and Pomfret Marbles, the museum houses a variety of items including the Alfred Jewel, which was said to have been made for King Alfred.

Woodstock

Blenheim Palace was originally given by Britain to John Churchill, the first Duke of Marlborough, to honor him for his 1704 victory at Blenheim. Sir John Vanbrugh designed the palace, and Capability Brown created the landscaping in 2000 acres of parkland. The Churchill family has lived there ever since, caring for the collections and preserving their heritage for future generations.

Inside, the **Great Hall,** with massive dimensions including its 67-foot-high ceiling, contains the arms of Queen Anne with two cherubs blowing horns. The ceiling painting, by Sir James Thornhill, depicts Marlborough kneeling and offering his plan for the battle of Blenheim. Don't miss the gigantic lock on the Hall door; it is a replica of one on the gates of Warsaw.

Sir Winston Churchill was born in a small room with pink and green floral wallpaper. The brass bed stands on an Oriental rug in this cozy bedroom. His reddish curls, tied with a white ribbon, are preserved, along with his baby vest. His "siren" suit and bedroom slippers stand beside the fireplace.

Outside, the water-terraces spout fountains in sculptured ponds, with ornate green hedges trimmed to perfection. The lake beyond, created by Capability Brown, provides a peaceful backdrop to the formal gardens.

Both Sir Winston Churchill and his wife, Clementine, are buried in the local village churchyard of Bladon, next to his parents. The tower of the church is visible from Blenheim.

The **Blenheim Park Nature Trail** begins at the Triumphal Arch at the Woodstock entrance and continues for two miles around the Queen Pool, past the Seven Arches Bridge, to the Grand Bridge, and back to the Palace.

Cotswolds

Beyond Woodstock lie the rolling hills of the Cotswolds. Placed mostly in Gloucestershire, the Cotswold Hills run from Cirencester up to Chipping Camden. The sheep that made a living in the Cotswolds are still there, baaing to each other as they munch across green fields. Cotswold villages are made of their own Cotswold stone in shades of blue gray to golden. Hikers can see one village after the next as they ramble up and down the hills.

Cirencester was once the largest Roman settlement in Britain outside of London. The **Corinium Museum** houses collections dating from prehistory with artefacts such as flints, a hand-axe, coins, jars, and mosaics.

North of Cirencester, in Withington, **Chedworth Roman Villa** has been excavated. Dating from the first half of the second century the villa increased in size and luxury over the next 200 years. A large number of mosaics were found at Chedworth.

Rich medieval wool merchants are immortalized in **Northleach Church;** if you want to rub brasses there be sure to think of a wall large enough to display them at home. I spent hours rubbing one that is beautiful but too large for available space. They are indeed handsome, larger-than-lifesize merchants, standing with one foot on a woolsack and the other on a sheep.

Stow-on-the-Wold lies at the junction of eight roads; it was once a thriving market town famous for sheep fairs. A model village that fascinates children who can peer in all of the windows, is **Bourton-on-the-Water,** just a few miles southeast. Our three-year-old, many years ago, found that everything was at just the right height for her. She could see into the houses, church, museums, and the model railway. There is even a tiny model village within the model village.

Moreton-in-the-Marsh had a thriving wool business that turned to the weaving of linen when wool went into decline. A museum of railway history has opened in the old railway station.

Broadway has a wealth of half-timbered houses facing each other across a wide street. It has been called the "painted lady of the Cotswolds." One mile to the southeast, **Broadway Tower Country Park** surrounds a 1799 tower built by the sixth Earl of Coventry. If you climb to the top, the view of 12 counties is rewarding.

Chipping Camden, another medieval wool market town with a covered market building, also has stone houses lining its main street. The "wool" church of St. James dates from the 15th century.

Stratford-on-Avon

The world's Shakespeare mania has made Stratford-on-Avon much more than the medieval market town it was long ago. Tourists arrive in hordes determined to see all of Shakespeariana from the cradle to the grave. It is a beautiful town, so try to visit it during the winter, if at all possible. Tickets for performances at the Royal Shakespeare Theatre or the Swan Theatre will also be easier to get—but still book ahead if you can.

Shakespeare's Birthplace, on Henley Street, is a half-timbered house probably dating from the late 15th or early 16th century. The house is furnished as it would have been during Elizabethan and Jacobean times.

One of our most pleasant memories is the early morning walk we took over 30 years ago from the center of Stratford out to **Anne Hathaway's Cottage** in Shottery. The grass and flowers were wet with dew, everything glistened in the morning sun, and we seemed alone in the countryside, free to breathe fresh garden scents deeply, and view the scene spread out before us in unusual clarity. It looked like a painting, and as we neared the cottage, the view of the house surrounded by brilliant gardens and topped with a thatched roof seemed almost unreal. No matter how many times we have visited again, images of that one magical time remain in our memory.

Anne Hathaway lived here while being courted by William Shakespeare. The house is large for a cottage—a 12-room farmhouse dating back to the 15th century. Most of the furnishings belonged to the Hathaway family including a carved Elizabethan bedstead. The living room contains an old wooden bench, or settle, where Anne and William sat beside the fireplace while courting.

Hall's Croft was occupied by Shakespeare's daughter Susanna and her husband, John Hall. The house looks similar to the birthplace, with a stone foundation, oak timber framing, lath and plaster, and a red tiled roof. The garden is enclosed by a wall on all sides.

New Place was Shakespeare's home in retirement until his death in 1616. Period furniture makes the house look lived in. In addition, there are historical and archaeological exhibits. The **Knott Garden** is a replica of an enclosed Elizabethan garden. Four "knots" or garden beds are separated by stone paths.

Mary Arden's House is a Tudor farmstead belonging to Shakespeare's mother. Because it was occupied until 1930 by farmers the farm remained in almost its original condition.

Warwick Castle

The River Avon, winding its way through central England, found a tougher crop of rock than that found in the rest of the countryside. The steep cliff remained as the river went around it. Early man recognized the strategic benefit of this rock and chose to build a defense-works there, the first said to be built by Ethelfleda, daughter of Alfred the Great in 914. Capability Brown designed the gardens, which are resplendent with topiary peacocks above the floral displays. Real peacocks roam freely in the gardens; we remember a mating dance by an enthusiastic male who did not succeed in attracting his chosen female, despite his brilliant feathers.

The **Great Hall,** the largest room in the castle, dates from the 14th century. In those days this all-purpose room would have had a fire in the center with an opening in the roof to let the smoke escape. Today this room contains a collection of armor including an example of "Maximilian" armor dating from 1520 and a child's suit of armor made for the son of Robert Dudley. Bonnie Prince Charlie's shield hangs on the right of the archway.

The **Private Apartments** now contain a new exhibition using 12 rooms to chronicle "A Royal Weekend Party, 1898." Wax figures are poised to look alive in each scene. Much of the furniture is original to 1898 at Warwick. In the library scene, the guest is the Prince of Wales, who became King Edward VII. In another scene the Prince of Wales is having a conversation with Lord Curzon in one of the bedrooms. The Countess of Warwick is relaxing taking tea with Millicent, the Duchess of Sutherland.

The **Watergate Tower** houses a ghost—that of Sir Fulke Greville, who was murdered by his manservant. Walk up to his study to hear a recording of the story of the murder. Banners of all of the Earls of Warwick hang in the armory. Armor of all kinds is collected there, including the horseman's helmet that once belonged to Oliver Cromwell. The **Dungeon** has displays of some of the unpleasant events prisoners were subjected to.

Kenilworth Castle

Here is the place to let off steam if you enjoy romping and climbing through ruins. The last time we visited, college students, let out of the confines of the bus, began scaling the walls and gleefully balancing as they made their way along the upper story. Dating from the 12th century, the castle was fortified and given to the Earl of Lancaster. John of Gaunt constructed the rooms overlooking the lake; later a harbor and pleasure garden was added by King Henry V. Sir Walter Scott's novel *Kenilworth* introduced the castle to many readers.

NORTH OF LONDON

Nottingham

Robin Hood has provided entertainment for legend lovers, who can still picture him feuding with the Sheriff of Nottingham from his lair in Sherwood Forest. His statue stands outside of Nottingham Castle. Some say that the "Major Oak" in Sherwood Forest is really the place where Robin Hood hid his booty.

Nottingham Castle stands high on a cliff; inside, an art gallery and museum display some of the historical remains of the area. Edward III, Edward IV, Richard III, and Charles I all lived there.

D. H. Lawrence's birthplace (8A Victoria Street, Eastwood) has been restored. Furnishings are typical of a Victorian home. Lord Byron lived at Newstead Abbey, which is 11 miles to the north. He took pleasure in scandalizing his friends and neighbors. Some of his work and belongings are on display.

There are a number of places in England where visitors can spend a pleasant day visiting charming churches in small villages. We chose to follow our noses in the area south of Nottingham near Oakham and Rutland Water, where we pushed creaking doors open in churches in Braunston, Brooke, Ridlington, Belton, and Hambleton. Sunlight streamed in on needlepoint cushions, statues, old box pews, balustraded screen, a medieval wooden chest that was carved from a solid tree trunk, stone font, stone coffin lids, a collection of church instruments, and monuments. The **Church of St. Peter** in Belton has used gargoyle heads as rainwater drains. Rolling hills, fields, sheep (with lambs when we were there), horses, twittering birds, beige stone houses, and rushing streams blended into our landscape.

Cambridge

Built on flat land, surrounded by fens (former sea marshes), and relieved only by a single, narrow river, the university city of Cambridge would not seem to have many of the qualities that would attract visitors, but it does. A city in population and a town in ambience, Cambridge achieves an almost perfect mixture of town and gown. The older colleges face the principal streets of the center, but many of them have extensive "backs" along the River Cam and the rest have enclosed gardens that bring the country within walls. In both cases, the colleges have an unmistakable rural flavor that suggests the pastoral tradition of removal from the world for contemplation. And like Oxford, the university is remarkably open to visitors, who may wander through the colleges at will during the day and track through the backs even during the evening. (In recent years, some restrictions have been established during the summer inundations of tourists, but the colleges maintain the general principal of welcoming visitors as long as they do not interfere with the life of undergraduates.) We have been fortunate enough to spend two academic years in Cambridge, separated by 14, and notice little difference in either university or city apart from increasing traffic problems as cars compete with bicycles for space.

Dating back to Neolithic times, then Roman, Saxon, and Norman, Cambridge provided what traders needed—a bridge across the River Cam. The trading route from eastern to central England went right through town. A group of Franciscans, Dominicans, and Carmelites founded Cambridge during the 12th century.

When town-and-gown disputes raged in Oxford in 1209, a number of scholars came to live in Cambridge. The first college, **Peterhouse,** was founded in 1284 by Hugh de Balsam, the Bishop of Ely. Today there are 24 colleges plus five post-graduate colleges in Cambridge. Each one is a separate self-governing body, with its students living and studying as members of the college. Students attend university lectures but hold tutorial sessions within their colleges. Colleges have dining halls, chapels, a library, common rooms, and sleeping rooms for their students.

King's College, familiar to many from the annual Christmas service beamed out to the world, has a magnificent Gothic chapel that took 70 years to build. Twenty-five 16th-century stained-glass windows portray the story of both the Old and New Testaments; they are said to be the largest and best preserved collection of old stained glass in the world. The Last Judgement west window dates from 1879. All of the glass was removed during World War II and hidden for safe-keeping.

Rubens's *Adoration of the Magi* stands at the far end. He painted this masterpiece in 1634 for the White Nuns at Louvain in Belgium. One's eye can't help but be drawn to this painting, even during a church service. Services are open to visitors and afterward one can stroll around to assimilate the glories of this building. The 16 choristers are joined by 14 undergraduates for services.

Roof-climbers are attracted by the pinnacles of the chapel; one left a coin up there dated 1760, in 1932 an umbrella appeared, flags fluttered from the pinnacles and a "Peace in Viet Nam" banner wafted in the 1960's.

Clare College is next to King's; it has three different renaissance styles in its buildings. Medieval buildings were destroyed by fire. Clare boasts the oldest bridge, dating from 1640. College gardens extend all the way to the river; something is in bloom from spring until fall.

Trinity College was founded by Henry VIII in 1546. The clock tower is known as the Edward III Gate. An ornate fountain, which was added during the time of Elizabeth, stands in the center of the Great Court.

St. John's College houses a number of courtyards and the Old Bridge, which looks just like Venice's Bridge of Sighs. Barred windows were designed to keep students in years ago.

Cambridge is also home to a number of museums including the **Fitzwilliam Museum,** which houses paintings, sculpture, furniture, coins, illuminated manuscripts, and rare books.

The **Cambridge and County Folk Museum** dates back to the 16th century when the building was the White Horse Inn. This timber-framed structure contains ten rooms full of items used by people during the last 30 years. Don't miss the toys and games, sure to delight children.

Next door, **Kettle's Yard** houses a collection of early 20th-century art collected by Jim Ede, who owned the home. His own chosen art objects and collectibles are found all over the house. A changing gallery offers contemporary art as well as video presentations.

The **Scott Polar Research Institute** contains displays of photographs, prints, drawings and manuscripts. Traveling gear and clothing used on the expeditions of Captain Scott and others helps tell the tale of their explorations.

Ely Cathedral

In 673 St. Ethelfreda founded an abbey, which was destroyed by the Danes in 870 on the site of the present Ely Cathedral. A Benedictine monastery was built on the site in 970. The cathedral was completed in 1351 and its towering peaks can be seen for miles away. The Norman nave and 14th- century choir lead the eye upward to the painted ceiling. Below the lantern tower is an octagon which separates the nave from the choir. Don't miss the **stained glass museum,** which explains the process of making stained glass as well as preserving old glass.

WALES

Allow at least several days for an excursion from London to Wales. There is much to enjoy in this western part of Great Britain, where mountains and rolling hills bring peace to harried city travelers. Waves crashing along the rocky coastline or breakers rolling up on long tidal beaches are also a part of the scene. In this land of castles, prehistoric gravesites, and relics from each era in the time-

line, one can retrace human history or just relax. **Snowdonia** is famous for
hiking, mountain climbing, and view. We are writing about Northwest Wales
for this excursion because that region provides both mountain and sea.

Wales holds special meaning for our family because Edward and Eleanor
Foulke left Bala, Wales in 1698 to settle in Gwynedd, Pennsylvania. The town
of **Bala** and the nearby village of **Cynwd** provided many immigrants to the
Philadelphia area, and those names stuck to an outer region of the city, Bala-
Cynwd. As Quakers during the Restoration of the Catholic monarchy in England and Wales, they were persecuted and had to go underground for their
Sunday meetings. The couple left a hillside farm, which we revisit every few
years; the beautiful land is in our blood. As ardent sailors, we also appreciate
the sailing center on Bala lake, the largest natural lake in Wales.

Not far beyond Bala lies **Snowdonia National Park,** the most mountainous region in Britain. For serious mountaineering, get contour maps that are
available for planning trips. For less strenuous hiking and walking, drive to the
height of the pass on A4086 toward Llanberis and walk in to **Llydaw,** near the
center of the group of peaks making up Mount Snowdon. There is a lovely lake
there and the walk is not difficult. In **Llandberis** there is a railway that climbs
to the top of the mountain complex.

Gray stone castles spread their wings along the seafront, or hover on a
hilltop out of reach of marauding bands. They can be seen from a distance
which must have been welcome to travelers slowly making their way hundreds
of years ago. Their ruins still hold romance and intrigue as visitors stumble up
darkened circular stairways to the battlements on top. Look down into gigantic
wells, dungeons, and cellars that must have been intensely cold and damp. The
remains of fireplaces dot the walls; inhabitants must have been either freezing
or roasting in those cavernous chambers and halls. North Wales has more than
enough castles to charm everyone. Imagine finding a secret passageway or two
during medieval times or today.

Although King Edward I built a number of castles in Wales, **Conwy Castle**
(1283–1292) is among the most fascinating. Its eight eastern towers rise up
from the water and loom over the town walls. The eastern four of the towers
were once accessible only from the water so that the sovereign could count on
security within his chambers.

Denbigh Castle was built by Edward I seven miles from the sea on a
hilltop that had previously supported a Norman castle. Henry de Lacy, the Earl
of Lincoln and also the chief military commander of King Edward's Welsh
armies lived in Denbigh. However, after de Lacy's eldest son, Edmund, fell
into the well inside the castle, the earl did not finish building.

Caernarfon Castle's past is one of historical importance. A thousand years
before the English kings chose to build there, the Romans established a fort
called Segontium. A castle made of timber and earth was in place by 1090; the
Bayeaux Tapestry pictures Norman knights along the coast of Wales. King Edward began building his castle there in 1283. His son, Edward II of Caernarfon,

was born in the castle in 1284. He was the first Prince of Wales, invested in 1301. In 1969 Prince Charles was invested there as the current Prince of Wales.

Anyone trying to break in would have had to cross the drawbridge, go through five doors and six portcullises (a lattice-like door) and survive attack from a number of ''murder holes.'' Arrow slits further enhanced the advantage of the inhabitants from the inside against any attacker.

Harlech Castle perches on a 200-foot-high craggy peak, once right on the water but now behind sand dunes. Edward I began to build Harlech in 1283. In 1404 Owain Glyndwr invaded the castle and remained there for four years until captured with his family. This castle was the last one to resist the Yorkists during the War of the Roses, undergoing a siege of eight years. Four towers and a gatehouse of three stories remain. Views of Snowdon are spectacular from its towers.

Beaumaris Castle, on Anglesey Island, was built between 1295 and 1298. It was the last of the great castles built by King Edward I in Wales. Its concentric circle plan, with the courtyard encased in walls, and surrounded by a wide moat, is similar to other castles.

A visit to **Anglesey Island** offers the chance to explore ancient gravesites dating back to prehistoric times. The sites include a variety of style from burial mounds and passage graves to flat-topped stones balanced on several uprights. Those living during the Mesolithic period, 8000–4000 B.C., were nomads who did not construct monuments, although some of their flint pieces have been found. The Neolithic period, 4000–2500 B.C., produced megalithic tombs, stone burial chambers made of slabs set on end and covered with a flat capstone. Most of these were group graves and there are signs that rituals or ceremonies were performed near the tombs. By the Bronze Age, individual graves were used, often covered with stones or earth mounds. Pottery, metal pieces, and stone objects were placed in these graves. During the Iron Age, weapons were buried, including spearheads, swords, bridle bits, and harness rings. The Romans left behind walls and hut circles.

Visitors will find it useful to obtain a map and a guide of the sites; little one-laned roads are pretty but often not well marked. We suggest moving in a clockwise direction from the A5 at Britannia Bridge to the A4080.

Bryn Celli Ddu Burial Chamber is a large mound within a stone circle, a bank, and a ditch. Inside, the passage grave is entered from the north-east and continues into a polygonal stone room. Spiral carving still remains on a south wall stone.

Nearby, **Caer Leb** is a pentagonal enclosure consisting of double banks and ditches within an area 200 feet by 160 feet. This Roman period site has yielded a 3rd-century brooch, a 4th-century coin, Roman pottery, quernstones (primitive hand mill for grinding grain), and a glass stud.

Bodowyr Burial Chamber takes a different form as it stands in a field without a mound to cover it. Of five upright stones, one has fallen, and three support an eight-foot-long capstone that looks like a giant mushroom top.

Barclodiad y Gawres Burial Chamber is a large mound reached by a path along the coast. The sea enhances this site with its crashing waves, and kayakers enjoying the surf. Two upright stones guard the entrance. The cremated remains of two men were found there in the western chamber.

Penrhos Feilw Standing Stones can be reached after walking through a field, perhaps still inhabited by a couple of young bulls who stared at us, then ran in circles. The standing stones are about ten feet high and may have been part of a stone circle.

Driving around Anglesey Island is pleasant, with hedgerows along one-laned roads in places, bouncing lambs in the fields when we were there, rolling hills, and views of Snowdonia on the mainland.

FINLAND

Currency unit • Finnish markka (FIM)
Language • Finnish and Swedish
Time difference from USA • six hours later (Eastern Standard Time)
Telephone access codes • to USA 990 or USA Direct 9800–100–10; from USA 358
National Tourist Offices • USA: Finnish Tourist Board, 655 Third Ave., New York, NY 10017, tel.: (212) 949–2333; Finland: Tourist Information, Unioninkatu 26, SF-00130 Helsinki, tel.: (9)0–144 511, postal address: Finnish Tourist Board, PB 53, SF-00521 Helsinki; Britain: 66 Haymarket, London SW1Y ARF, tel.: (071) 849–4048
Airlines • Finnair USA: (800) 950–5000 or (212) 689–9300; Britain: (071) 408 1222
Embassies • American Embassy: Itainen Puistotie 14A, Helsinki, Finland, tel.: 171931; British Embassy: 16–20 Uudenmaan Katu 00120 Helsinki 12, tel.: 64 79 22
Ferries • Viking Line

If you like the coast of Maine, the lakes of the Adirondacks and northern Minnesota, or the San Juan islands in Puget Sound, you will feel right at home in Finland. Seen from the air, the coasts are an unending panorama of bays, inlets and islands, and much of the land itself is filled with a vast series of interconnected lakes in heavily wooded land. You can take a trip from Turku to Aland through an unending archipelago on the most luxurious ferries in Europe; these very large ships wind through channels between the islands all the way to Mariehamn, halfway to Sweden across the Baltic. And the extended cruises through the chains of lakes offer a similar mix of land and water inland. Whether you go as a passenger or cruise on your own, Finland is a sailor's delight.

HISTORY..

Nomadic Lapps were the first inhabitants of Finland 3000 years ago. By 100 A.D. tribal people of Finno Ugric origin moved in and the Lapps went north.

The sparse population divided themselves into three tribes: Finns, Tavastians, and Karelians. Swedish crusaders arrived with Christianity and helped to create a unified Finland. Eastern and Western Finland were torn between Sweden and Russia, culminating in the 12th-century Peace of Noteborg, which gave most of Finland to Sweden. In 1809 Czar Alexander I confiscated Finland. She regained her independence in 1917. She is a parliamentary republic now with a democratic government.

HELSINKI

HISTORY......................................

King Gustav Vasa founded the city in 1550 as a trading center. He ordered inhabitants of four towns to move to the site on the Vantaa River and build Helsinki. She finally received protection from invaders after the Sveaborg fortress was built in 1748.

A fire in 1808 burned much of Helsinki, which was then rebuilt with the aid of Carl Ludvig Engel's great creativity. In 1809 Finland became a Grand Duchy of Russia under Czar Alexander I, who decided that his residence in Turku was too far away from Russia, and so Helsinki became Finland's capital in 1812.

SIGHTSEEING..................................

Visitors say that the place to feel the heartbeat of the city is the harborside **Market Square,** Kauppatori. Flipping fish, fresh from the sea, sold from fishing boats moored along the quay, and crayfish in late July vie with meat, dairy products, flower, and fruit for the housewife's attention. Fruit stands mound up a kaleidoscope of raspberries, blueberries, strawberries, currants, whortleberries, and sometimes cloudberries from the Arctic Circle. When we were there, people were eating peas, fresh from the pod, as a snack.

Benches are available for relaxing and taking in the scene. Ducks bob around in the water, sea gulls wheel and squawk, cruise ships head out, private yachts sit on their moorings, and launches ferry people out to islands.

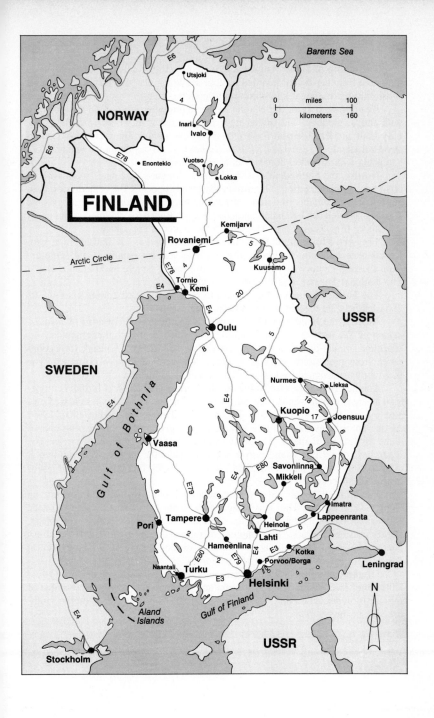

The **statue of Havis Amanda,** sculpted by Ville Vallgren, looks down on the scene from her perch, guarded by four sea lions. On May Day Eve, students swish through the moat and climb up to give her a hug.

Heading west from the Market is the **Esplanade,** a broad boulevard lined with shops, gardens, and linden trees interspersed with wooden benches. The **City Hall** and **Presidential Palace** overlook the harbor. The **Orthodox Uspensky Cathedral,** *(Uspenskin Kirkko* or *Kathedraali),* rises up on the Katajanokka peninsula with its onion domes—an easy landmark.

Nearby, the **Cathedral** *(Tuomiokirkko),* designed by Engel, soars with its crisp white stone exterior. The **university** stands opposite the cathedral on Senate Square; it contains museums of paleontology, agriculture, mineralogy, and zoology as well as botanical gardens. Walter Runeberg sculpted a statue of Alexander II of Russia, which stands in the center of the square.

The **Art Museum of the Ateneum,** *(Asemaaukio)* is housed in a neo-Renaissance building. The collection includes Finnish paintings and sculpture from the 18th century as well as work from French, Dutch, and Italian masters. The National Theater is just north of the museum.

The **House of Parliament** is hard to miss with its red granite exterior. Its 200 members are elected by proportional representation.

Nearby, the building with the tower is the **National Museum** *(Kansallismuseo* or *Suomen)* at Mannerheimintie 34, which contains ethnographical, archaeological, and historical displays portraying the history of Finland. Collections range from prehistoric artifacts to Ugric folk art and Finnish costumes. The building was designed by Gesellius, Lindgren, and Saarinen in 1910.

Another church to visit is the **Rock Church** *(Taivallahti)* in the Temppeliaukio area, which was carved out of granite bedrock. Rock Church was created by two brothers, Timo and Tuomo Suomalainen, and dedicated in 1969. As one approaches the church a low stone wall gives way to a dazzling copper dome 70 feet in diameter. Cooper wickerlike threads form a giant circle. The organ has copper pipes, and purple seats complete the picture. The building is used for services of the Evangelical Lutheran Church of Finland as well as for concerts and recitals.

Farther north stands the new Finlandia Hall, built in 1971 as a Concert and Congress Center. The Hall was designed by Alvar Aalto. Jean Sebelius's music is often on the program; his tubular steel memorial, which symbolizes music, stands in Sibelius Park. This monument took six years to make. Its columns contain patterned perforations as well as a variety of texture, which glisten in the sunlight against a backdrop of green trees.

Olympic Stadium *(Olympiastadion, Etela-Stadioninite)* went up in 1938. Climb the tower for a view of Helsinki and the countryside. A bronze statue of a Finnish runner called the "flying Finn," Paavo Nurmi, is poised on the southern side of the Stadium.

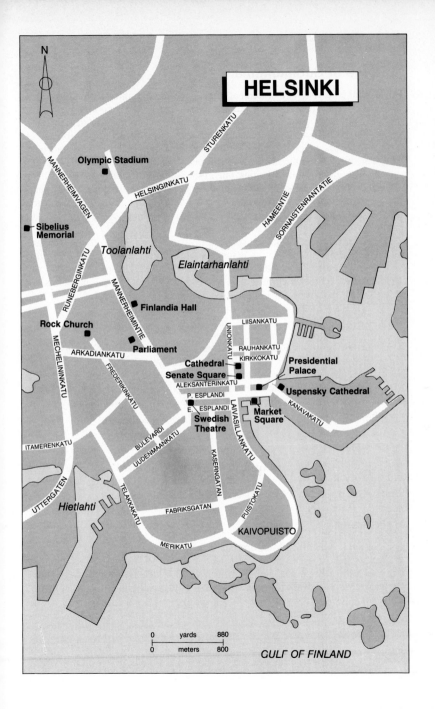

N

HELSINKI

Olympic Stadium

STURENKATU

HELSINGINKATU

MANNERHEIMVÄGEN

HÄMEENTIE

SÖRNÄISTENRANTATIE

Sibelius
Memorial

Toolanlahti

Elaintarhanlahti

RUNEBERGINKATU

MANNERHEIMINTIE

Finlandia Hall

LIISANKATU

UNIONKATU

Rock Church

RAUHANKATU

MECHELININKATU

ARKADIANKATU

Parliament

KIRKKOKATU

Cathedral

Presidential
Palace

FREDRIKINKATU

Senate Square

ALEKSANTERINKATU

Uspensky Cathedral

P. ESPLANDI

E. ESPLANDI

Swedish
Theatre

Market
Square

KANAVAKATU

ITÄMERENKATU

BULEVARDI

UUDENMAANKATU

LAIVASILLANKATU

UTTERGATEN

Hietlahti

TELAKKAKATU

KASERNGATAN

FABRIKSGATAN

PUISTOKATU

KAIVOPUISTO

MERIKATU

0   yards   880
0   meters   800

GULF OF FINLAND

Fortress of Suomenlinna

Ferries will take visitors to a number of islands including those of Suomenlinna, which protects Helsinki at the entrance to the harbor. Earlier called Sveaborg, the fortress, parks, gardens, an open-air theater, and two military museums are spread out on six islands. Suomenlinna is sometimes called the "Gibraltar of the North" because of its defensive position. Tours in English are given on a daily schedule during the summer; bring your walking shoes to tour the islands.

Sveaborg was built beginning inn 1748. Augustin Ehrensvard, an artillery officer, was in charge of the planning and construction of the fort for 22 years. The center of the fort is located on Vargon island, the largest of the six. Look for the dry dock, a marvel in its time, which was enclosed in the 1780s to provide winter storage for up to 15 frigates.

The fortress saw action in a series of invasions beginning with the Russians in 1808. Following a siege, its defenders surrendered in May 1808. The fort was again pounded by the Russians during the Crimean War between 1854 and 1856. Fire rockets zoomed inside the fort and the outmoded equipment was not able to reach its targets. In 1972 the last Russian troops departed.

Seurasaari

This **open-air museum** contains 17th-century farmhouses, an 18th-century manor house, and other buildings collected from various sections of the country. Visitors can wander through peasant houses, smoke saunas, shops, and a mill. The 17th-century Karuna wooden church holds services during the summer. Folk dancing is performed. Collections include folk tools, furnishings, and musical instruments.

Korkeasaari

Helsinki's **zoo** can be reached by a footbridge from Mustikkamaa or a ferry from the South Harbor. Visitors can wander around on paths in this wooded area to visit 60 species of mammals and 80 kinds of birds.

Hylkysaari

The **National Maritime Museum** can be reached by walking through the **zoo** grounds. After crossing on a bridge to the islands of Hylkysaari visitors can tour the brilliantly painted red lightship, *Kemi,* which is moored at the jetty. Here's a chance to walk through a working lightship and to explore her equipment.

Lightships are actually ships that are anchored to serve as lighthouses, radio beacons, meteorological stations, and pilot stations. The first lightship anchored in the Thames estuary in England in 1732. Now only about 30 lightships remain in the world. *Kemi,* originally christened the *Aransgrund,* was the last Finnish lightship in service, until 1974, when she was moved to the Maritime Museum.

The main building of the museum is the former pilot building, with three floors of exhibits. The ground floor exhibits detailed maritime history from the 11th century onward. The next floor contains models of some of the trades on board such as carpenter, boatswain, sailmaker, and cook. Most of the icebreakers, large, sturdy ships used all over the world, are built in Finland. The next floor presents conservation efforts as wrecks were explored over the years by divers. The top floor contains information on the *Mekrijarvi* boat find in the country of North Karelen.

Boat sheds on the property contain old fishing boats, the smell of tar still vividly present. A flat-bottomed **Seine Boat** dates from 1895. The pleasureboat shed houses an antique craft used by the President of Finland in the 1920s. Visitors gaze down on a row of boats including a Flying Finn that set a world record in 1964, an Olympia Jolley that won a bronze medal in Amsterdam in 1928, a British yacht from 1720, a Swedish yacht from 1830, an 1850 catboat, and a 1930 speedboat, to name a few.

DAY TRIPS FROM HELSINKI ················

Finland is a country with spectacular natural scenery. As glaciers receded in northern Europe, the landscape was revealed as rugged granite rock supporting pine forests lapped by lakes and fjords. Finland is a large country, at the same latitude as Alaska, but its population is sparse. Most of her people appreciate the beauty in the country enough to visit their vacation cottages frequently during weekends and holidays. Visitors cannot buy land in Finland, but they can visit breathtaking areas, fish in rivers and lakes, pick blueberries, strawberries, lingonberries, and whortleberries, and enjoy boating in the summer and skiing in the winter.

EAST OF HELSINKI
Poorvoo

One of the oldest towns along the south coast is picturesque in its location along the river. Its cobbled streets and wooden houses present Finland as it used to be. The 18th-century wooden buildings provide photo opportunities galore as the Old Town reaches up the hill from the river.

The 15th-century Gothic cathedral *(Tuomiokirkko)* towers over the town. It was here that Russian Czar Alexander I proclaimed Finland an autonomous Grand Duchy in 1809. Inside, there are frescoes to see. The historical museum, **Edelfelt-Vallgren Art Museum,** and **Town Hall** may be visited.

The main industry in Poorvoo is book publishing; many writers and artists have chosen to live there. J. L. Runeberg, the national poet, is buried in Poorvoo; his home is open for a visit. His son, Walter Runeberg, was a sculptor, and his collection is on display in the gallery across the street. Nearby, another house contains the collection of the sculptor Ville Valgren, who died in 1940, as well as paintings by Albert Edelfelt.

Kotka

The ruins of a fortress lend an air of historical significance to Kotka. The **Greek Orthodox Church of St. Nicholas,** which was constructed in 1795 in conjunction with the Russian naval base, is the oldest building still standing. In 1790 a combination Finnish/Swedish contingent defeated the Russians; this is explained in a museum on the islet of Varissaari.

The Czar's **fishing lodge** at Langinkoski is a reminder of those days of imperial power. Czar Alexander III used the lodge as a place for r & r in between St. Petersburg and Helsinki.

Hamina

Although Hamina dates back to 1336, it did not become well known as a seaport until the 18th century. The town hall stands in the center of town with two concentric, circular streets around it. Streets radiate out from the town hall like spokes of a wheel. During the early 1700s stone walls were built and still stand.

NORTHEAST OF HELSINKI—THE LAKE DISTRICT

Most of the 62,000 lakes in the Saimaa region are interconnected. This is the largest inland lake complex in Europe; boaters can cruise for a couple of thousand miles through this haven of lakes, inlets, islands, and harbors.

Lappeenranta

Once a Swedish garrison, the town is almost on the Russian border. It is located at one end of the lake district and connected to the Gulf of Finland by the Saimaa Canal. A local **history museum** is housed in the fortress. The guardhouse dates from 1722. Open-air summer theater is held in town.

Imatra

Catherine the Great, Richard Wagner, and Alexandre Dumas vacationed in Imatra, beside the white water of the Vuoksi River. Although the water has been controlled, it is free to cascade upon demand on summer Sundays. Imatra is famous for its waterfalls. Karjalainen Kotilalo is an **open-air museum** of 19th-century buildings.

Mikkeli

Dinosaur buffs will enjoy visiting **Dinosauria,** which is a complex displaying replicas of prehistoric animals as well as plants. In 1789 a small number of Finns were able to defeat the Russian army at Porrassalmi Battlefield. Field Marshal Mannerheim's museum is open in the headquarters he used during World War II.

Savonlinna

Olavinlinna Castle was built in 1475 as protection against invaders from the east. The castle was designed by Erik Axelsson Tott; three of its round towers still survive. This castle is one of the best preserved in Scandinavia and is the scene of grand opera, national dancing, and concerts in the summer.

The steamship *Salama,* which went down to the bottom of the sea in 1898, was brought up in 1971 and serves as a museum. The **Provincial Museum** explains timber floating trains. **Casino Park** is the site of baths.

Rauhalinna, another hunting lodge frequented by the czars, is just outside Savonlinna. The complex of turrets, balconies, and lattice-decoration, now a hotel, perches on a hill with a view of the lake.

Boat trips may be taken to **Punkaharju Ridge,** which is a slender strip of causeway between Lake Puruvesi and Lake Pihlalavesi. The town of Punkaharju is famous for its exhibition caves and labyrinths, which were whittled from the rock and turned into the Retretti Arts Center. Olavi Lanu created the amazing sculptures, which blend in with the landscape.

Nearby, the church in **Kerimaki** is the largest wooden church in Europe. It holds 3500 people. Some say the builder mistook feet on the plans for meters.

NORTH OF HELSINKI
Hameenlinna

Located amidst forests in the Lake Vanajavesi basin, Hameenlinna is known as the birthplace of Jean Sibelius. His house at 11 Hallituskatu is open to visitors. (Sibelius actually spent most of his life living in Jarvenpaa, which is south of Hameenlinna and closer to Helsinki. His house there, Ainola, is also open.) **Hameen Linna,** a medieval castle built by Birger Jarl, has been restored. The **Historical Museum** depicts the history of the town and the province of Hame.

North of Hameenlinna the former Karlberg Estate is now **Aulanko Park** *(Aulangon Puisto).* Colonel Standerskjold converted a rocky piece of land into a park with a golf course, ski trails, a slalom slope, riding, tennis and swimming.

NORTHWEST OF HELSINKI
Tampere

Located on the rapids of Tammerkoski on an isthmus between Lake Nasijarvi and Pyhajarvi, Tampere is a large textile center. The first cotton mill in town was constructed in 1820 by James Finlayson, who arrived from Scotland.

Kaleva Church *(Kaleva Kirkko),* is a modern granite structure. Finnish artists display their work in the gallery there.

For a bird's-eye view of the countryside, go to the top of **Nasinneula,** a 550-foot-high observation tower. **Sarkanniemi Park** houses a planetarium, aquarium, and zoo. The **Sara Hilden Art Museum** is nearby.

Summer theater is offered in Pyynikki Kesateatteri which is a revolving auditorium. Performances are offered in Finnish, with a translation in English.

WEST OF HELSINKI
Espoo

Espoo was an independent country parish until the 13th century, when it became a suburb of Helsinki. The parish church, with its unusually steep roof, dates from the 15th century. **Espoo Manor** was built by King Gustav Vasa of Sweden in the 16th century; it is not open to the public. Tapiola is a planned garden city that has served as a model for other planned towns.

Hvittrask

Finnish architects Eliel Saarinen, Armas Lindgren, and Herman Gesellius lived in a complex of wooden and stone houses connected by a studio. Saarinen's home is now open as a museum.

EXCURSIONS FROM HELSINKI.....................................

Turku

One of our favorite destinations in Finland is Turku, where visitors can walk up and down the river to many places of interest. With our maritime bent we headed first for two square-rigged sailing ships moored along the quay.

The frigate ***Suomen Joutsen*** first delivered saltpeter from South America to Europe. She served the Finnish Navy as a training ship beginning in 1930. As the "Swan of Finland," she invokes the symbol of Finland, especially during times of national stress. During World War II, she served as a mother ship for submarines and as a hospital ship.

From the top deck visitors can train their cameras on the bowsprit, fluttering flags, and the cathedral on shore beyond. The black deck and white masts contrast neatly with shady green trees alongside.

Nearby, the *Sigyn* dates from 1887, when she was launched in Gothenburg. She sailed to Canada, Africa, and South and North America, mostly carrying timber. Although originally a bark, she became a schooner after a collision off Jutland in 1913; during renovation she became a bark again. Look for the unusual water pump on her deck, which has a windmill as well as hand pumps.

The **Maritime Museum** is located on a hill in the former Observatory of the Academy of Turku. The view of the city from the terrace of the museum is worth the walk. Inside, displays detail the history of seafaring in Turku beginning with the Hanseatic merchants of the 12th century.

On the top floor, within the Wedgwood-like blue and white dome, the observatorium displays results of astronomical research dating from the 1830s. Ancient compasses, an hourglass astrolabe, parallel rules, spyglasses, and hand logs can be seen.

Turku Castle *(Turun Linna)*, dating from the 13th century, was restored between 1946 and 1961. Part of the castle is closed for renovation at this writing, but enough is open to make the visit worthwhile. Visitors can see the room where King Erik XIV was imprisoned in 1570. Guards constantly patrolled the corridor outside his room. Erik was moved from one castle prison to another; he finally died in 1577.

The **Turku City Historical Museum** is housed there. One of its exhibits is a sequence of prehistoric scenes from the Stone Age (7500–1300 B.C.) where a woman is portrayed cooking over an open fire, the Bronze Age (1300–500 B.C.) with a collection of grave cairns placed over cremated bones, the Iron Age (500–1150 A.D.) with agricultural implements and the Middle Ages (1150–1520).

Furnished rooms reflected the life of people in the 1600–1800s. An 18th-century kitchen offers a collection of early kitchen utensils. Two rococo rooms present ornate wallpaper, landscape wallpaper, and the curvaceous lines and bulging style of furniture from that period.

The **Cathedral** *(Tuomiokirkko)* was consecrated in 1290. It is now the mother church of the Lutheran Church in Finland. After the Great Fire restoration took place in the 1830's. Engel designed the pulpit and the reredos behind the high alter. A court painter, R. W. Ekman who is considered the father of painting in Finland, created the frescos on the walls and ceiling of the chancel. The black marble sarcophagus of Queen Karin Mansdotter, who was the wife of King Erik XIV, stands below a lovely stained glass window depicting the Queen with her children.

Although much of Turku was devastated by the Great Fire in 1827, a row of 17 houses survived and see new life as the **Luostarinmaki Handicraft Museum** where craftsmen ply their trades during the summer. The watchmaker works amid ticking works and faces on his walls. The shoemaker was not poor, as everyone needed shoes; today he makes shoes that are highly prized as they will last a long time. One of the sailors' homes contains a collection of shell decorations. The oldest residence in town is Qwensel House, which displays pharmacy items in its Apothecary Museum.

The **University of Turku** provides classes in Finnish, but there is also a Swedish-speaking university, which was founded in 1640. Because many Swedes moved to Finland years ago there is a large population of them. Swedish is the second language of the country.

The Archipelago

One of our favorite memories of Finland is a day cruise among the green islands in the archipelago surrounding Turku on a bright summer day. We joined groups of families with children dressed in their Sunday best ready for a day on the water. As we moved along the river toward the sea, we passed wooden villas dating from the 1700s, and 1800s painted mostly in pastels with gingerbread, lace curtains, and flowering plants. Cyclists on shore were going to the beach, and families in their summer homes waved as we passed. The green trees, grey rock, and painted houses blended together harmoniously and made us wish we lived there.

After enjoying a buffet lunch on board, we arrived in the town of Naantali, which dates from 1443 when a convent was built there. Nuns from the convent taught the local people to knit socks, which became an important export item. Visitors enjoy wandering around the old town, into the Church of Naantali and along the harbor where many yachts are moored. We were lucky enough to be on hand for folk dancing in the park.

Aland Islands

The Province of Aland contains over 6500 islands in a group halfway between Sweden and Finland. Runic artifacts reveal the existence of seafaring people there during the Middle Ages. Aland was governed by Sweden, then Russia, and finally Finland. However, it is an autonomous province with its own parliament and policies.

Mariehamn the principal European center for the last days of commercial sailing ships during the first three decades of the century, and its harbor was often filled with a large fleet of square-riggers. The **Aland Maritime Museum** in West Harbor, Mariehamn, explores the maritime heritage of the islands, with artifacts from windjammers among other treasures. The museum contains a wealth of maritime history from paintings, ship models, artifacts recovered from wrecks, displays on trading, sea chests with paintings inside, ships' instruments, bells, flags, and models of seamen plying their craft, to name a few. Visitors pass from the entrance directly into the bridge of a turn-of-the-century steamer.

Looking to the right we can have a close look at 15 figureheads mounted on the wall. The first one, in garish red, black, and gold, was mounted on the largest sailing ship of the 1930s, the bark *Moshulu,* which was anchored in Philadelphia before it burned in 1991. A lovely woman once sailed on the bow of the *Herzogin Cecilie,* which was wrecked on the Devon coast in England in 1936. The next lady in the row came from the bark *Lock Linnhe,* which went aground in Aland in 1933.

Turning to the left, we see the poop deck of a sailing ship, complete with the binnacle and wheel from the bark *Herzogin Cicilie.* A display in the museum features sailmaking. Because the sails on the **Pommern** were not usable, in 1984 local sailmakers were asked to make two sails using material from a Scottish company that still produced sailcloth. After 600 hours of works the sails were complete. The sailmakers had such fun making the first two, they asked if they could make another. They swapped sailing yarns while they worked, and are now on sail number 15. Between 8 and 35 sailmakers are involved in the project.

The four-masted bark *Pommern* was the last windjammer making the run from Australia to England into the 1930's as a member of Captain Gustaf Erickson's fleet. Now she is the last of her class existing in original structure. Built in 1903 near Glasgow, she is made of steel.

On deck, we noticed the massive windlass and giant turnbuckles. The galley contained a coal range that must have provided some heat. Don't miss the pigpen. The crew slept in the deck house in bunks with their chest below them and a group of tables in the center.

On shore again we noticed the **Midsummer Pole** with a wooden man on top waving his arms around and around, the Aland flag, a sun wheel, sails as good luck to sailors, bridal crowns for fertility, and Aspen leaves that whispered in the breeze.

In the harbor we went aboard the *Albanus,* a 19th-century Baltic schooner replica built in 1987 the traditional way with wood from the forests on Aland. She is double-planked with spur inside and pine outside. The vessel is owned by a society and was built for training with youth groups. Twenty students and four crew go out for five days at a time; the students work the ship.

Cruises are available out into the archipelago around Aland aboard the *Legend,* a vassal berthed in Mariehamn. Among other places, she sails to Kastelholm Castle, which dates from 1388. Duke John held his brother Eric XIV a prisoner there in 1571. Much of the castle was destroyed by fire in 1745; it is undergoing renovation at this writing.

The **Jan Karlsgarden open-air museum** portraying peasant life is located near the castle. The village contains thatched-roof houses, boat sheds, a windmill, a blacksmith shop, and a smoke sauna. When we were there, two men were working on building a fence in the traditional way. They burned slender branches until they became pliable enough to use for lashing, then fastened poles together at angles.

Lemland contains one of the largest Viking cemeteries in the islands. The ruins of the 13th-century **Lembote Chapel** lie near the cemetery.

Lapland

Lappi, or Finnish Lapland, is a vast area stretching south of the Arctic Circle that nearly reaches the Arctic Ocean. This wilderness area is inhabited by about 4000 Lapps, also called Sami. Forests cover the land in the south, then give way to dwarf birch and finally barren tundra. Reindeer wander during much of the year until fall, when they are rounded up for slaughter.

During the summer, the sun never sets around the Arctic Circle. Fall colors are so intense that the Finns call them *ruskaa* (red). During the winter, people enjoy cross-country skiing as well as watching the spectacular Northern Lights.

The capital city is Rovaniemi, located on the Kemijoki and Ounasjoki rivers. Although the retreating German army destroyed the city in 1944, a new city plan was designed by Alvar Aalto. He created the city in the shape of reindeer antlers. Alto's **Lappia House** is a civic center complex containing a theater, concert hall, and the Lapland Provincial Museum.

Nearby, the **Ounasvaara hills** area hosts an international skiing championship in March. Those who would like to learn how to drive reindeer can do so in Pohtimolampi, which is 17 miles northwest of Rovaniemi.

Farther north the town of Ivalo, on the Ivalojokri river, is the gateway for **Inari**. As a center for reindeer roundups, sports performances, fishing and hiking, Inari draws visitors from its own culture as well as tourists. To the south of Ivalo, the **Saariselka fells** area is popular with hikers. **Tankavaara** is well known for its gold prospecting; visitors can pan for gold if they wish.

To the west of Ivalo is the town of **Enontekio** with its modern church. At the northwestern tip of Finland, **Kilpisjarvi** is almost on the borders of Norway and Sweden. Hikers walk along a marked trail to the boundary stone in the **Malla Nature Reserve.**

FRANCE

Currency unit • French franc (FF)
Language • French
Time difference from USA • six hours later (Eastern Standard Time)
Telephone access codes • to USA 19 or USADirect 19 0011; from USA 33
National Tourist Offices • **USA:** French Government Tourist Office, 610 Fifth Ave., New York, NY 10020, Tel.: 1 (900) 420–2003 Maison de la France, 8, Avenue de l'Opera, 75001 Paris, tel.: (1) 42–96–10–23; **Britain** • 178 Piccadilly, London W1V OAL, tel.: (071) 499–6911 for recording or 491–7622.
Airline • **Air France** USA (800) 237–2747; **Britain:** (071) 449–9511
Embassies • **American Embassy:** 2 Ave. Gabriel, 75008, France, tel.: 42 96–12–02 or 42–61–80–75; **British Embassy:** 35 rue du Faubourg, St. Honore 75383 Paris, tel.: 4266–9142

HISTORY...

Caves in southern France have provided paintings dating back to the early Palaeolithic period, about 10,000 B.C. Megalithic artifacts in Brittany date to 2700–1600 B.C. The Celts were in residence from 500 B.C. and the Romans arrived in Provence around 121 B.C. with an interest in controlling the route from Spain to Italy and by 58 B.C. Caesar had the country within his grasp. Burgundian dukes settled in the area now called Burgundy in 443 A.D.; Celts from Britain arrived in Brittany in 449. In 511, three kingdoms included Austrasia, Neustria, and Burgundy. Charlemagne expanded his empire between 722–814; it became the first unified kingdom.

The Crusades, between 1096–1250, offered many opportunities of conquest for French nobles. By 1223 France became a hereditary monarchy under Louis VIII. The Hundred Years War took place between 1339 and 1453 and created a great deal of uneasiness between noblemen and peasants. France and the Habsburgs did not get along after the death of Charles the Bold in 1477. Religious wars continued from 1562 to 1598. By 1661, Louis XIV was in power as the "Sun King" who spent money wildly and basked in glorious ostentation. The court at Versailles was very active as nobles and everyone else congregated to receive favors during this reign of absolute monarchy. During the War of Spanish Succession, 1701–14, France was defeated by the Grand Alliance.

In 1789 the French Revolution exploded, and by 1791 France was controlled by a constitutional monarchy. In 1792 the country became a Republic. Robespierre perpetrated his cruelty from 1793 to 1794; Louis XVI and Marie-Antoinette were only ones who met their death then. The Reign of Terror ended with Robespierre's death in 1794. Napoleon crowned himself Emperor of the French in 1804. The Napoleonic Wars were fought all over Europe until 1815. Wars of Liberation protested Napoleonic domination in many areas of the continent.

In 1848 the February Revolution erupted in Paris as a protest against the monarchy and the voting qualification. France became a republic and its first leader was Napoleon III, nephew of Napoleon I. The Franco-Prussian War of 1870–71 resulted in the formation of a republic on September 4, 1871.

During the World Wars I and II France became a battleground. In 1929 the Maginot Line was devised when the French foreign minister, Briand, planned the evacuation of the Rhineland. In 1936 the German army entered the demilitarized Rhineland. In 1940 Paris was occupied by Germany. General de Gaulle ran his government in exile from London. Allied landings in Normandy in 1944 led to the liberation of France.

PARIS

Exploring the intricacies of Paris and discovering some of its many wonders is not an easy task for foreigners. We've been lucky enough to have relatives living in Paris for many years, and they have helped us appreciate the lineaments of the city from an inhabitant's perspective. It has been a treat for us to follow them to hidden treasures of the city and just to stroll along and learn where Parisians like to eat and amuse themselves. Our memories include a marvelous Alsatian dinner, and our children recall a special Twelfth Night meal complete with many courses and a cake hiding an object proclaiming the finder King for the night. In this city, enjoyment of daily living was high priority.

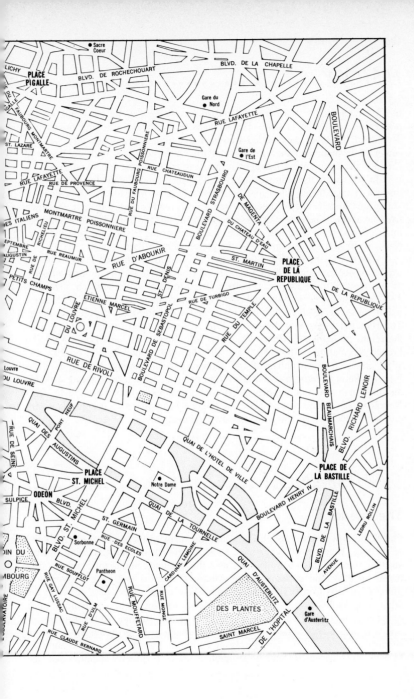

HISTORY..

In 53 B.C. a group of fishermen lived in a settlement along the Seine on the present site of Ile de la Cite. The Romans arrived under Caesar's power and developed the town they called Lutetia Parisiorum. This Gallic city was the center of Roman, and then Frankish, Paris. A fortress was built on Ile de la Cite and the town spread throughout the surrounding forest and swamp.

In 451 Attila the Hun marched 700,000 men toward Paris but surprisingly made a change in his plans and headed for Orleans instead. St. Genevieve, a young girl from Nanterre, became well known for her ability to save the town from invaders. When the city was starving to death, St. Genevieve brought boat loads of food from Champagne under the noses of the Franks and into the city. Needless to say, she is honored as the patron saint of Paris.

Clovis was the first Christian king, and in 506 proclaimed Paris to be the capital of his kingdom. Charlemagne ruled from 768 to 814 as the first emperor of the Holy Roman Empire. Philippe Auguste built walls between 1180 and 1210 and continued to expand his prosperous domain, which now included a major university and a great cathedral, and was considered a cultural center. The Hundred Years War during the 15th century stopped further building until the reigns of Francis I, Henry IV, Louis XII, Louis XIV, and Louis XV. The French Revolution (1789–1804) and the storming of the Bastille on July 14, 1789 produced much upheaval and abolished the monarchy. During the First Empire, Paris became the center of Europe. Napoleon forged ahead with his building plan and poured the spoils of his campaign into the city. In 1853 Napoleon III commissioned Georges Eugene Haussmann to design a modern city with wide streets instead of narrow medieval lanes.

SIGHTSEEING...................................

The Islands

The Seine flows right through Paris, and for many years has been the lifeblood of the city. Boats of all types have swished, glided, or chugged along its curvaceous route. Barges use the river as a thoroughfare, some with laundry fluttering on deck and curtains in the windows. Visitors can have a river-view glimpse of Paris from a sightseeing boat. Photo opportunities pass one after the other. I remember as a young student in 1952, looking up at a miniature Statue of Liberty and feeling a lump in my throat to see her standing so far from home. She was presented to France by Americans living in Paris during the late 19th century in thanks for the larger lady given by the French to grace the entrance to New York harbor. (There is yet another Statue of Liberty standing near the metro stop at Notre Dame des Champs, near the northwest part of the Jardin du Luxembourg.)

The womb of Paris and now the heart of the city, Ile de la Cite, is one place to begin a tour. The **Cathedral of Notre Dame,** 6 Parvis Notre-Dame, is on the site of an earlier Roman temple, a Christian basilica and a Romanesque church. In 1163, Pope Alexander III placed the first stone for the new cathedral; Maurice de Sully, who was the Bishop of Paris, was directly involved in the building process. By 1345 the cathedral stood intact. During the Revolution the interior was all but demolished. Napoleon crowned himself emperor there in 1804, and crowned Josephine empress.

Victor Hugo's novel, *The Hunchback of Notre Dame,* inspired the monarchy to restore the cathedral. Viollet le Duc spent many years working on this immense project. Recent cleaning has restored the original patina and brightness to the structure.

The facade is balanced by twin 220-foot-high towers. In the center the portal portrays the Last Judgment with Christ in the tympanum. The portal to the Virgin Mary is on the left and that of St. Anne on the right. Over the portals the Gallery of the Kings of Judah is a copy, the original figures were destroyed by the violent mob in 1793 who thought they were statues of kings of France.

Inside, the cathedral is famous for its rose window in the north transept, which dates from 1220. There is also a rose window in the west wall and another in the south wall. A 14th-century Virgin and Child (Notre Dame de Paris) is particularly revered. The choir screen contains 23 painted and gilded carved scenes from Christ's life. The tomb of the Comte d'Harcourt lies in one of the chapels. The largest organ in France, the Cavaille Coll, contains 8500 pipes. Visitors can climb up into one of the towers for a view of Paris.

We visited recently when Notre Dame was filled with worshippers for a Sunday morning mass. Music filled the air beneath the gray stone vaulted ceiling. Five priests conducted the service as incense wafted into the crowd. Afterward we wandered past chapels, pausing to savor a baptismal font given by the Corporation of Goldsmiths. The Sacristy contains the Cathedral's treasury. Relics include a nail and a piece of the True Cross and the Crown of Thorns. Church plate glistens on shelves.

The **Palace of Justice** *(Palais de Justice)* was built on the site of the ancient royal stronghold; only the Sainte Chapelle and four towers remain, along with a bit of foundation. Parliament occupies Conciergerie Palace. The name was changed to Palais de Justice after the Revolution.

St. Chapelle still has 50-foot-high, slender, stained-glass windows dating from the 13th century. The windows portray scenes from the Old and New Testaments. A rose window in the facade depicts the Apocalypse. St. Louis bought the Crown of Thorns from the Venetians in 1239 and brought it to St. Chapelle. It was preserved during the Revolution and now is housed in Notre Dame.

Inside, the lower chapel was used by servants, the upper for his Lordship. The lower chapel contains a number of slender columns to buttress the arches.

The stone columns and arches are painted in brilliant red, blue, gold, and green; fleur-de-lis and castle shapes dot each one.

The upper chapel is elegant with a navy blue vaulted ceiling polka-dotted with gold stars. There are no cracks in the vividly colorful 13th-century stained-glass windows. Louis XI, who was afraid of assassins, sat behind a grating where he could see and hear but remain protected.

The **Conciergerie** is recognizable from the right bank by its four towers. The Public Prosecutor, Fouquier Tinville, lived in apartments in one of the towers during the Reign of Terror. Another tower contained the royal treasury. Bonbec Tower was a torture chamber. A number of condemned prisoners awaited the guillotine in cells in the Conciergerie, including Marie Antoinette, Madame du Barry, Madame Elisabeth (sister of Louis XVI), Charlotte Corday (who stabbed Marat), Andre Chenier, Philippe Egalite, Robespierre, and many others.

Visitors today can read the names and occupations of those who were executed there. Among the unfortunates were an ex-president, ex-noble, judge, vivant de son bien (gentleman), domestique, perriquier (wigmaker), homme de loi (lawyer), ex-prince, hussier (bailiff), and homme de lettres. Those who had no money lay on the ground on straw; some with money had cots, other rich or famous prisoners had private cells with a table and chair. The rich were often executed quickly.

The **Guardroom** *(Salle des Gardes)* is next to the **Hall of the Men-at-Arms** *(Salle des Gens d'Armes)*. The executioner's quarters were entered from the Rue de Paris. The cells where Marie Antoinette and Robespierre lived are next to the chapel.

Marie Antoinette's recreated cell contains a model of her dressed in black sitting on a wooden chair looking at a crucifix. Her guards were on the other side of a partial screen at all times. The porcelain pitcher used by a woman to give her water just before being led to the quilliotine is on display. The cross she gave to her friend, Baroune de Poupar, is also there.

Place Louis Lepine is a breath of warmth and beauty as flowers brighten up the somber feelings left from a visit to the Conciergerie. Birds are for sale there on Sunday, adding another light touch.

The neighboring island of **St. Louis** was once two separate islands: the Ile Notre Dame and the Ile aux Vaches. This island, with its medieval charm, is the choice of artists and writers who feel inspiration just by living there. Inhabitants call themselves *insulaires* or islanders, and they take great pride in their almost-private domain. Tall poplars shade the promenade along the quays and most people shed cars for foot power.

The Right Bank

The **Arch of Triumph** *(Arc de Triomphe)* may seem like a haven in a storm of terrorized pedestrian, but how does a motorist escape from going around and around the vast circle? In 1959 I picked up a brand new car in Paris and, with my uncle for moral support and navigational aid, picked my way through busy streets until I came to the Arch. There we had to enter the swirling mass of cars to get to the other side; many streets led from the center like spokes of a wheel, so we went around a couple of times to determine which one we wanted. Then the question became one of trying to squeeze far enough toward the circumference to get out of the maelstrom. It was not a moment to admire the Arch.

The Arch sits in the middle of the Place Charles de Gaulle (the former Place Etoile) and it looks like an immense upside-down horseshoe when seen from below. Visitors can take an underground tunnel from the even-numbered side along the Champs Elysees to the Arch. **The Tomb of the Unknown Soldier** from World War I lies underneath; a flame of remembrance burns on his tomb. Napoleon commissioned Chalgrin to build the arch, which he began in 1806. By 1836 it was finished, except for the top, but Napoleon never saw it, although his casket moved under it in procession along the Champs Elysees to Les Invalides. Francois Rude designed the Departure of the Army in 1792 *(La Marseillaise)* in sculpture on one side. Many larger-than-life-size figures run around the frieze. Shields over the frieze list 172 battles; generals from those efforts are listed inside.

The observation deck is the place to go for a view of the circular traffic below as well as of the city. Visitors can ride an elevator or choose to climb 40 steps to the top. Outside, a lavender ledge lists information on areas and streets radiating out like the spokes of a wheel.

The Champs Elysees was once a promenade for fashionable ladies and gentlemen. Today it is a busy street lined with shops, airline offices, automobile showrooms, banks, and restaurants. We spent a pleasant hour in a glass cafe extension jutting out onto the sidewalk plotting our course for the day and watching passerbys. While we were there a motorcycle zoomed right up to an ATM for cash, a man lost his hat to the wind, which tossed it out into the frantic traffic, a gendarme with his coat up over his nose ambled past us, backpackers with black and white skunk-like mittens trudged along, and a girl in Turkish pants and a black leather bomber jacket waltzed by.

The Champs Elysees' straight stretch leads to the Place de la Concorde, which contains the 70-foot-high Obelisk. This 3000-year-old monument is decorated with hieroglyphics depicting the glory of Rameses II. Two large 19th-century fountains provide splashing coolness. The **Marly Horses** *(Chevaux de Marly)* stand at the edge of the square toward the Arc de Triomphe and the **Winged Horses of the Tuileries** stand on the other side. (These are replicas; the original marble statues are in the Louvre.)

Just off the Champs Elysees on the right side, before coming to the Place de la Concorde, stand the **Grand and Petit Palais.** Both were constructed for the 1900 World Exhibition. The Grand Palais is topped by a flat glass dome over its hall. Cultural exhibitions are held there throughout the year on a rotating basis. The west side contains the **Palais de la Decouverte,** which focuses on the history of scientific discovery complete with films, lectures, demonstrations, and experiments. The planetarium presents an introduction to the universe.

The **Petit Palais** houses a permanent collection of paintings, including work by Cezanne, Toulouse-Lautrec, Van Gogh, Monet, Courbet, and Bonnard. 18th-century furniture and art objects are housed in the Tuck collection. Temporary art exhibitions are mounted there.

The **Tuileries Gardens** *(Jardin des Tuileries)* grow on clay land once used for making tiles, which accounts for the name. In 1563 Catherine de Medici built a chateau near the Louvre; she extended her domain by using Tuileries land for her Italian garden. Bernard Palissy created terracotta statues for her garden; fountains and a grotto were added. In 1664 Le Notre, from a succession of Tuileries gardeners, was chosen to renovate the garden. He created terraces, two reflecting pools, walkways, and formal flower displays.

Two pavilions now house art galleries. The Orangery contains mostly impressionist paintings, including work by Cezanne, Renoir, Rousseau, and Soutine. Two oval rooms house Monet paintings from the garden of his Giverny house in Normandy. *Water Lillies (Les Nympheas)* is there. **Jeu de Paume Museum,** once a real-tennis club, housed exhibits from the Louvre until 1986. It is now a center for temporary exhibitions.

The **Arc de Triomphe du Carrousel,** which looks like the Arch of Severus in Rome, was placed there to memorialize the victories of Napolean over Austria. At one time the arch was topped by the four bronze horses Napoleon snatched from St. Mark's in Venice. They were replaced in 1828 with a four-horse chariot commemorating the Restoration.

The **Louvre** was originally a fortress built by King Philippe Auguste in 1200. Recent archaeological excavations have revealed the base of a circular building 100 feet high. Treasures, archives, and valuable furnishings were kept there. The 1230 crypt of St. Louis has been restored.

Charles V chose to live in the Louvre beginning in 1364, but later kings resided in other palaces. In 1527 Francoise I decided to make the Louvre his principal residence and proceeded to pull down and rebuild it to suit Renaissance tastes. Catherine de Medici extended a Long Gallery from the Louvre to her chateau in the Tuileries. After the monarch moved to Versailles in 1682 the Louvre fell into disrepair. A number of artists used the galleries for their studies. Renovation was undertaken by Napoleon I and completed years later by Napoleon III. In 1871 the Tuileries Palace was destroyed by fire and replaced with a garden.

The Louvre Museum began with the collection of Francois I including work by Leonardo da Vinci, Titian, and Raphael. Each monarch added to the collection, and finally, in 1793 the Grande Gallery was opened to the public. Today the Louvre extends from the Cour Carree, on the site of the old fortress, with two giant arms culminating in the Tuileries.

Added in 1989 was the **I. M. Pei pyramid** at the entrance to the Louvre. It stands 71 feet high at the apex and 108 feet wide at the base. Begun in 1985, the building adds underground museum space as well as a new entrance. Today fountains and nearby buildings are reflected in the glass. The controversy over this starkly modern structure will probably never end. There are those who say it doesn't fit in with the stolid, sturdy classical Louvre; others say it gives pizzazz to it. Were all Frenchmen crazy about the Eiffel Tower?

The size of the Louvre is so staggering, with its extensive collection of paintings, sculpture, antiquities, and furniture that we suggest visitors obtain a current guide at the door. Collections are constantly being moved around or closed for rearrangement, so timely information is essential.

Most visitors want to see the most famous painting of all, Leonardo da Vinci's *Mona Lisa*. When we first saw her enigmatic smile in 1952, we could walk right up to her for a better look. The next time we found a roped barrier around the painting. Now there is glass in front of it and presumably whistles and bells should anyone cross over the marked barrier. In any event, it's still worth the trip to gaze into her eyes.

One of our favorite haunts is the Galerie Medicis where Peter Paul Ruben's series of 21 canvases hang. He painted them for Marie de Medici who appears in each one beginning with her birth in 1575, marriage in 1600, birth of her son Louis XIII at Fontainebleau in 1601 and continuing throughout her life.

The Marais

Marais means swamp, and this area was a low spot until it was drained in 500 A.D. It was fashionable during the 17th and 18th centuries and elegant homes were built here. The Place des Vosges was the home of Victor Hugo, Cardinal Richelieu, and the Marquise de Sivigne. At the other end of the quartier Les Halles market was in operation from the 12th century until the 1970s when it was razed; the shops have been moved near Orly Airport.

The **Jacques Cousteau Museum** *(Parc Oceanique Cousteau)* opened in 1989 on the former site of Les Halles. Visitors can ride in a gondola, come eyeball-to-eyeball with fish, and, just like Jonah, walk through the belly of a whale.

On the other side of Boulevard Sebastopol from the site of Les Halles stands the new **Beaubourg Center** (Georges Pompidou National Center of Art and Culture). This structure has to be seen to be believed. Towering above the Marais, this mass of cylindrical tubes, girders, and glass looks as if it has just been begun. Inside, there is a cinema, library, children's workshop, and industrial design center. The **National Museum of Modern Art** is there.

Some of the grand old hotels have been turned into museums. Hotel Carnavalet (23 Rue de Sevigne) is now the **Museum of the History of Paris.** It contains a collection of antique Parisian signs from merchants, taverns, tobacconists, and more. These were handy in the days when people were mostly illiterate.

The new **Picasso Museum** (5 Rue de Thorigny) is housed in the Hotel Sale, which was originally built by Pierre Aubert de Fontenay. He had become wealthy by collecting taxes on salt for the king. Unfortunately, he was jailed for pocketing salt money.

Picasso's work inside includes pieces from his early Blue Period (1895–

1903) as well as from the Late Period (1961–71). Picasso's heirs gave the collection to the French government instead of paying inheritance taxes after his death in 1973.

The Left Bank

Gustave Eiffel designed the **Eiffel Tower** for the 1889 World's Fair, amid the hue and cry of the population. The tower took 300 acrobatic skyjacks two years to rivet in, piece by piece. Soaring up 984 feet under its television mast, the tower is one of the most popular sites in Paris. After the World's Fair was over, the tower was almost taken down but saved to be used as an antenna for French radio telegraphy. By 1916 it had become the terminal for the first radio telephone to America, then a radio transmitter in 1918, and television transmitter since 1957.

One of our favorite photographs is one we took in 1952 looking straight down from the very top of the tower. We always ask friends who are viewing the slide for the first time to guess what it is. The tiny cars and people are, of course, in miniature against the patterns of the walks and flowers. Another slide with part of a leg showing gives the secret away.

The **Invalides** was constructed by Louis XIV for soldiers who had been wounded in battle. Thousands once lived there, being reduced to begging for their daily bread. Today less than 100 men live there. An **Army Museum** is located in both wings of the building. Napoleonic souvenirs include his tent and the stuffed skin of his white horse, Vizier. The museum displays an extensive collection of armor, arms, and uniforms.

Napoleon's remains are interred in a crypt in the Dome des Invalides. His red porphyry tomb holds the successive coffins in which lay his remains. Although he died on St. Helena in 1821, his body arrived in Paris in 1840. It is said that the coffin was opened for a few minutes, after nineteen years, and his body was perfectly preserved. Also buried in the crypt are Napoleon II, Marshal Turenne, the military engineer Vauban, Joseph Bonaparte, Jerome Bonaparte, Marshal Foch, and Marshal Lyautey.

The **Church of St. Louis des Invalides** contains many captured enemy banners hanging from the upper galleries. In 1814, as the Allies were entering Paris, the Invalides governor set fire to 1417 of the flags. Berlioz's *Requiem* was played for the first time there in 1837.

The **Rodin Museum** (77 rue de Varenne) is housed in the Hotel Biron. Built in 1729 by Abraham Peyrenc, the next owners were the Duc and Duchesse du Maine who were both involved in the political life of the times, including a conspiracy to do away with the Duc d'Orleans. The museum's 20 rooms contain sculptures, plaster casts, and drawings. Favorites include *The Kiss* and *The Hand of God*. The garden contains castings of *The Thinker, Balzac, The Burghers of Calais,* and *The Gates of Hell.*

Luxembourg Palace was built by Marie de Medici as a reminder of her happy youth in Italy. salomon de Brosse designed a palace similar to the Pitti

Palace in Florence. After living there for two years she was sent into exile in Cologne because she opposed Richelieu. The palace became a prison, a parliamentary assembly and is now the seat of the Senate.

The **Luxembourg Gardens** were designed for Marie de Medici; the Medici Fountain stands between the Palace and the Rue Medicis. Polyphemus, the jealous cyclops, is poised to get rid of Acis and Galatea. Statues stand all over the gardens amid formal flower beds; a favorite is that of Georges Sand in a crispy crinoline.

Museum Orsay *(Musee d'Orsay)* is housed in a former train station and hotel. Opened in December, 1986, this stretched-out museum presents a collection of 19th- and 20th-century French painting and sculpture. Its voluminous interior is interlaced with galleries, salons, and sculpture courtyards connected by ramps, many of them bathed by natural light from the elongated station dome. Both for the interior architecture and the collections, the musuem ranks among the best in Paris.

Montmartre

During the 19th and early 20th centuries artists chose to live and work in Montmartre. Renoir, Utrillo, Bernard, Gauguin, Dufy, Valadon, Poulbot, and Picasso all considered it home.

Up on a hill perches Montmartre's star, **Sacre Coeur Basilica.** This stark white church can be seen from many parts of Paris, and it stands out as a beacon. Its dome and 262-foot-high campanile are unmistakable. Visitors should be prepared to navigate endless steps up to the church.

Inside, mosaics dazzle with brilliant color. Stained-glass windows destroyed during World War II have now been replaced. The bell tower houses La Savoyards, which is one of the largest bells anywhere. Visitors can go up to the gallery around the dome for a view of Paris.

DAY TRIPS FROM PARIS ....

SOUTH OF PARIS
Fountainebleau

Long ago Capetian kings, such as Philip the Fair, considered it a favorite residence where they could be secluded and also hunt within their woodlands. Francois I removed the medieval palace and created a new one using Florentine and Roman artisans. Henri II and Catherine de Medici added refinements, Henri IV enlarged the chateau and Louis XIII finished his father's plans. Louis XIV expanded the gardens and redecorated for his favorite, Madame de Maintenon.

During the Revolution, the castle was not harmed although some of the furniture disappeared.

After Napoleon was defeated, he retired to Fontainebleau, signed the abdication, and said farewell to his Old Guard in the courtyard sometimes called *La Cour des Adieux*. The famous horseshoe staircase there is the one Napoleon descended on that day. More than a century later, the palace was liberated by General Patton in August 1944 and became the military headquarters of the Allied forces in Europe.

The gardens include a formal garden created by Le Notre for Louis XIV, a long canal ordered by Henri IV extending toward the east, Carp Lake, which houses ancient carp, and the Jardin Anglais where the original spring spouted, the *Fontaine Bleau*. The Forest of Fontainebleau surrounds the estate. There are gorges, forests of oak and beech, moorlands, and rivers to explore.

SOUTHWEST OF PARIS
The Loire Valley

The Loire Valley is a fairyland filled with magic palaces to visit. Some of the chateaux there are enormous; many are medieval fortresses, while others are ostentatious pleasure palaces. The memories of these retreats for kings are hidden—if only walls could talk! Tales of intrigue and scandal stir up the imagination as you walk through the pages of French history in these halls, chambers, galleries, and gardens. The chateaux offer a rare opportunity to see with your own eyes the elegance and splendor of aristocratic life in former centuries. You can easily visit the larger, tourist-laden chateaux, but we hope you will also find one of the less well-known chateaux, which, for us, had a more special, personal atmosphere; we were lucky to discover and stay in one that has a fascinating history that the marquis who owns it related. Take a trip down some of the enchanting smaller roads and into quiet villages in search of your chateau—it's fun!

The Loire is a wide, quiet river beginning in the Massif Central, flowing through Orleans and past the orchards, vineyards (try some of the local white wines), and gardens of the Touradine, slowly widening as it passes through Blois, Tours, Saumur, Angers, Nantes, and out into the sea estuary. Fishermen enjoy the variety of fish in the rivers and streams in the valley, and hunters find wildlife plentiful.

Although it is not easy to pick a favorite Loire castle, one cannot go wrong visiting **Chenonceau,** which is said to be the most popular (after Fontainebleau) in all of France. We find the setting of Chenonceau very appealing because its beauty is reflected in the waters of the River Cher. You may have seen pictures of this magnificent, elegant, building atop stone arches over the river, with formal gardens adjacent—green foliage, blue water and sky contrasting with the white stone. The approach along a wide boulevard of plane trees builds up anticipation for the treasures ahead.

Also known as the "Chateau of Six Women," Chenonceau was developed through the influences of six women who lived there over a 400-year period. The first woman was Katherine Briconnet, who was involved in the chateau's placement on the site and its interior design. Diane de Poitiers, mistress of Henri II, received Chenonceau as a gift from the king in 1547. She was responsible for the lovely formal garden as well as for a bridge from the castle to the bank of the River Cher. This red-haired beauty was hated by Catherine de Medici, who turned Diane out after the King died. Catherine added a park and a gallery on the bridge; she gave fetes there, including the first display of fireworks in France. Louise of Lorraine housed nuns in the attic rooms; they had a drawbridge they could pull up at night to isolate themselves from the outside world.

In the 18th century, Madame Dupin attracted a following of intellectual visitors including Voltaire, Monesquieu, and Jean-Jacques Rousseau (who was her son's tutor). Madame Dupin was respected and loved by the villagers, and perhaps the feeling they had for her was responsible for the lack of damage to Chenonceau during the French Revolution. In the 19th century, Madame Pelouze devoted herself to restoring the castle. Pick up a brochure in the language you prefer as you buy your ticket; the rooms are listed in order with an explanation of the contents of each.

Chambord, the largest and most ostentatious of the chateaux, was built by Francois I as a hunting lodge in 1519. It is hard to believe that this 400-room palace was used as a retreat for hunting and entertaining; it seems the height of extravagance. Just keeping 365 fireplaces supplied with wood must have taken many francs. Chambord is set in a large deer park that is now also a wildlife preserve. As you approach, you will be struck by the immense scale of the building, with its towers, turrets, dormers, and chimneys in a potpourri of design. Grand though it is, this is probably not the castle of your dreams; a weekend might be fun but you "wouldn't want to live there." In any event, it is impressive.

The keep, or main structure, was developed by Leonardo Da Vinci; on each level there is a Greek cross with apartments around it. You can't miss the famous double-ramp spiral staircase, which ascends from the first floor to the roof, in the middle of the Greek crosses. You can go up or down on one ramp never meeting people you can see on the other ramp; it must have been a tantalizing arrangement in those days of intrigue and seduction.

Francois I built this castle with firm resolve, even when he did not have enough money to pay the ransom for his sons, languishing in captivity in Spain. He forced French citizens to give up their silver for the cause.

Chartres

The **Cathedral of Notre-Dame** in Chartres is perhaps one of the most impressive medieval cathedrals in the world. Its tall spires soar upward from the hill that dominates the flat plain of La Beauce and can be seen across miles of fields from all directions. The Druids worshipped on the site, the Romans called it Autricum, Philip the Fair ruled there in 1286, the Huguenots arrived in 1568, and Henri (Henri IV) of Navarre captured the town in 1591. A number of churches have shared the site since the 4th century. In 1020 a disastrous fire ravished the 9th-century structure; it was rebuilt only to succumb in 1194 to a fire that left only the facade and the towers. The new cathedral was consecrated in 1260 and with a few changes remains to this day.

A circular maze created on the floor of the nave may have been used by the dedicated, as they followed it on their knees. The labyrinth is over 40 feet in diameter and its paths wind back and forth, wormlike, until reaching the flower in the center.

In the choir 40 sculptures depicting the Life of Christ and the Virgin are framed with delicate tracery work. The treasury contains a garment said to have been worn by the virgin. It was presented by the Empress Irene to Charlemagne and then to Chartres in 876 by Charles the Bald, Charlemagne's grandson. It is said that during the 10th century, when the Normans were invading Chartres, the bishop climbed up onto the city gates and showed the precious garment, called the Sancta Camisia. The Normans turned around and left, not wishing to defy the sanctity of the relic. In 1194, after the disastrous fire, many thought the garment had been lost. However, it was found by the bishop in a secret place in the crypt.

WEST OF PARIS

Versailles

On our last trip to Paris we chose to stay in Versailles, where we could savor parts of the magnificent palace at a slower pace every day, rather than limit ourselves to a single, hurried tour. Not that we had delusions of grandeur; but it was nice to look up the street as we walked around the town and see the palace standing there. We had just been reading a novel about Marie Antoinette, which added zest to the charm of the place. Versailles also proved to be an extremely convenient and inexpensive base for forays into Paris, only 30 minutes away by clean, quiet, and fast trains.

Although some have tried to copy Versailles, no structure has yet appeared as grand and spectacular. The Sun King, Louis XIV, built a golden palace on the site of Louis XIII's hunting lodge. He commissioned three great architects— Le Notre, Le Vau, and Le Brun—to create his masterpiece. France almost went bankrupt over this building.

Louis XV added an opera house, then the Petit Trianon for his mistress, Madame Dubarry. The Revolutionists broke into the palace, the king and queen could not contain them, and Versailles lost its royalty forever. Versailles' paintings were removed to the Louvre and the furniture sold at auction. Louis Philippe undertook the formidable task of renovating the palace. Recent restoration began in 1978 when the French government allocated over $37 million for the project.

As a statue in the courtyard, Louis XIV still rides a horse. Two wings extend out sideways from the central section of the palace. The gardens are symmetrical, complementing each side and continuing out in front of the central section.

Inside, the **Hall of Mirrors** *(Galerie des Glaces)* is unquestionably the favorite room of all. This 246-foot-long gallery, lit by 17 windows reflected in 17 mirrors, is ornate and opulent. Scenes from the Sun King's reign were painted on the ceiling. One can almost imagine Marie Antoinette and Louis XVI walking to their wedding there under sparkling chandeliers and over Savonnerie carpets.

The **Queen's Apartments** *(Grand Appartement de la Reine)* include the bedroom created for the Infanta Maria Teresa, who married Louis XIV. Nineteen royal children were born in the room. Marie Antoinette spent her last night in Versailles there; her jewel chest is on display.

The **King's Bedroom** has been renovated and is just as it was when Louis XIV reigned as the Sun King. The royal bed was the scene of formal ceremonies as members of the Court gathered to watch the king rise and retire. He died of gangrene poisoning in that very bed in 1715.

The **King's Private Suite** was more comfortable for Louis XV; he retired and arose formally in the state bedroom, but then crept out of the state bed to actually sleep in this room. He died of smallpox there in 1774.

The **King's Private Apartments** on the second and third floors were Louis XV's favorite retreat with his friends and mistresses. Gardens on the rooftops were alive with aviaries. Madame du Barry's suite was on the second floor; Madame de Pompadour's on the third floor.

The Gardens were laid out by Le Notre from 1667. Pools, fountains, pavilions and statues were carefully placed for balance. The fountains spurt at limited times, culminating in the Neptune and Dragon Basins where 99 fountains rise up to 138 feet.

Also on the grounds are the **Grand Trianon,** a small chateau decorated with blue and white tiles. Louis XIV enjoyed retreating there with his intimates. The **Petit Trianon** was a favorite with Louis XV. Marie Antoinette felt at home there as well as in the little hamlet with thatched roofs, built as a reminder of her home in Austria. When we last visited, the woods were quiet and peaceful, the silence broken only by the twittering of birds.

NORTHWEST OF PARIS

Bayeux

The **Bayeux Tapestry,** an exquisite work of art, is unique in the world. Scholars felt that this lengthy, embroidered chronicle was commissioned by Bishop

Odon of Conteville and was created by the Saxon School of Embroidery in England over a 10-year period. The wool yarn, in vivid red, blue, green, gray, black, and yellow is amazingly well preserved. The story, fashioned almost like a cartoon strip, relates the conquest of England by Duke William of Normandy. In addition to the large central narrative strip, you will see a border running at the top and bottom that features scenes of rural life at that time. The design was made with intelligence and humor; there are hidden surprises, like surprisingly risque drawings, to intrigue visitors. (By the way, if you are confused by the characters, remember that the English wear mustaches and the Normans do not.)

Bayeux is one of the best examples of a well-preserved historic town anywhere. Don't miss the cathedral with its Gothic spires on top of Romanesque towers. The tapestry was originally designed to be displayed there. Look for the story of Thomas Becket's murder in the south transept; there are a number of chapels, the treasury and the crypt to visit.

The **Baron Gerard Museum** is housed nearby in the Old bishopric, with a collection including porcelain and ceramics on the ground floor, paintings and tapestries one flight up.

Normandy Landing Beaches

American men who fought and died in 1944 lie in the **Normandy American Cemetery** above Omaha Beach; 9386 American war dead are buried there; 14,000 others who were originally buried have been returned home at the request of their next of kin. The headstones are of white Italian marble, marked by a Star of David for those of Jewish faith and a Latin Cross for all others. There is a long series of pools with a loggia at each end. The southern loggia contains several large maps depicting the landings, naval support for them, and air operations on that day. The bronze statue, *The Spirit of American Youth*, stands 22 feet high on the platform. The chapel has a lovely mosaic ceiling, with an altar made of gold and black "Grand Antique" marble from the Pyrenees. As you look out over Omaha Beach spread below the cemetery, filled with soft, fine sand, you may begin to feel the anguish of the day. Men landed behind the beaches from three Airborne Divisions as the Allied Naval forces assaulted Omaha Beach with heavy equipment at 6:30 a.m. The enemy had prepared continuous mine fields in the water and on the beach; their fortifications were connected by tunnels and enhanced by machine-guns in trenches. It must have taken a great deal of courage to jump into waist-deep water (if they were lucky) and wade ashore knowing the danger of mines and whizzing bullets coming down from the cliffs above. Yet they persevered, in spite of horrendous losses, slowly opening up one avenue after another for their buddies to follow. By 2:00 p.m. the Allies had weakened the enemy's fortifications enough to move inland to the highway by the entrance to the cemetery.

Eight miles to the west is another historic spot, **Pointe du Hoc.** Visiting this site five days before the 40th anniversary of D-Day, as we did, aroused strong but conflicting emotions. As we looked out over the wide panorama of beach and sea, with only a few peaceful sailboats tacking slowly in the sunlight, we tried to imagine that day: June 6, 1944: the bustling, crashing, frenzied activity of vessels unloading men and equipment onto a narrow strip of beach, and then the Rangers struggling to climb the cliff. We knew from living in south Devon, where the practice for the landing took place, what had preceded that ordeal. The Channel crossing was not calm, and many of the men were seasick. At 4:30 a.m. British assault landing craft arrived with 225 men from the U.S. 2nd Ranger Battalion. As they looked up at the cliffs of Pointe du Hoc, one said, ''My God, they are up there waiting for us.''

As that initial force hit the beach, the enemy opened fire, and 15 Rangers were killed wading through the waves and running across the very narrow strip of beach below the base of the cliffs. Lieutenant Colonel James Earl Rudder, a rancher and former football coach from Brady, Texas, led his group to climb the 100-foot-high cliffs and capture the guns at Pointe du Hoc. This assault was rather like assaults on fortified castles in ancient times, with rocks and stone walls to scale. Eighteen U.S. bombers confused the enemy by dropping bombs on them minutes before the Rangers began to climb up. The Rangers used rocket-fired equipment to anchor ladders to the top, then began to ascend. Of the 225 Rangers, but 90 reached the top alive. Ironically, when they reached the gun emplacements that were the objective of the whole operation, they found them empty; the large guns had been moved back by the enemy in anticipation of invasion. Later the guns were located some distance from shore; had their location been known they could have been taken without such a tragic loss of life.

Pointe du Hoc remains as it was when the Rangers left it; bunkers were mostly destroyed, crater holes are everywhere, and there is one bunker you can walk into to look out through the gun slot down the cliff toward the now peaceful sea.

GERMANY

Currency unit • Duetschemark (DM) divided into 100 Pfennige (Pfg)
Language • German
Time difference from USA • six hours later (Eastern Standard Time)
Telephone access codes • to USA 00 or USADirect 0130–0010 (not available in former East Germany yet); from USA 49
National Tourist Offices • **USA:** German National Tourist Office, 747 Third Ave., New York, NY 10017, tel.: (212) 308–3300; **Berlin:** Europa-Center, Tauentzienstrasse, 1000 Berlin, tel.: (30) 2–12–34; **Cologne:** Unter Fettenheunen 19 D-5000 Cologne, tel.: (221) 221–3340; **Frankfurt:** Gutleutstrasse 7-9, D-6000, Frankfurt 1, tel.: (69) 313–3677; **Munich:** Postfach, D-8000 Munchen, tel.: (89) 2–39–11; **London:** Nightingale Rd., 65 Curzon St., London W1Y 7PE, tel.: (071) 495–399
Airlines • **Lufthansa, USA:** (800) 645–3880; **Britain** (071) 408–0442
Embassies • **American Embassy,** Deichmanns Ave., 5300 Bonn 2, Germany, tel.: (0228) 3391; **American Consulate,** Cleyellee 170, 1000 Berlin, 33 tel.: (30) 819 75; **American Consulate,** Koniginstrasse 5, Munich, tel.: 089 23011; **British Consul,** Uhlandstrasse 7/8 1000 Berlin, tel.: (030) 309–52–92–4; **British Embassy:** Friedrich Ebert Allee 5300 Bonn 1, tel.: (0228) 234061; **British Consulate,** Amalienstrasse 62, 8000 Munich 40, tel.: (089) 39–40–15/9

HISTORY..

Prehistoric remains include the lower jaws of *Homo Heidelbergensis* found near Heidelberg, a skull discovered at Steinheim an der Murr, and a skeleton of "Neanderthal man" near Dusseldorf. Pile dwellings were found on Lake Constance, dating from 8000–1800 B.C., and megalithic tombs on Luneburg Heath. Celtic hill forts were found at Heuneburg, near Sigmaringen. Roman legions lived in the country from the 1 A.D. Arminius, a German, defeated them in 9 A.D.

Writings of Tacitus describe the Tungri tribe's customs in his *Germania*.

Migrations took place between 300–918 A.D. In 919, Duke Henry of Saxony became King of the Germanic people.

The Holy Roman Empire began under the leadership of Frederick I (Barbarossa) in 1152. By 1356 the Golden Bull decreed that emperors had to be chosen by seven electors. These electors consisted of the Archbishops of Mainz, Trier, and Cologne and four lay electors: the Duke of Saxony, the Margrave of Brandenburg, the Count of Palatine, and the King of Bohemia. The Reformation beginning in 1517 diminished the power of the Roman Church. By 1618 the Thirty Years War had begun with its battles between Catholics and Protestants.

In 1648 the Peace of Westphalia saw the decline of German Imperial power and the rise of Brandenburg-Prussia. In 1701 Frederick of Brandenburg was crowned King of Prussia. In 1814–1815 the Congress of Vienna provided for the establishment of the German Confederation of 39 states. The Franco-Prussian War took place in 1870–71 and Germany became the German Empire in 1871.

Germany was named a Republic in 1918 during the armistice signed at Compiegne. The Treaty of Versailles stripped the country of much of its area and Germany admitted responsibility for the war. Adolf Hitler was appointed Chancellor in 1933 and the real trouble began. After a horrendous number of years, Germany surrendered in 1945. The Berlin Wall went up in 1961 and was torn down in 1989, leading to the reunification of Germany in 1991.

BERLIN

The dream of visiting all of Germany without any hampering restrictions has finally become a reality. The Berlin Wall, now reduced to a broad swath of rubble snaking across the city, reshaped political geography and blocked normal communication between the two halves of the city for three decades. Seven months after the wall went down, my husband and I visited sites in East Berlin that had special meaning for us. When I was a baby, my aunt spent a year studying in Berlin. She and I had re-lived that time together, and talked about the turmoil surrounding the collapse of the Weimer Republic and the rise of Hitler. Our last day together before her death was spent remembering the atmosphere of Berlin in 1931. Just 60 years after her visit, those scenes came alive again as I walked into the courtyards of Humboldt University.

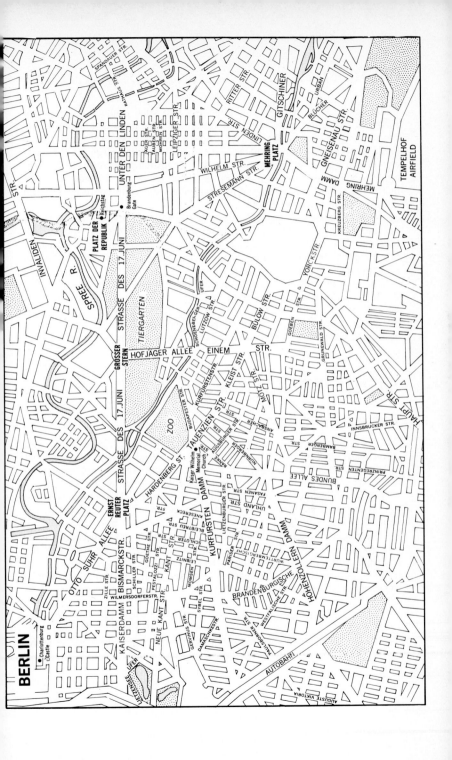

HISTORY......................................

Berlin emerged in 1307 from the joining of two small fishing villages on the shores of the River Spree. The first castle was built there in 1443 by Count Frederick II of Hohenzollern. The Thirty Years War decimated Berlin, but Frederick William of Brandenburg went to work building quays on the river, and a canal linking the Spree and the Oder. He invited persecuted French Protestant scholars and craftsmen as well as Dutch artists and architects to settle there. The culture and learning of the Huguenot settlers was not insignificant in the growing prosperity of Berlin.

During the Age of Enlightenment of the 18th century, the first King of Prussia, Fredrich I, built the Chateau of Charlottenburg for his wife Sophie-Charlotte. The next ruler, Friedrich Wilhelm I, expanded the town by adding Friedrichstadt. Frederick (II) the Great added monuments along the Unter den Linden and the Forum Fredericianum.

In 1810 the University was founded, bringing more scholars into the city. By 1871 Berlin had become the capital city of Germany. Two World Wars wreaked havoc on Berlin, and in 1945 the outcome of the Yalta conference meant four-power government for the city. Although much of the city had been destroyed, many of its baroque buildings have now been reconstructed.

SIGHTSEEING....................................

Tiergarten and Area

For some time to come, visitors will want to visit the **Brandenburg Gate** *(Brandenburger Tor)*, which was built in 1791 to stand as the major triumphal arch into Berlin. The Propylaea in the Acropolis in Athens gave impetus to fashion the same kind of Doric columns. Napoleon carted off the Goddess of Victory after invading Berlin in 1806; it was returned in 1814. Now everyone can rejoice to see the Brandenburg Gate stand again in glory, unmarred by the horrendous Berlin Wall.

Nearby, the **Reichstag,** Platz der Republik, which was damaged by a fire in 1933 and in 1945 by bombs, has been restored although the surface of the building is still pockmarked with light spots from bullets. It was originally opened in 1894 as the German Parliment of Imperial Diet. A permanent exhibit, ''Questions Addressed to German History,'' describes German history since 1800.

Eight white crosses mark the spot in the river where eight persons died while trying to cross. Their names are written in black on the crosses; when we were there a young man was freshening the paint. Standing there staring at the river, noting guard stations still visible, we wonder at the great amount of courage it took for those who slipped in to the water on the other side.

Detail of these tragedies is given in the **Checkpoint Charlie Museum** on Friedrichstrasse, which stands just a few doors away from the old guard station. From the date of the wall, August 13, 1961, collections were assembled to commemorate the efforts of those who lived or died trying to escape. The first exhibit opened Oct. 16, 1962 opposite a series of houses where windows had been bricked over; an expansion opened later in the present location.

Inside, poignant photographic reminders are on display with printed descriptions written in several languages. For example, a steamer crew got their captain drunk, locked him in his cabin, and crossed in the boat in 1962. In 1979, eight persons were successful in a hot-air balloon. Twenty-year-old Hans Meyer passed the last wire while trying to climb the wall. As he was fired upon, an American, Hans Pool, climbed the wall and shouted, "Let go of the boy." After an underwater blockade was spiked, a diver removed one section, and 14 persons got through with breathing tubes.

To the west of the Reichstag stands **Congress Hall** *(Kongresshalle)* which was given by the USA in 1957 as the International Building Exhibition. Although the roof fell in during 1980, it was reconstructed in 1987. It is sometimes referred to as the "pregnant oyster."

Tiergarten Park is bisected by the Strasse Des 17 Juni running from west to east. Friedrich III devised the idea for the park and it was landscaped by Peter Josseph Lenne beginning in 1789. Although the landscaping was ravaged during the war most of the statues remain.

Schloss Bellevue in the northern section of the park was constructed in 1785 by Prince Ferdinand who was the brother of Frederic the Great. The President of the Federal Republic has lived there since 1959. Behind the residence, **Bellevue Park** houses an English garden among other botanical groupings.

The **Victory Column** is 222 feet high and memorializes the battles of 1864, 1866, and 1870. Colorful frescoes and gold cannon barrels glisten in the sunlight. 285 steps lead to the top and views of the Tiergarten and the Spree.

The **Berlin Zoo** *(Zoologischer Garten)* is the largest and oldest zoo in Germany. The **Crocodile House** is one of the newest additions. Many of the animals are known to visitors by their nicknames.

Nearby the west tower ruin of **Kaiser Wilhelm's Church** *(Kaiser Wilhelm Gedachtniskirche)*, which was built from 1891 to 1895 in his memory, can be seen on Breitschieldplatz. This reminder of the ravages of war still stands, and next to it the new church and campanile. Blue-tone stained-glass windows were created by Gabriel Loire in Chartres. An "eternity" mosaic stands behind the high altar.

To the west is the famous **Schloss Charlottenburg,** Luisenplatz, which is the place to enjoy some of the old flavor of Berlin, pre-Berlin Wall and ravagement. Queen Sophie Charlotte created a large garden there reminiscent of Versailles. A temple-style mausoleum stands under the trees behind the palace.

Inside, royal tombs include those of Friedrich-Wilhelm III and Queen Louisa, Emperor Wilhelm I, and Empress Augusta.

Queen Sophie Charlotte was a popular monarch who spent much of her life supporting the arts. She was part of the movement in 1700 to form a scientific group known as the Royal Academy of Science and Fine Arts.

Here baroque architecture can be seen as a result of post-World-War-II restoration. Visitors can stroll through the apartments of Frederick I and Sophie Charlotte, which contain portraits of the royal family by Antoine Pesne, the official court painter. Tapestries line the rooms of Queen Sophie Charlotte.

The **Knobelsdorff Wing,** built between 1740–1749, contains Friedrich Wilhelm II's summer apartments, rich in Chinese decoration, galleries, and a banquet hall. The **Museum of Decorative Arts** houses works from the Middle Ages. The **Guelph Treasure** *(Welfenschatz),* a reliquary that contained the head of St. Gregory after it was returned in 1173 from Constantinople and the Guelph cross are also there.

The **West Wing,** or Orangery, contains a theater and the **Museum of Pre- and Proto-history** *(Museum fur Vor und Fruhgeschichte).* Here is the place to trace the history of man from ancient times. See the skeleton of a man who died a violent death 20,000 years ago in Combe Capelle in the Dordogne in France. He was dismembered and buried with snail shell ornaments.

Opposite Charlottenburg Palace stands the **Egyptian Museum,** which contains a marvelous head of Nefertiti. The gateway portrays the Roman Emperor Augustus making an offering to Isis. The museum contains funerary masks, sarcophagi, statues, and terracotta vases.

The **Museum of Greek and Roman Antiquities** *(Antikenmuseum)* houses a wealth of ancient treasure on the lower floor. The Schatzkammer collection contains Hildesheim silver—a cup dating from the end of the first century B.C. shows the goddess Minerva, seated and looking pensive.

Museum Island

Formerly in East Berlin, Museum Island offers a number of buildings housing a variety of subjects. The **Pergamon Museum** contains ancient art dating from the 6th-century B.C. The 160 B.C. **Pergamon Altar** from Asia Minor was brought stone by stone from Turkey. The frieze portrays a battle of gods and giants with fragments of human heads, bodies, lions, and serpents entwined. A 2nd-century market gate and mosaic floor from Miletus, Greece and the 580 B.C. Ishtar Gate from Babylon are also there. The Babylonians must have enjoyed color, as they used brick-shaped tiles in navy blue, gold, green, aqua, and white in their walls.

The **Bode Museum,** Am Kupfergraben, is handsome inside, with a curved black and gold stairway and a huge white dome decorated with eagles. The museum contains Egyptian and Byzantine artifacts, coins, sculpture, altar triptychs, mosaic frescoes, sarcophagi, and paintings. An impressive papyrus collection is encased in glass. Mummies include those of humans, crocodiles, cats, birds, and fish—complete with x-rays of their bones. European paintings date from the Gothic period.

The **Altes Museum,** Marx Engels Pl. features 15th–18th century lithographs and engravings. Botticelli's work for Dante's *Divine Comedy* is there. This museum was originally built by Schinkel in 1825; it has been renovated and its dome inside is freshly painted with rose-colored squares.

The **National Gallery,** Bodestrasse, houses German Impressionist works as well as modern paintings, drawings, and sculpture. Art from the Soviet Union and other Eastern bloc countries is on display. Part of the collection is housed in the Altes Museum, the Otto Nagel House, and in Friedrichswerdersche Kirche.

Humboldt University is partly housed in a restored palace once built for Prince Henry, the brother of Frederick the Great. Professors who taught there include Albert Einstein, Georg Hegel, and Max Planck. The front gate is alive with cherubs, and roses were blooming in the courtyard when we were there.

Nearby, a changing of the guard was in process—as we approached, three soldiers came out of an adjoining building wearing black boots and helmets, holding guns in their right hands. They went through a goose-stepping routine that made shivers run up and down our spines. (Since then we have heard that this painful reminder of Nazi militarism has been eliminated.) Inside a memorial building, the eternal flame glows within a glass prism that casts light in all directions.

The **Schinkel Museum** is located in the old Friedrichswerdersche Kirche, handsome with stained-glass windows above a black altar, wooden arches on the sides, and two modern chandeliers. The statues and monuments inside include ones of Dionysos and Ariadne, Persephone, Electra, Eros, as well as the tomb of Princess Luise von Preufzen.

We visited the headquarters of the German Army and had another moment of poignancy as we gazed at the yellow mums and daisies tied with a German ribbon beside a red wreath. On July 20, 1944 the "Officer's Rebellion" that might have ended the war a year earlier and saved millions of lives reached its own fatal end on this spot. A bomb had been placed under an oak table to assassinate Hitler, but when it exploded the heavy table deflected the force. Of course, the high-ranking officers involved in the plot were executed in the courtyard, and their names are engraved beside the flowers.

Alexanderplatz

Before World War II the square was lined with many buildings. Today the 13th-century **St. Mary's Church** *(Marienkirche)* remains as a reminder of the old days. A fresco in Tower Hall, called *Dance of Death, Totentanz* dates from 1484. Its 1703 marble pulpit and 1721 organ are also there.

The **City Hall** *(Rathaus)* is a block-sized red brick neo-Gothic building which was damaged during the war, but rebuilt after 1945. Its frieze portrays important events in the history of the city.

The 1190-foot-high TV tower soars upward from Alexanderplatz. Inside there is a revolving restaurant at the 650-foot level.

DAY TRIPS FROM BERLIN.....................

POTSDAM

Potsdam dates back to the 11th century, when it was founded by Slavs. In 1660 the Prince Elector of Prussia, Friedrich Wilhelm, built a palace there. During the 18th century, Frederick the Great continued to give attention to Potsdam, as the importance of the Hohenzollerns grew. Succeeding Kings of Prussia imitated French kings in building palaces similar to Versailles with gardens to match.

Sans-Souci

We entered the gardens of Sans-Souci through the Obelisk Portal, which looks like an Egyptian monument. Flowers, fountains, paths, and statues draw the visitor from one end of the park to the other. **Neptune's Grotto** is on the right side of the path. Water splashes from one shell to another until it reaches the pool at the bottom. Neptune stands on the top holding up his trident, and two naiads carry water pitchers.

The **Chinese Pagoda,** or tea house, was built with a tent-like roof and three bays with porches in between. Look on top of the cupola for a mandarin perched under an umbrella. The building and statues glitter with at least 260 grams of gold. The pagoda contains a collection of Japanese and Chinese porcelain and Meissen.

The **Orangery** was originally built to keep plants over the winter. Czarina Charlotte of Russia and her consort, Czar Nicholas I resided in apartments here when they visited Potsdam.

The **New Palace** is located at the end of the path opposite the Obelisk. Frederick II built it at great expense after the Seven Years War, calling it a *fanfaronade*.

Inside, the ceilings are ethereal, with angels and clouds bathed in soft light. The **Hall of Shells** looks like the inside of a mosque with arches, striped fabric, and alcoves with sculpture. Shells are set into the walls and pillars. The marble floor ripples like an ocean bottom.

The **Concert Room** is ornate with gold around each painting, mirrors, gold cherubs, animals, birds, leaves, grapes, fountains, and a spider's web on the ceiling.

Cecilienhof Palace

Built in 1916 this half-timbered building looks like an English country house. Negotiations during the Potsdam Conference of 1945 were held there. Thirty-six rooms were redecorated to serve as studies for the delegations of each major government. Delegates lived in other parts of Potsdam and congregated at Cecilienhof for meetings.

The **Red Salon,** once a writing room, was the study of the Soviet delegation. Red wallpaper, a red carpet, an oriental rug, and the desk used by Stalin are in place.

President Truman and the American delegation used a former living room and smoking room with panelled walls. The classical style furniture was made in 1790.

Sir Winston Churchill and his delegates were placed in the former library and reading room. Books are still there in cases along wood panelled walls.

EXCURSIONS FROM BERLIN ....

Weimar

In Weimar one can see and feel three centuries of German history and culture, from apogee to nadir. As Germany's Stratford, it is associated with Goethe and Schiller, who lived and worked there during the flowering of German literature, but it also has a larger history of major artists, writers, and musicians that made it a far richer place than Shakespeare's birthplace village. Such cultural riches, however, cannot obscure the other face of Weimar as a site of political and moral disaster in the twentieth century. Here, in the theater of Goethe and Schiller, the Reichstag of the shaky Weimar Republic met until it collapsed before Hitler's onslaught, and just a few kilometers west of the beautiful city center lies Buchenwald. Memories of the dark underside of German history commingle with monuments of high culture.

Weimar provided the name and center for the abortive Weimar Republic born in August 1919 after World War I. The coalition of Social Democrat, Catholic Center, and Democratic Parties tried to maintain order and promote peace. During 1923–1929 Germany was a peaceful nation with some economic recovery. Then came the crash of 1929. In the shambles that followed, Hitler gained power and the Third Reich began in 1933.

Earlier, a series of scholars and artists came to live in this pretty section of Thuringia. Among them—Martin Luther, Lucas Cranach, Johann Sebastian Bach, Johann Wolfgang von Goethe, Friedrich Schiller, Franz Liszt, and, in the 1920s, Walter Gropius and the Bauhaus group of architects and painters, including Vasily Kandinski and Paul Klee.

We found the old center Weimar to be a jewel with its winding streets, wooded parks, and river Ilm—all in a low-key, semi-pastoral atmosphere. Historical houses, castles, and museums are there to be savored—slowly. When we were there, people sat on benches, and strolled on shaded streets, and we listened to two young girls playing violins and tapping their feet to an organ grinder who cranked out music with his top hat on.

Goethe lived in a house on Frauenplan from 1782 to 1789 and again from 1792 until his death in 1832. Today visitors can walk up the staircase Goethe designed, looking up at the ceiling painting in five rainbow colors called *Iris*.

The **Goethe Museum** includes prints of a Faust production in 1981, two large wooden marionettes of Faust and Mephisto, a bronze relief of Goethe, paintings of his family, his mother's round pin box, playing cards, and a Bible.

Walk through the park to his garden house, which is a plain building with a lovely garden. Inside, his floral table and chairs, writing desk, another stand-up desk with a padded seat, and a black trunk are reminders of his presence.

Wittums Palace was where Duchess Anna-Amalia entertained scholars and artists. She brought the poet Christoph Martin Wieland to Weimar. The museum in her house is dedicated to him. Each room contains pieces original to the house.

The **Gallery in the Castle** *(Kunstsammlungen zu Weimer)* houses a large number of Lucas Cranachs including *Hercules* with dwarfs shooting arrows at him, sawing his foot, and poking him with spears. In the next painting Hercules rises up and they scatter. Also on display: *David and Bathsheba, Samson and the Lion, Charitas, Adam and Eve, Salome and Herodes,* and *Samson and Delila.*

COLOGNE

When we think of Cologne we always recall the cathedral as we first saw it, left standing alone with rubble all around. Like St. Paul's in London, it became the symbol of the few remnants of hope left amid the barbaric destruction of World War II that saw European nations turn inward and obliterate the civilization they had created. Now the cathedral is the centerpiece of an elegant rebuilt square including museums, restaurants, shops, and archaeological exhibits going back to the Romans.

HISTORY......................................

Cologne was founded by the Romans in 38 B.C. They built a wall, and Constantine built a bridge across the Rhine four centuries later. Roman ruins are still visible, including a gate in front of the cathedral, old fortifications, the Praetorium, a palace, and the original drainage system. During the Middle Ages the city first became powerful as a center for the church, then rich as a member of the Hanseatic League. By 1881 medieval walls were taken down and wide boulevards laid out. More bridges were built over the Rhine and industry moved in. World War II devastated the city, but by 1985 all 12 of the old churches had been rebuilt.

SIGHTSEEING................................

The **cathedral** is probably the first site most visitors want to visit. Begun in the 13th century but not finished until the 19th century; it was patterned after the ambitious cathedrals at Amiens and Chartres. The facade is definitely Gothic with stepped windows and gables. Look for the 14th-century tympanum over the main door. St. Peter is being crucified head down by his own request as a mark of respect for his beloved Master. The spires soar upward for 515 feet. Visitors can climb the 500 steps to the top of one of the spires for a view of the city. A gold shrine on the altar contains treasures of the Magi brought in 1164 by Frederick Barbarossa from Milan. The Cross of Gero dating from the 10th century is also there. The triptych in the chapel on the southeast side presents Stephan Lochner's scenes of groups of saints of the city with a Madonna and Child in the center.

The **Roman Germanic Museum** *(Romisch Germanisches Museum)* has a wealth of exhibits from Roman days in Cologne, and its exhibits are beautifully designed. The most memorable for most visitors is the almost undamaged large **Dionysian Mosaic** that once enhanced the floor of a villa on that very spot.

Next door stands the **Wallraf Richartz Museum,** Bischofsgartenstrasse 1, which contains medieval art, 17th- and 18th-century Dutch masters, and contemporary work by German and French artists.

Schnutgen Museum, Cacilienstrasse 29, is housed in a lovely old church, once St. Cecilia's. The collection was begun by Alexander Schnutgen, a local priest who enjoyed finding and buying sacred art.

The **Metropolitan Historical Museum** *(Kolnisches Stadtmuseum),* is housed in the former arsenal, surprisingly not obliterated during World War II. Visitors can trace the development and life of Cologne through exhibits of arms, battle photographs, armor, maps, paintings, and more.

DAY TRIPS FROM COLOGNE ....

A Cruise on the Rhine

With the Rhine flowing along the east side of the city center most visitors feel an urge to enjoy it afloat. From Cologne you can take a cruise to various cities upriver including Koblenz, from which it is possible to return to Cologne by train the same day. Or you can take an overnight trip past more castles and vineyards on the Rhine to Mainz, or even farther south toward Strasbourg, Freibourg, and Basil in Switzerland.

We have driven both sides of the Rhine; the left (west) bank has a faster road (it is possible to drive from Cologne to Bingen in three hours); different castle views unfold on both sides. Heading south you'll pass **Rolandsbogen ruin,** the town of **Remagen** with its Roman gate, **Sinzig** and its 13th century Romanesque/Gothic church, **Rheineck** as a view point, and **Koblenz** with its well preserved old town.

Continuing upstream from Koblenz, one can't help but see **Marksburg Castle** across the river, the only castle on the Rhine to have escaped destruction. If you want to cross over, this is a good one to tour, with changing views on each level. Throughout the drive, steep slopes of vineyards alternate with craggy rock outcroppings and castles, including **Burg Maus** (mouse) and **Burg Katz** (cat). **Lorelei Rock** is a Germanic isle of Sirens, legendary for the beauty that lures ships to their destruction.

East of Cologne

The 13th-century **Altenberg Cathedral** is located 12 miles east of Cologne. It is known locally as the Bergische Dom, and contains tombs of the Berg family. Once a Cistercian abbey, the cathedral contains the largest stained-glass window in Germany. Protestant and Catholic services are now held alternately in this lovely Gothic cathedral.

South of Cologne

Bruhl Castle *(Augustusburg),* is located eight miles south of Cologne. Elector Clement Augustus built the castle in 1725 as his residence. the interior was designed by Francois Cuvillies and includes an exceptional staircase by Balthasar Neumann. This rococo staircase is alive with telamones and caryatids (columns of male and female figures similar to those in the Acropolis in Athens.) The park contains a hunting lodge, Falkenlust, also created by Cuvillies.

FRANKFURT

Many business travelers land in Frankfurt, do their business, and head back home before they have a chance to enjoy a remarkably interesting city. Besides being a financial center and site of trade fairs, Frankfurt has a vibrant historical past to explore. It is also well situated for trips to Heidelberg, Rothenburg, and the Rhine Valley.

HISTORY.....................................

Frankfurt was an important trading center during prehistoric times when the Celts lived there. Germanic tribes moved in, then the Romans, and later the Franks. The name came from Franks' ford across the river. Ludwig, Charlemagne's grandson, proclaimed Frankfurt as the capital of the German Empire. By 1152 all of the Holy Roman Empire's German leaders were inaugurated in Frankfurt. The Golden Bull of Karl IV (which was the law of the Empire) came into effect in 1356.

Frankfurt developed into the printing center of Europe with Johann Gutenberg's printing press in the 15th century. In the 16th century, money was minted there and the city began to prosper as a financial center. When the Rothschilds opened their banking doors in the 18th century, Frankfurt was well on its way as a powerful banking center.

SIGHTSEEING.....................................

The **cathedral,** near Fahrstrasse, dates from 852. Inside there is a tombstone for Count Gunther von Schwarzburg, the man who unsuccessfully sought the title of Emperor in the 14th century. A painting from Van Dyck's school, *Deposition from the Cross,* is in the north transept.

Saalhof Rententurm stands as a remnant of the 12th-century castle built by "Red Beard," Emperor Frederick I, Barbarossa. The chapel dates from 1175. The building became a trade-fair center and warehouse. Look on the wall to see dates of major floods.

Nearby, the **Church of St. Nichol** *(Nikolaikirche)* stands on Romerberg Square. Dating from the 13th century, this church is known for its 40-bell carillon, which plays four times a day. Its gallery was popular with officials and their families, who watched celebrations there.

The Romer contains a number of reconstructed 15th-century burghers' homes. The **Zum Romer house** in the middle is colorful, with four statues of emperors flanked by imperial eagles. Coronation banquets for Holy Roman emperors were once held in the Imperial Hall. Portraits of the 52 emperors from Charlemagne to Franz II hang on the walls.

St. Leonard's *(Leonhardskirche)*, on Mainkai, west of Eiserner Bridge, has 13th-century octagonal towers. The original Romanesque basilica doors are handsome with carved fronts.

Also on Romerberg, the **Historisches Museum Frankfurt** houses a large-scale model of the old city prior to 1944. We were intrigued by a collection of coronation coins for ten kings from Maximilian II in 1562 to Franz II in 1792.

Goethe's House *(Goethehaus)*, Grosser Hirschgraben 23, has been reconstructed to show his childhood home. The bedroom where he was born is there, and the study contains his marionette theater near the desk. Goethe's father had a large window inserted near his desk in the library so that he could be aware of the activities of his children without getting up.

The **Stadel Museum** *(Stadelsches Kunstinstitut)*, Schaumainkai 63, contains paintings of masters from all over Europe. Masters include Pablo Picasso, Renoir, Hans Memling, Pieter Brueghel the Elder, and Hans Holbein.

The **Senckenberg Museum** *(Naturmuseum Senckenberg)*, Senckenberganlage 25, houses a collection of fossils, dinosaur skeletons, stuffed animals from five continents, and minerals.

The **zoo** *(Zoologischer Garten)*, Alfred-Brehm Pl. is quite large. Rare animals that are often difficult to breed live there and multiply. The aviary is an enormous free-flight area with birds of all species enjoying life. The exotarium was built to house reptiles, insects, and penguins in proper climatic conditions. Don't miss the beehive, where you can watch the activity of countless bees.

DAY TRIPS FROM FRANKFURT......................................

Heidelberg

Heidelberg has a medieval town (enclosed in a larger modern city) with an enormous castle and Germany's oldest university. Many believe that its irreplaceable center survived the bombing of World War II by allied design. It was also the site of a prehistoric settlement; the jawbone of "Heidelberg Man" was found in a sandpit and now resides in the University Museum.

As in most cities, we like to rise to a high point—in this case to **Philosopher's Pass,** which is a garden area on the bank opposite the city. The view includes the Neckar River, the castle, and the highest mountain at 1800 feet.

The 13th-century rose-tinted castle, which stands above the town and the river, is now in ruins. It could be the scene of a romantic operetta and, in fact, is during the summer. The castle was destroyed along with the town in 1689 during the Orleans War. In 1764, the rebuilt castle was struck by lightning and has remained a ruin ever since, but a large part still stands with many interesting rooms, terraces, towers, and gardens to visit.

The sixty-foot-deep moat was once filled with wild animals including wolves, bears, and lions. Filling it with water would have destroyed the use of corridors under the castle. We heard birds twittering and watched them dart in and out of vine-covered walls. The gunpowder tower, even though 21-feet thick, exploded, and today part of it stands at an angle. Goethe liked that view and stood there in 1779 for inspiration.

The 1556 **facade** of the Heinrich's building is standing with statues of strength in the bottom row—Joshua, Samson, Hercules, and David. The next row is the five virtues; over them stand gods of antiquity, with Jupiter and Zeus at the top. On the terrace look for the footprint of a knight in armor who jumped out to save his lady's virtue. Try the footprint to see if it fits!

You can also see the **Heidelberg Tun,** a gigantic cask dating from the 18th century. According to legend, its guardian, a dwarf named Perkeo, had a tremendous capacity for wine and was able to drain it to the last drop.

In town you can visit the **Student's Jail** *(Studentenkarzer),* where rowdy students carved inscriptions, their silhouettes, and coats of arms on the walls. The Dean would send up students who drank too much, sang too loudly, or swam in the Neckar without clothes. They usually stayed three days, living on bread and water; if they remained longer, their landlords could bring in food. Each student tried to be incarcerated at least once—the party fever there was enticing.

The **Library** *(Universitatsbibliothek)* contains rare manuscripts, including the *Codex Manesse*—a volume of medieval love songs created by over 140 poets from 1305–1340. Each poem is printed on the right with its vividly colored picture on the left. This book had disappeared and was later found in Paris. There is also a beautiful old lecture hall with frescoes and carving preserved in the university.

The **old town,** with its narrow cobbled streets, has squares where one can have a coffee and watch the scene. The **Church of the Jesuits** is a pure baroque style with chandeliers and gold decoration at the top of the pillars. The **Church of the Holy Spirit,** in Gothic style, contains a mural discovered fairly recently. A winding staircase leads up to what was once a library in the galleries. There used to be a wall in the church to separate Catholics from Protestants.

St. George's Church dates from the 12th century and St. George stands with his sword on the west gable. Look for the scene of the Last Supper on the outer wall of the choir. Judas Iscariot holds the money bag on the far right.

Inside, the center aisle has carved wooden pew ends and 11 pillars lead the eye upward to the vaulted ceiling. The high altar depicts the crucifixion, with St. George slaying the dragon above. A wooden screen portrays the Ten Commandments, including the punishment for not obeying them. Frogs cascade down from heaven, the Nile flows in blood, and sinners are afflicted with mosquitos, painful sores, locusts, hail, and darkness. The remains of St. Sebastian lie in his tomb, decorated with gold and visible to the viewer.

Rothenburg Ob Der Tauber

Rothenburg is one of the favorite "romantic" places to visit in Europe. You may have seen the photograph of the junction of two picturesque streets with their half-timbered buildings and clock tower, called Plonlein; now you can take your own photographs. For some of the best views, especially of secluded courtyards, walk around the city on the old wall and climb up into the 197-foot-high belfry. This small city, with its cramped quarters and crooked streets, will transport you back to town life in the 14th century.

Dinkelsbuhl

Another charming town farther south is Dinkelsbuhl, with its wide, cobbled streets, a Romanesque tower to climb, and dungeons in the town hall. Since the 19th century, artists have wanted to capture the painted oriel windows that look down into the streets from upper stories, gilt and wrought-iron signs, half-timbered buildings, and gabled roofs. This town is also a photographer's dream.

MUNICH

HISTORY......................................

The emblem of Munich is a little monk *(Munchner Kindl)* dating back to its earliest 9th-century beginnings when the village was built near a Benedictine abbey. *Munchen* is the High German word for monk. The village did not grow until it received market rights in 1157. The year before, Emperor Frederick Barbarossa gave part of Bavaria to Henry the Lion, Duke of Saxony. Henry wisely chose to ensure Munich's financial security by changing the route of the old salt-water path from Reichenhall to Augsburg. He eliminated the old bridge and built a new one in town, which meant that traders had to pay salt trade taxes in Munich.

The Wittelsbachs were avid patrons of the arts, supporting and encouraging musicians, writers, and artists. They built theaters, concert halls, art galleries, churches, gardens, and elaborate residences. Maximilian I is responsible for the famous **English Garden.** His son, Ludwig I, added a Mediterranean flavor with his **imperial gate,** called the Propylaea, which looks as if it should be in Athens, and the **Glyptotheque,** a museum of ancient sculpture. His liaison with the Spanish dancer Lola Montez forced him to abdicate in favor of his son, Maximilian II.

Ludwig II received the crown at age eighteen; he became a patron of Richard Wagner. Ludwig II suffered from depression but cheered himself up by building three extraordinary castles long after there was any need for fortification: **Neuschwanstein, Linderhof,** and **Herrenchiemsee.** Eventually "Mad Ludwig" was deposed as king and within a few days threw himself into a lake and drowned. Ludwig's uncle, Prince Luitpold, came into power and continued the family tradition of promoting the arts. His son, Ludwig III, reigned until 1918, when he was forced to abdicate and flee to Austria. Munich was in a state of chaos, and the Nazi Party took hold. During World War II, Munich was devastated by bombs, but the city was rebuilt in its traditional manner from old blueprints and plans.

SIGHTSEEING.............................

MARIENPLATZ AND AREA

Most visitors head first for Marienplatz, which is the crossroads, or center, of Munich. Medieval trade routes used to cross there; the action is still concentrated on the square. One can sink into a chair, owned by the municipality and therefore free, or pull up to a table in a chair owned by a cafe and order a little something. Then the fun begins, as the moving scene changes by the minute against a backdrop of medieval and modern buildings framing the square. As you look around you'll realize that there are no skyscrapers; just turrets and towers atop churches and palaces. In the center of the square soars the **Mariensaule,** which is a 1638 statue honoring the Virgin. The "Queen of Heaven" is constantly bestowing her blessing on the city.

In 1909 a glockenspiel was placed in a tower of the **New City Hall** *(Neu Rathaus).* A 15th-century tournament is replayed every day at 11:00 a.m. Copper figures that are larger than life-size become the stars of the show as the carillon music begins. Bavarian Duke Wilhelm V and Renata of Lorraine celebrate their wedding in 1568 as a parade of knights and trumpeters march around below them. Jousting begins with two mounted knights brandishing their lances.

One is dressed in the blue and white colors of Bavaria, the other in the red and white of Lorraine.

The opening below features folk dancers dressed in traditional costume. Their red jackets signify that they belong to the coopers' guild. In 1517 coopers danced through the streets to cheer the citizens who had lived through the Black Plague.

At the top perches the rooster who crows three times and flaps his wings. He is telling the town that all is well. Visitors' cameras continue to click until the performance is over.

Hofbrauhaus, once the court beer shop dates from 1589. Since 1830 the restaurant and beer hall has been open to the general public. Beer flows and the food is hearty.

St. Peter's Church was founded in 1050 and is the oldest parish church in Munich. Inside, the rococo style hits the eye with ornate gold decoration, including a sunburst. One can climb up the tower's 297 steps for a fine view.

The **Food Market** *(Viktualienmarkt)* is the place to go for all kinds of fruits, vegetables, meat, cheese, and other edibles. A blue and white maypole stands ready for annual festivity. Statues of six theater artists stand in the square. We were especially taken with one fountain sporting a man with his umbrella.

Twin onion domes, one of the symbols of Munich, top the **Church of Our Lady** *(Frauenkirche)* located west of Neues Rathaus. Although the red brick church was ravaged during World War II, it has been restored. Inside, the white nave soars upward on octagonal pillars to the reticulated vault. Although the interior is modern, the sculpture and paintings contrast *and* blend with it. Erasmus Grasser created the 24 carved wood busts of saints, prophets, and apostles. Original stained-glass windows have also been restored. The Princes of the House of Wittelsbach are buried in the crypt.

The **Church of St. Michael** *(Michaelskirche)* was built for Jesuits in 1583. Statues of Bavarian kings stand in the niches on the facade. The gable sculpture portrays Christ watching the victory of Otto in 955 at Lech. A bronze Archangel Michael stabs the dragon by the center doors. Ludwig II was buried in the crypt.

The **Palace** *(Residenz)* was inhabited by rulers of Bavaria who lived in the palace from the 14th century onward, each one building a little more until there were seven inner courts and a conglomerate of style.

The **Altes Residenztheater,** designed by Francois de Cuvillies, is the place where Mozart produced his opera *Idomeneo* for the first time. The **Opera House** *(Bayerisches Nationaltheater)* is there as well.

The **Hofgarten** was planned in 1613 by Heinrich Schon for Herzog Maximilian I in French style. Arcades and a temple are on the grounds. The **grave of the unknown soldier** by Bernhard Bleeker lies to the east. The **residence of the Bavarian president,** the Prinz Carl Palais, stands on the northeastern corner of Hofgarten. The **Academy of Fine Arts** is now housed in the building.

From the northeast corner you can cross over into the famous **English Garden,** which is a large park constructed from 1789 until 1795. This garden contains pavilions, such as the Chinese building, a Japanese teahouse, lakes, and the Monopteros Temple.

Oberewiesenfeld is the northwestern section of Munich, famous as the site for the 1972 Olympic Games. The television tower is the place to head for a view of the Olympic Village, the city, and the Bavarian Alps. The stadium seats 80,000. The village includes training areas, swimming pools, a cycling track, gymnasiums and an open air theater.

MUSEUMS

The **National Museum of Bavaria** *(The Bayerisches Nationalmuseum),* 3 Prinzregentenstrasse, contains Bavarian collections from the Middle Ages through the 18th century. Here is the place to see folk costumes, porcelain, gold, silver, armor, furniture, and Christmas nativity scenes. King Maximilian II started this museum with his personal collections.

Oskar von Miller founded the **Deutsches Museum** in 1903 and it opened in 1925. High ceilinged rooms house planes, early automobiles, and railway locomotives. It is one of the finest science and technology museums in the world, and visitors can see the latest developments in many areas. Working models provide a learning experience for all ages.

Glyptothek, 3 Konigsplatz, houses a world-famous Greek and Roman sculpture collection. The building was designed by Leo van Klenze in 1816 and restored in 1972. This building is a pleasure to visit, with its simple white brick walls inside and sculpture arranged with plenty of breathing space.

Across the square stands a neo-classical building built in 1838 and restored in 1967, which contains the equally impressive **State Collection of Antiquities** *(Antikensammlungen.)* Scholars from all over the world come to study Greek, Roman, and Etruscan artifacts, including bronzes, glass, jewelry, and terracotta.

The **Propylaea** on the west side of the square is a triumphal gateway copied from the Propylaea in the Acropolis in Athens. Crown Prince Ludwig traveled in the Mediterranean in 1817 and became enamored of Greek and Roman antiquity; hence the influence found in Konigsplatz Square.

Old Pinakothek *(Alte Pinakothek),* Barer Strasse 27, was designed by Leo von Klenze in Venetian Renaissance style. It contains the Wittelsbachs' paintings collected from the beginning of the 16th century. Paintings date from the 14th through the 18th centuries. This museum has the largest Rubens collection anywhere.

New Pinakothek *(Neue Pinakothek),* located next door, originally opened in 1846 as a contemporary museum; it was rebuilt by Alexander von Branca in 1981. Over 500 18th- to 20th-century paintings and sculptures are displayed in the new building.

DAY TRIPS FROM MUNICH...................

Schloss Nymphenburg

This former summer home of the Wittelsbach family dates from 1664. King Ludwig II of Bavaria was born in Nymphenburg in 1845. Ludwig and his brother Otto grew up in this lovely palace, which was then out in the country. The group of buildings is surrounded by a formal park of woods, streams, and lakes. The **Great Hall** *(Steinersaal),* the **semi-circular wings** reminiscent of Versailles, and the **Nymphenburg Porcelain Factory** on the north side are well worth a visit.

Amalienburg Palace is a baroque hunting lodge created by Francois Cuvillies for Princess Amelia. The circular **Hall of Mirrors** is a favorite with visitors.

Pagodenburg Pavilion was designed with Chinese design in an octagonal shape. A **Carriage Museum** houses 18th- and 19th-century coaches, broughams, and sedan chairs used by the Wittelsbachs. Karl VII's coronation coach is also there. The **Badenburg Bathing Pavilion** contains scenes of playful nymphs.

Schloss Herrenchiemsee

After Ludwig II's trip to Versailles, when he noted the lavish lifestyle of the French Bourbon monarchs in the 17th and 18th centuries, he was inspired to plan his new castle in similar style. Construction of Schloss Herrenchiemsee began in 1878 and by 1886 20 million marks had vanished. The facade looks like a replica and inside many of the rooms are larger than those at Versailles. The Hall of Mirrors contains a lovely Meissen fireplace.

The castle is perched on an island that is accessible only by boat. Visitors see the French formal gardens encircling the castle as they approach.

A museum in the palace tells the sad story of the mad King. At the age of 40 Ludwig was deeply in debt and thinking of suicide. His family moved to have him deposed and declared unfit to rule. He was taken to Schloss Berg, where he was last seen with his doctor by the lake. It has been surmised that they took out a boat and both drowned, although some say that he was murdered.

Garmisch-Partenkirchen

Prehistoric tribes, the Illyrians, first settled in this beautiful mountain setting followed by Celts and Romans who named their town Partanum. It became a market town in 1361 as well as a favorite stop along the trade route into Italy. Garmisch also became prosperous, and both towns were popular with the Dukes of Wittelsbach who built a castle there.

Today the large Bavarian murals painted on houses and hotels give Garmisch-Partenkirchen a warmth that visitors enjoy. And summer folk festivals provide the chance to see folk costumes worn by families for many years.

Churches are ornate with Bavarian rococo decoration, frescoes on the ceilings, and carved altars. **Alte Kirche** has been renewed with the removal of paint covering old frescoes. **St. Martinkirche** stands out with its carved and gilded altar. **Pfarrkirche** houses a number of paintings as well as panels behind the altars. **St. Antonkirche** is the pilgrim's church of the area, with Stations of the Cross on the way up to the church and a pieta inside.

The twin towns joined just before the Olympic Games of 1936 and have been considered Germany's major winter sports center. Heavy snowfall, even at an altitude of 2363 feet, provides excellent skiing all winter. The 1978 alpine skiing world championships were held there. The **Ski Stadium** *(Skistadion)* contains two runs for competition and two for practice. The **Olympic Ice Stadium** *(Olympia Eisstadion)* has three skating rinks for figure skating and ice hockey. Adjacent to that you will find five indoor and one outdoor swimming pool, as well as a solarium.

Germany's highest mountain, the **Zugspitze,** is one to reckon with in both winter and summer. Visitors can climb up the 9700 feet in summer or choose to ride up on a railway from Garmisch, transferring to a cable car from Schneefernerhaus. We spent an exhilarating day up there in late spring, crunching around on the snow and wishing we had time to join other skiiers. The air seems pristine and the sights enough to encourage any photographer.

Oberammergau

In 1632 a miracle occurred when the Black Plague halted its progress just before reaching Oberammergau; the inhabitants were safe until a villager who had been living away returned and without meaning to infected his own villagers. After 84 persons had died the inhabitants of the town vowed to offer a play honoring the Passion of Christ every 10 years if they were delivered from further deaths. The deaths ceased.

The Passion Play was presented first in 1634 and continued every ten years until 1674 when it was decided to schedule it at the beginning of each decade. The 17th-century script was rewritten in 1750, 1810, 1850, and in 1980. An additional year was added for a special anniversary celebration, in 1984, then the year 1990. The next year will be that of 2000. About 1700 actors participate in this day-long pageant, all of them residents of Oberammergau for at least 20 years.

The town is in an attractive setting in the Ammer valley, encircled by the foothills of the Ammergau Alps. People visit to enjoy winter sports as well as to visit a health spa. Frescoes decorate many of the walls in town. The **Heimatmuseum** contains woodcarving and carved nativity displays. The State School of Woodcarving is there, and many local residents are passionate woodcarvers.

Schloss Linderhof

King Ludwig II of Bavaria built his castle in Italian Renaissance and French rococo styles. Originally a farm within the Ettal monastery, then the home of the Linder family, Georg Dollmann built the castle for Ludwig II in 1870. There are portraits of Louis XIV, Madame du Barry, Madame de Pompadour, and Louis XV, as well as a hall of mirrors to see. The gardens contain pools, fountains, and a grotto similar to Capri's Blue Grotto with a royal boat that looks like a shell. There is a Moorish pavilion with a peacock throne and a temple of Venus. Inside the castle, the state bedroom is spectacular, with gold leaf and midnight-blue velvet.

Schloss Neuschwanstein

If you're ready for a look-alike Disneyland in Germany head for Neuschwanstein with its white turrets playing stair-steps. Ludwig II began building this, his dream castle, in 1869; it was not finished when he died in 1886. His favorite swan motif was used with flair, and there are painted reminders of the legends of Wagner's operas. The view from its perch provides visitors with a blend of lake, snowcapped peaks, gorges, and forests.

Schloss Hohenschwangau

This Neo-Gothic castle dates to the 12th century when it was built by the Swan Knights, whose family disappeared by the 16th century. During the Napoleonic Wars the castle was ravaged, later restored by King Maximilian II in 1832. Ludwig II lived there during his youth. A mural portrays Lohengrin, the famous knight who used swans as horses to pull his boat along. Ludwig became obsessed with swans and with Wagner, who played the piano for him at Hohenstaufen.

Augsburg

Augustus Caesar founded Augsburg in 14 B.C. The town became an important trading center on the route to Italy. By the Middle Ages it was a major banking center supporting the families of Fuggers and Welsers, among the wealthiest in the world at that time. In 1555 the Peace of Augsburg was signed there in an effort to allow Protestants freedom of worship.

The **Cathedral** *(Dom)* has some of the oldest stained-glass windows anywhere in the world, called **Windows of the Prophets.** Hans Holbein created the altar paintings.

The **Town Hall** *(Rathaus)* is a Renaissance structure dominated by two towers. The pediment features a pine cone, a symbol of fertility. Nearby stands the **Augustus Fountain** with bronze figures for German rivers. The **Perlach**

Tower was once a watchtower. A yellow flag flies when the Alps can be seen on a clear day.

An area known as **Fuggerei** was constructed in 1519 by Fugger the Rich to provide housing for the poor. Sixty-six gabled houses still stand on the eight streets in the area. Citizens who need a home stay there for a minimal rent—in exchange they pray for the souls of the founding fathers. The gates are closed every evening as they have been for many years.

Maximilian Museum, located in two burger's houses dating from the late 15th century, houses collections of sculpture, goldsmith's work, displays of the history of Augsburg, furniture, maps and documents.

Mozarthaus is the birthplace of Leopold Mozart, father of Wolfgang Amadeus Mozart.

GREECE

Currency unit • drachma (DR)
Language • Greek
Time difference from USA • seven hours later (Eastern Standard Time)
Telephone access codes • to USA 00 or USADirect 00–800–1311; from USA: 30
National Tourist Offices • **USA:** National Tourist Organization of Greece, 645 Fifth Ave., New York, NY 10022, tel.: (212) 421–5777; **Canada:** Greek National Tourist Organization, Upper Level, 1300 Bay St., Toronto, Ontario M5R3K8, Canada, tel.: (416) 968–2220; **Britain:** Greek National Tourist Organization, 4 Conduit St., London W1R ODJ, tel.: (071) 734–5997; **Greece:** Greek National Tourist Organization (E.O.T.) 2 Amerikis St., P.O. Box 1017, Athens GR-101 10, tel.: (01) 322–3111.
Airlines • **Olympic U.S.:** (800) 223–1226; **Britain:** (081) 846–9080
Embassies • **American Embassy,** 91 Vasilissis Sophias Blvd., 10160 Athens, Greece, tel.: 721–2951 or 711–8401; **British Embassy:** 1 Odos Ploutarchou, Athens, Greece 10675, telephone: 72 36 211

We have a special affinity for Greece because we have spent much of the last decade studying ancient seafaring in relation to the wanderings of the semi-historical hero, Odysseus. It has been fun to trace the routes of ancient mariners, including Odysseus, Menelaus, Agamemnon and Nestor as they plied the waters between islands, hoping to stay within sight of land. But our strongest early impression of Greece was ashore at the place most tourists head for, Delphi.

We spent a spring day of pure delight slowly exploring the archaeological sites and the museum. The delight emanated from the warm, clear day, the shapes of the trees, the abundance of blossoming flowers, and the uncanny quiet—all despite the arrival of many loaded tour buses. They were all there—Germans, Dutch, Italians, Austrians, English, Americans, Japanese, even a few Greeks—but the hillside of ruins seemed to contain them easily and noiselessly. Novelist John Fowles is right: there is a special, absolute quality to the silence one encounters at certain times and places in Greece, one that can absorb the noise of people and even of machines. Part of this effect is hillside acoustics, part your own imaginative perception of older civilizations that lasted far longer

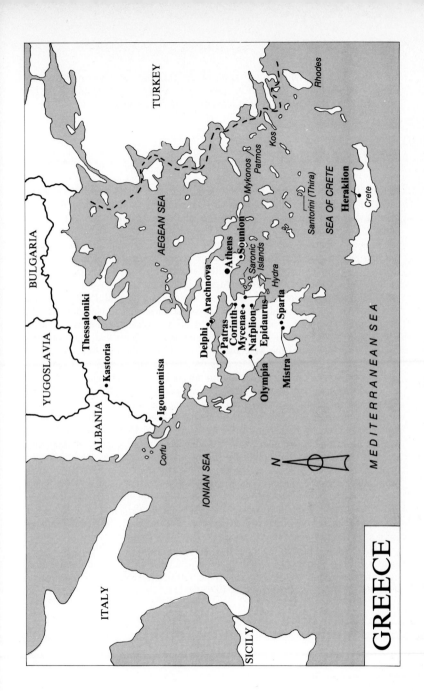

than ours probably will. So, in spite of the trappings of tourism in modern Delphi—all the hotels, shops, restaurants, and tour buses—the magic of the hill of the Oracle seems to survive, at least on beautiful spring days.

HISTORY....................................

A Neanderthal skull dating from the Stone Age was found near Salonika and caves in the Louros Valley indicate habitation from 4000 B.C. The House of Tiles at Lerna in the Argolid is typical of the early Bronze Age, from 2800–2000 B.C. Minoan civilization during the early Bronze Age can be explored at Knossos and Phaistos on Crete. The palaces on Crete were destroyed by earthquakes, but they were rebuilt in the same style. Minoans created branches of their civilization on Thera, Kythera, Rhodes, and Miletus. Later, palaces were built at Mycenae and Tiryns in the Argolid around 2000 B.C.

The Minoans were at the height of their power around 1550 B.C.; then Minoan sites were suddenly devastated. Some ancient historians attribute the destruction of Minoan civilization to the massive volcanic eruption of Thera, which blew a hole in the middle of the island and sent huge tidal waves toward Crete. Power passed to the Mycenaens who gained control of the colonies established by the Minoans, and Mycenae became the capital. Linear B, which is an early version of Greek, was found on tablets in Crete and Pylos.

According to oral tradition, each of the local rulers sent men and ships to fight in the Siege of Troy in about 1250 B.C.; the account was recorded by Homer in the *Iliad*. By 1200 B.C., Mycenean civilization had collapsed, perhaps through invasion by barbarians from the north called Dorians, who destroyed everything in their path, leaving the Myceneans without control of their own sea and cut off from each other by mountains. Five centuries later, after the Greek Dark Ages, Hellenic city-states were established, such as Athens, Corinth, and Sparta. Temples were constructed on top of the palaces at Mycenae, Tiryns, and Knossos. The Persian Wars took place in the early fifth century, and Athens succeeded in turning back much larger Persian forces. Classical civilization flourished in the fifth century B.C., particularly in Athens, but fell apart after the Peloponnesian Wars had ravaged the land.

Greece fell under Roman and Byzantine rule from the 2nd century B.C. to 1453 A.D. The Turks began their invasion of Greece in 1453 and continued to fight their way into Europe for many centuries. In 1830 Greece became an independent state, and a republic in 1974.

ATHENS

HISTORY..

According to myth, Athens has a long history with legendary kings dating back to Kekrops, who was part serpent and part man. He was known for introducing the alphabet, counting people, making laws, and advocating monogamy. While he was in control, Poseidon and Athena had a major battle over Attica; Athena won and planted an olive tree as a symbol of peace. Kekrops's tomb is reported to be under the Porch of the Caryatids in the Erechtheion. The 10th mythical king was Theseus, who lived during the 12th and 11th centuries B.C. He was known for killing the minotaur, which then stopped the required Athenian payment to King Minos of Crete. Theseus led an active life, fighting centaurs and Amazons, as well as snatching Helen from Sparta and taking her to Attica.

Athens grew during the 6th and 5th centuries B.C. under the leadership of Solon and then Peisistratos. The town expanded outside of the Acropolis area to include a lower town. At the end of the Persian Wars in 479 B.C., Pericles began to work on the reconstruction of Athens. The Propylaia, Parthenon, Erechtheion, and Temple of Athena Nike ascended in white Pentelic marble. The Peloponnesian War, which ended in 404 B.C., caused Athens to sink for a time. St. Paul brought Christianity to Athens in 53 A.D. Athens rose again and continued to thrive until sacked by the Saracens in the 12th century.

During the Crusades, Athens was passed around to invaders including the Turks who used the Parthenon as a powder magazine; unfortunately it was blown up in 1687. Otho of Bavaria, the son of Ludwig I of Bavaria, reigned with his queen, Amalia, from 1832. Otho created a city of straight streets and raised neoclassical style buildings including the Royal Palace.

SIGHTSEEING................................

THE ACROPOLIS

As with many sites containing ruins, we suggest wearing solid walking shoes. The terrain is very uneven, with lumps of stone and chunks of marble of all sizes to climb on and over.

Visitors enter through the Beule Gate, which was named after a French archaeologist who found the gate in 1852. Walk up a couple of flights of stairs to the **Temple of Athena Nike.** It was there that some say Aegeus, King of Athens, watched for his son, Theseus, to return home. It seems that every year, 14 Athenian men were sent as a sacrifice to the minotaur in Crete; Theseus chose to be one of them. His father made him promise to hoist white sails if he was successful in slaying the Minotaur; he forgot and Aegeus threw himself over the cliff in despair at losing his son.

The **Propylaia,** which was constructed by Mnesicles as a formal gateway between 437 and 432 B.C., is on several levels. It includes the propylon, or center section, and two asymmetrical wings. The northwestern wing once housed the art gallery, or *pinakotheke;* the southwestern wing contained a portico. Straight ahead up the hill to the left of the Sacred Way looms the **Erechtheion,** a small Doric and Ionic temple known for its caryatids.

The largest structure by far is the towering **Parthenon.** This Doric temple was built during the reign of Pericles and dedicated to Athena. A sculptured frieze of 525 feet portrays the Panathenaean Procession. Ninety-two sculptured metopes portray battles with giants, the Amazons, centaurs, and scenes from the Trojan War. Pedimental sculpture portrays the birth of Athena from the head of Zeus on the eastern side and a quarrel between Poseidon and Athena on the western pediment.

Today the Parthenon is in a state of preservation, with a great deal of controversy raging around the method. From the 1890s to the 1930s, architects tried to strengthen the Parthenon by adding iron clamps and rods. But they did not seal the irons, which rusted and caused the marble to crack with normal expansion and contraction of the iron. In addition, no one knew what the pollution of Athens would do in a few short years to the sculpture that had withstood everything else.

The **Erechtheion** was the first project completed in 1988. There, the rusty iron was replaced with titanium, which is rust-proof. The caryatids, almost destroyed by the polluted air, are in the Acropolis Museum (except for one in the British Museum) where they live in a glass case filled with nitrogen to preserve them from further deterioration. They have been replaced on the Erechtheion by plaster likenesses.

The Parthenon, eight times the size of the Erechthion, will take a great deal more effort. Because of the explosion in 1687 a lot of the stones are scattered around the building. The interior chamber, called the cella, will be completely rebuilt using stones from the original structure. In addition, the frieze and pediments are being removed and placed in the Acropolis Museum; marble replicas will take their place. Fifteen of the metope reliefs are in the British Museum and one is in the Louvre. When the Seventh Earl of Elgin was British Minister to Turkey he received permission to remove some of the sculptures and take them to the British Museum. Although there is a great deal of controversy about the ''Elgin Marbles'' and their proper home, those that have been

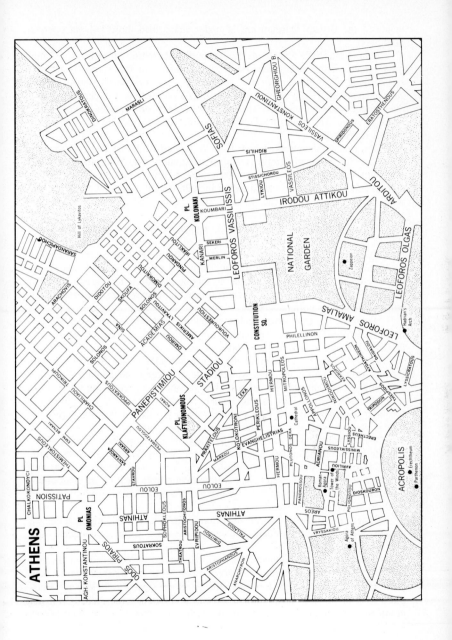

inside in the British Museum are in better shape than those left out open to pollution.

Behind the Parthenon stands the **Acropolis Museum,** which no one should miss—many of the pieces once decorating buildings of the Acropolis are preserved there. Two 6th-century B.C. pedimental sculptures depict Heracles (Hercules) slaying the Hydra and a lioness slashing a bull with two serpents observing the carnage. Another sculpture shows the battle between Heracles and the three-bodied Triton. The head of a Gorgon with her tongue sticking out dates from the 6th century B.C.

Don't miss the **sphinx,** which faces frontward while her body is turned to the side. Her enigmatic smile is almost beckoning. The **Rampin Horseman** rides with his original body and a replica head, as his real head is in the Louvre. Votive statues to Athena, called *Kore,* include beautiful almond-eyed maidens with mysterious smiles. The western side of the Parthenon frieze portrays Olympian gods in the Panathenaic procession.

North of the Acropolis spreads the **Agora,** once the center of Athens' religious, political, and social life. Evidence of life in the Agora dates back to Neolithic times, before 3000 B.C. The **Doric Temple of Hiphaistos** *(Hephaestus)* is also called the **Theseion.** Dating from 449 B.C. this temple is one of the best preserved in Greece. During the Byzantine period the temple was changed into St. George's Church, with a new entrance on the west end. The east portico still has its marble coffered ceiling.

Down the hill stands the **Tholos,** which is a round building where 50 public officials dined every day and conducted government business. A set of standard weights and measures were also kept there.

In 1956 King Paul dedicated the **Agora Museum** in the **Stoa of Attalos.** Dating from 159 B.C., the Stoa was the site of trading and promenading, and watching the Panathenaic Procession. The building was reconstructed in 1953 using limestone from Piraeus and Pentelic marble. Burial offerings from the Neolithic Age and Bronze Age include an ivory griffin devouring a deer. A bronze head of Nike and a headless statue of Apollo are there.

Not far away stands the **Roman Market,** where daily business took place. Its entrance is on the east end near the **Tower of the Winds,** called the Horologion (clock) of Andronikos Kyrrhestes, which is a well preserved octagonal building. Reliefs near the top depict wind blowing from each of the eight directions indicated on the compass. A bronze weathercock shaped like a triton used to stand on top of the tower.

Hadrian's Library, located next door, was a large building containing a theater, a library, and a garden. The central room was a library complete with depressions for manuscripts.

The **Theater of Dionysos** *(Theatro Dionissou)* is located down the hill almost under the Acropolis on the north side. Dionysiac festivals have taken place since the 6th century B.C. and still do. Sophocles, Aeschylus, and Euripides were involved in the production of classical drama there. Athenians loved drama and would take a holiday to travel in the early morning from their homes to be on time for a performance. The tiers of seats in this theater are in remarkably good condition, enhanced by odd pieces of stone lying around where they fell.

The **Odeon of Herod Atticus** *(Odio Irodou Atikou)* was originally built by Herod Atticus in 161 B.C. Part of the skene, or stage, still survives. This two and three-story backdrop provides a perfect frame for evening performances with lights playing on its shadows. The theater has been completely renovated and the Athens Festival is held there every summer.

Hadrian's Arch *(Pili Adrianou)* is a large free-standing gate built of Pentelic marble to honor the Emperor Hadrian. Statues once stood in the upper frames of the arch. When it was built in 131 B.C. the arch separated the new Roman city, Hadrianopolis, from the old Greek city. An inscription on one side reads: "This is Athens, the ancient city of Theseus"; the other reads: "This is the city of Hadrian, not of Theseus."

The **Olympieion** *(Naos Olimpiou Dios)* is the largest temple ever built for Zeus on mainland Greece. The building was begun in 515 B.C., then stopped until 174 B.C. when the Syrian King Antiochus IV Epiphanes changed the style from Doric to Corinthian. Work stopped after his death and Hadrian finished it in 131. Fifteen of the original columns still stand. The view of the Plaka and the Acropolis is worth the trip up there.

The **Stadium** *(Stadio)* has been completely restored and can seat 70,000 persons. Lycurgus planned the Stadium in the 4th century B.C. and Herod Atticus rebuilt it in 144. For many years it lay under a wheatfield until it was reconstructed in 1896 for the Olympic Games. A tunnel at one end may have been used for animals in Roman performances.

Philopappos Hill *(Lofos Filopapou)* was dedicated to the muses and is sometimes called the *Mouseion*. Travelers who climb up the hill will pass troglodyte cave-dwellings, including one said to be the place where Socrates was kept. He could have escaped but chose not to, finally drinking hemlock. The **Philopappos Monument** honors an exiled Roman prince who was also a benefactor of Athens. Reliefs on the facade depict the Prince standing in his chariot.

Lycabettos *(Likavitos),* also called the wolves' hill, rises for 909 feet up to the chapel of St. George. This hill is about three times the height of the Acropolis and can be ascended by funicular railway, or by car as far as the open-air theater. Legend reports that Athena carried the large rock of Lycabettos on her way to the Acropolis, but when she heard that Aglauros and Herse had defied her and opened the chest containing Erechtheus, the rock slipped out of her hands.

Museums

The **National Archaeological Museum** *(Ethniko Archeologiko Moussio),* 1 Tossitsa, is the place to go to see relics from ruins you have been climbing around in Greece. In 1876, Heinrich Schliemann the German archaeologist, began excavating several sites, and many of his finds are in this museum. As he removed a brilliant gold mask, Schliemann said that he had gazed upon the face of Agamemnon; however, scholars point out that this mask probably belonged to a king who lived four centuries earlier.

Classical art includes a bronze statue of Poseidon, which was found in the ocean off Cape Artemision near Euboia. He stands, strong and sturdy, ready to throw his triton (which is no longer in his hand). His sightless eyes once held ivory eyeballs. The Jockey of Artemision rides his bronze horse as they gallop away with vigor. This 2nd-century B.C. bronze was also found off Cape Artemision.

The **Santorini frescoes** are found on the second floor. Professor Marinatos discovered them in the 1970's and they were moved into this museum for safe keeping. Cycladic life is portrayed by a fisherman with his catch, two boys boxing with each other, a spring scene, and a painting of the fleet with cities in the background.

Antonis Benaki, who died in 1954, had collected both Greek and Asian art; the collection is displayed in his mansion, **Benaki Museum,** Vassilissis Sophias & Koubari sts. His Greek art includes jewelry from Thessaly in filigree and enamel. Two gold cups from 3000 B.C. came from Euboia. Byzantine jewelry and icons include two icons said to have been created by El Greco. Chinese ceramics from the T'ang dynasty are displayed on the second floor.

Downstairs, Greek costumes are on display, as well as embroidery and traditional jewelry. Wooden carvings from the Ottoman period are there as well.

Byzantine Museum, 22 Vassilissis Sophias, is a residence of the Duchess of Plaisance, Sophie de Marbois, who was a member of the French aristocracy. Religious artifacts are placed in rooms that look like chapels or churches. 18th- and 19th-century folk artists once had their work displayed in now abandoned churches out in the country; some of it is has been collected in the Byzantine Museum.

The icon collection in this museum contains a 14th-century mosaic icon from Bithynia which portrays the Virgin Mary and Child, a wood-carved relief of St. George from Kastoria, the Crucifixion from Thessaloniki, and one of the Archangel Michael.

Plaka

The Plaka is the place to stroll through narrow streets, exploring squares, Byzantine churches, shops and tavernas. Greek cuisine and music makes the place very popular at night.

DAY TRIPS FROM ATHENS ·················

Attica is the name given to the area surrounding Athens. The word comes from the Greek word *akte,* which means where the waves break, or peninsula. The entire peninsula, down to Sounion and over to the Euboea channel is included in Attica.

SOUTHEAST OF ATHENS
Sounion

Cape Sounion is the place to go for a beautiful sunset; we drove down while watching a full moon rise. It took longer than we expected, with all of the undulations of the road along the coast. When we arrived the site was closed, but we could still enjoy the twelve Doric columns of the **Temple of Poseidon,** which is what we wanted.

On the way back we stopped for dinner in a taverna with tables right on the water. A family near us gathered around a table, eating and watching the World Cup on a little TV perched on top of their car. The sea was on one side and the world of sports on the other.

Ancient sailors rounding the cape could look up at the dazzling white temple and realize their ship was almost home, or they could wave good-bye on an outbound voyage. The rocky headland rises 197 feet, and the height adds to the majesty of the standing columns. Lord Byron wrote about Sounion and even carved his name on one of the pillars.

SOUTHWEST OF ATHENS
Piraeus

Piraeus has been the port of Athens since ancient times. In 493 B.C., Themistocles moved Athens' harbor from Phaleron, where the wind hit it dead on, to Piraeus. After the Corinth Canal opened in 1893, the port of Athens became very busy.

Ferries and cruise ships dock there, waiting to take passengers to the Greek islands. There are actually six harbors, including Kendriko Limani, Alon, Herakles, Kolpos Elefsinas, Zea, and Mikrolimano. The yacht basins in the latter two house a changing scene of pleasure vessels of all sizes and types.

The **Hellenic Maritime Museum** is one of our favorite museums anywhere, partly because of our own research and development of the Odyssey Project over the last ten years. Founded in 1949, the museum houses a variety of artifacts, mementoes, and displays portraying the history of Greek seafaring.

If you have seen the **Attican urn** in the British Museum portraying Odysseus voluntarily tied to the mast of his ship so that he could hear the sweet song of the sirens without being mesmerized by them, you will already know what some of the ancient vessels looked like. The Hellenic Museum has many models of ancient vessels.

The museum houses a large model collection of merchant ships, sailing ships and steamships. On display is a rare model of Admiral Nelson's flagship

Victory, which was made by French prisoners out of bone during the Napoleonic Wars.

WEST OF ATHENS
Dafni Monastery

The most important Byzantine site in Athens is Dafni Monastery, built on the site of a shrine honoring Apollo Daphnios. The name came from the bay laurel, daphne, which was a favorite with the god. When built in the 5th century, the monastery had a basilica. A new church was constructed in the 11tth century in octagonal shape with a large dome. The mosaic work includes a sternly staring Christ as Pantocrator in the dome, Christian saints and prophets around the drum of the dome, and the Virgin Mary surrounded by archangels in the apse.

EXCURSIONS FROM ATHENS..............

Delphi

Trying to describe ancient Delphi leaves one at a loss for the right words to capture the amalgam of impressions that make a visit memorable. The setting is beautiful, with varying shades of green in the olive trees and cypresses, and wild flowers among the ruins, all cradled in a valley protected by a crescent of soaring rock behind Delphi. The mountains all around on the other sides complete a perfect circle; this "center of the earth" is magnificent. The entire scene looks like a giant amphitheater, with Delphi isolated from the rest of the world, a perfect shrine. Variations in light change the intensity of the red color in the rock throughout the day. Mount Kirfis stands behind with the two red cliffs, Rodina and Flambouko, and the valley filled with olive trees. Below all is the pure blue of the Gulf of Itea.

From early times, a number of deities were worshiped at Delphi, including the Earth Goddess, Gaea, Themis, Demeter, Poseidon, Python (the son of Gaea), Apollo, and Pythius. Pythius, through the Priestess Pythia, gave cryptic prophecies to those who came to seek wisdom from the Oracle, and by the 6th century B.C., Delphi had become an international diplomatic center, which led to the building of many temples and treasuries.

In terms of planning your time, you can reach the top section of the ruins in about 30 minutes, with a few stops to catch your breath. We spent several hours up there, then walked down slowly to explore the **Sanctuary of Apollo,** the **theater,** the **stadium,** the **Temple of the Pronaia Athena,** and the **Palestra.** After a leisurely lunch in a taverna, we returned to spend most of the afternoon in the museum, which contains many fragments and a magnificent bronze charioteer from 478 B.C.

The Peloponnese

The Peloponnese *(Peloponissos)* looks like a large maple leaf, with graceful inward swoops inbetween sharply pointed headlands and points. Rugged mountains rise on this peninsula, making inland travel, especially in the south, difficult. Many of the little villages along the shore depend on contact by sea only. We found the perfect, pure Greek, undeveloped village of **Yeraki** *(Gerakas),* which we entered by boat. There were no tourists in this idyllic place as the existing roads on the map are infinitesimally tiny.

We climbed up the hill to the **acropolis,** wearing long pants after plenty of scratched legs on our last hike, and found one cyclopean wall after another, with large sections almost intact. In fact, much of the outer walls remain in place. These walls were made from huge blocks of stone cut straight across or five-sided, with a peak at one end. The British School explored them in 1905 and concluded that they date from Mycenean times of the Middle Helladic period. The site was peaceful, with cicadas, katydids, and grasshoppers rasping away, wind fluttering the olive leaves, and a brilliant sun beating down on the scene. We sat on the walls and watched waves crashing on the rocks far below; the sound swished around in our heads long after we went back to the real world.

As luck would have it we were still on board getting dressed for dinner when the ferry came in. It backed up to the pier a few feet from us, and let down the gangway. A huge crowd assembled to watch. Some people got on, with their plastic bags and suitcases, and a few got off. Lots of people lined the rail above the car deck; colored lights glowed above their heads. As the ferry got ready to leave, lines were thrown off and it went out into the harbor. We watched it steam around the corner and disappear from sight.

The moon was almost full, shining on the water setting a romantic scene. Tables, covered with plastic, were set outside the taverna on the harbor. Greek music boomed from a tape deck set in the doorway. Families came together for dinner; one next to us had three little boys relishing their meal.

Most tourists are familiar with the rich ruins on the Peloponnese; many historical cities lie within a small driving range. Day tours leave from Athens, but we suggest spending several days on the Peloponnese to see a number of sites.

Corinth

Ancient Corinth dates from the Neolithic Period, 5000–3000 B.C. Ruins include the **Agora,** with some walls of its shops remaining, the **Fountain of Peirene,** the **Bema,** where the Apostle Paul spoke to the Corinthians, and the **ancient theater.** The museum contains many statues, but unfortunately, few of them have heads.

No trip to Corinth is complete without a visit to the canal. The walls are 260 feet high and the canal is four miles long and 27 yards wide. Cutting this canal through solid rock took a number of tries from 1882 until 1893. When it was finished, Piraeus became the most important port in Greece.

We stood on the bridge, shaking with every truck or bus that rumbled over. A tug pulled its ship against the current, moving through the canal at a very slow pace. Waiting for the ship gave us plenty of time to look at the layers of the walls—from marine sand on top, to clay and limestone farther down.

Mycenae

"Mykenai, the strong-founded citadel," as described in Homer's *Iliad,* is an impressive site on a hill, with barren mountains beyond. This "City of Agamemnon" has a sense of peace and quiet. The rustling of wind through the trees and grasses moves visitors to settle on a rock, or the ground, and drink in the quiet beauty of the place.

We found it strange to feel so peaceful there, considering the violent past of the house of Atreus. Legend reports that Atreus murdered his nieces and nephews and served them for dinner to their own father, Thyestes. The gods were so enraged that they took it out on Atreus's son, Agamemnon, after he returned from the Trojan War. Agamemnon's wife, Clytemnestra, and her lover Aegisthus killed him. His death was avenged by his son Orestes.

The main entrance to Mycenae is through the **Lion Gate,** which was shaped by hammer and saw into four immense conglomerate blocks. The two lions carved on the stone over the gate are thought to be the oldest remaining sculpture in the western world. Unfortunately, the heads of the lions have been lost. Lions are the symbol for the royal dynasty of Mycenae; they are set in stone to guard the family, probably members of the House of Agamemnon.

The first circle of **Royal Tombs** is located just inside the Lion Gate. A double row of stones date from the 16th century B.C. Heinrich Schliemann began to dig on the site in 1876, finding six shaft graves that held nine women, eight men, and two children.

The **palace,** dating from the 15th century B.C., is large and constructed in three sections. The **megaron** is a royal room containing a round hearth in the middle, which was once topped by four pillars under the roof.

On the other side of the hill, steps lead down to the **sally port,** which could be a handy exit or entrance for the inhabitants. Myceneans could dash out to intercept intruders in a surprise attack.

The **Tomb of Clytemnestra,** dating from 1220 B.C. lies near the entrance to the area on the left. A passageway leading to the tomb is impressive, with large stone blocks still in good condition.

Tiryns

"Tiryns of the huge walls," or "wall-girt Tiryns," as described in Homer's *Iliad,* was built on a hill beside the sea. Today it lies 59 feet higher than the plain that surrounds it, next to a road, railroad tracks, and a prison. Legend claims that Tiryns was built by seven Cyclops from Lycia in Asia, to help Proetus, the King of Tiryns. They were the only beings who could lift such heavy stones, some weighing 14 tons.

Invaders found it difficult to enter Tiryns, as they passed up an inclined ramp to a pair of thick stone towers. The ramp may have been constructed for use by animals pastured outside, as well as chariots. Even if they were able to crash through this section, they could be picked off easily by guards from above.

One of the most intact structures is a curved, crescent-shaped staircase that descends outside the wall to a source of water, crucial in times of siege. Any invaders could be removed easily as they came up the stairs. If they did reach the top, there was a clever device waiting for them. A well, seven meters deep, was covered with a wooden lid, which could be removed suddenly, throwing invaders to their deaths. A gate and square tower could further daunt anyone who got that far.

Epidaurus

Epidaurus (*(Epidavros)* is well known for housing the best preserved theater in the ancient world. Polykleitos the Younger created the theater during the 4th century B.C. Fifty-five rows of seats shaped in a semi-circle all provide perfect sound and vision. We climbed to the top row and listened as someone spoke from the center of the circular stage. Then we tried a number of other seats until we were convinced that rumors were true—there isn't a bad seat in the house. Classical Greek performances are given there during the summer.

The **Sanctuary of Asklepios,** who was the god of healing, dates from the 4th century B.C. A Doric temple was designed by Theodotos. Sick patients came to take a cure and to rest, hoping to become healthy; they lived in a dormitory called the Abaton. Some say that harmless snakes were let loose during the night in the hopes that their presence would heal the sick. The Tholos, a circular building, contained concentric circles in a labyrinth pattern. It has been said that patients were supposed to crawl in the dark until they encountered healing serpents.

Nauplion

Nauplion *(Nafplion or Nafplio)* is a village set on a peninsula on the Argolic Gulf. We spent a lot of time sitting in one of the *tavernas* in the harbor, watching the boat traffic as well as local goings on.

According to legend, Poseidon's grandson Nauplios was the founder of Nauplion. His descendant Palamedes was a busy man, who invented some of the letters of the Greek alphabet, games of dice, knucklebones, the science of navigation, and lighthouses. He was also a doctor and astronomer. Odysseus and Diomedes killed Palamedes during the Trojan War.

Palamedes Fort dates from the Venetian occupation in 1711. 857 steps up lead to the Fort; there is also a road. Eight bastions with watchtowers and secret passages encircles the Fort. Views from the parapet walk includes the harbor of Nauplion, the bay, the Argolid plain, the coastline of the Peloponnese, and another fortified complex, which is the island of Bourdzi.

The citadel **Acronauplia** has walls of polygonal Greek style, then Frankish, and finally Venetian, influences. Views from the citadel include the harbor, the bay, and Palamedes Fort.

HUNGARY

Currency unit • Hungarian forint (FT)
Language • Hungarian
Time difference from USA • six hours later (Eastern Standard Time)
Telephone access codes • to USA: 00 (await second dial tone) 36 0111; from USA: 011 36 1
National Tourist Offices • **USA:** Ibusz Hungarian Travel Company, North American Division, One Parker Plaza, Suite 1104, Fort Lee, NJ 07024, tel.: (201) 592–8585; **Hungary:** Ibusz head office, 1075 Budapest VII, Tanacs krt. 3/c, tel.:142–3140; **Britain:** Ibusz Hungary, Conduit Street 6, London W1R 9TG, tel.: (071) 493–0263
Airlines • **Malev USA** (800) 223–6884 or (212) 757–6480; **Budapest:** 184–333; **Britain** (071) 439–0577
Embassies • **American Embassy:** v. Szabadsag Ter 12, 1054 Budapest, Hungary, tel.: 112–6450 or 112–6451; **British Embassy:** Harmincad Utca 6 Budapest VI, tel.: 182–888

My husband thinks of Hungary in topographic terms, especially the importance of water in a totally landlocked country—the broad Danube that separates the rolling hills of the west from the great plains of the east, huge but shallow Lake Balaton, and the profusion of mineral springs gushing up throughout the country.

HISTORY......................................

Celts settled in Hungary by the last few centuries B.C., but in 10 A.D. the Romans invaded and established their province of Pannonia (now known as Transdanubia, which is south and west of the Danube). There was a Roman settlement at Aquincum, the site of present-day Budapest. A series of invaders included the West Goths in 408, and Attila and his Huns in 451. Magyars invaded in 896, using the Danube Basin as a base from which to raid Europe.

In 1000, Stephen I was crowned the first king and patron saint of Hungary. Hungary was a powerful state during feudal times; its area included Transylvania, now in Romania, and Croatia, now in Yugoslavia. Mattias Corvinus ruled from 1458 to 1490, during the Golden Age of the Renaissance. Beatrice of Aragon, his second wife, brought Italian scholars and artists to Hungary.

By 1526 the Turks had demolished the Hungarian army. They occupied Buda in 1541, and controlled the country for 145 years. Other armies in Europe helped Hungary to overcome the Turks, who finally left in 1686. The Habsburgs ruled Hungary for 200 years, gaining land and power through strategic marriages and wise leadership. In 1740 Maria Theresia came to the throne; her 40-year reign brought both administrative and financial reform to Hungary. By 1867 the Austro-Hungarian Monarchy came into power and promoted a joint effort toward industrial development.

In 1941 Hungary joined Nazi Germany in an attempt to regain former territories and people, but in fact, more of Hungary's land was lost to Czechoslovakia, Yugoslavia, and Romania following World War II. The Soviet Union liberated Hungary in 1945, and large estate owners saw their land parceled out to peasants, as Communist and Social Democratic ideologies combined. Further, conflict between Bela Kun's socialist government and counterrevolutionary fighters resulted in devastation for the Hungarian people. By 1956 a rebellion was imminent as Prime Minister Nagy proclaimed that Hungary should renounce the Warsaw Pact and thereafter be neutral. The Soviet Army invaded and demolished the rebellion, and Hungary regained its independence only when the Warsaw Pact began falling apart thirty years later.

BUDAPEST

HISTORY......................................

The Danube River divides Buda, the old historic section, from Pest, which is more recent and commercial. Eight bridges span the river; all were rebuilt after they were bombed during World War II. The **Bridge of Chains,** first connecting Buda and Pest in 1849, is lit at night by small bulbs on its graceful suspension wires.

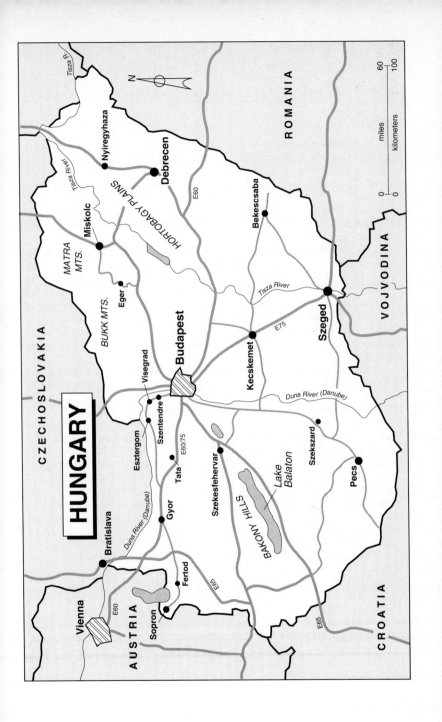

SIGHTSEEING..

BUDA

The Castle District on the right bank of the Danube is called Varhegy; most of the historic sites and monuments are there. Unfortunately the German Army used this high ground as headquarters so the 1944–45 siege left the area destroyed. There was one compensating advantage however; archaeologists were then able to sift through the area's ruins and distinguish different layers of civilization. Work progressed slowly in order to restore accurately remains buried under 20 feet of rubble. Now old walls and ramparts have reemerged and they have been reconstructed with great care.

Cars are not allowed on Castle Hill, although taxis and the no. 16 bus scoot up there. Visitors can also ascend on the funicular, which was originally built in 1870, destroyed during the war, and then rebuilt by May, 1986. It glides up almost 96 meters, carrying eight passengers per car.

Forever facing the Danube River *(Donau)*, the statue of Prince Eugene of Savoy on horseback greets visitors in front of the Royal Palace *((Budai Var)* of Buda Castle. Prince Eugene was a 17th-century army commander who saved Hungary from the Turks. The terrace provides a panoramic view of Pest across the river.

The neo-baroque structure containing the Royal Palace and museums was designed by Miklos Ybl, who followed plans laid out by Alajos Hauszmann; it was under construction from 1890 to 1903. After World War II, a number of medieval sections of the old castle were uncovered and restored.

Visitors enter into the center of the building, which houses the **National Gallery** *(Nemzeti Galeria)*. Hungarian art on display ranges from medieval stone carvings, Gothic paintings, and carving from the 14th and 15th centuries, renaissance and baroque art up to 1800, and 19th- and 20th-century works of art. Masters Mihaly Munkacsy, Laszlo Paal, Szinyei Merse, and Csontvary are well represented in the collection. Concerts are held in the gallery. We were especially impressed by the 15th-century large, golden, wooden figures of the Virgin Mary, St. Peter, and St. John. Gigantic 16th-century triptychs with lots of gold, gothic spires on top, and carved wooden figures with ancient wormholes are on display. A 15th-century wooden pieta expresses tender Mother/Son feelings.

Walk up wide marble stairs to the top floor to see a collection of Hungarian sculpture. You'll come face to face with a fisherman created by Somogyi called *Navvy,* as well as Kerenyi's *The Rape of Europe,* which looks like a huge Russian bear with a woman lying on top, and Svervatiusz's *The Burning Throne,* which is a grotesque partial skeleton in bronze of Gyorgy Dozsa, who was burned alive on a throne of red-hot iron. On the next floor down there are collections by Karoly Ferenczy, Reti, Grunewald, Utiz, Perlmutter, and Koszta.

The south wing houses the **Budapest History Museum** *(Budapesti Torteneti Muzeum,* which contains Gothic statues and ruins of the medieval royal

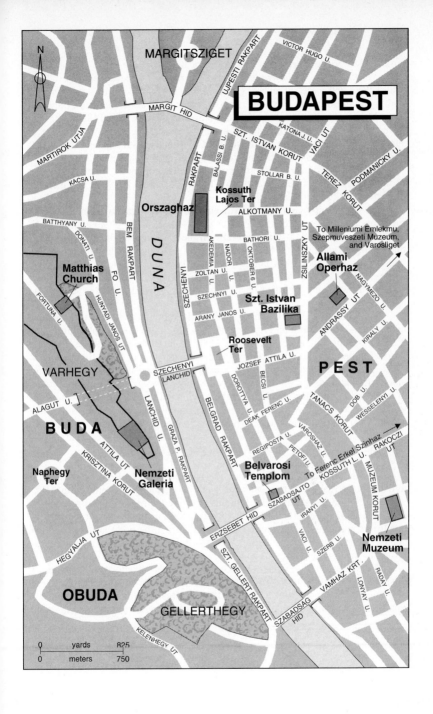

palace. Here visitors can trace 2000 years of history of the castle and of Budapest. Walk down to a labyrinthian series of rooms to see collections of grotesque faces and pieces of arches, green tile pieces of a decorative stove complete with a new tall replica, clay pots, ancient armor and sword, the coat-of-arms of King Matthias on carved stone doors, a panel of cherubs from 1480–1490 with different expressions on their faces, headless statues, the seals of the Court of Justice, and a chapel. The **Medieval Hall of the Knights** captures the feel of the past. Choral musical performances are given in the palace on Sundays.

The **National Library** *(Szechenyi Konyvtar),* comprises the western wing of the building. It contains over two million books about Hungary and includes everything written in Hungarian.

The north wing contains the **Museum of the Hungarian Labour Movement,** including items from the Worker's Movement and a photo collection.

Don't miss the **Matthias fountain** on the wall in a courtyard. King Matthias enjoyed walking and hunting incognito. According to legend he was invited home to dinner by a hunter, met the daughter Ilonka, and fell in love without telling her he was king. She happened to see him ride by in Buda, realized he was king and died of a broken heart. When he went to see her the house was empty.

The Church of Our Lady, **Matthias Church,** dates to the 13th century when it was first built in French Gothic style. It was a mosque during the Turkish occupation, almost ruined in 1686 when Buda was under seige, and restored in neo-Gothic style by Frigyes Schulek beginning in 1873. Burial crowns, rings, and a cross belonging to King Bela III, who died in 1196, and his wife, Anne of Chatillon, are on display there. A tiny copy of the Gospel was found in an enamel chest, the encolpium; it also belonged to King Bela. The surprise in this church is that every inch is covered in small geometric patterns of many colors. Don't miss the unique non-concentric window with a stained-glass lamb decorating it. The **Treasury Museum** houses a collection of vestments, chalices, and other church treaures. An orchestra plays during High Mass on Sundays.

Outside, on Szentharomsag Ter, the baroque **Trinity Column** stands tall to express the thanks of those who survived the plague. It was erected in 1712.

The **Hilton Hotel** has melded into its structure the ruins of the oldest church on Castle Hill, dating from the 13th century. Dominican friars built the church; one tower and ruins of the church still stand. Inside the hotel visitors can look out on the chapel and walk around the cloisters where ancient pieces are attached to the wall and arches.

The statue of St. Stephen on horseback stands next to the **Fisherman's Bastion,** the entrance to the palace complex from the river side. The first king of Hungary, he lived from 977 to 1038. The **Bastion,** or *Halaszbastya,* is a handsome set of white stone towers connected by a series of arches; one round tower contains a cafe.

Continuing north in the Castle District, the **Museum of Musical History,** on Tancsics Mihaly, contains musical instruments and music medals of Hungary. Beethoven stayed in 1800 when playing in Buda, and Bela Bartok's workshop is there as well. Right next door stands the building containing the dungeon where Lajos Kossuth was imprisoned for three years; he led a revolt in 1848 to unseat the Habsburgs.

The Square of St. John Capistrano, *Kapisztran Ter,* once was the site of the Gothic Church of St. Mary Magdalene. The tower, now restored, is all that remains.

The **Museum of Military History** traces military development from feudal times, the Bourgeois revolution and war of liberation in 1849, the Austro-Hungarian Monarchy, and World War I.

Part of the enjoyment of the Castle District is coming upon older buildings that survived the war. Some of the most interesting are numbers 29–31, 32–33 and 61–66 on Uri utca and, number 14 on Tarnok utca. Original painted walls remain. Some of the houses have Gothic seats in their gateways. Streetlamps from the past set the stage during the evening.

Squeezed between Castle Hill and the river is a narrow section that once held many old houses separated by cross streets or flights of steps up the hill; unfortunately, many of the houses have been destroyed. A promenade runs along the river, and **Main Street,** or *Fo Utca,* begins at Chain Bridge.

The **tomb of Gul Baba,** a dervish and poet, stands in **Mosque** *(Mecset)* utca. Four windows in the shape of ovals were placed in his stone tomb. This has been a place of pilgrimage for Turks for many years. It will be the site of an Islamic Center. Bela Bartok's house on Csalan ut 29 contains exhibits.

Gellert Hill, or *Gellerthegy,* is now a park that overlooks the city. During the 11th century the Venetian missionary Bishop Gellert was martyred there by being tossed off the hill. A fortress was built in 1854 by Austrians to help them maintain control of the restive Hungarians. The huge statue of a soldier was erected to commemorate Soviet soldiers who died in the fight to free Hungary in 1945. In 1956 it was removed during the revolt against Hungarian Stalinism, but a replacement was put up in 1957.

Gellert Hill is a good place to view some of Budapest's eight bridges. Retreating Nazis blew them all up in a senseless act of destruction. To the south Petofi Bridge joins the Buda and the Pest sides of the Grand Boulevard.

The **Liberty Bridge,** or *Szabadsaghid,* stands at the bottom of Gellert Hill. **Elizabeth Bridge,** or *Erzsebethid,* is a single arched suspension bridge, the last to be rebuilt (in 1964). A statue of the Empress Elisabeth, wife of Franz Josef, sits near the bridge. The **Chain Bridge,** or *Lanchid,* was originally designed in 1839 by William Clark, who designed London's Hammersmith Bridge. **Margaret Bridge,** or **Margit,** lies at the southern end of Margaret Island. It takes a jog to the north in the center to connect with the island itself. On the other end of the island stands **Arpad Bridge,** which is the only way for cars to reach the island. There is a railway bridge on both the southern and the northern end of these bridges.

MARGARET ISLAND

Margaret Island is a 2.5 km/1.5-mile-long island containing two thermal hotels, a large park and swimming pools. Thermal water spouts into a number of baths and hotels offer programs for health and treatments for various conditions of the skin and joints. The island was named after Margit, daughter of King Bela IV. He sent her to a new Dominican convent (where she died at age 28) to honor his pledge after the country was saved from the Mongols. Visitors enjoy pedaling on four-seater pedal bicycles two by two.

PEST

Pest is the larger of the two halves of Budapest, stretching out over the Great Hungarian Plain. Once a walled city, Belvaros, the inner medieval part of the city is still the commercial and government center. Three ring roads form concentric semicircles around Pest.

Near the Chain Bridge, statues of two great leaders stand in Roosevelt Square. Count Istvan Szechenyi and Ferenc Deak both lived on this square and now stand there for all time. Szechenyi generously gave up a year of his income in order to build the Academy of Sciences on the square. Ferenc Deak was responsible for the Compromise of 1867.

The **Parish Church of the Inner City** *(Belvarosi Templom)*, V. Marcius 15, began life as a 12th-century Romanesque structure. It now has Gothic, Turkish, and baroque overtones. The chancel is Gothic, and a Muslim prayer niche, the *Mihrab,* is a reminder of Turkish occupation. Chapels contain renaissance altars and red marble tabernacles. Franz Liszt, who lived nearby between 1867 and 1875, played the organ in the church.

Pest's largest church, **St. Stephen Basilica** *(Szt. Istvan Bazilika)*, has a neo-renaissance dome that can be seen all over the city; it rises to a height of 312 feet. Hungary's first king, St. Stephen (Svent Istvan) reigned during 1001–1038. His Carrarra marble statue stands in the center of the high altar. Bronze reliefs portray his life. A painting by Gyula Benczur shows St. Stephen giving his crown to the Virgin Mary before he died. He asked her to protect Hungary. Saint Stephen's right hand is kept as a treasured relic in the rear chapel.

The **State Opera House** *(Allami Operahaz)*, Nepkoztarsasag Utja 22, was built in the 19th century in Italian-Renaissance style. The architect was Miklos Ybl. The **National Ballet School** is located in Drechsler Palace across the street. The **Ferenc Erkel Theater** is the other opera house in Budapest; it is also used as a theater and concert hall.

To the south, the **National Museum** *(Nemzeti Muzeum)*, Muzeum Korut 14-16, contains a major collection of Hungarian artifacts dating back to prehistoric times. Stone, bronze, and iron pieces are on display along with Roman antiquities. The history of Hungary from the 9th century onward is one of the permanent displays. In 1848 Sandor Petofi read his revolutionary poem, *The National Song,* there, as he incited citizens to overpower the Habsburgs. The

crown jewels, held by the United States for safe keeping from 1945 until 1978, are now in the Hall of Honor. An enormous Byzantine crown dates from the 12th century. The gold rim is brilliant, with precious gems, pearls, and cloisonne plates. The top part is ornate with gold filigree and enamel plates. The crimson silk coronation robe is embroidered with gold threads. The head of the scepter is rock crystal and the orb gold-plated bronze.

Near the Chain Bridge stands **Parliament** *(Orszaghaz),* which presents itself in duplicate, mirrored in the waters of the Danube. This building reminds us of Parliament in London; in fact, it was modeled after it. The halls on the ground floor contain frescoes, tapestries and paintings. A red star stands on top of the central dome.

To the northeast, at the entrance to **City Park** *(Varosliget),* lies **Heroes' Square** *(Hosok ter).* The **Millennial Monument** stands in commemoration of the thousandth anniversary of the Magyar conquest of 893–96. The **Tomb of the Unknown Soldier** is there. Statues of important Hungarian leaders stand in niches around the colonnade beginning with St. Stephen *(Szt. Istvan),* who gave his crown to the Virgin Mary as mentioned above, St. Ladislas, King Coloman, who was against burning witches, and Andrew II, a crusader who was instrumental in developing the Golden Bull, which was similar to the Magna Carta. One can continue to follow Hungarian history through Bela IV, who was saved during the Mongol occupation, Charles Robert, who was the first Anjou King, Louis the Great, Governor Janos Hunyadi, who was a hero in wars against the Turks, King Matthias, who ruled during the golden age of Hungary, Princes of Transylvania Gabor Bethlen, Istvan Bocskai, Imre Thokoly, Prince Ferenc Rakoczi II, who was the leader of the War of Independence, and Lajos Kossuth of the 1848 Hungarian Revolution.

Also on the square, the **Museum of Fine Arts** *(Szepmuveszeti Muzeum),* Dozsa Gyorgy Ut 14, and the Mucsarnok, or Art Gallery, face each other. Old Masters are on display in the first; there are temporary exhibits in the second.

The **Museum of Fine Arts** contains the foreign works collected by the Hungarian National Museum, and the private Esterhazy Collection, which came home from Vienna in 1870. We were very impressed with the El Greco collection.

City Park contains playgrounds, gardens, a zoo, amusement park, and baths. **Vajdahunyad Castle** was built for the Millennium with a variety of architectural style from the 11th through the 18th centuries. Visitors can see a Transylvanian tower, Gothic church, Romanesque church, and baroque dwellings. Don't miss the statue of "Anonymus," King Bela III's scribe. He sits with hooded face, pen in his right hand, a book in his left. Another statue, of Karolyi Sendoi, sits on a couch with books spread around him. He was a politician and minister of agriculture at the beginning of the century.

The **Agricultural Museum** (Mezogazdasagi Muzeum) is also in the park. Its five sections explore Hungarian animal husbandry, forestry, horticulture, hunting, and fishing.

The **Franz Liszt Museum,** Vorosmarty ut 35, is located in the composer's home. Chamber concerts are given on some Saturdays.

AQUINCUM

The remains of the Roman city of Aquincum, located north of Buda on the road to Szentendre, date back to the 2nd century B.C. Excavation has revealed evidence of a floor heating system as well as running water and sewage systems. A basilica, forum, and public baths have been excavated and reconstructed. An unusual Roman water organ is housed in the museum. A Roman amphitheater stands next to the railway station. Part of the Roman aqueduct still stands in the median of the highway. Hercules Villa, located nearby in Meggyfa Utca, displays mosaic floors.

DAY TRIPS FROM BUDAPEST.................

Buda Hills

One of the nicest ways to begin a trip to the Buda Hills is to take the cog railway, which has been making the run since the 1870s. It starts on Szilagyi Erzsebet Fasor, opposite Hotel Budapest and near Moszkva ter Metro station. The railway climbs up to Szechenji Hill, where travelers can catch a train on the **Pioneer Railway** *(Uttorovasut)* for a further eight-mile journey. The Pioneer Railway is unusual because except for the engine driver, the railway crew is made up of 12- to 14-year-old Pioneers (similar to scouts). Travelers can ride up to Huvosvolgy Station or get out at Janos-hegy Station for a chairlift up Janos Hill. The lookout tower on Janos Hill provides a wraparound view.

The Danube Bend

North of Budapest, the Danube River makes an ''s'' shape as it passes through the Pilis and Borzsony mountains. **Palaces** were built by medieval kings along the west bank of the river. Visitors can reach these palaces and attractive towns by taking a Danube cruise, train ride, or automobile drive.

Szentendre

Szentendre, 12 miles from Budapest, was the spot where 17th-century Serbian and Greek settlers chose to escape the Turks. Their baroque houses stand on cobblestone streets. The **Blagovesztenska Greek Orthodox Church** stands on the main square; the **Serbian Belgrade Church** can be spotted with its soaring red tower. Near the Serbian Church, a **museum** displays Serbian ecclesiastical art including icons, textiles, and goldwork. Galleries in town include the **Kovacs Margit Museum,** the **Ferenczy Museum,** the **Kmetty Museum,** and the **Szentendre Picture Gallery.**

Szabadteri

The **Open-Air Ethnographical Museum** *(Szabadteri Neprajzi Muzeum)* is located three miles northwest of town. The collection portrays 19th-century Hungarian peasant life and architecture. Both buildings and objects were collected from villages in the area.

Visegrad

Visegrad is 26 miles from Budapest; King Charles Robert of Anjou built a royal palace there during the 14th century. In 1458 King Matthias Corvinus built his palace on the shore of the river. Although the Turks demolished it, the **palace** has been excavated and restored. The coat of arms of King Matthias decorated the red marble well, which was designed by an Italian architect. Some of the original wall decorations are still visible. **Solomon's Tower** in the Lower Castle has walls that are eight meters wide. More of the artifacts are housed in the **King Matthias Museum.**

Visegrad Citadel, built in 1241 after the Mongol invasion, is located above Solomon's Tower—follow signs *Fellegvar* along a hiking trail. Bus service is also available during the summer from a street near the King Matthias statue beside the wharf. It is also possible to drive up. Views from the top of the Danube Bend are a photographer's dream. The **Nagy-Villam Lookout Tower** provides more views from a different angle.

Esztergom

Esztergom was the capital of Hungary from the 10th to the 13th centuries; now it is the seat of the Cardinal-Primate of Hungary. Geza, who was the father of St. Stephen, was born there, and his son was crowned in Esztergom in 1000. Its **cathedral** is the largest in Hungary and it is impressive as it stands on a high hill over the river. The skull and a bone of St. Stephen are kept in a glass container in a side chapel. The neo-classical-style structure contains a red marble chapel, which was moved there from another church. The treasury contains a priceless collection of medieval art objects. The **Kereszteny Museum,** in the primate's palace, contains European art including wooden statues of the Apostles guarding the "Coffin of our Lord," 16th-century Flemish paintings, and French tapestries.

Lake Balaton

The largest fresh-water lake in central Europe, Balaton is 48 miles long. The flat southern shore has sandy beaches and warm, light green, shallow water.

The Romans had settled at Siofok, even constructing locks in order to control the level of the water in the lake. Six miles away, at Sagvar, there are Roman ruins to visit. The southern shore contains one resort after another, some of them old, with attractive promenades, parks, and private villas.

Along the northern shore extinct volcanoes dot the landscape. The largest, **Badacsony,** contains grotesque and strangely beautiful lava rock formations. Along the upper side, 200-foot-high basalt columns stand in a semicircle. Vineyards surround the volcanoes, and winetasting is popular. The Hungarian poet, Sandor Kisfaludy lived on the top of the mountain until 1844; his house still stands. A wine-press that belonged to his wife, Roza Szegedi, has been turned into a museum.

The peninsula of Tihany has been a **National Park** since 1952. It contains a variety of ruins, including **Celtic walls of the Ovar,** or Old Castle, a **Roman watchtower,** pieces of **ancient churches** and the **Tihany Abbey crypt.** King Andrew I began to build the crypt in 1055, and he is buried there. The Abbey charter, written in Latin, is a precious historical document now kept at Pannonhalma, in western Hungary. The Abbey church is decorated with silver-gilt altars and angelic cherubs on the ceiling.

IRELAND

> **Currency unit** • the Irish pound, also called punt, divided into 100 pence
> **Languages** • English and Gaelic
> **Time difference from USA** • five hours later (Eastern Standard Time)
> **Telephone access codes** • to USA 16; from USA 353 for the Republic of Ireland and 44 for Northern Ireland
> **National Tourist Offices** • **USA:** Irish Tourist Board, 757 Third Ave., New York, N.Y. 10017, tel.: (212) 418–0800; **Canada:** 10 King St., Toronto M5C 1C3, Canada, tel. (416) 364–1301; **Britain:** Irish Tourist Board, 150 New Bond St., London W1Y OAG, tel.: (071) 493–3201, Northern Ireland Tourist Board, 11 Berkeley St., London W1, tel.: (071) 493–0601; **Ireland:** Bord Failte, 14 Upper O'Connell St., Dublin 1, tel.: (01) 747733
> **Airlines** • **Aer Lingus USA:** (800) 223–6537; **Britain:** (081) 569–5555
> **Embassies** • **American Embassy:** 42 Elgin Rd., Ballsbridge, Dublin, Ireland, tel.: 688777; **British Embassy:** 33 Merrion Rd., Dublin 4, tel.: 695211

In one sense, the rapid move of high-tech industries into Ireland is reversing the great emigration to America after the devastating potato famine in the 19th century. But in another, perhaps renewed prosperity and development is not transforming the pace of life there that much, at least in the countryside. Whenever we travel in Ireland, we recall a number of friends who have chosen to settle there for a year while on sabbatical leave. Their reports of pastoral peace and quiet in a little cottage by the sea or in green rolling hills seemed both impossibly romantic and simultaneously an ideal way to live. How many times have we returned from a spell abroad away from stress, tight schedules and daily frustration to vow we would change our lifestyle. Perhaps, even now, Ireland may be the perfect place to learn how to do it and set a pattern for life.

HISTORY.................................

Ireland is romantic because ancient monuments from the past still stand there, shrouded in mystery, their legends and myths rattling around, and true facts often remain unrevealed. The first settlers were probably hunters who came across a strait from Britain in 6000 B.C. These Mesolithic people lived along the coasts, in river valleys, and beside lakes; they used boats called *curragh,* which fishermen in the west of Ireland still use today.

The Celts, who used iron in their tools and weapons, settled by 600 B.C. in Ireland. Their dwellings were encircled by ditches and earth rings to keep livestock in and intruders out. By 841 A.D., the Vikings had installed a fortified settlement on the site of Dublin, near the mouth of the River Liffey. The Normans built stone castles and intermarried with Irish families, which expanded their power. In 1172 Dublin became the seat of government by charter from Henry II. Henry VIII tried to demand allegiance by the Irish and remove Catholicism from the country. In 1690 William of Orange defeated Catholic forces and by 1800 Ireland had become part of England. In 1916, the Easter Rising when Irish Volunteers took over the Post Office, City Hall, South Dublin Union and other buildings, was followed by the Anglo-Irish Treaty of 1921 which formed the Irish Free State of the 26 southern counties. Northern Ireland became the Independent Republic of Ireland in 1949.

DUBLIN

SIGHTSEEING.................................

The Old Town

The oldest part of Dublin centers on the **Hill of Dublin,** or the Christ Church Cathedral area. King Sitric, or "silkbeard," built a wooden church there in 1038, on a ridge that was once a border dividing Ireland in two sections. The cathedral was begun in 1172 by Richard de Clare, the second Earl of Pembroke, called "Strongbow," upon the advice of Saint Laurence O'Toole, the archbishop (from 1162 to 1180) and patron saint of Dublin. Saint O'Toole's heart lies in a chapel to the right of the high altar. The ten-year-old pretender, Lambert Simnel, was crowned Edward VI of England in 1487 in the cathedral. In 1562 the south wall of the nave collapsed into its foundations in a peat bog. A major restoration was begun in 1871; the north wall of the nave, which leans outward 18 inches at the top but is secure with its flying buttresses, and the transepts are original. Underneath the cathedral lies the Crypt, which is the original from 1038 complete with wooden wedges used in construction. Christ Church is the cathedral for the Anglican Archdiocese of Dublin.

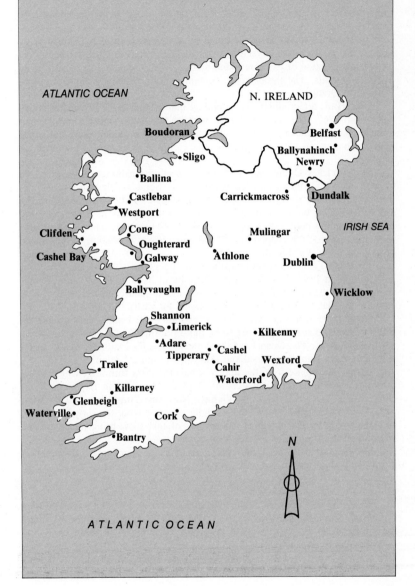

IRELAND

ATLANTIC OCEAN

N. IRELAND

Boudoran

Belfast

Ballynahinch

Sligo

Newry

Ballina

Dundalk

Castlebar

Carrickmacross

Westport

Clifden

Cong

Mulingar

IRISH SEA

Oughterard

Cashel Bay

Galway

Athlone

Dublin

Ballyvaughn

Wicklow

Shannon

Limerick

Kilkenny

Adare

Tipperary

Cashel

Tralee

Cahir

Wexford

Waterford

Killarney

Glenbeigh

Waterville

Cork

Bantry

N

ATLANTIC OCEAN

Dublin Castle, dating from 1204, was begun by Henry I's grandson, Myler FitzHenry. A fortified castle was needed to repulse the raids of local clansmen; this one needed to be enlarged and made more secure following each attack.

The **State Apartments** are entered by walking up the grand staircase, elegant with its Waterford crystal chandelier. **St. Patrick's Hall** has been used for the inauguration of Irish presidents since 1938. Ceremonial flags hang along two of the walls. The throne room contains a throne dating from the time of William of Orange.

City Hall, a Corinthian-style building that was once the Royal Exchange, dates from 1769. The central rotunda, with its seal in the center of the circular floor, contains statues of famous Dublinites such as O'Connell and Dr. Charles Lucas. Charters in City Hall include the earliest one from 1172 granted by Henry II.

St. Patrick's Cathedral, on Patrick Street, the national cathedral of the Church of Ireland (Protestant), dates from 1190. Some say that St. Patrick baptized converts at a well on the same site. Jonathan Swift, who was dean from 1713 to 1745, is buried there. His "Stella," Esther Johnson, lies at his side. Look for the old door with a hole in it—in 1492 two earls had a dispute, one of them retiring to the chapter house, and when it was over someone cut a hole in the door so they could shake hands.

Elizabeth I founded **Trinity College** on the site of a confiscated Priory of All Hallows in 1592; it is the oldest university in Ireland. The 40-acre campus is an oasis in the center of a busy city; its parklike landscaping, complete with gardens and statues, can be a welcome respite for weary tourists.

One of the wonders of Ireland is the illuminated manuscript called the **Book of Kells,** painstakingly created by monks during the 8th century to glorify the life of Christ. The Gospels of the New Testament, Matthew, Mark, Luke, and John, have been transcribed and illustrated in minute detail.

Across the square from the library stands the **Arts Building,** which offers a multi-media show on the history of Dublin. "The Dublin Experience" includes early Christian Ireland, the Vikings, Normans, Elizabeth I, Oliver Cromwell, Georgian Dublin, the famine, Catholic emancipation, the early Irish state, and modern Ireland. The sights and sounds of this show bring into focus the chronological order of Dublin's development.

The **Examination Hall,** or Theatre, contains an organ case that was made in the Netherlands, then put on its way to Spain by ship. Admiral Rooke captured the ship at Vigo in 1702. The Duke of Ormond took the organ as part of his treasure and gave it to the college when he served as Viceroy.

The **Chapel,** also containing a stucco ceiling, was designed by Sir William Chambers. Stained glass windows give color to the altar and draw the eye along the ceiling as well.

The **Campanile,** designed by Sir Charles Lanyon, contains the large bell of the college and also the smaller "Provost's Bell," which may have once stood in the monastery of All Hallows.

The oldest buildings on campus are called **"the Rubrics,"** and they stand on the east side of Library Square. Oliver Goldsmith once lived there.

Southeast Dublin

The **National Gallery of Ireland,** Merrion Square, was designed by Francis Fowke and opened in 1864. Over 2000 works are on display; it is one of the largest galleries in Europe. J. M. W. Turner's watercolors were given with the stipulation that they only be shown during the month of January to preserve the colors. George Bernard Shaw bequeathed one third of his estate to the gallery, claiming that he received his education there; his statue stands by the entrance.

The **National Library** contains a collection of first editions and works of 17th-century Irish authors including Swift, Goldsmith, Yeats, Shaw, and Joyce. The famous literary debate in James Joyce's *Ulysses* took place there.

The **National Museum,** Kildare St., exhibits some of its extensive collection of Irish antiquities dating from 6000 B.C. The **Treasury Gallery** has gathered gold pieces from pre-Celtic to pre-Viking times.

Leinster House, Kildare St., the seat of Dail Eireann (House of Representatives) and Seanad Eireann (The Senate) make up the **National Parliament.** Originally built in 1745 as the mansion for the Dukes of Leinster, this house was at that time out in the country. When others questioned the Duke on his choice of land he insisted that society would follow him across the River Liffey—and they did. The Kildare St. side looks like a town house and the Merrion Square side has a country look.

North of the River Liffey

The **Custom House** is said to be the most beautifully proportioned structure in Dublin. Designed by James Gandon, the classical facade, with its 120-foot-high copper dome, stretches along the river.

The **Abbey Theatre,** on Lower Abbey St., founded in 1904 by W. B. Yeats, Lady Gregory, and others, is now in its second building on the site; the first was destroyed by fire. The Anglo-Irish idiom comes through clearly in plays such as J. M. Synge's *Playboy of the Western World* and Sean O'Casey's *Juno and the Paycock.*

The **General Post Office** was the meeting place of the Irish Volunteers in 1916, headed by Patrick Pearse and James Connolly. Shells from an English gunboat in the River Liffey set the building on fire, and Pearse, Connolly, and fourteen others were executed in Kilmainham Jail.

The **Custom House,** called the Four Courts, was completed between 1786 and 1802. The copper-covered lantern dome rises above six Corinthian columns. Two adjoining wings enclose quadrangles on each side. Inside, the circular main hall leads to the original "four courts"—Exchequer, Common Pleas, King's Bench, and Chancery.

DAY TRIPS FROM DUBLIN ....

To the south lies **Sandycove** and the **James Joyce Tower and Museum.** In 1904 Joyce lived with Oliver St. John Gogarty (Buck Mulligan) in a Martello tower. Today the Joyce Tower is a museum, housing a variety of Joycean memorabilia.

While Joyce was visiting his friend Gogarty in the tower, another friend, Samuel Chenevix Trench, joined them. Trench had a nightmare about a black panther, reached for his gun, fired into the fireplace, and fell asleep. Gogarty grabbed the gun, shouted "leave him to me," and shot at saucepans, which were just over Joyce's bed. Joyce left the tower and never returned.

Just south of Sandycove is the little town of **Dalkey.** During the summer, visitors can take a boat trip to **Dalkey Island** where there is another Martello tower. This island, a **bird sanctuary,** also has the ruins of a **Benedictine church.**

The **Wicklow Mountains,** which are within easy reach of Dublin to the south, are granite hills with deep, steeply sloped glens complete with rivers and lakes. The area has not been developed—scattered cottages and a few villages provide room to breathe. The **Vale of Glendalough** contains two lakes and the remains of St. Kevin's 6th-century monastic settlement. Although he came to live there as a hermit, he was chased by a beautiful redheaded girl, Kathleen, who had eyes of "unholy blue." Some say that St. Kevin rolled himself and Kathleen in nettles to reduce their passion; others say that he threw her from a cliff into the lake.

Although **Powerscourt's** mansion was destroyed by fire in 1974, it still contains landscaped gardens and the highest waterfall in the British Isles. Visitors enter the gardens through wrought-iron gates, which came from the Cathedral of Bamberg in Bavaria. The view from the highest point of the terrace takes in both Little and Great Sugar Loaf Mountains. Some say that the designer, Daniel Robertson, was wheeled about the place in a wheelbarrow grasping a bottle of sherry. When the sherry was finished Mr. Robertson ended his designing for the day.

Russborough is an 18th-century Palladian House designed by Richard Castle for the First Earl of Milltown in 1740. The house contains famous paintings from the **Beit Art Collection.** In 1974 two supporters of the IRA stole some of the most famous paintings and held them for ransom. Both paintings were recovered and the two thiefs convicted.

EXCURSIONS FROM DUBLIN..............

West of Dublin

The **Burren,** a stark region of karstic limestone in the uplands south of Galway Bay, reminds one of a lunar landscape. The rock formations of the 50-square mile area resemble those along the Dalmation Coast of Yugoslavia. The place seems to be incredibly lonely and is fascinating. Its porous carboniferous limestone rock, molded and scraped by Pleistocence ice sheets, now lies in bare, fissured, sometimes flat pavements called "clints" in between open crevices called "grykes" that extend in rows. "Turloughs" are grassy hollows that receive water from underground springs, which flood in times of wet weather. "Swallow holes" are the places where the water flows in and out. Subterranean caves lie underneath, like the holes in swiss cheese, challenging even experienced speleologists. **Ailwee Cave** is the only one open to the general public.

The beauty of wildflowers peeking out from the somber grey stone seems almost magical—they dare to grow there amid a seeming lack of life and movement. Every little bit of soil holds a miniature rock garden of plant life. Surprisingly enough, the plants found there are from two different climates—both arctic and alpine plants are found side-by-side. It is thought that the ice age glaciers carried seeds from the arctic and alpine regions and placed them beside local plants, which were of Mediterranean heritage.

We approached **Corkscrew Hill** at sunset and were treated to a long view of desolate landscape, enough to whet our appetite for exploration in the morning. Archaeological remains are everywhere on the Burren—megalithic tombs, earthen and stone ring-forts, walls, churches, and castles—to tell us something about the people who once lived there.

The **Burren Display Centre,** located in Kilfenora, provides an overview of the Burren. A scale model shows the geological strata as well as early settlement patterns. The flora and fauna of the Burren are shown in silk and wax. There's more to see in the Burren than one would expect from the description of one of Cromwell's men: "a country where there is not water enough to drown a man, wood enough to hang one, or earth enough to bury him."

While in Kilfenora visitors might want to visit the **Kilfenora Cathedral** with its east window still standing. Also in the cathedral is a 15th-century wall tomb and two tomb effigies. Four high crosses stand there—the most interesting is the 12th-century Doorty Cross with carving on both sides.

One of the earliest archaeological finds, from 2500 B.C., is the **Poulnabrone Dolmen,** which stands tall above its upright slabs. This portal dolmen has a tilting trapezoidal capstone measuring twelve feet by seven feet; it almost looks like a sail ready to take off.

Hundreds of **ring-forts** are scattered in the Burren; these reminders of the Celts are easy to find. **Cathair Mhor** has a standing gateway with a long flat slab on top. **An Rath** is an earthen ring-fort with water all around it in wet weather. Some of them have several banks and ditches.

Aillwee Cave was first discovered by a local farmer, Jack McCann, in 1944. He crawled into its three-foot hole almost to the end. Today, after blasting, the cave has been widened to allow tourists easy lighted access along paved walkways with no danger. This is the only cave most of us should enter—experienced pot-holers or speleologists explore others.

Newtown Castle is surprising as it has a square base with a round tower above. The house rises up five stories high to mullioned windows on the parapets. It was till occupied by Charles O'Loughlin in 1837; the O'Loughlin family had been very powerful since 950 A.D.

In the southern part of the Burren, **Leamaneh Castle** is a tower-house dating from 1480, belonging to the O'Brien family. The tower-house has five stories with a stone vault on the top floor; it also has a "murder hole" over the doorway.

Just east of the Burren, Lady Augusta Gregory entertained a number of writers including G. B. Shaw, A. E. Sean O'Casey, and W. B. Yeats in her home at Coole Park. As a dramatist and folklorist Lady Gregory was also the co-founder with Yeats of the Abbey Theatre in Dublin. Coole Park was purchased in 1768 by the Gregory family; in 1928 it was sold to the state. The house is gone but the **Autograph Tree** remains, a copper beech with the initials of her literary friends.

Yeats lived for 12 years during the summers near Coole Park in his 16th-century tower-house, Thoor Ballylee. He first saw the tower when visiting Lady Gregory and bought it for 35 pounds.

The coastal side of the Burren is well known for its majestic **Cliffs of Moher,** towering up to 700 feet above the sea. They stretch for five miles along the coast, undulating in a scalloped fashion most of the way. Many seabirds nest there and spend their time squawking, flapping and soaring. Visitors will find the best view from the top of O'Brien's Tower, built in 1835 as an observation spot. One can see the Aran Islands looking like humpback whales in the distance, the Kerry mountains, Loop Head, and the Twelve Bens of Connemara.

Southwest of Dublin

An excursion of several days to the southwestern section of Ireland brings visitors into a magical kingdom of great natural beauty. County Kerry was formed by geological rising and sinking over the last 400 million years, resulting in drowned rivers, or bays of Bantry, Kenmare, and Dingle. These fingers of the sea penetrate inland to form the peninsulas of Beara, Iveragh, and Dingle. All three are beautiful; the Beara is less traveled as its roads will not accommodate tour buses.

Glengariff is a sheltered resort town at the entrance to the Beara Peninsula.

From Glengariff's wooden pier, visitors can take a boat to Garinish Island, famous for its Italian gardens. Although once Garinish Island was just a barren rock, John Allen Bryce turned it into a botanical garden early in the 20th century.

At the end of the point lies Dursey Island and three large rocks named the Bull, Cow, and Calf. A cable car connects the mainland with Dursey Island.

Healy Pass, a winding road up and over the mountain, was constructed as famine relief work under Tim Healy, the first governor-general of the Irish Free State. As you climb, there will be lots of hairpin turns, some peat squares lying around, and great slabs of tilted rock with a little grass blowing in the wind. The shrine at the top looks down into country Kerry. Several lakes stud the landscape up there including Glanmore and Inchiquin, where there is a small stone circle near the bottom of the lake.

Derreen, the home of the Marquess of Lansdowne, descended from Sir William Petty. The fourth Lord Landsdowne enlarged the house and the next Lord planted an extensive garden. By 1884, 400 acres were landscaped, some with giant conifers from America, including both red cedar and western hemlock. Tropical flowers and shrubs grew rapidly in the mild climate.

The **Ring of Kerry,** a scenic road, travels all around the Iveragh Peninsula; it is the most extensive of three rings and requires some selectivity depending upon available time. Most local people suggest driving the Ring of Kerry in counter clockwise fashion to catch the best views. However, for a shorter taste of the ring, you might drive to Sneem, then take the road over the mountain to Caragh Lake for a bit of both coast and interior views.

Muckross House, built by Henry Arthur Herbert in 1843, is now a folk museum. The house contains locally carved period furniture, maps, and prints. Craft workers, including a weaver, potter, and blacksmith, are engaged in their traditional work. Both the house and gardens belong to the National Parks Service. Nature trails are marked through the gardens and beside the lake.

Muckross Friary, the ruins of a medieval Irish Franciscan monastery, was founded in 1448 by MacCarthy Mor. A larger tower was added during the 16h century. Plaques honor the four gaelic poets of Kerry; three of them (Aodhgan O Raithile, Geoffrey O'Donoghue, and Eoghan Rua O Suilleabhain) are buried in the church. The fourth poet, Piaras Ferriter, was hanged in Killarney and is buried in the graveyard.

Killarney itself is a popular tourist town, complete with horse-drawn traps.
Ross Castle, built by the O'Donoghues in the 15th century, was the last stronghold that held out against the Cromwellians in Ireland. It was also the inspiration for Tennyson's *The Princess*. Once a ruin, the keep has been restored complete with corner towers and 94 steps up to the top.

Ballymalis Castle, on the banks of the River Laune, was one of the first castles built by the Anglo-Normans in the 13th century. Today a tower house has been restored with four stories—the bottom for storage, the first for defense, the second for sleeping, and the top, a living room.

Killorglin is famous for its **Puck Fair** in August, which is a time of great merrymaking. A wild male goat is captured and dressed with ribbons on its horns, then displayed in the center of town as a carrot-crunching mascot. These festival origins may stem from worship of the Celtic god, Lug. Killorglin is thought of as the northeast end of the Ring of Kerry.

Caragh Lake, which looks like a sickle, is framed with woods below its steep slopes. At Glenbeigh stand the ruins of 1860's towers built by Lord Headley.

Derrynane contains several wedge-gallery graves, artifacts from the Beaker people, and a dolmen from Neolithic days. **Derrynane House,** the home of Daniel O'Connell, contains mementos belonging to the family.

The village of **Sneem** is signposted "National Winner Tidy Towns Competition 1987." The homes look like dollhouses—each one kept tidy and refreshed with a coat of paint every year. When we were there a caravan of gypsy wagons was just going through town, adding a bit of color.

Another ring, on the Dingle Peninsula, takes place on the most northerly of the peninsulas in southwest Ireland. This peninsula contains a great many early Christian monuments and iron age fortifications.

Dingle is still an old-world fishing village in some respects; its fishing fleet still goes out at night. At one time it was the most important harbor in Kerry; it was also famous for smuggling in the 18th century. Legend reports that a local resident, James Rice, had prepared a house in Dingle to receive Queen Marie Antoinette, but she chose not to be rescued.

ITALY

Currency unit • lira (LIT)

Language • Italian

Time difference from USA • six hours later (Eastern Standard Time)

Telephone • access codes: to USA 001 or USADirect 172 1011; from USA 39

National Tourist Offices • **USA:** Italian Government Tourist Office, also called ENIT, 630 Fifth Ave., Suite 1565, New York, NY 10020, tel.: (212) 245–4822; **Britain:** Italian State Tourist Office, 1 Princes St., London WIR 8AY, England, tel.: (071) 408–125. **Campagnia Italian Turismo (CIT) in Italy:** Firenze 50121 (Toscana) Via Manzoni, 16, tel.: (055) 247–8141/2/3/4/5; Genova 16121 (Liguria) Via Roma, 11, tel.: (010) 581–407; Milano 20123 (Lombardia) Via Marconi, 1, tel.: (02) 870–016; Napoli 80121 (Campania) Via Partenope, 10-A, tel.: (081) 418–988; Roma 00185 (Lazio) Via Parigi, 11, tel.: (06) 461–851; Vicenza 36100 (Veneto) Piazza Duomo, 5, tel.: (0444) 544–122; **Britain:** ENIT, 1 Princes St., London WIR 8AY, tel.: (071) 408 125

Airlines • **Alitalia USA:** 800 223–5730; **Britain:** (071) 602–7111

Embassies • **U.S. Consulate,** Via Vespucci, 38, 50123, Firenze, tel.: (055) 298–276; **U.S. Consulate General,** Banca d'America e d'Italia Building, Piazza Portello, 6. 16134, tel.: (010) 282–741; **U.S. Consulate General,** Largo Donegani, 1, 20121, Milan, tel.: (02) 652–841; **U.S. Consulate General,** Piazza della Republica, 80122, Napoli, tel.: (081) 660–966; **United States Embassy,** Via Vittorio Veneto, 121. 00187, Roma, tel.: (06) 46741; **British Embassy,** Via XX Settembro 80 A 00187 Rome, tel.: 4755–441/551, **British Consulate,** Lungarno Corsini 2, I 50123 Florence, tel.: 212–594, **British Consulate,** Via San Paolo 7, I 20121 Milan, tel.: 869–3442, **British Consulate,** Via XII Ottobre 2, 13 Piano, I 16121 Genoa, tel.: (010) 564–833/6, **British Consulate,** Box 679, Dorsodoro (Accademia) 1051, I 30100 Venice, tel.: 041 522–7207, **British Consulate,** Via Francesco Crispi, 122, I 80122 Naples, tel.: 663511.

HISTORY......................................

Seafarers from the Near East landed in Italy and settlements date from 3500 B.C. Early Metal Age copper daggers dating from 1800 B.C. were found near Brescia. Minoan and Mycenean burial pieces from around 1500 B.C. give evidence of the arrival of Greek sailors. Homeric legends about the Cyclops, Sirens, Aeolus, Scylla, and Charybdis in the 13th century B.C. may be placed in regions the Mycenaeans had been familiar with in southern Italy and Sicily.

By 1000 B.C. Etruscans from Asia Minor moved in and formed city states. Between 750–550 B.C. Greek settlements appeared in Sicily and southern Italy—Cumae, Pithecusae, Reggio Calabria, Neapolis, Agrigento, and Syracuse. Rome was founded in 753 B.C. by Romulus. During the Punic Wars, Rome expanded its power over the western and then eastern Mediterranean. By 50 A.D., Rome was the largest city in the world and the Roman Empire stretched through most of Europe.

In 79 A.D., both Pompeii and Herculaneum were destroyed when Vesuvius erupted. Around 375 the Huns began invading Europe and German emperors began their rule in 493. In 772 Charlemagne took control of the Lombard kingdom in northern Italy and combined it with the Frankish kingdom. In 800 Charlemagne was crowned Emperor. Italy was governed by German emperors from 951 until 1268. Two parties developed: the Guelfs, who sided with the Pope, and the Ghibellines, who supported the Emperor. From 1250 onward independent city states were formed in Italy. Each large town or city was ruled by a powerful family. Wars were fought for supremacy between some of the towns during the next centuries. Napoleon became King of Italy in 1805.

In 1915 Italy fought with the Allies in World War I. By 1922 Mussolini took over Rome and became Prime Minister and dictator of the country. In 1940 Italy declared war on Britain and France and signed a pact with Japan and Germany. By 1943 Italian troops fell in North Africa, the Fascist regime collapsed, and Mussolini was arrested. In 1947 the Treaty of Rome was signed and Italy lost its colonies. Floods hit northern and central Italy in 1966 and earthquakes caused devastation in 1976 and 1980.

FLORENCE

Have you ever enjoyed being sick in a room alive with curvaceous frescoes from the baroque era? My husband spent a day lolling in bed with our small

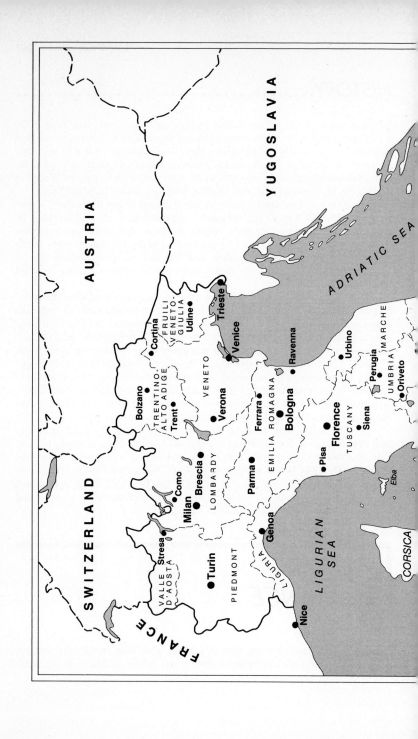

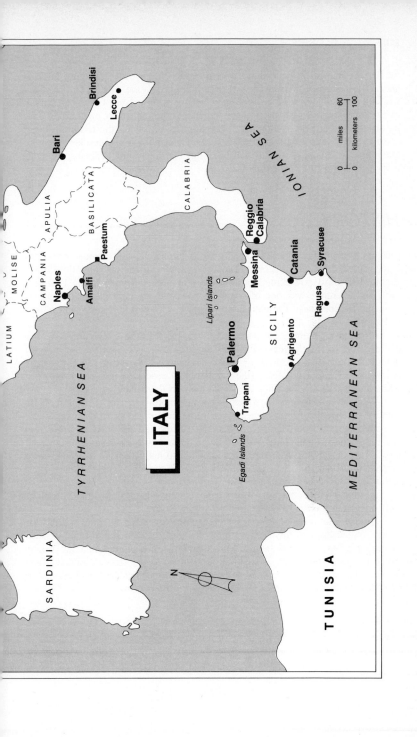

toddler for company while the rest of us were out savoring antiquity in Florence. The residence we had chosen once belonged to the Medici family and it was our pleasure to soak in the ambience for a few days. On another more recent occasion, we visited convents and chapels not generally open to the public and discovered an astounding "Last Supper" in which the faces of all the apostles were contorted with the whole gamut of human expressions. There is much hidden behind the facades of buildings that look quite ordinary. Florence is indeed, a city one never tires of.

HISTORY......................................

Little is known about prehistoric Florence. During the first century B.C., Romans settled there and it grew to become a provincial capital when the Roman Empire was most powerful. Medieval city-states were formed in the 11th century, and Florence was one of the most powerful. Florentine art appeared in Romanesque churches. The gold florin, the first coin used in trading, was minted in Florence.

Florentine Guelphs, the papal party, fought with the Ghibellines, the imperial party, for many years. Families ganged up on one another and some of them had connecting overhead passages into each other's towers. In 1303 Dante Alighieri, a "white Guelph" (the Guelphs had separated into two factions—white and black) left Florence to go into exile in Ravenna.

Warfare ended when the Guelphs became more powerful. During the 15th century the Medici family rose to rule Florence for the next three centuries. Giovanni de Bicci de Medici and his son Cosimo left the banking profession and turned into rulers. Lorenzo the Magnificent, who was Cosimo's grandson, took down the towers and turned his attention to his patronage of Renaissance artists. Michelangelo, da Vinci, Brunelleschi, Botticelli, Galileo, Dante, Donatello, and Boccaccio were among those who lived and worked in Florence.

In 1865 Florence became Italy's new capital. When the final unification of Italy became a fact in 1871, the honor went to Rome.

Almost total disaster devasted Florence on November 4, 1966, when flood waters surged through town. Everything was under water, and torrents swished through piazzas, bridges, homes, and churches. Around midnight the waters began to lower, but great damage had been done to priceless treasures. Many of us sent money from the U.S. to help with the cleanup and restoration. We visited recently and the water marks were still grim reminders.

SIGHTSEEING......................................

Cathedral Center

The **Cathedral of Florence** *(Duomo di Santa Maria del Fiore)* on Piazzo Duomo, was begun in 1296 with designs by Arnolfo di Cambio, and finally finished several hundred years later. Its pattern of green, red, and white marble is distinctive and a source of pride for Florentines. The duomo is also the third (behind St. Peter's in Rome and St. Paul's in London) largest church in the world.

Filippo Brunelleschi designed a dome for the cathedral in 1417 that was most unusual. It was actually two domes, placed like two bowls of different sizes, one within the other. He used ribbing to tie them together and lessen the strain of their weight. As you walk between the layers of the dome you may be reminded of the backbone of a giant fish. A Roman herringbone pattern of the brickwork strengthened the entire structure. The dome measures 149 feet in diameter and there are 463 steps up to the top for a view of the structure as well as the city.

Some of the cathedral's famous frescoes have been placed in its museum, but among those that remain are Andrea del Castagno's *Niccolo da Tolentino* and Paolo Uccello's *Sir John Hawkwood*. Look for the flood marks on the wall and then look above for Domenico da Michelino's portrait of Dante in his red robe, safe above the flood. Florence is shown on the right, hell on the left, and heaven above.

Paolo Uccello painted a large clock high on the wall in the 1400s. The face is unusual in that the Roman numerals go around counter-clockwise. The hand shows the hours on a 24-hour basis and it still works!

The **Cathedral Museum,** *Museo dell'Opera del Duomo,* is at the east end of the piazza, near the rear of the cathedral. Over the years many works of art have been removed from the outside of both the duomo and the baptistry to preserve them from pollution. On display are a number of Arnolfo di Cambio's sculptures destined for the facade of the duomo, which was unfinished when he died.

The original wooden model of the duomo created by Brunelleschi is on display. Andrea Pisano's sculptures from the Campanile, and Luca della Robbia's dancing and singing galleries, Michelangelo's unfinished *Pieta* and Donatello's *Mary Magdalen* are all there. Two panels from the Paradise Doors have been restored and now are contained in a plexiglass housing where inert gases can circulate and preserve them.

The **Baptistery** *(Battistero)* standing in front of the cathedral dates from 1000 and is another green and white Romanesque structure. It is dedicated to St. John (San Giovanni Battista) who is the patron saint of Florence. The 14th-century bronze Renaissance doors are magnificent. Lorenzo Ghiberti was the craftsman who designed the north and east doors. The north doors portray the life of Christ and the east doors are from the Old Testament. Michelangelo remarked that the east doors could have been placed at the entrance to heaven, and they are called the "Doors of Paradise." Four of the east doors now reside in the cathedral museum to protect them from pollution.

Inside, the Byzantine-style mosaics depict scenes from the Creation, the Life of St. John, and the Last Judgment. Look up into the 14th-century cupola at the figure of Christ the Universal Judge with his hands outstretched and the circle of angels around the dome. Years ago Florentine children were baptized there. A black bean was counted for each male child and a white bean for each female—a means of taking the census.

The Bell Tower *(Campanile)* dates from the 14th century. Designed by Giotto and completed by Andrea Pisano and Francesco Talenti, this 267-foot-tall bell tower has scenes from the Old Testament sculpted by Giotto and Luca della Robbia. 414 steps to the top lead to another view of Florence.

Renaissance Sights

The **Pallazzo Medici-Riccardi,** Via Cavour, now Florence's prefecture and seat of Provincial Administration, which dates from 1444, contains a chapel full of paintings including Benozzo Gozzoli's 15th-century fresco of the *Journey of the Magi to Bethehem.* Lorenzo the Magnificent and Catherine dei Medici were born there. Michelangelo lived in the palace when he was studying with Bertoldo.

The **Laurentian Library** *(Biblioteca Laurenziana)* is entered by climbing stairs from the cloister up to the balcony. Michelangelo created the wooden desks, which hold manuscripts from all ages.

Nearby, the **Church of St. Lorenzo** (Chiesa de San Lorenzo) contains a Brunelleschi-designed **Old Sacristy** and a Michelangelo-designed **New Sacristy,** as well as **The Princes' Chapel** *(Cappella dei Principi),* and the **Medici tombs.** Michelangelo created his *Twilight and Dawn* for the tomb of the Duke of Urbino and *Night and Day* for the Duke of Nemours. The figures, complete with realistic features, have an impact on visitors.

Museo Nazionale

The **National Museum of the Bargello** *(Museo Nazionale),* Via Proconsolo, was famous during the Renaissance as the place to see a picture of Medici enemies and crooks painted on the outside walls. The police chief *(Bargello)* ran his notorious prison within these walls. It has been the scene of sieges, fires, and executions.

The main focus of this museum is sculpture, including a grouping of Michelangelo's *Drunken Bacchus,* with grapes in his hair and unsteady feet, Brutus, with a stern stare and powerful neck, *Tondo Pitti* and an unfinished *David-Apollo.* Donatello's *Youthful David,* and *David* in bronze, wearing a hat, with his helmet on the ground and his sword in hand. Two panels placed in competition for the baptistery doors, by Lorenzo Ghiberti and Filippo Brunelleschi, are there. Luca della Robbia's glazed terracottas are also on display, as are works by Michelangelo, Bandinelli, Sansovino, and Cellini. Other collections include Venetian and Islamic glass, Roman and Byzantine ivory, Limoges, Medici jewelry, tapestries, and majolica.

Piazza Santa Croce

The **Church of Santa Croce** *(Chiesa di Santa Croce)*, dating from the 13th century, contains the remains of Michelangelo, not in the sarcophagus but to the left under one of three slabs (his father and brother lie under the other two). Allegorical sculpted figures on the sarcophagus depict painting, sculpture, and architecture. Look at his bust on top—his flat nose was the result of a fight as a young man.

The allegorical figure on the tomb of Niccolo Machiavelli represents diplomacy. Tombs of Galileo Galilei, Lorenzo Ghiberti, and Gioacchino Rossini and a memorial to Dante Alighieri are also there. Two Giotto frescoes portray the lives of St. John the Evangelist, St. Francis, and St. John the Baptist. Donatello's *Annuciation* portrays an angel announcing to Mary that she will have a virgin birth. Mary pulls away in shock with her hand over her heart. The museum was reorganized after the 1966 flood to house art from the church and the cloister.

Piazza San Marco

The **Academy of Fine Arts** *(Accademia)*, on Via Ricasoli, displays a number of sculptures by Michelangelo, including the original *David,* moved there in 1873 from the Piazza della Signoria. David stands 13 feet tall—Michelangelo didn't waste an inch of his 13-foot-high block—the top of the head is a little flat when seen from above. David, ready to kill the giant Goliath, symbolizes the Florentines, ready to defend the liberty of their city. In 1527 David's right arm was damaged by falling debris but it was repaired. This humanistic figure stands resolute. Some say it represents Michelangelo's glorification of renaissance man.

Michelangelo created the unfinished *Pieta* here at age 65. (He completed the one in Rome at age 23). His own mother died when he was very young; perhaps over the years his attitude toward a mother figure softened. The statue of St. Matthew, also unfinished, seems to be trying to free itself from the block of marble. Four prisoners also stand uncompleted. Sixteenth and 17th-century tapestries hang behind Michelangelo's work.

The **Museo San Marco** is now in the **Monastery of St. Mark.** A memorial for Fra Angelico, who painted frescoes on the walls beginning in 1437, is there. Later his other works were brought into the museum. His paintings are also in the monks' cells and each one is different. We were taken with one depicting Christ being welcomed into heaven, with devils from hell pushed away, including one flattened by a door. His *Descent from the Cross* and *Last Judgment* are also there.

Ghirlandaio's *Last Supper,* dating from the 15th century, is on the walls. This Last Supper is different, with two angels in front, a crucifix above, and Christ's eyes gazing upward. Another version of the Last Supper in the same building features the table set in a cloister, peacocks, fruit trees, a grey cat, and two women disciples on the right. The library contains a series of illuminated manuscripts that were created in the convent.

Nearby, the **Museo Archeologico,** on Piazzo Santissima Annunziata, houses Estruscan artifacts and exhibits, as well as Greek and Egyptian antiquities. Cosimo (the Elder) d' Medici collected treasures in marble, bronze, and terracotta crockery. The famous *Chimera* bronze of Arezzo is there, as well as ceramic pieces, coins, gems, and sculpture. Don't miss the large Francois vase, which contains a variety of scenes, including the wedding of Peleus and Thetis and also scenes from the Iliad.

Uffizi Gallery

The **Uffizi Gallery** *(Galleria Degli Uffizi),* 6 Loggiato degli Uffizi, is housed in the 1565 Uffizi Palace, which reaches from Piazza Signoria to Palazzo Vecchio. Giorgio Vasari designed the horseshoe-shaped building as government offices and workshops for Duke Cosimo; it also served as the mint for Florence's florin. The Medici family placed some of their favorite paintings in a gallery on the third floor; the last heir, Anna Maria Luisa, gave the collection to the state.

Botticelli's *Birth of Venus* shows Venus, the goddess of love and beauty, standing in a scallop shell in the center. Zephyr winds on the left blow through her hair, which swings to the right and also blow the pink blanket and Flora's dress. Leonardo da Vinci's *Adoration of the Magi* presents a calm Virgin and child with animated spectators in the background.

Nearby, the arcaded **Loggia dei Lanzi** houses a number of sculptures including Benvenuto Cellini's *Perseus Holding the Head of Medusa,* Giambologna's *The Rape of the Sabine Women,* and *Hercules and the Centaur.* Bartolommeo Ammannati's *Neptune Fountain* is also there. The Piazza della Signoria contains Donatello's *Marzocco* and *Judith and Holofernes,* a copy of Michelangelo's *David,* and Baccio Bandinelli's *Hercules and Cacus.*

In the Piazza della Signoria, there is a bronze plaque marking the spot where the monk Savonarola instigated the "bonfire of the vanities" in 1497; it included "masquerading costumes and masks, false hair and rouge pots, musical instruments and dice-boxes, books of Latin and Italian poets, priceless parchments and illuminated manuscripts, works of art and paintings, especially such as represented female beauty." Savonarola was burnt at the stake there a year later.

Hofburg Fountain in motion,
Vienna, Austria

BELOW: Fishing Nets Along Belgian
Coast—a Working Fleet

Sculpture with a view at Louisiana Museum, Humlebaek, Denmark

Shakespeare's Birthplace, Stratford-upon-Avon, Britain

Horologue on Prague's Town Hall, Czechoslovakia

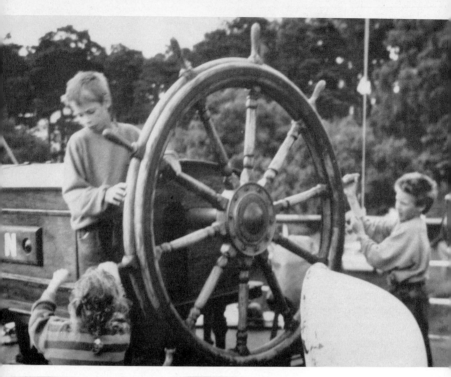

Children at the *Pommern's* wheel, Aland, Finland

LEFT: Sacre Coeur, Paris, France

A row of Houses in Dinkelsbuhl, Germany

A woman with her donkey, Corfu, Greece

Modern statues in Old Buda, Hungary

OPPOSITE PAGE: View from Cernobbia, Lake Como, Italy

BELOW: Poulnabrone Dolmen on The Burren, Ireland

**Bock Casements,
Luxembourg City,
Luxembourg**

**Amsterdam's Canals,
The Netherlands**

Statue of Edward Grieg from his home
in Troldhaugen, Norway

Wawel Cathedral, Krakow, Poland

Cabo da Roca, the Western-most
point, Portugal

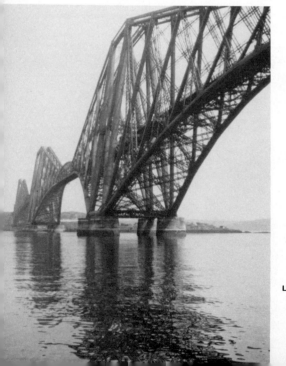

LEFT: **Firth of Forth Bridge, Scotland**

The Escorial, Spain

Ales Stones, Kaseberga, Sweden

Clock Tower, Zurich, Switzerland

Trojan Horse, Troy, Turkey

Ponte Vecchio

The name means "old bridge" and it is old—dating back to 1345 when it replaced an even older bridge that was washed away by a flood. One shop after another line the bridge over the Arno. In the old days these shops were used by butchers, grocers, blacksmiths, and a host of merchants. In 1593 the Medici Grand Duke Ferdinando I removed them and replaced them with upscale goldsmiths and jewelers. A bronze bust of Benvenuto Cellini watches the strollers from the center of the bridge.

Pitti Palace

This palace was started during the second half of the 15th century by Luca Pitti. Cosimo I d' Medici's wife, Eleanora of Toledo, acquired the building in 1550 and it was turned into the official residence of the Grand Ducal family.

Today the palace houses a number of Florentine museums including the **Palatine Gallery,** the **Silver Museum,** the **Gallery of Modern Art,** and nearby, in the Palazzina del Cavaliere of the Boboli Gardens, the **Porcelain Museum.**

The **Boboli Gardens** date from 1549, when Niccolo Pericoli Tribolo laid out plans for Eleanora of Toledo. Here's the place to work off some of that pasta as you stroll by fountains, statues, grottoes, and loggias. And behind the Boboli Gardens, one of the best views of Florence can be had from the Belvedere Fortress.

Santa Maria del Carmine

The **Church of Santa Maria del Carmine,** on Piazza del Carmine, contains an unusual collection of Renaissance painting in the newly cleaned Brancacci Chapel. Masaccio's twelve frescoes in the chapel have been given new life after fig leaves as well as grime were removed during cleaning.

DAY TRIPS FROM FLORENCE...............

NORTHEAST OF FLORENCE
Fiesole

The Etruscans lived in the area of Fiesole. The Romans arrived during the first century B.C. and began building with a vengeance. The remains of the Roman theater were uncovered in 1792; restoration has provided a theater that will seat 3000 persons and is in use today. Here's the place to run up and down the steps of an amphitheater—great for young legs needing some stretching. The **Roman**

baths include a gymnasium and hot and cold baths. The **Archaeological Museum** contains artifacts from Etruscan as well as Roman days.

SOUTHWEST OF FLORENCE
Siena

Reportedly Siena was founded by Senius and Aschius, who were the sons of Remus, whose brother Romulus founded Rome; others say that Augustus founded the city around the time of Christ's birth. Florence and Siena feuded for years—in 1260 the Sienese conquered the Florentines at the battle of Montaperti. A great surge in building—the cathedral, the Palazzo Pubblico, and many palaces rose after the victory at Montaperti. By 1559 Siena was part of the Grand Duchy of Tuscany and ruled by Florence.

The **Piazza del Campo** is the first place to head for in town; its crescent shape looks like a giant scallop shell. Traditionally the *Palio*, a horse race that has been held every summer for hundreds of years, takes over the Piazza. Silk banners, special colorful Renaissance costumes worn by pages, musicians, flag-twirlers and men-at-arms, and the tradition of pageantry provide more than enough for photographers to capture. Ten of the 17 parishes *(contrade)* of Siena are chosen by lottery to race every year at breakneck speed. These bareback riders can be ruthless, whipping horses and other jockeys if they wish. A few years ago members of a contrade beat their own jockey after he fell from his horse.

The **Palazzo Pubblico,** the town hall of Siena, has a 335-foot-high bell tower visitors can climb for a view. **Cappella di Piazza,** the chapel at the base of the tower, was built to commemorate Siena's escape from the plague of 1348. **Museo Civico** is the museum housed upstairs.

The **duomo,** with its zebra-style black/green and white marble exterior, is located up one of the three hills of Siena. Inside the blue-vaulted ceiling, marble floors and gilded dome set off the octagonal carousel pulpit carved by Nicola Pisano in 1265. **Museo dell'Opera Metropolitana,** the Cathedral Museum, is also there.

The **Pinacoteca Nazionale,** 29 Via San Pietro, contains the largest collection of Sienese paintings in the city.

WEST OF FLORENCE
Pisa

Visitors still have a couple of hundred years more in which to see the **Leaning Tower of Pisa** before it tumbles. At this time it leans fifteen feet off center. This is not surprising, considering the fact that "pisa" means "marshy land" harboring extremely soft, sandy soil. The foundations of the tower are just nine feet deep because of the high water table. And 15,000 tons of white marble do more than make a dent in the earth. The tower was closed to visitors in February 1990.

People say that Galileo Galilei dropped two metal balls of different weights from the top of the tower; they arrived on the ground at the same moment. Others reported that while attending Mass in Pisa Cathedral, Galileo timed his own pulse while watching a swinging lamp and concluded that the width of the swing does not alter the timing of a pendulum.

The duomo dates from 1063 but took three centuries to be completed. Roman inscriptions remain on some of the building stones on its walls, an early venture into recycling. Bronze doors portray the Life of Christ; visitors rub the doors for good luck.

The baptistery was built to baptize infants, who were thought to be pagan until the rites had been performed. Originally the baptistery did not have a roof; the dome, a lantern turret and the statue of St. John the Baptist were added later. Inside, the acoustics are considered perfect.

The **Museo dell'Opera del Duomo,** which opened in 1986 in a former Capuchin convent, houses a collection of art gathered from the area over the centuries. An unusual collection of Islamic pieces include an amusing bronze griffin which emerged from the cathedral.

EXCURSIONS FROM FLORENCE ....

Assisi

Francesco di Bernardone, later St. Francis of Assisi, was born in 1181. He was a wild, spoiled youth until he reached 23. After being thrown into a Perugia jail, suffering a serious illness, and receiving a vision while in the Chapel of San Damiano, he was forced to redefine his lifestyle. St. Francis accepted a life of austerity, penitence, and prayer and founded the mendicant Franciscan Order in 1210. His preaching converted many, and the example of his devotion to birds and animals brought others to him as followers. St. Francis was the first person to receive the stigmata (the wounds in his hands, feet and side similar to those received by Christ) while on a mission to Monte La Verna, near Arezzo. The Franciscan Order is still strong in the Catholic church today.

The **Basilica of St. Francis** *(Chiesa de san Francesco)* is really two superimposed churches that share a common apse. His tomb lies in the crypt, coming to light as late as 1818 after being hidden from Perugian invaders. Access is down a long flight of marble steps.

The **Church of St. Clare** *(Ciesa di Santa Chiara)* honors the founder of the Poor Clares. St. Clare was an ardent follower of St. Francis and founded the Order of St. Clare as an imitation of the Order of St. Francis. The body of St. Clare, with visible blackened bones, is lying on her bier in full black habit with a floral wreath around her head.

GENOA

Although a cloud of secrecy surrounds Christopher Columbus's birthplace, many scholars pinpoint Genoa as the likely place. According to Samuel Eliot Morison in *Admiral of the Ocean Seas,* "There is no mystery about the birth, family, or race of Christopher Columbus. He was born in the ancient city of Genoa sometime between August 25 and the end of October, 1451, the son and grandson of woolen weavers who had been living in various towns of the Genoese Republic for at least three generations." One can picture him as a young boy with red hair perched on the dock watching the activity aboard a sailing ship. Merchant ships sailed in to deposit their cargo of spices and herbs from the Levant and take on fruit, vegetables, and Lugurian-produced velvets and damask. Some of them carried armor made in Milan, such as lances and shields. Christopher Columbus was probably yearning to be on board one of the ships as it left port.

HISTORY......................................

Genoa dates back to pre-Roman times when the town was located on the hill of Santa Maria di Castello; it was capital of the Ligurians in 218 B.C. The town was destroyed in 205 B.C. by Mago, then became a Roman center by 381 A.D. During the next several hundred years, Genoa concentrated on setting up colonies in the Mediterranean as well as on taking part in the Crusades. By the 10th century Genoa was an independent republic, losing this status through internal disention until Admiral Andrea Doria restored the republic in 1528. Genoa was involved with sieges and occupations by several foreign powers including France, Austria, England, Spain, and Sardinia; it took the unification of Italy to give the city back its own identity.

SIGHTSEEING................................

Although schooners no longer sail in and out of Genoa, modern shipping makes the city the largest Italian port. The harbor with its five basins, is enclosed by two breakwaters. The oldest section, Porto Vecchio, dates from 1250. The Lanterna, a lighthouse built in 1544 during Andrea Doria's tenure, soars upward 360 feet from its base in the center of the harbor. If you'd like a view of the harbor and city from above, take the Granarolo Funicular, which is a cog railway, up to Porta Granarolo. The 17th-century city walls up there guard one of several fortresses.

The **Royal Palace** *(Palazzo Reale, once called the Balbi Durazzo)* 17 via Balbi, dates from 1650. The palace contains Genoa's **Department of Fine Arts and Antiquities** and displays tapestries, sculptures, paintings, and ceramics. One room is devoted to Sir Antony Van Dyck who lived and worked in Genoa for six years beginning in 1621.

A number of palaces are grouped on Via Garibaldi, where patrician families built sumptuous homes filled with art treasures. **Palazzo Bianco,** 11 Via Garibaldi, is Genoa's most important gallery, containing a selection of local painters plus Flemish and Dutch works.

Next door is the **Town Hall** *(Palazzo Tursi)* 9 Via Garibaldi. The building was built by Nicolo Grimaldi in the 16th century. Inside, the **Guarnerius violin** owned by Paganini is on display; it is played on October 12 every year. Reportedly some of the ashes of Christopher Columbus are kept in the building.

Across the street stands **Palazzo Rosso,** 18 Via Garibaldi, which dates from the 17th century. Built for the Brignole Sale family, the house contains a large courtyard with loggias on each floor and a frescoed ceiling at the peak. Van Dyck family portraits are featured here.

The **National Gallery** *(Palazzo Spinola)* was owned by the Grimaldi family and given to the state in 1958. Frescoes portray the life of the family painted by L. Tavarone in the 17th century. The Spinola family restored the palace between 1730 and 1737.

The **Church of San Matteo,** dating from the 12th century, holds the tomb of Andrea Doria. Besides working on the constitution for Genoa in 1529, Doria was also a famous admiral.

Piazza San Matteo is a well preserved medieval square and the center of the Doria family residences.

The **Church of San Lorenzo** is the medieval church to visit in Genoa. Black and white horizontal lines extend across the facade and the tower, thin vertical columns hover around the three arched doors. A 15th-century rose window gives life to the otherwise dark interior. An unexploded shell remains after its firing from an English ship in 1941. The **Cathedral Treasury** contains a **sacred basin** of green crystal, which some say was on hand for the Last Supper, and the **Cross of Zaccaria,** which contains a piece of the original cross under its emerald and ruby decoration.

Incongruous as it seems, the **Piazza Dante,** which contains the first skyscraper in Genoa, is perhaps also the site of the house of Christopher Columbus. The ruin of the little medieval house, renovated during the 18th century, may or may not have been his childhood home.

DAY TRIPS FROM GENOA...................

Portofino

Portofino, called Portus Delphini or Port of the Dolphins by Plinius, is an attractive village with its wide piazza on the harbor and craggy mountains all around. Once a quiet fishing village with boats sailing out carrying fishermen, merchants, traders, ancient navigators, and soldiers off to the Crusades, the village harbor also attracted larger ships who were grateful for the deep harbor and shelter from the sea.

Modern seafarers come to Portofino to race in the Portofino Regatta or to moor in the harbor for a relaxing vacation. It is almost easier to come by boat than by car as the only road into town is often clogged with traffic.

The **Church of St. George** *(Chiesa de San Giorgio)* contains the relics of St. George, which were returned by the Crusaders. There is a view from the terrace. The **Castle of St. George** *(Castello di San Giorgio)* also features a view. Farther on, the views from the lighthouse include all of the coast as far as La Spezia.

San Margherita Ligure

The next village is also pleasant, ringed with mountains and open to the sea. The **Basilica of St. Margherita di Antochia** has two steeples and a number of paintings inside. The **Centurione Palace,** which was built by the Durazzo family in 1560 contains a large Italian garden.

Rapallo

Rapallo is tucked into the innermost spot of the Tigullio Gulf, where it gave sanctuary to bishops from Milan who fled from the Lombard invasion in 568. In 1549 the dreaded pirate, Dragut, invaded and ruined the town. The castle dates from the 16th century when it was built to defend the town from the Saracen raids.

Visitors can drive up the mountain to the **Madonna de Montallegro,** a church dating from 1557. The church is well known for its picture of the Virgin, which disappeared and then miraculously reappeared in the same spot. Other treasures include a pieta by Luca Cambiaso and an apparizione by Nicolo Barabino. Poignant reminders of the lonely lives of sailors are votive offerings for safe voyages, handmade and hung on the walls.

Gulf of La Spezia

Farther down the coast near the next promontary lies the town of La Spezia, where Percy Bysshe and Mary Shelley spent part of the summer of 1822 at

Villa Magni in nearby San Terenzo. It has been nicknamed Golfo dei Poeti, as other writers found inspiration in its pleasant hills. Its **Castel San Giorgio** dates from the 12th century. The **Church of St. Mary,** first built in 1271, then destroyed and rebuilt during the 15th century, was once outside the wall; now it is inside. A number of paintings and statues and a polychrome terracotta by Andrea Della Robbia are in the church.

Napoleon first thought of planning a naval base there and it is still in use today. The **Naval Technical Museum** houses model ships representative of Columbus's caravels, Roman galleys, Bourbonic vessels, and recent ships. The figurehead collection is outstanding, including one of a bare-breasted young woman named Atalanta, found in the sea in 1864.

The **Archaeological Museum** *(Museo Archeologicao Lunense)* contains prehistoric artifacts from Palmaria Island *(Grotta dei Columbi)*. The collection also includes items from the Roman era.

The Gulf of la Spezia has a town on each end—Portovenere and Lerici. Lerici holds special memories for us, as we walked along the harbor, there after our children were tucked in bed, stopping to enjoy an aperitif and savor the moment. In the morning our son was enthralled with the fish market, running from one basin of freshly caught fish to the next.

Lerici's castle, originally called Borgo Pisano by the Pisans who built it, dates from 1256, with other sections added 300 years later. It is now a youth hostel. The 16th-century **Oratory of San Rocco** has an unusual Romanesque campanile. St. Francis's parish church houses a wood statue by Maragliano, several marble statues, and a number of paintings.

Portovenere has a 13th-century **Genoese Gothic Church of St. Peter,** zebra-striped in black and white. An earlier pagan temple on the site may have been dedicated to the goddess of the sea. The **Church of San Lorenzo** dates from 1131. Its treasury contains three Syrian caskets and a first century Byzantine sarcophagus, marble statues, two triptychs from the 15th century, and a fresco from the same vintage.

The castle stands firm above the church, its earlier ruins dating from Roman times, with 16th-century additions. Crenellated walls are still standing here and there in the town. A blue grotto at Isola Palmaria may be entered from the sea. Byron's grotto, Grotta Arpaia, is on the cliffs below St. Peter's. Besides swimming across the gulf to visit Shelley in San Terenzo, Byron wrote *Childe Harold* there.

MILAN

Our efforts to visit Leonardo da Vinci's *Last Supper* seemed doomed to failure as we inched through thick fog on the outskirts of Milan over 30 years ago. We gave up and found a room for the night after following red taillights to a corner where we spotted a taverna with rooms. The next time we tried to visit the church was closed. Finally we made it and were able to feast our eyes on the painting we had visualized from countless reproductions. It was worth the trip.

HISTORY.....................................

Situated as it is at the juncture of three navigable rivers, the Adda, Ticino, and Po, and just south of the mountain passes of the Alps, Milan has been in the position of attracting most invaders over the last 2500 years. It has been under the power of Gauls, Romans, Goths, and Franks as well as later rulers of France, Austria, and Spain. During its one period of Milanese rule, the Visconti and Sforza families were in power. Today Milan is known as an industrial and commercial center.

SIGHTSEEING.....................................

Travelers come to Milan with a strong desire to see Leonardo da Vinci's *Last Supper*. Unfortunately, when Leonardo began his work in 1495, he was intent on having the option of working in a medium that would not dry rapidly and so chose oil paint. In only ten years, when he was still alive, the painting began to deteriorate. Atmospheric pollution has contributed to the decay also. Over the years restorers have tried techniques to preserve it that did not work. Layers of clumsy pigments were added, destroying his lines. Now, with more sophisticated techniques, restorers are trying to uncover his original work and leave blank that which has been destroyed. *Last Supper* is in the refectory of the church of Santa Maria delle Grazie, on Via Caradosso.

When we were last there restorers had cleaned the right side of the painting using a microscope; it is noticeably lighter. The focal point is the head of Christ, probably just after he has announced that one of the disciples will betray him. They seem frozen in their disbelief, grouped in threes, with Judas grasping the bag of money. The two hands—one of Christ and one of Judas—almost touch the plate of fish—another sign perhaps.

The *Crucifixion* fresco by G. Donato Montorfano is on the back wall. It is thought that Leonardo da Vinci added figures of Beatrice d'Este, her son Francesco, and Lodovico il Moro with his son Massimiliano. This fresco has a slight 3-D effect as the tops of helmets jut out from the wall.

The **Cathedral,** is a mammoth pile of Gothic turrets, buttresses, spires, arches, and belfries and the building is the largest cathedral in Italy. Part of the fun is climbing 158 steps to the roof amid the peaks, pinnacles, flying buttresses, and statues. Galeazzo Visconti III, the first Duke of Milan, started building the cathedral in 1386. Stained-glass windows dating from the 15th century are magnificent; they portray the Old and New Testaments. The tomb of Gian Giacomo Medici de Marignano dates from the 1560s. We were taken with the blackened skeleton of Cardinal San Galdino, 1166–1176, who lies in a glass tomb wearing a red robe and pointed slippers.

Don't miss the gold line on the floor near the entrance. Look up to see a hole at the top—an ancient sundial. At noon the light falls on the line; before clocks someone would wait until the sundial indicated noon, then go up to the castle and fire the noon cannon. Astronomers of Brera designed this curiosity in the late 1700s.

Visitors can walk through the cathedral and under the piazza to see the remains of a 4th-century baptistery. Some say that St. Augustine was baptized there by St. Ambrose in 387.

The **cathedral museum** contains architects' wooden models for the building. Working models of statues for the duomo, tapestries, and paintings are also there. Vestments from the 16th to 20th centuries are on display.

Take a stroll through the **Galleria Vittorio Emanuele,** which is a gigantic cross-shaped arcade built of glass and steel, with frescoes high on the walls and a 19th-century style.

On the other end you will be near **La Scala,** in the Piazza della Scala. Its acoustics are considered to be perfect all the way up the six tiers of horse-shoe shaped balconies. Statues of Verdi, Bellini, Rossini, and Donizetti stand in the foyer.

Museo Teatrale alla Scala is the museum with a musical focus, obviously. It houses drawings of Verdi during his last hours when the street was covered with straw so carriages clattering by would not disturb him. His death mask, lock of hair, cast of right hand, and a bronze figure of him sitting on a rock are on display.

The **Brera Museum,** 28 Via Brera, Pinacoteca di Brera, is in a 17th-century Jesuit palace. Over 500 paintings were brought back after World War II restoration.

Castello Sforzesco, Piazza Castello, a large brick fortress dating from the 15th-century, contains Michelangelo's *Pieta Rondanini,* which was his last work, unfinished before his death in 1564. Collections of prehistoric and Egyptian culture are in the basement of the Roccetta courtyard. Look for the bronzes from the first Tomb of the Warrior of Sesto Calende (6th century B.C.) in the center of the prehistoric room.

Biblioteca Ambrosiana, Piazza Pio XI 2, was once the palace and library of Cardinal Federigo Borromeo. Leonardo da Vinci's *Portrait of a Musician* is an unfinished but well preserved painting.

DAY TRIPS FROM MILAN ....

ITALIAN LAKE DISTRICT

The Italian Lake District, with its long silvery slivers of fingers peaked by mountains, has been the scene of visits by a long line of travelers. Medieval and renaissance cardinals built villas on the shores, and royalty from many nations came for a holiday. Poets and novelists went to write in peace—Pliny, Dante, Goethe, Stendhal, Flaubert, Mann, Wagner, Byron, Shelley, Napoleon, and Hemingway found inspiration and beauty there. Most of the lakes were formed during the Ice Age.

Lake Maggiore

Lake Maggiore (also called Verbano), to the northwest of Milan, has its northern leg in Switzerland, extending through Italy for at least 40 miles in a "y" shape. Artifacts dating back into the Iron Age, from the 9th century B.C., have been found in burial grounds.

The town of Stresa is a resort and the jumping-off place for boat tours. Located on the west shore of Lake Maggiore, Stresa is popular in summer and in winter when a cable car rises from Stresa-Lido to Mattarone for skiing and more views of the lakes and the alps. Ernest Hemingway set part of his *A Farewell to Arms* in Stresa.

The jewels of Maggiore are the **Borromean Islands,** romantic with baroque palaces and sumptuous gardens. The Borromeo family story is romantic indeed. Originally from San Miniato in Tuscany, they moved to Florence. Filippo De Borromeo was beheaded for his political beliefs and the family moved to Padua. They increased their wealth through banking, including lending money to Gian Galeazzo Visconti, the Duke of Milan. The Viscontis gave land to their loyal friends, including several islands in Lake Maggiore. During the 1500s the Borromeos began building both palaces and gardens on their islands.

Isola Bella has a large **palace** *(Palazzo Borromeo)* where Mussolini slept the night before the 1935 Stresa Conference after his aids had checked the bedroom thoroughly for possible assassins. The gardens contain a shell-shaped stone amphitheater where concerts are held, graced by the presence of white peacocks. The famous "Garden of Love" has a lily pond, statues, exotic plants, fountains, and clipped hedges, all overlooking the sea. The name of the island is attributed to Isabella, who was the wife of Count Carlo Borromeo.

Isola dei Pescatori is a little fishing village on an island that looks very much like all three islands did before the Borromeos transformed them. This island is quarter of a mile long and its winding lanes cross less than 100 yards in width.

Isola Madre, which is farther out from shore, contains the palace, a family chapel dedicated to San Carlo Borromeo, and botanical gardens. Peacocks roam here as well as both silver and gold pheasants.

Lake Como

Lake Como *(Lario)* is the deepest lake in Europe at almost 1350 feet. Its 30-mile length holds a series of villas, gardens, towers, cloisters, castles, basilicas, and museums. Como, the city on the southern tip of Lake Como, is an industrial place. Heading north along the southwestern leg one comes to Cernobbio, which is famous for its Grand Hotel Villa d'Este, which was once home to Caroline of Brunswick, estranged wife of King George IV of England. (See Inns.)

Villa Carlotta, an 18th-century mansion farther up the coast, has terraced gardens renowned or spring blossoms. A morning visit is preferable before shadows fall on the blooms from towering Monte di Tremezzo. The villa was built for Marquis Giorgio Clerici beginning in 1690.

Continuing north to Tremezzo one comes upon a view of the open lake, just above the "y" and a view of the town of Bellagio on the opposite shore. The ferry to **Bellagio** leaves from Tremezzo. Bellagio is a romantic place with stone steps heading up tier after tier. Gardens of Villa Melzi compete with those of Villa Serbelloni for choice blooms.

NAPLES

Mount Vesuvius towers over Naples as well as the Sorrento Peninsula—its presence is constant. To get a closer look many years ago, we took a perilous journey up the wrong side of the volcano on a makeshift road and hiked the rest of the way to a narrow, unfenced lip. As we peered down into the terrifyingly deep crater we noticed wisps of white steaming upward from cracks as if to warn "I'm not dead yet." Visits to both Pompeii and Herculaneum reinforce the sense of foreboding that the volcano could spout fire once again. And yet life goes on, right under its very nose.

HISTORY......................................

The siren Parthenope was the legendary inspiration for Naples. Originally a Greek colony called Palaeopolis (or old city), this area was founded by settlers from Cumae in the 7th century B.C. During the 5th century B.C. settlers came from Chalcis and Athens to found Neapolis (new city). In 328 B.C. Palaeopolis was invaded by the Romans and the city dissolved. Neapolis probably surrendered because it was given the privileges of a "civitas foederata." Pyrrhus tried to conquer Neapolis, unsuccessfully, in 280 B.C. Neapolitans spoke Greek and continued their Greek customs until the end of the Empire. Wealthy Romans such as Tiberius, Nero, Augustus, and Virgil spent winters in Naples. Virgil wrote much of his *Georgics* there and asked to be buried on the hill of Pausilypon. In 543 Naples was conquered by the Goths but by 553 was again under Byzantine control. In 1130, a Norman, Roger II became King in Palerno. Naples became the capital of the kingdom during the reign of Charles of Anjou. Spanish viceroys moved in from 1503 to 1707 but after the War of the Spanish Succession Naples was controlled by the Hapsburgs, then the Bourbons, until the unification of Italy in 1860.

SIGHTSEEING.....................................

Castle Nuovo or *(Maschio Angioino)*, on Piazza del Municipio, was built as a Franciscan monastery called Santa Maria ad Palatium in the early 13th century. Charles I of Anjou turned it into a fortress between 1279–82 and it has been enlarged several times since then. In 1446 Guillermo Sagrera was brought from Spain to redesign the building and add the five towers there today. Everything seems on such a large scale as one looks at this sturdy square fortress, with its massive, round, grey stone towers. It wouldn't be easy to break in or out of this place. The **Triumphal Arch,** of Renaissance origin, was built in honor of Alfonso I of Aragon. Castel Nuovo is not open to visitors.

The **Royal Palace** *(Palazzo Reale)* dates from the early 17th century when it was designed by Domenico Fontana. The facade contains marble statues of eight kings who ruled Naples. The bronze door at the bottom of the stairway was removed by Charles VIII during the campaigns of Italy but eventually returned. Look for the cannon ball thrust into the door. Napoleon's sister Caroline lived here with her husband Joachin Murat during his short reign in Naples.

Nearby stands the **St. Charles Theater** *(Teatro San Carlo)*, which was built by Charles of Bourbon in 1737. Ionic columns in the loggia give this theater a classical look.

Farther along the waterfront stands **Castel dell'Ovo,** called the Egg Castle, which is a 12th-century fortress. Its remains look out on a view of the entire harbor. The last of the German Hohenstaufens, Conradin, at only 16 years of age, was thrown in prison there by Charles I of Anjou in 1268 and later beheaded on the Piazza del Mercato.

The **National Archaeological Museum** *(Museo Archeologico Nazionale)* is the place to go *before* you head for Herculaneum or Pompeii. Many of their treasures, including mosaics, sculpture, and paintings, have been preserved and collected there.

Capodimonte Palace and National Gallery was built as a palace in the 18th century by the Bourbons. The **Banqueting Hall,** with its frescoed ceiling and gigantic hanging chandeliers, is elegant indeed. The **Porcelain Boudoir** is a delicate tracery of oriental figures, flowers, curves, and detail from floor to ceiling.

The duomo dates from the 1300s although it has been altered since, including the insertion of 110 old columns taken from pagan buildings. Some mosaics can be seen in the baptistery and in the Chapel of San Gennaro. The relics of St. Januarius (San Gennaro) are there and it is said that his dried blood becomes liquid during special services in his honor every May.

DAY TRIPS FROM NAPLES ....

SOUTHWEST OF NAPLES

Herculaneum

Herculaneum *(Ercolano)* was founded by Greek settlers using the name Herakleion, or according to legend, by Hercules. The city was right on the sea and supported a fishing fleet and drew wealthy vacationers who built villas there. Herculaneum was divided into five sections with three main roads. Although the upper part of town is still underneath modern buildings the lower part has been uncovered.

Mount Vesuvius exploded in 79 A.D. burying Pompeii in volcanic ash and Herculaneum in volcanic mud that filled all air space within buildings and hardened into stone, rising over 65 feet high. This hard crust protected some second stories as well as wooden frames, beams, walls, doors, stairways, and furniture. It also made looting and vandalism difficult so many pieces were not removed before systematic excavation began. Well diggers in the early 18th century first noticed parts of the hidden city. The Austrian Prince of Elboeuf began digging privately, then with directors in 1738. Excavation stopped from 1765 to 1828, then began again until 1875. In 1927 organized excavation was begun in earnest.

Visitors walk along a tree-lined promenade over views of the city below, which gives one the chance to really look at the dazzling display of homes and buildings still standing before descending down the ramp into the streets. The main street is called Decumanus Maximus and it runs from west to east. Near the Hercules Fountain are some shops containing crockery and tools.

The **House of Argus** was one of the first houses to be uncovered after 1828. The name came from a fresco portraying Io guarding Argus, which was in the hall of the peristyle. Pantries were found still containing carbonized foods. The **House of the Carbonized Furniture** still contains a couple of pieces of furniture including a couch and a small table with carved feet.

Baths were divided for men and women. They have seats along the walls. One mosaic floor features a Triton and four dolphins. The **Gymnasium** has a portico where the officials sat to watch games. A pool in the shape of a cross is fed by a bronze fountain featuring a five-headed snake.

Pompeii

Pompeii dates back to the 8th century B.C. when it was founded by a group of shepherds and peasants. Mount Vesuvius erupted in August of 79 A.D. and showered the town with volcanic ash up to a layer of 23 feet. It was discovered during the 16th century when roadwork was in progress. Excavation began in 1748 under Charles of Bourbon.

Pompeii was built on a ridge 130 feet above sea level; the ridge was made by a lava flow in prehistoric times. The land slopes from north to south toward the sea. Pompeii was planned with a grid pattern; two main streets intersect each other. Streets have pavements above street level for pedestrians with the addition of a few steppingstones across the road.

Inside the entrance at Porta Marina stands the **Antiquarium,** which houses molds of humans and animals in the moment of their death.

The **Forum** was the center of life in town and the first buildings were probably built around it. It measures 124 feet by 466 feet and was once surrounded by a portico. Daily markets, the slave markets, public speeches, and religious ceremonies took place there.

The **House of the Tragic Poet** has a mosaic over the door picturing a black dog with the caption, *Cave Canem* or "Beware of the dog." Another mosaic in the tablinum portrays a group of players before a performance. Mythological paintings include one of Iphigenia's sacrifice.

The **Amphitheater** is the oldest Roman amphitheater in existence. Games were held between animals, gladiators and any combination. A gymnasium and a small theater are nearby.

Mount Vesuvius

Once you have looked at the result of the eruption, you may want to see the volcano close up. We made the mistake of driving up the "back" way on the south face in 1968 with our two young children. The road tilted, made more noticeable in our tall VW camper, and lava had drifted over the road in the wind. We walked up the last part and gazed down into the crater without a guard rail. With this in mind, we suggest visiting the volcano on the west face if you have young children. On a later trip we took the chair lift up on that side and found the view exhilarating.

SOUTH AND SOUTHEAST OF NAPLES
The Sorrento Peninsula

The town of Sorrento lies on the eastern side of the Bay of Naples, partway out the peninsula that bears its name. The terrace Villa Comunale provides views of the bay and of Mount Vesuvius, which are enhanced by the crisp fragrance of lemons and oranges, growing prolifically in Sorrento.

The **Correale Museum** (*Museo di Correale*) houses a variety of collections in an 18th-century palace. The poet Tasso is featured, with his death mask on display as well as first editions of his books. The terrace behind the museum also provides striking views of the sea.

The Amalfi Drive

Imagine driving a winding corniche road along a craggy coast with sheer drops into an intense blue sea in front of a madman who wants to go twice your speed. It can and does happen that way, but the trip is worth the panic. Each hairpin turn provides another glimpse of cliff, sea, brightly colored boats far below, a Saracen tower, deep gorges, perhaps a roof part way down and—the screeching tires of your friend behind. He will probably honk and blink wildly meaning "Get out of my way," but don't let it bother your concentration. At some point he will zoom by and disappear in a flash around the next curve.

On the other hand you may be tied up in a long line of cars and coaches during high season or a holiday. We were foolish enough to drive the Amalfi coast during Easter weekend when everyone was going somewhere. No one went very fast that day. We were amused by the coach drivers who couldn't pass each other from opposite directions on the turns. They got out and waved their arms around with much shouting. Finally one of them had to back up and all the rest of us as well. At least the delays gave us time to really soak in the views as well as catch a little glimpse of life during a holiday.

You can drive the Amalfi Drive in either direction: from Sorrento to Salerno or the reverse. Its 43 miles are just as pretty and exciting either way and there is an Autostrada at each end for the trip back to Naples at the end of the day. If you start from the Sorrento end, turn left at Meta and follow signs for Colli di San Pietro and then for Positano.

Positano

Positano was a fishing village for centuries, accessible only by sea or by pack mule. Some say it was founded by people from Paestum who were trying to stay out of the clutches of Saracen pirates. The flat-roofed white or pastel colored houses perch on the cliff from the sea upward, spilling their flowers over walls and terraces. Trader's ships used to come in from the East bringing silks and spices during the 16th century; now hydrofoils zing out to Capri.

Amalfi

Pisa and Genoa were rivals of Amalfi when the town was a powerful maritime center, especially up to the 11th century. The Amalfi Navigation Tables originated here and are kept in the town hall. A monument honoring Flavio Gioia, who invented the compass, stands in the square. Amalfi was founded during the 4th century when a group of Romans were shipwrecked there while on their way to Constantinople.

The duomo, **Cathedral of St. Andrew,** was begun in the 9th century, with renovation taking place several times since then. The bell tower, with its mullioned windows and arches, is from the original structure. High on the gable of the facade shines the mosaic of Christ on a throne among the Evangelists. The black and white marble stripes are interwoven with an Eastern touch. Eleventh-century bronze doors came from Constantinople. St. Andrew's remains are kept in the crypt. The **Cloisters of Paradise** date from the 13th century and are Moorish in style. Concerts are held there during the summer.

Trips to visit the **Emerald Grotto** *(Grotto dello Smeraldo)* can be taken from Amalfi. Discovered in 1932 near Conca dei Marini, the grotto looks green as light is filtered in through the rocks.

Ravello

The drive up the Dragon Valley to Ravello is steep and long, which cuts down on tourist traffic. The duomo was founded in 1086 and renovated in the 18th century. Its facade is quite plain, but there is a bronze door dating from 1179. Its 54 panels depict stories of the Passion. Inside, the blood of St. Pantaleo, who was beheaded in 290, is said to liquefy on the anniversary of his death every July. A mosaic depicts the whale swallowing Jonah. The pulpit has twirled columns resting on six lions and mosaic patterns as well.

The **Church of St. John the Bull** is just above the cathedral. Its Arabian style provides delicate arches and mullioned windows. The pulpit has mosaics and frescoes.

Palazzo Rufolo was built as a villa during the 11th century by the Rufolo family. Several popes have lived there, as well as Charles of Anjou, and Richard Wagner. Wagner had the inspiration for his *Parsifal* from the arcaded cloister in the Villa. Wagnerian concerts are held here during the summer. The gardens are planted in raised shapes with palms giving some shade.

Villa Cimbrone is a modern structure built in medieval style. The main building has two towers and a courtyard containing sculpture and gardens. A small temple hovers over the statue of Bacchus.

Maiori

Maiori was once encircled with towers and fortifications dating from the 9th century. Today ruins remain, including a Norman tower built on a pile of rock on the sea. Its long beach attracts visitors.

Cape Orso has another outcropping of grotesque rocks and a view each way toward Maiori Bay and Salerno Bay. The Autostrada leads from Vietri, and the end of the Amalfi Drive, back to Naples.

Salerno

The medieval section of Salerno is up on the hill complete with a castle dating back to the Lombard Prince Arechi in the 8th century. The duomo has a plain facade with three windows and a gable. The Romanesque belfry is from the 12th century. Inside, Byzantine mosaics lead the eye up to the dome with its brilliant reds and gold on a dark blue background. The crypt is ornate with marble decorations and frescoes in baroque style. San Matteo's tooth is kept in the Crypt.

Paestum

Originally called Poseidonia, Paestum was an ancient Greek seaport city dating to the 6th century B.C. As with other ancient cities, malaria led to its demise. The remaining temples stand majestically in meadows of green, their buff-colored limestone columns pockmarked with age but still standing.

The **Temple of Neptune** was thought to have been dedicated to Hera Argiva, the goddess of motherhood and wife of Zeus, as was the basilica. Its Doric lines have perfect proportions with tall elliptical columns reaching upward. The size of this temple is 200 by 80 feet. It is one of the best preserved in Europe, along with the Temple of Theseus in Athens and the Temple of Concord in Agrigento.

The **basilica** dates from the 6th century B.C. Its 50 original Doric columns are tapered at the top with swelling in the middle. The basilica is the oldest temple in Paestum. Its measurements are 177 by 82 feet.

The **Temple of Ceres** was dedicated to Athena, and is still has its gable perched precariously on the end. The Ionic columns from this temple are preserved in the museum.

The **Archaeological Museum** contains the contents of tombs from Paestum and nearby Sele. Thirty-four metopes dating from the 6th century B.C. portray Greek myths including that of Hercules.

WEST OF NAPLES
The Phlegrean Fields

The **Phlegrean Fields** *(Campi Flegrei)* cover a volcanic section west of Naples along the Gulf of Pozzuoli from Cape Posillipo to Cape Miseno. Molten lava is in constant turmoil not far from the surface, producing warm earth, spouts of steam, and a pungent sulphurous odor. Greek and Roman writers were not imagining things when they wrote about the underworld from this place.

Solfatara is actively producing fire, whisping steam, bubbling mud, and a smell of rotten eggs, but the last eruption was in 1198. As one walks through the sunken crater all of these assail the senses plus the sight of white and yellowish-green deposits on the ground. There is no vegetation within the floor of the crater.

Pozzuoli

Pozzuoli was founded in the 6th century B.C. under the control of the Greek colony of Cuma. The Sammites ruled until 338 B.C. and finally the Romans took over. As an active seaport serving both Rome and Naples, the town attracted wealthy merchants and patricians who lived in villas on the hills. Two amphitheaters, a theater, and a circus were constructed to provide entertainment.

The **Flavian Amphitheater** is the third largest in Italy after the Coliseum in Rome. Its stone basements are in good condition with lots of small rooms and passageways where the animals were kept. It was also flooded with water for marine battles, as was the Coliseum. When we were there it was quiet, except for the twittering of birds in the trees outside. With a little imagination one could hear the roaring of the crowds from the past.

The **Macellum,** or market, was a busy place until it began sinking into the ground with the invasion of subterranean water. During the 3rd century a new floor was laid above the old one but it continued to sink. Then, during the 11th century, the ground level started to rise. Now the marble columns are slowly sinking again. They show the effect of marine molluscs up to a height of 19 feet. The Macellum was earlier called the Temple of Serapide because a statue of the goddess Serapide was discovered there in 1750.

St. Paul landed in the harbor in 61 on his way to Rome. Although his ship was wrecked near Malta, he completed his journey on a grain ship from Alexandrea, the *Castor and Pollux.*

Lake Avernus *(Lago d'Averno)* was considered by the ancients to be the entrance to hell. Orpheus, Aeneas, and Odysseus may have used this site. It is said that birds could not fly over the lake without being overcome by the fumes and perishing here. The color is definitely green, distinct from the blue sea beyond.

Cumae

Cumae, or Cuma, was inhabited since prehistoric times and founded by the Greeks in the 8th century B.C. The famous **Cave of the Sibyl** *(Antro della Sibilla)* was dug out of the rock in the 5th century. Virgil wrote about her in *The Aeneid,* Book 6: "Thus from her sanctuary does the Cumaean Sibyl spread the sacred horror of her ambiguous oracles and moans in her cave, where truth is shrouded in shadow." The ancients believed that this prophet was able to speak with those in another world. Rulers, businessmen, farmers, and ordinary people came to learn from the Sibyl. The Cave of the Sibyl is a long tunnel with a striking vaulted opening and stones tapering to a flat top. Light comes in at intervals from the side. One can walk from one end down the length of the tunnel to a cave where the Sibyl delivered her oracle.

Up on top, the **acropolis** stands with the remains of two large temples. The **Temple of Apollo** has been destroyed down to the bases of huge columns and ankle high remnants of the walls of the rooms. The **Temple of Jupiter** was constructed on the highest terrace of the city so it can be seen from the sea. This temple was used by early Christians as a basilica, and its red bricks still stand as arches and walls. The circular font has a marble facing. We shared the beautiful sunny day with lots of buzzing bees enjoying the wild flowers.

EXCURSIONS TO THE ISLANDS NEAR NAPLES......................

Many tourists visit both Ischia and Capri on day trips from Naples, Sorrento, or Pozzuli. If you have the time it is pleasant to stay overnight and have more hours to enjoy the island leisurely.

Ischia

Ischia, a jewel of an island, is located at the northwest end of the Bay of Naples. Much of the island contains volcanic hills; the largest is **Mount Epomeo.** Today there is no primary volcanic activity; secondary activity takes the form of hot springs and mineral waters. Many people come for thermal treatments where the minerals are claimed to heal.

The ancient town of **Pithekoussai,** settled by Greeks in the 7th century B.C., has an **archaeological museum** located in a crypt under the church of San

Restituta. Artifacts are displayed in the entrance room, which is only a part of this fascinating site. Visitors are free to wander deeper and deeper under the church to view excavations which have produced walls, urns, tombs, bones and other objects. The musty dampness and eeriness add to the atmosphere.

Ischia Ponte's bridge leads to the **Castle of Ischia,** which dates from the 15th century. Vittoria Colonna, who was a poet and friend of Michelangelo, lived there at one time.

Capri

Capri has been called the "island of dreams" and we can't argue with that. Happiness seems to flow as one thinks in anticipation of this romantic place. The craggy, jagged, limestone rocks, rising in two enormous masses from the sea form two distinct sections with a cleft in the middle. From the pinnacles soaring into the sky to the blue grottoes along the sea, Capri is striking. The vegetation is prolific and lush, with colorful cascades of flowers overlaying the green foliage everywhere.

Every time we visit Capri we do some hiking. One of the walks from the piazza leads around to a natural arch, framed in pines with the blue-blue sea sparkling below. Sheer rock cliffs drop into turquoise water below and the surf pounds.

The walk up to the **Villa of Tiberius** *(Villa Jovis)* is about three kilometers. Tiberius's reputation for throwing his enemies and wives off the cliff into the sea is still remembered. Tiberius arrived here in 27 and ruled Italy from his villa, which is in ruins. When we reached the chapel at the top we heard a chorus of four tourist priests singing around the monument of the Madonna and child.

The **Blue Grotto** may be entered only by small boats, and only when the sea is calm as the opening isn't large enough for anything bigger. When the sea is too rough, swimmers may enter by hanging on to a rope along the left side so as not be dashed onto the rocks. Inside, the grotto really is blue, with light coming from another opening below the waterline. The grotto is 177 feet long, 98 feet wide, and 49 feet high.

The **chairlift ride** to the top of Mount Solaro brings visitors to the highest point on the island. The view from the top included Naples, Mount Vesuvius, Pompeii, the Sorrento Peninsula, the Amalfi Drive, and nearby islands.

The **Villa San Michele** was built by Axel Munthe, who wrote *The Story of San Michele* while living there. His sculpture collection is extensive and the garden views extend to Mount Tiberius. In 1949 Sweden received Munthe's villa; it is used as a center for young musicians and artists. Concerts are given there during the summer.

ROME

With *Three Coins in the Fountain* humming in our heads we turned around and threw coins into the water, hoping for a return visit. The year was 1968 and we had spent the morning playing "Alice in Wonderland" in the ruins of the Forum with our six-year-old. Since then we have returned three times, with more to come. On each visit we plan our days to suit our companions, but nothing can match that first time when we savored Rome through the eyes of children.

HISTORY....................................

Whether you choose to believe in the legendary origin of Rome or the historical data collected from artifacts, the city has been around for a long time. Livy's *Roman History* and Virgil's *Aeneid* relate details about the marriage of Aeneas, son of Venus and Lavinia, daughter of the king of Latium. Their son, Ascanius founded Alba Longa in 1150 B.C. Amuius, the last king of the Alban dynasty removed his brother Numitor from the throne and Numitor's daughter, Rhea Silvia, was sent to the Vestals. The god Mars conceived with Rhea twin boys, Romulus and Remus. Crafty Amulius threw them into the Tiber but they were found, nursed by a she-wolf and lived with two shepherds, Faustulus and Larentia. By 753 B.C. the twins had placed their grandfather, Numitor, on the throne and went back to the spot where they had spent their childhood to create a new town. Romulus drew a line around the sacred place for the new city. It is said that when Remus stepped over the line in fun, no-sense-of-humor Romulus killed him. Romulus went on to provide Sabine women for the bandits who chose to live in his new town.

Earliest artifacts, which are on display in the Forum Antiquarium, are from tombs dating back to 1000 B.C. A cemetery in the Roman Forum has revealed pieces dating to the 8th and 7th centuries B.C., the era of Romulus. Also three huts from the same period were uncovered on the Palatine. A 6th-century B.C. monument was discovered underneath black marble slabs in the Forum; it may possibly be the tomb of Romulus.

The Sabines and the Latins lived in small villages of huts surrounding a swampy circle that was often flooded by the Tiber. It is thought that the Etruscans were the people who created a sewer system to drain the marsh, then used the land for a new forum. Etruscan kings ruled Rome from 616 to 509 B.C., when Tarquin the Superb was removed and the Republic was formed. Over the

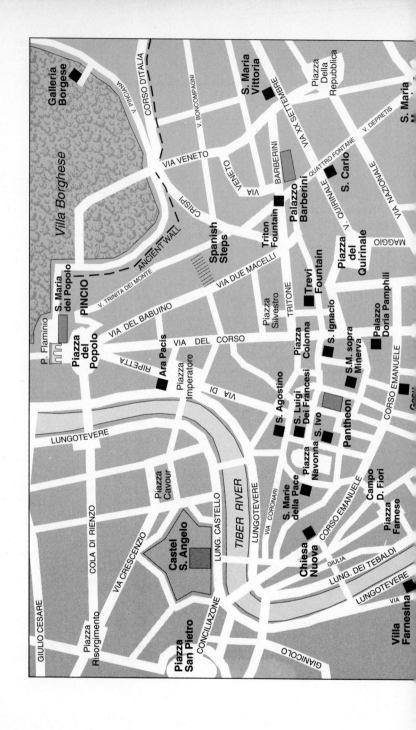

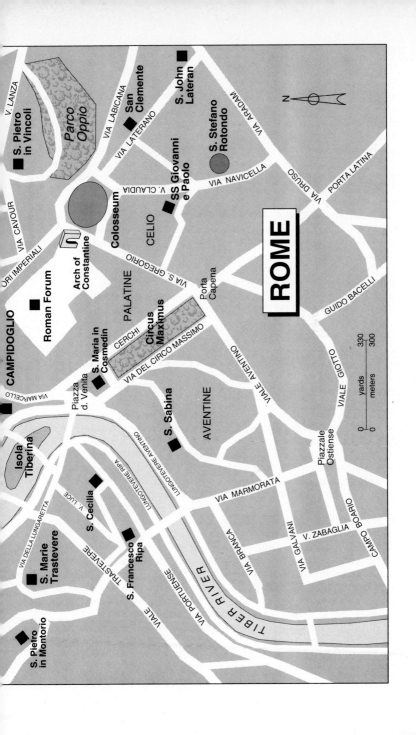

next five centuries, senators listened, harangued, and made choices on local, military, and foreign policy. By 312 B.C. the first aqueduct had been built. Caesar directed a major reconstruction in 44 B.C. to expand the size of the forum. In 27 B.C., Augustus continued Caesar's expansion; it is said that he found Rome in brick and left it in marble. Augustus was followed by Vespasian, Domitian, and Trajan, who continued raising statues and buildings.

Faith in Christianity was renewed with the worship of one god and preaching by Paul of Tarsus from 60 A.D. In 313 Constantine the Great ordained religious freedom, and by 391 the pagan temples were eliminated. Some of their stone was used in building new churches.

The forum suffered in 410 when Alaric the Goth destroyed part of it by fire. An earthquake in 442 and invasion by several armies finished off the active life of the forum. The site further deteriorated into a pasture by the 15th century.

The regions of Italy were united by King Victor Emmanuel II in 1861 after a number of years of infighting between the church and the state. Rome became the capital in 1870. In 1929 the Lateran Agreements settled the age-old problem of church and state and the Pope settled into the Vatican.

SIGHTSEEING..................................

The Palatine

Some visitors like to pick up a picnic lunch before heading up one of Rome's seven hills: the Palatine, the Aventine, the Quirinale, the Esquiline, the Celio, the Pincio, or the Janiculum.

We like to begin with the oldest inhabited hill—the Palatine. It was here that Romulus plowed the furrow around his proposed city; the line that his brother Remus stepped over and then had to be killed. Reportedly the legendary wolf's cave and the shepherd's hut were on the southwest side of the hill.

This once residential section in ancient times was home to Cicero, Antony, Agrippa, Octavian, Tiberius, Caligula, Caudius, Nero, and Domitian. The palaces on the Palatine eventually fell into ruin, and during the Renaissance the hill supported vineyards, gardens, and country houses.

For views below of the Forum, Colosseum, Capitol, and the city from the Lateran to the Janiculum, walk through the **Farnese Gardens,** on the site of the **Palace of Tiberius.** Cardinal Alexander Farnese, who was the nephew of Paul III, designed the gardens during the 6th century. A cascade of terraces rise up step by step to the top, where a botanical garden was planted.

Although most of the Palace of Tiberius lies underneath the Farnese Gardens, a row of massive arcades stand facing Cybele's temple. These arcades were part of the rear of the palace. At one point in time the building extended all the way to Via Nova, overlooking the forum.

Livia's house, where the Emperor Augustus lived with his wife Livia, contains a fresco, that of Io and Hermes. Legend reports that Zeus loved Io, turning her into a heifer so that his wife, Hera, would not realize his deception. Argus, with his hundred eyes, was sent by Hera to scrutinize Io until Zeus sent Hermes to rescue her.

Beyond the Temple of Apollo, ruins of the **Flavian Palace** *(Domus Flavia)* contain the official state rooms including the **Lararium,** which was a chapel, the **throne room,** where the emperor gave audiences, and the **basilica,** where he dispensed justice. A peristyle contains an octagonal basin or fountain in the middle. Domitianus used to walk around the peristyle; hated as he was for his cruelty he probably did not feel comfortable turning his back on anyone. Underneath the Lararium is a room with griffins; some of the frescoes have been removed to the antiquarium for preservation.

The Palace of Augustus **(Domus Augustana)** contains the private imperial rooms arranged in upper and lower levels around two peristyles. The **Antiquarium Museum** is housed in a convent building between the two palaces. Artifacts unearthed on the Palatine are displayed in the museum, including an unfinished statue of Diana.

The **Stadium** has an oval track, and there has been great debate about its use. It looks like a place to run or to watch private games, or maybe it was even a garden. Steps lead up to the ruins of the **Palace of Severus** and also the **Belvedere,** a three-storied terrace with views of the Circus Maximus.

The Roman Forum

If you'd like a bird's eye view of the **Roman Forum** take a walk up the steps to the **Campidoglio,** or Capitoline Hill, where you can gaze down on the pattern of ruins below. One can almost see emperors riding through the gates, senators gathering, and people going about their everyday lives in the Forum. You can see all of the way down the **Sacred Way** *(Sacra Via)* once the route of triumphal processions. Near the **Temple of Vespasian,** Roman orators held forth and their platform remains; at one time the prows of enemy ships were mounted on the stand.

The **Temple of Castor and Pollux,** dating to the 5th century B.C., still has three columns standing. Legend reports that Castor and Pollux, the sons of Jupiter and Leda, were involved in a battle beside Lake Regillus in 496 B.C. After the battle, the two brothers came to Rome to speak with people in the Forum.

The **Temple of Vesta** is thought to be the place where a communal fire continually burned; Vesta was the goddess of fire. The temple's circular shape has its roots in the round hut where Romulus lived. Next to the Temple of Vesta stood the House of the Vestal Virgins. Girls were selected from patrician families to spend at least 30 years, sometimes their whole lives within the service. If a girl let the fire flicker out she was punished; if she broke the chastity vow she was buried alive.

Colosseum

The **Colosseum** *(Coliseum* or *Amphitheatrum Flavium)* can hardly be missed as its red-brick bulk eclipses everything else in Rome. Its elliptical shape stands on the site of a marshy lake where the Palatine, Caelian, and Oppian hills meet. Although some of the structure is in ruins, the four stories are intact on one side. Gladiatorial performances were popular, with slaves fighting each other. Cruel "hunts" were planned where the arena was set to look like a setting in nature and the hunters and hunted were wild animals and men. Naval battles, with the arena filled with water, were staged as well. Visitors can still see the underground tunnels and passageways where animals and men were kept and escorted into the arena.

Go up to the second level for views looking down into the elliptical pit. Walk around looking for arched frames of gardens outside, pines, and closeups of the arches to photograph.

Nearby, the **Arch of Constantine,** built in 313 to commemorate the victories of Constantine, sport sculpture removed from other monuments such as the four Dacian prisoners on the top, which came from Trajan's monument. Reliefs depict Marcus Aurelius in a series after his return to Rome in 174.

From the Colosseum, take the San Giovanni in Laterno directly to the cathedral of the same name. Don't miss the large door that originally hung in the Curia of the Forum in the 1st century B.C. Inside, two saints on a high platform portray St. Paul, who, as a Roman, was allowed to be decapitated with a sword, and St. Peter, who was subjected to crucifixion.

On the left side of the basilica stands a building housing the **Holy Staircase** *(Scala Santa),* which was brought by Constantine's mother, St. Helen, from Jerusalem. It is thought that Christ climbed those steps when he went to see Pontius Pilate in the Praetorium. Those who want to ascend the 28 steps today must go up kneeling and praying.

Another of the four main basilicas in Rome is **Santa Maria Maggiore** on Piazza dell'Esquilino. According to legend a wealthy Roman dreamed that the Virgin suggested he build a church where freshly fallen snow appeared the next morning. The Esquiline was covered with snow and the church was built there. Inside, the mosaics in the nave portray scenes from the Old Testament. Walk down the steps into a chapel containing a large white marble statue of the kneeling Pope of 1854, who promulgated the doctrine of the immaculate conception. Five pieces of the Bethlehem cradle of Christ are preserved in a glass case.

Also in the church is the **Porta Santa,** a holy door that is opened every 25 years for one year. Anyone who passes through the door will have all sins forgiven. The next opportunity is the year 2000.

The Capitoline

The smallest of the hills in Rome is the Capitoline, now the civic center of Rome. Its square, the **Piazza del Campidoglio,** is enclosed on three sides by the Palazzo Senatorio, the Palazzo Dei Conservatori, and the Musei Capitalini. The square was known as Goat Hill during the Middle Ages because of the goats grazing around the ruins. Pope Paul III asked Michelangelo to design plans for Capitoline Hill before the visit of Charles V in 1536; work continued for the next hundred years.

The **Palazzo Senatorio,** which is the official residence of the Mayor of Rome, was constructed over the ancient Tabularium, where all of the laws inscribed on "tabulae" were kept in ancient times. The **Capitoline Tower** houses the **Patarine Bell,** which is rung on special occasions. The cross at the top signifies Christianity in Rome. The **Palazzo Senatorio** is not open to visitors as it is an office building for the city.

The **Palazzo Dei Conservatori** is now a museum of art. The courtyard contains gigantic pieces of a head and hand from the immense statue of the Emperor Constantine that once stood in Constantine's basilica in the Forum. Bernini's statue of Pope Urban VIII and Algardi's statue of Innocent X are in the **Horatii Room** and **Curatii Room.** The **Triumph Room** contains the famous *Boy with the Thorn,* by Spinario, where a little boy is seated, concentrating on removing a thorn from the bottom of his foot. The **Wolf Room** is one everyone wants to visit to see the bronze statue of a she-wolf, the motto and emblem of Rome, suckling Romulus and Remus.

The **Capitoline Museum,** in the New Palace, has a display of the "talking" statues who apparently made caustic or satirical comments about local figures. The Egyptian collection includes granite heads of monkeys, which were once on the Temple of Isis. A large statue of Mars stands in the atrium. The *Dying Gaul* in the Gladiator Room dates from the 2nd century B.C.

The **Church of Santa Maria D'Aracoeli** stands high up on Capitoline rock. This church was the center of religious life in medieval days. It houses the famous *Bambino d'Aracoeli,* which is a wooden statue of the baby Jesus, carved from olive wood from the Garden of Gethsemane.

Other Famous Landmarks

The **Pantheon,** on Via Palombella, was built in 27 B.C. by Marcus Agrippa, then reconstructed by Hadrian. This Hellenistic-style building was built with perfect symmetry and balance. The bronze doors are original, although many of the other bronze and marble decorations were stolen by Roman emperors and the popes. It is rumored that when Pope Urban VII Barberini removed the bronze beams from the portico to construct the canopy over the altar for St. Peter's, people said, "What the barbarians didn't do, Barberini did."

Inside, the only light comes from the hole in the cupola at the top of the dome. The space inside is circular, leading the eye upward to the dome. The weight of the dome is borne by the alternating arches and protruding platforms of masonry. The platforms contain shrines. Victor Emmanuel II, who was the first king after the unification of Italy, lies in his tomb in one of the chapels. Raphael, who died in 1520, is also buried there.

The **Trevi Fountain** is one place all visitors want to see so they can throw in a coin to ensure a return visit to Rome. Marcus Agrippa ordered a canal dug to bring water to Rome in 19 B.C., called Acqua Vergine because a virgin found the source of the spring. Pope Clement XIII decided that a fountain should be created at the end of the canal. Nicola Salvi designed the fountain with Ocean, riding in a chariot that is drawn by two tritons and sea horses, in the center. Salubrity and Abundance stand on either side. Water pours over its craggy rocks and visitors line the rim to watch and toss in their coins. The 1954 film *Three Coins in the Fountain* has spread the legend even further.

The **Spanish Steps** are climbed by most visitors; there is a view at the top that makes the climb worthwhile. Previously, there had been a diplomatic difference of opinion between the Holy See and France. During the 17th century, there had been talk of building steps in between the Spanish Square and the Church of Trinita dei Monti, but haggling continued concerning statues and designers until Pope Innocent XIII settled the question. De Sanctis planned three flights of steps, with varying widths and patterns, and they were finally built. People begin by walking up the center, with blossoms on both sides, then splitting either right or left around a central wooded area, emerging into a graceful tapering series of steps, and finally splitting again to reach the top.

Vatican City

The Vatican State is the spiritual center of the Roman Catholic faith. Pope John Paul II, who was elected in 1978, is the supreme head of the Roman Catholic Church, which has over 700 million members. He controls legislative, executive, and judicial matters assisted by the Cardinal Secretary of State, a Governor, and the College of Cardinals. Swiss Guards wear Renaissance-style uniforms in yellow, red, and blue as they stand guard at the Vatican.

The Emperor Constantine ordained that the first Christian basilica should be placed over St. Peter's tomb; the present building was placed on the same site as the 4th century structure. **St. Peter's Basilica** was begun in 1506 according to plans drawn by Bramante, followed by Raphael, Antonio da Sangallo, and Michelangelo, who designed the dome. The last architect was Carlo Maderna, who designed the baroque facade, which was finished in 1614. The bronze door was original to the first St. Peter's.

Inside, this largest of all churches in the world is almost unimaginable, difficult for the senses to absorb such immense proportions. The length is 692 feet, which includes the porch. Marks on the floor indicate the length of other great cathedrals (all in meters) including St. Paul's (London; 158.10), Florence (149.28), Bruxelles (140.94), Cologne (134.94), Paris (130), Prague (124), Assisi (114.76), St. Paul's (Brazil; 111.45) and Westminster Abbey (110) to name a few.

The **Pieta Chapel** is to the right. Michelangelo created this piece when he was 25. When enemies stated that it was not his work, Michelangelo inscribed his signature on the sash of the Virgin; it is the only work he signed. The white marble gleams with careful spotlighting and the marble behind is an amber shade. A glass shield stretches from the floor to the arch.

The high altar stands below the **Baldaquin,** a black and gold canopy created by Bernini in 1624. This 95 foot-high canopy contains some bronze taken from the Pantheon. St. Peter's tomb lies underneath the high altar. The bronze figure in the nave is St. Peter; his right foot has become smooth from the kisses of his followers.

Visitors can take an elevator up to the terrace, then walk up to a walkway inside the dome to see mosaics eyeball to eyeball, as well as to look down on the canopy. It is a further 330-step climb to the top of the dome emerging on a gallery outside the lantern for a view of the city.

The **Vatican Palace** houses eight museums, five galleries, a library, the Borgia Apartments, Raphael Rooms, and the Sistine Chapel. There is so much to see before reaching the Sistine Chapel; one is torn between moving along at a reasonable pace and hurrying on to the chapel.

The **Sistine Chapel,** named after Pope Sixtus IV, is where conclaves and special ceremonies are held. Pope Julius II gave Michelangelo the task of covering 10,000 square feet of ceiling. Although some of us have had the vision of Michelangelo lying on his back for four years of conscientous effort, he apparently threw back his head and painted with a permanent crick in his neck. In early 1990 cleaning was completed, amid much controversy on proper methods of conservation. The rich colors have been revealed and the life in the faces enhanced by the removal of grime. Nine scenes from the Old Testament include: The Separation of Light and Darkness, the Creation of the Sun and Moon, the Separation of Land and Water, the Creation of Adam, the Creation of Eve, the Fall and Expulsion from Paradise, the Sacrifice of Noah, the Great Flood, and the Intoxication of Noah.

From 1535 to 1541 Michelangelo created the *Last Judgment* on the wall above the altar. Christ sits in judgment with the Virgin. Prophets and saints either ascend to heaven or fall into hell. The walls are covered with frescoes by Botticelli, Pinturicchio, Ghirlandaio, Rosselli, and Signorelli.

Catacombs

The catacombs of Rome are Christian cemeteries used from the 2nd to 4th centuries. We visited the **Catacombs of St. Callistus,** on Via Appia, which stretches for 20 kilometers in five layers. Each layer has rectangular openings, one on top of the other up to the ceiling. Small openings were for babies and small children. Some family tombs have several spaces on each side of a small room, like built-in beds, and perhaps an arched entrance. Christian symbols on the tombs include a boat, a dove, the good shepherd, several fish, and the three magis. Bodies were wrapped in linen and sealed, and lit candles were placed near them. Mass is celebrated in the crypt where 16 popes were buried.

A marble statue of St. Cecilia lying on her face shows marks on her neck where she was slashed in real life. She held up three fingers as she died—for the Trinity.

Baths

Caracallas Baths, on Via delle Terme, were once an important meeting place where people could relax, do a little business, use a library, have a meal, or enjoy a sauna. These baths date from 212 A.D. and cover 27 acres. A central building housed the frigidarium, tepidarium and caldarium with adjacent rooms on each side. During the summer, opera is held in the ruins of the caldarium.

DAY TRIPS FROM ROME......................

East of Rome
Tivoli

Tivoli, earlier called Tibur, was founded by Tiburtus. Located at the foot of the Sabine Hills, Tivoli is where the Aniene River meets the Tiber.

Hadrian's Villa *(Villa Adriana)* built by the Emperor Hadrian beginning in 118, is the largest and richest Roman villa ruin. The eight-mile boundary encircled an estate containing lakes, canals, fountains, and gardens. Hadrian built an imperial palace, a maritime theater, a library, and baths. His interest in architecture around the world led him to imitate some favorites from his travels. As an astute art collector, he decorated his palace with many treasures. Barbarian invaders sacked the villa and many of his statues and works of art were taken to Villa d'Este.

The **Maritime Theater** was a round villa with a portico encircled by a canal, accessible by swing bridges. Here, the emperor could escape from his busy life and restore himself. He had only to pull up the drawbridges to seclude himself.

Hadrian saw a place in Thessaly, Greece, that caught his eye and so created his own Terrace of Tempe. A statue of the goddess Venus stands within a round temple that has been reconstructed.

The baths come in all sizes from small to large and in octagonal, circular or rectangular shapes. The **Great Bath** contains a bit of vaulting in its ruin.

Villa d'Este, once a Benedictine monastery, was the home of Cardinal Ippolio d'Este. The gardens are alive with fountains, grottoes, reflecting pools, and waterfalls. Cypress provide a dark green and cool backdrop to the rushing water. The **Organ Fountain** used to be controlled by water jets that actually played an organ. Claude Venard created this unusual work in the 16th century. The **Avenue of a Hundred Fountains** contains a floral display as well as one fountain after another in the form of animals, eagles, lilies, obelisks, and boats.

The **Oval Fountain** is circular and flows into a pool; statues of naiads pour water from jugs. The **Rometta Fountain** contains some of the emblems of Rome, a few ruins, and a sculpture of the she-wolf that raised Romulus and Remus. The **Dragon Fountain** was built to commemorate Pope Gregory XIII; his family coat-of-arms contains dragons.

Villa Gregoriana is the place to go for a hike to see a number of water-falls. The River Aniene runs through a double tunnel called the **Traforo Gregoriano,** which was built in 1826 for flood control. As the water emerges, it falls as the Cascata Grande. At the **Siren's Grotto** the water falls into a cavern with great force. The **Grotto of Neptune** contains strange contorted rocks which have been worn by the force of the water.

VENICE

As a giddy young girl I arrived in Venice with three others and we booked into a once-grand, now decaying hotel right on the Grand Canal. We left our luggage in a heap and set out to walk all over Venice. Getting lost was half the fun, and we giggled our way over canals and sought more corners to turn with surprises right and left. Every now and then we chose to enter a palace where we listened intently to a guide who told us what it was like hundreds of years ago. We were just serious enough to learn a little and then spin off to run around more corners. Later visits with my husband and children have had their own adventures and pleasures but never quite the magic of that first encounter with the grande dame of the Adriatic.

HISTORY.....................................

As northern invaders surged across Europe, taking everything they wanted, those living in northern Italy escaped into the mud flats and islands of the lagoon. They pounded tree trunks as pilings into the soft mud and built a city. Their refuge during the Dark Ages turned out to be sturdy and strong. They were able to keep others at bay and develop their city into a powerful trading center. Venice was built on 118 islands contained in the archipelago with more than 150 canals to serve as her water-routes. She became a dominant force in the sea-world of the Adriatic Sea and the eastern Mediterranean. The first doge was selected in 697 with the advent of the Most Serene Republic.

Byzantine craftsmen came to create brilliant mosaics in the city's churches. Grand palaces were built during the 11th to 13th centuries. By the 15th century Venice had reached her peak; after the 16th century her sea-power declined as the Ottoman Empire took control of traditional trade avenues. During her Golden Age sumptuous buildings went up and Tintoretto, Titian, and Bellini decorated them. In 1797 Napoleon got rid of the old republic. In 1866 the Italian city-state took over.

Since then Venice has been threatened by the sea; floods have devastated her treasures. Algae turned the canals green with the balance of nature upset by flood control measures. However, Venice is still dreamlike, with the romance of the centuries to explore.

SIGHTSEEING...............................

Piazza San Marco is the place to sit in the sun and have a cappuccino while soaking in the activity of the square. This gigantic square is framed on three sides by old world arcades housing shops and cafes. Chairs are set out or stacked up with the weather but there is always a place to rest for a while. And this is the place to take in the grandeur of **St. Mark's Basilica.** St. Mark's *(Basilica di San Marco)* glitters in the sun, and even on a dark day is resplendent with its combination Byzantine/Romanesque/Islamic/Greek/Gothic facade. Five domes perch as a backdrop to the soaring spires and ornate facade. All of this hovers over the basic floor plan, which is a Greek cross.

The church was begun as a tomb for St. Mark after two Venetians stole his body from Alexandria in 828. It is said that the saint's body was hidden in a barrel under some pickled pork until safely past Islamic guards. This story is portrayed in a mosaic, the *Transfer of St. Mark's Body,* over the doors. Earlier mosaics in the atrium of the church date from the 11th century, illustrating Mary and the Apostles. Mosaics in the domes date from the 12th and 13th centuries. This "church of gold" is aptly named, as the glow from the many mosaics brightens the interior.

St. Mark's tomb is under the high altar, handsome with an alabaster canopy. Behind the altar stands a golden altarpiece, the **Pala d'Oro,** vivid with jewels and enamel panels. It is said that the number of jewels on the altarpiece once numbered 2486. The **Treasury** also contains many pieces that were confiscated from Constantinople as well as other places over the years.

Four gilded horses are kept in the **Museo Marciano** upstairs; copies have replaced them on the balcony outside. The organ gallery is also the place to view the inside of the church. Walk into the outdoor gallery for more views of the piazza.

The **Campanile** soars up 324 feet, sturdy at the moment. (The earlier structure collapsed in 1912.) The **loggetta** designed by Jacopo Sansovino in the

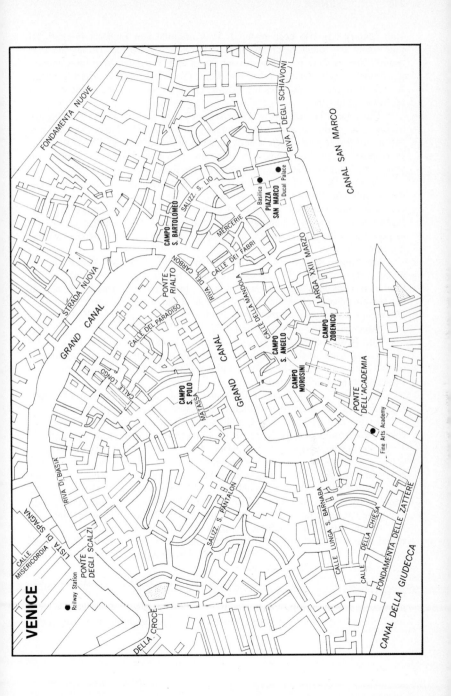

16th century has also been restored. It is rumored that Emperor Fredrick III rode round and round the spiral ramp on horseback to the top. During the 15th century thieves were placed in wooden cages and suspended from the Campaniel. Some of them lived on bread and water for a time, others starved to death. A view from the top includes the Piazza, lagoon, Lido, and the countryside all the way to the Alps.

The **Clock Tower** *(Torre dell-Orologio)* was built in 1496. Two bronze Moors, with muscular arms and grim faces, strike the bell on the hour. Visitors can go up to get a really close look at these punctual figures. The Lion of St. Mark poses just below them, with one paw on a book inscribed "Peace unto you, my evangelist Mark," and a smile on his face.

At the other end of the square, Napoleon destroyed an old church and built the **Napoleonic Wing** *(Ala Napoleonica),* which is now *Museo Correr*. This collection once belonged to Teodoro Correr, who gave it to Venice in 1830. Jacopo de Barbari's wood engraving of Venice from 1500 is on display, as well as portraits of the doges, models of galleys, Venetian armor, and robes belonging to the doges.

The **Doges Palace** *(Palazzo Ducale)* was built in the 14th century as the home of the doges and the seat of government for the republic. Its pink Gothic-Renaissance facade looks like a large cake, but with lacey frosting arches on the bottom instead of the top. Take a look at the sculptures on its corners— *Drunkenness of Noah,* by the Paglia Bridge, *Adam and Eve,* on the Piazzetta, and *Judgment of Solomon* near the basilica.

The **Bridge of Sighs** (Ponte dei Sospiri), leads from the east wing to the prison. The name of the beautiful bridge recalls often harsh and cruel treatment of individuals in a magnificently wealthy society. Casanova described walking over the bridge in his memoirs.

Across the Grande Canal in Dorsoduro stands the **Accademia Art Gallery** *(Accademia Delle Belle Arti),* which is a treasure of Venetian painting.

To the east on the Grand Canal in San Gregorio stands **Peggy Guggenheim's Collezione.** Peggy Guggenheim lived here until her death at age 81 in 1979. She purchased her unfinished palace, dating from 1749, in 1949 for $80,000; it had a garden with pine and linden trees where her Lhasa Apso terriers could run, and a terrace on the Grand Canal. She remodeled from 1949 to 1951 and then opened her doors to the public three afternoons a week. Her home was near that of Isabella Stewart Gardner, who lived in Palazzo Barbaro. Peggy rode along the canals in her private gondola which was ornate with golden lions.

Santa Maria Della Salute, a church standing at the entrance to the Grand Canal, was dedicated to the Virgin Mary after the plague of 1630. This octagonal church with its familiar white dome, has a Byzantine icon from Crete dating from 1670 on the high altar.

Also in the Salute is a gilt throne, which was given by Pope Benedict XV in 1921 as a memorial to his predecessor, Pius X. It is said that when Pius X journeyed to Rome from Venice for the conclave to elect a Pope he bought a return ticket. Apparently when he was elected he felt such humility that Cardinal Gibbons, Archbishop of Baltimore, had to strong-arm him into putting on the papal robes.

Looking out to sea one can spot the **San Giorgio Maggiore** on its own little island. Andrea Palladio designed this 16th-century church. Inside Tintoretto's *Gathering of the Manna,* and *Last Supper* are on display.

Everyone wants to take a gondola ride, at least once, in Venice. (More about that later). But we suggest a vaporetta ride along the Grand Canal to the **House of Gold,** *(Ca'd'Oro),* which has its own stop. This marble early 15th-century Gothic palace contains the Galleria Franchetti collection. For the last fifteen years restoration has been in progress in the Ca'd'Oro. We visited there in 1952, when it was in a state of decayed elegance, and applaud the renovation effort.

The **Rialto Bridge** *(Ponte di Rialto)* was the only bridge across the Grand Canal until 1854. A busy place, it still has little shops lining its rails.

The **Naval History Museum** *(Museo Storico Navale)* at the Arsenale houses a collection of boat and ship models, as well as the real thing. Peggy Guggenheim's gondola, the last private gondola in Venice, is on display there. Although all gondolas were decreed to be black, hers had gilded lions as well. There is also a model of one of the doges state barges called the *Bucintoro.*

DAY TRIPS FROM VENICE TO THE LAGOON ....

If you're interested in a tour of the islands of the lagoon, we suggest taking the vaporetta so you can get off and on at your will, not at the will of a tour guide who wants you to buy glass baubles. One time we were forced to watch while craftsmen blew little toy animals for our children, with the implied understanding that we would buy lots of glassware.

Torcello is the island where northern Italians landed in their hurry to escape the barbarians during the 5th century. Here you can see what the islands looked like, as this one is not overly populated. The 7th-century cathedral is considered by many to be among the finest of the Venetian-Byzantine churches.

Burano is a little fishing village with a thriving lace industry run by fishermen's wives. The **Lace Museum** *(Consorzio Merletti di Burano)* is the place to go to learn how authentic handmade lace is created.

Murano is well known for glassworks; glassblowers have lived there since the 13th century. Visitors can have a demonstration if they wish. The church of San Pietro Martire has Giovanni Bellini's *Madonna and Child* and Veronese's *St. Jerome.*

San Michele is the smallest island in the group. Its San Michele in Isola was designed by Coducci in 1478. The cemetery there contains the graves of Igor Stravinsky and Ezra Pound, among others.

The Lido boasts sand beaches for sunning and walking, not swimming, and a resort atmosphere. The church of San Nicolo and its monastery are on the north end of the island. If you've read Thomas Mann's *Death in Venice,* you can picture what the island looks like. Cars are allowed—a surprise after Venice.

EXCURSIONS FROM VENICE...............

SOUTH OF VENICE
Brenta Riviera

On our last trip we discovered another jewel in the Brenta Riviera where villas line the banks of the peaceful river, which is hidden a few miles away from the busy industrial coast road to Venice. During the 15th century, Venetians began to build these sumptuous villas, so they could vacation in peace and quiet amid lush gardens, peacocks, statues, farmland, and cool breezes. Gentlemen could supervise farms as well as enjoy family holidays there. They decorated their gardens with statues and their villas with frescoes, including cycles of mythological scenes. Today visitors can tour the river by burchiello, a tour boat since the 17th century, by car or cycle.

Starting from Venice the first villa is Villa Foscari at Malcontenta, built by Palladio in 1574. A foscari wife was once imprisoned—hence the name "Malcontenta." Zelotti created frescoes with mythological scenes there.

Villa Widmann Foscari, at Mira Porte, contains frescoes by Angeli, including mythological scenes of Agamemnon poised, with dagger in hand, to kill Iphigenia.

The Villa Pisani at Stra is referred to as the "Doge's Palace of the Mainland." A park and a maze delight visitors.

Ravenna

Ravenna is the place to see wonderful mosaics, preserved over so many years after others were destroyed. Once a powerful seaport on the Adriatic, Ravenna now lies six miles from the sea. Emperor Honorius ruled the Western Empire from Ravenna beginning in 402. His sister, Galla Placidia, followed his rule and was known for her support of Christians.

The **Tomb of Galla Placidia** and the **Church of San Vitale** hold some of the finest mosaics in the world. The tomb was built in the shape of a Latin cross. Inside, the royal blue mosaic is bright with golden stars, resembling a planetarium. Jesus is depicted as the Good Shepherd in a purple robe with his sheep. Eight apostles stand around the dome. Doves straddle the edge of a large bowl, drinking from the water of faith and salvation. Their white bodies and the bowl stand in contrast to the deep blue sky behind them. Although there are three marble sarcophogi in the tomb, no one knows if the body of Galla Placidia was ever brought home after she died in Rome in 450.

San Vitale, dating from 547, contains Byzantine works throughout. Behind the altar, the Emperor of the East, Justinian, and the Bishop of Ravenna, Maximian, stare unwaveringly. Empress Theodora resides on the other side of the chancel, still holding her goblet of communion wine. She wears a decorated gown with jewelry including earrings. Her jeweled crown was a model for that of Mary in the Chartres Cathedral many years later.

The **Church of San Apollinare Nuovo** has divided sides for men and women. On one side, 22 virgins offer crowns for Jesus, who is held on the Virgin's lap. On the other side, 26 men carry jeweled crowns and palm fronds of martyrdom to Christ.

The **Church of San Apollinare,** a few miles out of town in Classe, has rich mosaics inside. Christ in Judgment is one of the oldest mosaics. The hand of God emerges through clouds to bless a large, jeweled cross.

Dante's tomb stands on Via Ricci, next to the church of St. Francis. After he was exiled from Florence for his political beliefs, the poet moved to Ravenna where he wrote *The Divine Comedy.*

Pesaro

Still farther down the coast lies Pesaro, the birthplace of the composer **Rossini.** His house, 34 via Rossini, is a museum; his *Swan of Pesaro* was composed there. The Rossini opera festival is held in Pesaro every August.

The **Ducal Palace** *(Piazza del Popolo)* was built by Alexander Sforza between 1450 and 1465. On June 8, 1494, the Ducal Palace offered hospitality to Lucrezia Borgia, who was the 14-year-old wife of Giovanni Sforza.

The **Municipal Museum** contains Giovanni Bellini's masterpiece *Pala di Pesaro,* which is a large, colorful altarpiece. The Virgin graces the center panel, along with St. George and the Dragon, the Conversion of St. Paul, the Crucifixion of St. Peter, the Nativity, St. Jerome, St. Francis, and St. Terenzio.

We were fascinated by the facade of the **Villa Ruggieri,** on Piazzale Liberta, which was built in the 1st decade of the 20th century. A local artist created the patterns of flowers, and designs in white on light green.

Urbino

Inland, 23 miles west of Pesaro, is Urbino, which stands on two hills. Duke Federico da Montefeltro reigned during 1444–82; his forebears ruled from the 12th century.

The **Ducal Palace** contains a wealth of paintings in the **National Gallery** of the Marches. Masterpieces include Verrocchio's *Madonna*, Uccello's *Profanation of the Host*, Titian and Raffael's *The Mute*.

Raphael's home there contains his first work, that of a Madonna. His mother posed for the Virgin and Raphael himself as Jesus. Raphael lived in the house until he was 14 years of age.

NORTHWEST OF VENICE
Verona

Shakespeare's *Romeo and Juliet* was supposed to have taken place in Verona around 1302. As you probably remember, Juliet and her family, the Capulets, were Ghibellines and supported the Emperor Frederick I, while Romeo and his family, the Montagues, were Guelphs, supporting the Pope. The series of events including the ball, the balcony scene, their secret marriage, their farewell, Romeo's suicide, and then Juliet's, were all set in Verona.

The following sights offer visitors an idea of some of the key events in Romeo and Juliet's lives. **Juliet's House** *(Casa di Giulietta Capuletti)* is on Via Cappello—marked with a sign and complete with a balcony. **Romeo's House,** Via Arche Scaligieri, 2, is a disappointment in its present state as a coffee bar. **Juliet's tomb** *(Tomba di Giulietta)* is located in the Capuchin cloisters on Via del Pontiere. The marriage of Romeo and Juliet took place in the adjacent church.

The **Roman Arena,** in Piazza Bra, is one of the largest Roman amphitheatres; it holds 25,000 spectators. Its origins go back to the first century; only four arches are still standing from the outer rings. Summer opera is staged there every year.

Herb Square *(Piazza delle Erbe)* was once the place of the Roman Forum. A 14th-century fountain stands in the middle of umbrellaed market stalls. Venetian columns include one dating from 1401. Medieval houses line the square.

Dante's statue stands in the middle of the Piazza dei Signori. The **Lamberti Tower** next to the Town Hall stands on the south side; the **Governor's Palace,** once the residence of the Scaliger family, is on the east side.

The **Tombs of the Scaligers** stand between their church and palace. The tombs are ornate with sculpture, marble balustrades and wrought iron grill-work.

Castlevecchio, a 14th-century fortress and palace, is now the home of the **Museum of Art.** Most art is of the Venetian school.

NORTH OF VENICE
Cortina D'Ampezzo

Cortina is located in the beautiful Dolomites, known for their pink cast and craggy peaks. Also called the "Pearl of the Dolomites," the setting is heady, with mountains encircling the valley. We spent a few days skiing there just after the 1956 Winter Olympics, which were held there. Cable cars will take skiers and summer hikers to the summit of Tofana di Mezzo and Tondi di Faloria.

In town, the parish church contains paintings by Franz Anton Zeiller dating from 1774. Climb the tower for fine views of the mountains. Local inhabitants still speak in their traditional Latin-Romansh dialect, which was derived from Latin.

LUXEMBOURG

Currency unit • Luxembourg franc
Time difference from USA • six hours later (Eastern Standard Time)
Telephone access codes • to USA 00; from USA: 352
National Tourist Offices • USA: Luxembourg National Tourist Office, 801 Second Ave., New York, NY 10017, tel.: (212) 370–9850; **Luxembourg:** Office National du Tourisme du Grand-Duche de Luxembourg, 77, rue d'Anvers, B.P. 1001, L-1010 Luxembourg, tel. 400808 or 487999; Syndicat d'Initiative et de Tourisme, Ville de Luxembroug, B.P. 181 L-2011 Luxembourg, Place d'Armes, tel. 22809/27565; **London:** 36-37 Piccadilly, London W1V 9PA, England, tel. 014342800
Airline • **Icelandair USA** (800) 223–5500; **Britian** (071) 388–5599
Embassies • **American Embassy,** 22 Blvd. Emmanuel-Servais, 2535 Luxembourg, Luxembourg, tel.: 46 01 23; **British Embassy,** 15 Bouldevard Roosevelt, Box 874, L 2018 Luxembourg Ville, tel. 29/864/6

For many years we flew in and out of Luxembourg because Icelandic Airlines, not part of the cartel, offered far lower prices than other carriers for flights to Europe. After landing, we usually picked up the car we had ordered and headed off for Britain for study and research. One year, when we weren't in such a hurry to get settled, we lingered in Luxembourg and realized how beautiful and varied this tiny country is—with mountains, rolling hills, river valleys banked with vineyards, castles, and a single historic and attractive city. In terrain, it is Europe in miniature, a wonderful place to explore in a leisurely way with never a worry about hordes of frenzied tourists, even in high season.

HISTORY . . . .

The heart of Europe, the Grand Duchy of Luxembourg is located at the juncture of three countries, yet maintains its independence as a constitutional monarchy. Belgium, France, and Germany border it and their influence has undoubtedly swayed its history.

BELGIUM

Lieler

Troisvierges

Clervaux

N

miles 6

kilometers 10

Wiltz

Vianden

GERMANY

Esch-sur-Sure

Bourscheid

Sure R.

Eschdorf

Sure R.

Diekirch

Ettelbruck

Beaufort

Berdorf

Sure River

Grosbous

Colmar-Berg

Mullerthal

Echternach

Useldange

Larochette

Consdorf

Mersch

Hollenfels

Wasserbillig

Septfontaines

Grevenmacher

Gaichel

Eisch River

Eischen

Alzette River

Dommeldange

Moselle River

Arlon

Luxembourg

Findel

Ahn

Koepchen

Wormeldange

Ehnen

Hamm

Remich

Petange

Rodange

Alzette River

Mondorf-
les-Bains

Moselle R.

Esch/
Alzette

Schengen

FRANCE

GRAND DUCHY OF LUXEMBOURG

Long ago, Stone Age people arrived from the west; their stone and bone tools were left behind. During the Bronze and Iron Ages, people lived along the Moselle and in the south of Luxembourg. Burial mounds and signs of fortifications are evidence of their presence. Caesar conquered Gaul and Luxembourg became part of the Roman Empire; traces of Gallo-Roman country homes are still visible. The Franks arrived from Germany and Luxembourgers adopted Westfrankish language. Christianity developed in Luxembourg and in 698 Saint Willibrod built Echternach Abbey.

In 963, Count Siegfrid of the Ardennes built a castle, Lutzelburg, on the rock *(Rocher du Bock)* where the city of Luxembourg now stands. He inaugurated the Luxembourg Dynasty within a fortress known as the "Gibraltar of the North." Others were jealous of Luxembourg and invaded time and again for the next 400 years. By 1050 a second city wall was constructed to contain expansion and a third in 1320. During the 17th century, Marshal Vauban strengthened the castle once again; some of those walls are still standing today.

A series of counts and dukes ruled Luxembourg, including Henry IV (in 1136), Countess Ermesinda, who extended the boundaries of the country by marriage (1196–1247), Henry VII, who was the first German emperor (1308), and Emperor Charles IV (1354). Luxembourg was acquired in 1443 by Philippe le Bon of Burgundy, bringing the country under French rule. Spanish domination began in 1506, then French in 1684, Spanish in 1697, Austrian in 1713, and French in 1794.

Finally, in 1815, the Treaty of Vienna established Luxembourg as a grand duchy under William I of the Netherlands. In 1867 the Treaty of London proclaimed Luxembourg's neutrality. Grand Duke Adolf I of the House of Nassau succeeded as ruler of Luxembourg in 1890.

Although Luxembourg maintained neutrality, she was occupied by the Germans during World War I. After the war, Grand Duchess Charlotte ruled with an iron hand and a soft heart; she was beloved by all of her people. Again, World War II brought German occupation and the royal family and government left for exile. Grand Duchess Charlotte lived in Estoril, Portugal, where she could keep the world informed on Luxembourg. She spoke on BBC and was the symbol of independence for her country. In defiance of the Germans, people wrote "Long Live Charlotte" on city walls. Some of those who were to be shot called her name in their last minutes. One of the darkest moments occurred in 1944 and 1945 during the Ardennes Offensive, which brought devastation to the country. Many Luxembourgers fought with the Allied resistance movement and many were forced to join German armies.

In 1950 Luxembourg, Belgium, and Holland formed the Benelux customs union and later joined the Common Market. By the 1980s, Luxembourg had become one of the major European banking centers. Twenty-five percent of the population are foreigners; 7000 of them are involved in the Common Market financial district. People enjoy the quality of life in Luxembourg; they can enjoy life in the green countryside and reach work in the city in 20 minutes.

LUXEMBOURG CITY

SIGHTSEEING......................................

Luxembourg City is an oasis with parks and forests on different levels within it. The upper town is on the level of the first fortress; down below in the valley reconstruction is going on within treasured old buildings.

Visitors often want to begin sightseeing where Siegfrid first built his castle in 963 at the bridge containing the Memorial of the Millenial; ruins were discovered there in 1963 on the Bock Plateau. Legend relates the story of Melusine who fell in love with Siegfried and agreed to marry him. Her one condition was that he was not to see her on Saturdays. Unable to contain his curiosity, Siegfried peeked through the keyhole to her room. Aghast, he found that she was really a mermaid. When he screamed she disappeared under the city, never to be seen again. Some say that a mortal will find her, take the key from her mouth, kiss her, and love her—and something special will then happen to the city.

It is possible to walk through the **Bock Casemates,** a system of underground tunnels spreading for 23 kilometers under the city. Empress Maria Theresia of Austria was responsible for this defense avenue. The funnels are open from April through October.

The view from the bridge includes the Grund area in the valley below, St. John's Church, the Rham Plateau, the "Hollow Tooth," which is the local name for one of Vauban's towers, once used as a watchtower over a city gate, Spanish turrets, barracks, built by Vauban in 1685, and the towers from the Wenceslas wall from 1390.

St. Michael's Church dates back to Count Siegfrid's time, when the court chapels were built inside. It had been destroyed and rebuilt countless times, until 1688, which was the last building. Bartholomeus of Namur designed the baroque high altar portraying the Assumption of the Virgin Mary. St. Michael's statue stands near the entrance and a painted pieta dates from 1690. The promenade behind St. Michael's is the place for a fine view of the valley and the old fortifications.

The **Fish Market** was a lively place as people lived very close together in that area. This historic center of the old town was the center of roads leading out to Reims, Metz, Trier, and Aachen. Visitors can walk through a 13th-century building to visualize the crowded conditions of years ago. A number of restaurants are now housed there.

The **National Museum** *(Musee de l'Etat)*, Marche aux Poissons, contains the original collection of a wealthy German. Luxembourg, from prehistoric days to the 20th century, is on display in the extensive decorative arts collection. Gallo-Roman artifacts include tools, part of a funeral monument, bronze vessels, a bronze oil lamp, a beaker encircled with hunting scenes, a stone head, and glass bottles. The numismatic collection includes Celtic coins from the Titelberg, a bronze medallion of Lucius Verus from the days of the Roman Empire, coins of the Merovingian era, and Luxembourg coins and medals.

Favorite paintings include: a large work of Bacchus, which was originally created for Fontainebleau. Apparently the owner did not like its nudity so the painting was removed.

The **Grand Ducal Palace** contains three different architectural styles, including the oldest from 1572 with Renaissance facades and Moorish strapwork around the window frames. The palace was built on the site of the original town hall, which was devastated by an explosion in 1554. Since 1895 the royal family has used the building as a formal residence. Next door, the neo-Gothic structure now houses the Chamber of Deputies, or Parliament.

The **Town Hall,** dating from 1838, stands on Place Guillaume, called the *Knuedler* by Luxembourgers. Bronze lions guard the front doors; they were created by Auguste Tremont in 1931. A statue of King William II, who was King of the Netherlands and Grand Duke of Luxembourg, sits on horseback in the square. A memorial to Michel Rodange, a famous Luxembourg poet, stands to one side. When we were there on a Saturday, the square was alive with color and movement, as the biweekly market of flowers, fruit, and vegetables was in full swing. Photographers can capture a kaleidoscope of color as well as children enjoying the playground on one side of the square.

The **Cathedral of Notre Dame,** Blvd. F. D. Roosevelt, is unmistakable with its three towers; one sports a rooster on top. A Belgian Jesuit, Father Jean du Blocq, designed the building, which was built between 1613 and 1618. The doorway was created by Daniel Muller in 1613. Inside, Muller also designed the choir stalls, which feature alabaster cherubs playing musical instruments. A portrait of Our Lady, who is the patron saint of both city and country, is particularly cherished. Stained-glass windows portray the medieval history of Luxembourg in brilliant color. The crypt contains the sarcophagus of John the Blind, guarded by bronze lions.

A statue of Grand Duchess Charlotte stands in Place Clairefontaine. She is waving with her palm up, which was characteristic of her. Her earrings were the only ones she wore from the age of 23 until she died at 89.

Place d'Armes was once a parade ground. The **Cercle Municipal Building** contains a frieze portraying Countess Ermesinda granting the charter of 1244. The **Tourist Information Center** is the place to go to find out about tours of the city. We can recommend the tourist train, which guides passengers

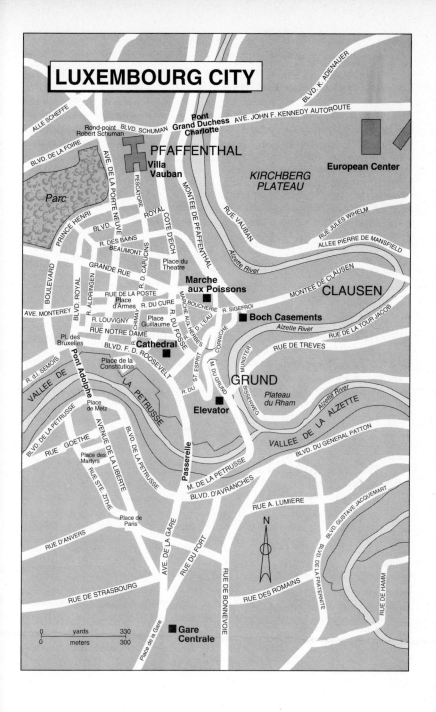

LUXEMBOURG CITY

ALLE SCHEFFE

BLVD. K. ADENAUER

Rond-point Robert Schuman

BLVD. SCHUMAN

Pont Grand Duchess Charlotte

AVE. JOHN F. KENNEDY AUTOROUTE

BLVD. DE LA FOIRE

PFAFFENTHAL

Villa Vauban

KIRCHBERG PLATEAU

European Center

BLVD. DE LA FOIRE

Parc

PESCATORE

AVE. DE LA PORTE NEUVE

PRINCE HENRI

ROYAL

COTE D'EICH

MONTEE DE PFAFFENTHAL

RUE VAUBAN

RUE JULES WIHELM

ALLEE PIERRE DE MANSFIELD

BLVD.

R. DES BAINS

BEAUMONT

Alzette River

GRANDE RUE

R. D. CAPUCINS

Place du Theatre

MONTEE DE CLAUSEN

CLAUSEN

BOULEVARD

BLVD. ROYAL

R. ALDRINGEN

RUE DE LA POSTE

R. DU CURE

Marche aux Poissons

BOUCHERIE

R. SIGEFROI

MONTEE DE CLAUSEN

RUE DE LA TOUR JACOB

AVE. MONTEREY

R. CHIMAY

R. LOUVIGNY

Place Guillaume

MARCHE AUX HERBES

R. DU FOSSE

R. DE L'EAU

Boch Casements

Alzette River

RUE DE TREVES

Pl. des Bruxelles

RUE NOTRE DAME

R. d.l. SEMOIS

Pont Adolphe

Place de la Constitution

BLVD. F. D. ROOSEVELT

Cathedral

CORNICHE

ST. ESPRIT

R. DU GRUND

MUNSTER

GRUND

VALLEE DE

LA PETRUSSE

R. DU

M. DU GRUND

Plateau du Rham

Alzette River

BLVD. DE LA PETRUSSE

Place de Metz

RUE GOETHE

AVENUE DE LA LIBERTE

BLVD. DE LA PETRUSSE

Elevator

BISSERWEG

VALLEE DE LA ALZETTE

BLVD. DU GENERAL PATTON

Place des Martyrs

RUE STE. ZITHE

Passerelle

M. DE LA PETRUSSE

BLVD. D'AVRANCHES

RUE A. LUMIERE

BLVD. GUSTAVE JACQUEMART

Place de Paris

RUE D'ANVERS

AVE. DE LA GARE

RUE DU FORT

N

RUE DES ROMAINS

BLVD. DE LA FRATERNITE

RUE DE HAMM

RUE DE STRASBOURG

RUE DE BONNEVOIE

| 0 | yards | 330 |
| 0 | meters | 300 |

Place de la Gare

Gare Centrale

along the valley with an accompanying narration (available in several languages) received through headphones.

DAY TRIPS FROM
LUXEMBOURG CITY......................

A drive through the "Valley of the Seven Castles" leads visitors to the pretty town of Esch-sur-Sure, which was once a market town. The River Sure winds horseshoe-shaped through town, and its banks are dotted with fishermen relaxing in the sun. The town nestles at the foot of craggy peaks, and medieval castle ruins perch on top. The 10th-century keep is still intact. Hikers will find 30 kilometers of footpaths, which are linked with the national network. A dam built in 1963 provides much of Luxembourg's drinking water.

A memorial monument in honor of General George S. Patton stands in Ettelbruck. The eagle on top overlooks an army tank used in the Ardennes Offensive. Patton is respected as the American general who stopped the German invasion.

The **Battle of the Bulge Museum** (Diekirch Historical Museum) is housed in a former brewery in Diekirch. It opened in 1984 to commemorate the liberation after the Battle of Ardennes. Ten lifesize dioramas, complete with mannequins wearing a variety of military clothing of that period, depict the misery and horror of the battle. Interviews with veterans on both sides led to accurate detail. Men are shown pushing a boat through the deep snow, tending bleeding wounded; there are also a U.S. signalman climbing a telephone pole, a German mortar crew, an American foxhole, and bunkrooms at the Tambow Prison Camp. In the hall hangs an American flag stitched by local ladies using red fabric from a German swastika for the stripes.

The **Castle of Vianden** dates back to the 4th century, when a Roman fort existed there. The first Count of Vianden was Bertolph and several more followed him until the Counts of Luxembourg took over in 1264. By 1417 the House of Nassau was in control. A fire in 1667 and an earthquake in 1692 took their toll, but the castle was repaired. In 1820 Wilhelm I, King of the Netherlands and Grand Duke of Luxembourg, sold the castle, which was classified as a ruin in 1827. In 1978 Grand Duke Jean proceeded to rebuild the castle for the state.

Inside visitors enter through a great hall where the count received guests. A collection of armor stands in glass cases. The crypt has lighted panels depicting the development of the castle from the Romans, the Counts of Vianden in the 9th centruy, Romanesque additions in the 11th century, Gothic additions in the mid-13th century, and Renaissance in the 16th and 17th centuries. The oldest wall is on the side of the crypt. A collection of coats-of-mail, swords, and rifles are housed in one room.

Upstairs, the **Byzantine Hall** is where Count Henri I was married to the daughter of the Emperor of Constantinople. The windows make attractive frames for photographers. Up farther still is a room containing models of the reconstruction of the castle. On the walls, there are photographs of Victor Hugo, Grand Duchess Charlotte, Eleanor Roosevelt, Margaret Truman, Perle Mesta, Queen Elizabeth, Queen Beatrix, and Prince Claus, among others.

The **Banquet Hall** contains an original chimney and a tapestry. A large conference room is hung with immense tapestries including one of Ulysses dropping anchor at the Isle of Circe. Vianden Castle is illuminated at night—it is spectacular.

The **Folklore Museum** *(Musee d'Art Rustique)* houses antique furniture and treasures from ordinary homes. Also within the Folklore Museum is a new **Doll Museum** *(Musee de la Poupee et du Jouet)*, which delights all ages. Besides priceless dolls, there are a number of Steiff and other bears.

The **Victor Hugo House** contains some of his letters, sketches, and furniture. After he was thrown out of Belgium, the French writer chose to live in Vianden.

A chairlift on the right bank of the River Our takes visitors to the Belvedere summit for a fine view of the Our Valley and Vianden. Hikers can take a number of footpaths up there.

The Little Switzerland of Luxembourg is located in the northeastern corner. The forest contains mammoth rock outcroppings of layered sandstone, grotesque rock formations, and sheer drops into gorges. Wind erosion creates honeycombed stone, which is actually more chalk than stone. Caves are an added attraction to this dappled sunlit green haven. It seems cool there even on a hot day.

Many people come to **Bergdorf** to hike and walk along the many footpaths. We took one past an outdoor chapel with an altar, pieta, benches, and flowers. Our trail led down to the S1 path, part of the national network. We proceeded up again, climbing an iron ladder and stone steps to a view of the valley, the mill, and a castle.

Back in Bergdorf, we waited patiently for a herd of black and white holsteins to parade home through town. Jokes went around about the few who ran—producing whipped cream or a milk shake! The town is attractive, with stucco houses, geraniums in window boxes, and well-kept gardens. The church has a Roman votive stone, which forms the base for the altar. It pictures the four deities: Apollo, Hercules, Minerva, and Juno. Eighteenth-century houses are grouped near the church.

Echternach was once a Roman center, and remains of villas, vases, and coins have surfaced there. It is said to be the oldest settlement in Luxembourg. Fortifications on the hill near the Church of St. Peter and St. Paul date to Roman times. The foundations of a palace have been found on the Schwarzuecht.

St. Willibrod founded a **Benedictine Abbey** during the 7th century. Around

800 a basilica was built and the crypt still remains. A fire in 1016 and the sack of the town in 1795 by the French was followed by German troop destruction in 1944. The basilica today is similar to the 11th-century structure.

The **Echternach School of Illumination** was thriving during the 10th and 11th centuries. The monks owned a great deal of land and became imperial princes in the 10th century. In 1795 the tomb of St. Willibrod was robbed by the French and the monks escaped with their manuscripts.

Every year on Whit Tuesday, there is a dancing procession, which dates back to the 16th century. Over 100 adult and youth groups come to dance from all over Luxembourg. In 1990 the procession honored the 1250th anniversary of Saint Willibrod's death.

Although the town was all but destroyed during the Ardennes Offensive in 1944–45, it has been rebuilt and now stands as a major cultural center. An **International Music Festival** is held during the summer there.

The **Wine Road** along the Moselle is 42 kilometers long. One of the most pleasant ways to enjoy the country is by a cruise vessel, the *Princess Marie-Astrid,* from Wasserbillig to the south. The vineyards lining the hills in neat rows slip by as the boat glides along the river. A cluster of kayaks dipped along with their paddles gleaming in the sun. We went through a lock and rose up about six meters.

Bernard Massard Winery offers tours and wine tasting in its plant in Grevenmacher. These wines are famous for quality; we especially enjoyed their champagne. The winery also owns a **butterfly garden** *(Jardin des Papillons),* which houses a wide variety of butterflies in a tropical garden setting. Visitors can learn about the life cycle of different species and perhaps witness a birth.

The little village of **Bech Kleinmacher,** near Remich, is the site of a **Folklore Museum** *(A Possen).* Dr. Kayser Prosper bought the house of a wine grower in 1965, restored the 1617 building, and furnished it. Dr. Kayser said during an interview that he is a conservator—he doesn't change much but preserves the pieces he collects. He felt lucky to be collecting just when people were throwing things away 25 years ago. The museum opened in 1972.

The kitchen has a *hoascht,* which is a large chimney tapering up to the ridge of the roof. Hams hang there now, just as in olden days. Housewives cooked in a pan perched on a tripod or in a large cast-iron pot hanging from a *heil,* or potholder. While cooking, the heat was transferred into the adjoining living room through a cast-iron plate mounted on the wall. At least eight to ten loaves of bread would be baked in the large oven using dried vines for fuel. A woody flavor was characteristic of winegrowers' bread.

The living room is furnished with a large oak table where bread kneading was done. Chairs were carved by traveling craftsmen. An oil lamp gave light to the room at night. A four-poster bed with blue and white linens stands next to a cradle in the bedroom. Clothing is displayed on the walls. A winding stone staircase leads up to the spinning room where visitors see the procedure in detail.

The wine museum houses a collection of wineglasses as well as displays detailing the wine growing process. Wine casks were made with tools in the cooper's shop.

On the upper floor there are collections of dolls, toy soldiers, a Noah's Ark, doll houses, a train set, and a rocking horse. One room is devoted to religious articles, including colorful altarpieces.

Mondorf les Bains is a famous health spa at the edge of the wine route. Within an area of gardens, the hot mineral springs spurt up and into a large swimming pool. Bathers can swim from the indoor pool into the outdoor pool. A series of waterfalls, geysers, and jets spew water and bubbles out to soothe the back of necks or the entire body. Guests at the spa will find a number of sports available including tennis, squash, golf, fencing, archery, body-building, and swimming. A casino featuring roulette, blackjack, and slot machines is also there.

Don't miss the fountain just outside of the spa portraying one of Aesop's fables. *Maus Ketti* is the story of a fieldmouse named Katie who made a visit to her cousin in town.

The **Luxembourg American Cemetery and Memorial** is the final resting place for 5076 American soldiers who died during World War II. Many of the soldiers were killed in the Ardennes Offensive. Gilded laurel wreaths hang on tall iron gates at the entrance to the cemetery. Gilded bronze eagles perch on the pillars. A tall stone memorial shaft soars upward; inside, a chapel awaits those who would like to remember loved ones. Two pylons stand near the graves—each carries the names of 370 missing Americans. A large map detailing military operations was placed on each of the pylons.

Visitors look out on the sea of white marble grave markers, which stretch in rows and curves. I walked down the slope to a grave that had a fresh floral display on it. The ivory mums and purple blooms were placed in a wreath of pines. My eyes filled with tears as I bent down to read a note thrust amongst the flowers—Father's Day. His children had been there on that Sunday.

THE NETHERLANDS

Currency unit • Guilder (HFL)
Language • Dutch
Time difference from USA • six hours later (Eastern Standard Time)
Telephone access codes • to USA 09 or USAdirect 06–022–9111; from USA 31
National Tourist Offices • **USA:** Netherlands Board of Tourism, 355 Lexington Ave., New York, NY 10017, tel. (212) 370–7367; VVV Amsterdam Tourist Office, P.O. Box 3901, 1001 As Amsterdam, Holland, tel.: 020–26–64–44; **Britain:** 25–28 Buckingham Gate, London SW1E 6LD, tel.: (071) 630–0451
Airlines • **KLM USA:** (800) 777–5553; **Britain:** (081) 750–9000
Martinair U.S.: (800) FON–HOLLAND; **Britain:** (0784) 250–251
Embassies • **American Embassy,** Lange Voorhout 102, The Hague, tel.: 070–62–49–11; **British Embassy,** Lange Voorhout 10 2514ED, The Hague, tel.: 64 58 00

HISTORY..................................

Prehistoric *hunebeds* or long burial graves have been found in the province of Drenthe; they may date to 3000 B.C. In the province of Friesland, settlers lived on top of *terpen,* which were mounds designed to avoid flooding. Julius Caesar arrived around 50 B.C. and took over the Celtic and Germanic tribes there. The Franks invaded and Roman control began to weaken. King Clovis became a Christian in 496 but could not convert the Frisians who remained pagan until Willibrord succeeded around 714.

Charlemagne became Emperor of the West in 800, but after his death in 814 the Netherlands endured a number of rulers including Charlemagne's grandson Lothair. By the 9th century, Norsemen engaged in pirate raids, enslaving and murdering villagers. Castles were built at river mouths, and fortresses helped

NETHERLANDS

NORTH SEA

N

Zwolle

Edam
Volendam
Haarlem
Zandvoort
Amsterdam
Laren
Aalsmeer
Wassenar
Utrecht
Schevenigen
Woerden
Arnhem
The Hague
Oudewater
Gouda
Rotterdam

GERMANY

BELGIUM

to guard the inhabitants. During the Middle Ages, the Netherlands was under the power of the Dukes of Brabant, Limburg, and Gelder, the Bishop of Utrecht, and the Count of Flanders, among others.

The Burgundians took control in 1384, with Philip the Bold, Duke of Burgundy, succeeded by Philip the Good, who bought and inherited more territory. He diminished the power of both Bruges and Ghent. Maximilian became regent for his infant son in 1482 and Philip the Handsome took over at age fifteen in 1494; his son became Emperor Charles V in 1519. William the Silent was crowned in 1544. By 1572 the Netherlands had become anti-Catholic and anti-Spanish after towns were destroyed by Spanish troops.

English separatists moved to Leiden and then sailed on the *Speedwell* (until the leaking ship forced them to continue in the *Mayflower*) to America in 1620 where they settled in Plymouth. The Treaty of Westphalia was signed in 1648, but the Dutch continued to have problems with the English at sea. They also disagreed with the French over part of Belgium. In 1667 Dutch ships successfully blocked the Thames, which caused trouble in London.

The "golden age" of the Netherlands brought prosperity during the 17th century through worldwide exploration and trade. The Batavian Republic of 1795 gave way when Louis Bonaparte was named king in 1806. By 1815 the House of Orange was again in power. Queen Wilhelmina succeeded the last of three King Williams in 1898; she abdicated in 1948 in favor of her daughter Juliana. During World War II she moved with her family to England to form a government in exile. Beatrix, Wilhelmina's daughter, has been queen since 1980.

AMSTERDAM

HISTORY.....................................

An apocryphal legend suggests that in ancient times a couple of fishermen landed at the junction of the Amstel River and the IJ, found it a pleasant place to live, and began a settlement that eventually became the extraordinary city we know. Ships found that they could sail from Amsterdam into the Zuider Zee by the 13th century. When Antwerp succumbed to Spain in 1576, merchants relocated in Amsterdam. By 1602, when the East India Company was founded, Amsterdam was a center of trading and prosperity. The canals were a boon to traders and more were dug during the 17th century. Shippers realized the advantage of unloading their cargo from ships to warehouses right in the city. Some of the homes on the canals still have giant hooks used to haul spices, tea, and silk up into the top floors.

Disaster struck when the Zuider Zee slowly and steadily collected silt. Vessels with deep keels could not make their way into the city; only flat bottomed barge-style boats could continue to move in and out. In 1825 the North Holland Canal was completed, as was the North Sea Canal in 1876—both made deep-tonage shipping more possible.

SIGHTSEEING..................................

Museum Corner

The canals in Amsterdam are grouped in concentric circles, and it is said that 1000 bridges span them. We suggest a boat trip on the canals as the perfect way to grasp the uniqueness of this city in water. Look up at the wonderful bell gables, neck gables, and stair-steps meeting at a point on the top of narrow houses. The houses are mirrored in the placid canal until a tour boat comes along rippling the water from side to side.

Visitors can also take the "Museum Boat" around in a circle through the canals. It stops five times at scheduled docks and allows access to 20 museums. Ask at the VVV near the railroad station, or look for the first stop nearby on the water.

The National Museum (*Rijksmuseum*), 42 Stadhouderskade, is unmistakable with its clustered turrets and old-world style. This building was constructed in 1885, although Louis Bonaparte founded the museum in 1808. Inside, the collection of Dutch masters from the 15th to the 19th century is the largest in the world. In 1975 *Night Watch* was slashed by a lunatic; the rip has been repaired and guards are watchful. This 1642 painting portrays the company of Captain Frans Banning Cocq. Originally the canvas was much larger, but when it was moved to the Royal Palace 26 inches were removed from the width and 11 from the height.

1990 was the "year of van Gogh," celebrating the centennial of his birth on March 30. The **Rijksmuseum Vincent van Gogh,** 7 Paulus Potterstraat, opened in 1972. This museum houses the largest van Gogh collection in the world with its 200 paintings and 500 drawings. Here's the place to go to revel in van Gogh's rich colors from ocean-blue seascapes with colorful boats, a riot of sunflowers, fields of golden corn, night skies, murky-green cypress trees, delicate almond blossoms, and his house in Arles, to name but a few.

The **Stedelijk Museum,** 13 Paulus Potterstraat, contains a modern art collection including works by Chagall, Cezanne, Picasso, Monet, Matisse, Pollock, Toulouse-Lautrec, Dubuffet, Mondrian, Kandinsky, and Vasarely. In 1957 a collection by a Russian artist, Kasimir Malevich, came to the museum. In

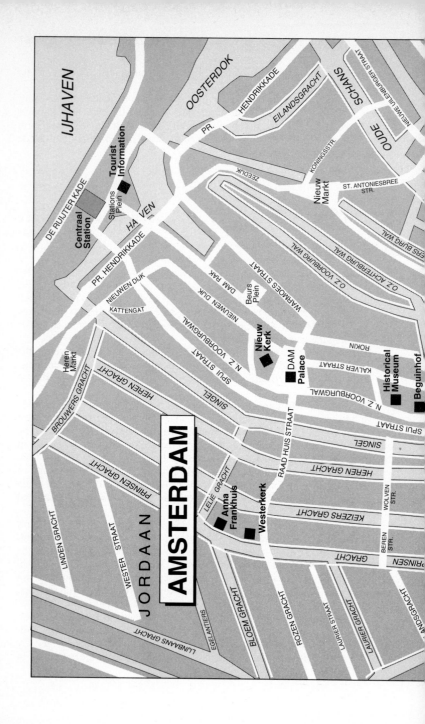

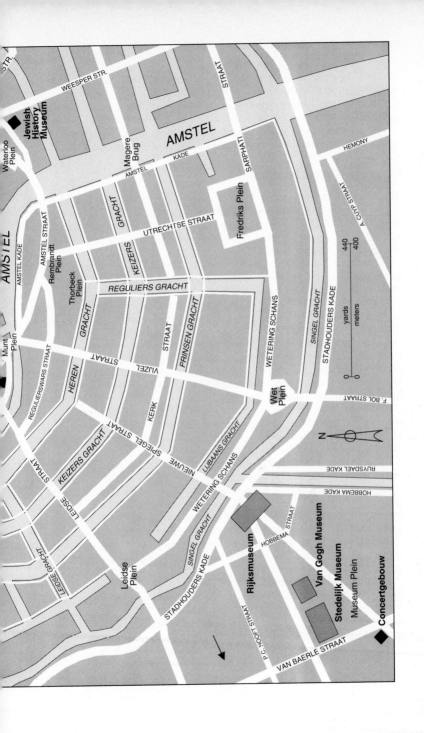

addition, the museum displays changing exhibitions. There is a Sculpture Garden and area in front of the New Wing to visit.

Nearby, the **Concertgebouw,** on Museumplein, is a concert hall with almost perfect acoustics. Two national orchestras, the Amsterdam Philharmonisch and the Concertgebouworkest, present concerts there, as do a number of visiting orchestras. Chamber music can be heard in the smaller auditorium.

Historical Amsterdam

The **Alms House** *(Begijnhof),* 130 Kalverstraat, dating from 1346 offered lodging to "beguines," women who wanted to live in a convent. Number 26 was the residence of the last beguine, who died in 1974. This quadrangle of little houses is now home to elderly female pensioners. This is a peaceful oasis in the middle of bustling Amsterdam.

Madame Tussaud's, 156 Kalverstraat, contains wax statues of international figures as well as Dutch famous persons including Erasmus, Anne Frank, and Queen Beatrix. Rembrandt stands in a special exhibition area.

The Mint *(Munttoren),* not far away from the Begijnhof, was constructed in 1618 on top of a medieval gate. Coins were made there, which accounts for the name "Mint Tower." Now the tower contains a carillon.

Amsterdam Historisch Museum, 92 Kalverstraat, houses a variety of paintings, sculptures, models, maps, drawings, and photos, which portray the history of the city. Located in a former orphanage, the museum offers visitors the chance to walk up and down, to peer out of large windows, try button and light displays, and listen to carillon bells.

Exhibits range from 14th-century shoes, 15th-century daggers, a model showing the growth of the dam and the city, fragments of a gown of Mary Magdalene, armor and swords, a 1566 drinking horn, china cabinets shaped like row houses, paintings, models, a glockenspiel, and more.

The **Allard Pierson Museum,** 127 Oude Turfmarkt, contains a collection of Greek, Egyptian, and Roman archaeological finds; it is also a teaching museum for the University. Displays of ancient Mediterranean civilizations include artifacts from Egypt, Crete, Mycene, and Cyprus on the first floor. Visitors can see mummies, stone and wooden coffins, a Book of the Dead, written on papyrus, cuneiform writing on clay tablets, pottery vessels, and marble idols. The **Cyprus Room** houses an exceptional in-depth study of an important crossroads between Europe, Asia, and Africa. It features the skillful crafts of metal-working as well as trading displays.

Royal or **Dam Palace** *(Koninklijk Paleis),* on the Damplein, is the official royal residence of Queen Beatrix. Originally constructed as the town hall in 1648, the building was finally finished around 1700. Louis Napoleon, who was the French Emperor's brother, lived there. In 1808, the palace was converted into the royal residence for the Dutch ruling family, the House of Orange. Formal receptions such as those for heads of state are held there.

Also on the Dam stands the **National Monument** to Dutch victims of

World War II. Earth from the 11 provinces of the Netherlands and also from Indonesia stands in 12 urns.

The **New Church** *(Nieuwekerk)*, is the place where royal coronations are held; Queen Beatrix took her oath of allegiance there in 1980. Although the original building dates from 1400, a fire in 1645 forced reconstruction, this time in Renaissance style.

West Church *(Westerkerk)*, on Westermarkt, was begun in 1620. The imperial crown given by Emperor Maximilian of Austria perches on top of the 275-foot-tall tower. Queen Beatrix was married in the church. Rembrandt and his son Titus lie together in Westerkerk. There is an observation deck for views of the city; perhaps you will be up there when the carillon chimes.

The **Anne Frankhuis,** 263 Prinsengracht, is a canal house famous as the hiding place for the Frank family during World War II. After Hitler came into power, the family left Germany and moved to Amsterdam in 1933. As a Jewish family, life became dangerous. They went into hiding in this house, with its secret passageway.

Anne, a teenager, kept a meticulous diary during those years, from 1942 to 1944, which was published as *A Diary of a Young Girl*. The family was caught and sent to Auschwitz; the only person to survive was Anne's father. Holocaust exhibits are on display in the house as well as efforts by the Anne Frank Foundation to track racism.

Old Church *(Oudekerk)*, on Oudekersplein, is the oldest building in the city. Consecrated in 1306, the church has its original belltower, a carillon, and some 16th-century stained-glass windows. Visitors can climb the tower for a fine view of the old town.

Nearby, on Prins Hendrik and Geldersekade, stands **Schreierstoren,** which means ''weeping tower.'' It was here that sailor's wives wept and said goodbye to their husbands. Henry Hudson trimmed his sails on *Half Moon* in 1609 as he left on his voyage to Nieuw Amsterdam, now New York.

Our Lord in the Attic *(Amstelkring Museum or Ons'Lieve Heer Op Solder)*, 40 Oudezijds Voorburgwal, really does have a church in its attic. Dating from the 17th century, this merchant's house was a place where Catholics could worship in secret during the Reformation. It seems that the city officials turned a blind eye toward the 62 such churches in Amsterdam. Look for the swinging pulpit that can disappear from view.

Rembrandthuis, 4–6 Jodenbreestraat, was the great artist's home from 1639 to 1660. Two hundred and fifty of his original etchings are on display. Don't miss the expressive self-portraits with the artist wearing variations of a cap with feathers and curly hair peeking out. The lower floor was home for the family; his studio was on the upper floor. After his wife, Saskia, died in 1642, Rembrandt went into a decline and was finally forced to sell his house. His presses and tools are on display.

The **Netherlands' Maritime Museum** *(Nederlands Scheepvaart Museum)*, 1 Kattenburgerplein, is now in the arsenal of the Amsterdam Admiralty. Ships that were built in nearby shipyards were outfitted with rigging, sails, lines, weapons, and nautical instruments from the arsenal. The Royal Dutch Navy left the building in 1971 and the Maritime Museum moved in.

The development of Dutch maritime history is illustrated with paintings, ship models, anchors, charts, instruments, maps, arms, and memorabilia. Major themes of the museum include navigation, cartography, commerce, fishery, war at sea, and yachting. Archaeological finds, such as the v-shaped piece from a medieval wooden boat, have given credibility to historians. Votive ship models made by sailors and given to a parish church in thanks for a safe voyage are on display.

During the 17th century, Amsterdam was a center of cartography. Skippers brought their findings, and the House of Blaeu made charts and atlases. A six-ton royal barge dating from 1816, with Neptune seated in a shell pulled by three sea horses as a figurehead, is on display. She sailed the last time in 1962 to celebrate the silver wedding anniversary of Queen Juliana and Prince Bernhard.

We always head for the maritime book shop, which offers a variety of titles including some that are out of print and difficult to find.

The replica of the *Amsterdam,* with its fierce lion bowsprit, is moored there. Neptune stands with a goat and a cock in green and gold splendor on the stern. The original *Amsterdam* foundered near Hastings, on the southern coast of England. Shortly after leaving the Netherlands on its maiden voyage to Asia in 1749, she lost her rudder in a gale. We first saw the new *Amsterdam* at "Sail Amsterdam" in 1990 as she led the procession of beautiful tall ships into Amsterdam.

DAY TRIPS FROM AMSTERDAM ••••••••••••••••••••••••••••••••

The relatively small size of The Netherlands and its superb road system make exploring the country from a base in Amsterdam possible. The following day trips can all be completed comfortably in a single day each; if you want to combine several, you may want to stay overnight.

SOUTHEAST OF AMSTERDAM
Otterloo

The **Rijksmuseum Kroller-Muller,** located in **Hoge Veluwe National Park,** contains one of the most important art collections in the Netherlands. The unusual park setting draws visitors back time and time again because there is so much to do there beyond enjoying the beautifully designed museum, such as visiting a "hunting lodge" with the magnitude of an English country house, looking at extensive exhibits in the nature center, and walking along wilderness trails through a variety of terrain in the midst of one of the most densely populated countries of Europe. We first visited this extraordinary museum and park when our children were toddlers and look forward to bringing our grandchildren there in the future.

Willem Kroller and his wife, the former Helen Muller, lived in St. Hubert Hunting Lodge in the park until 1934, when the collection was given to the state. The lodge is open to visitors during the summer.

Vincent van Gogh's works form the centerpiece of the Museum. Our favorites include *Drawbridge with Cart, Cypresses, Cypress with Star,* and *Olive Orchard.* Other painters represented in the collection include Picasso, Corot, Van der Leck, Renoir, Cezanne, Mondriaan, Seurat, and Leger.

The twenty-seven acre sculpture garden, the largest in Europe, contains works such as Rodin's *The Kiss,* and *Men of Calais,* which we saw almost 40 years ago and have not yet forgotten. Classical bronzes are also there. The floating sculpture hovers in Marta Pan's pond. Fourteen sculptures by Barbara Hepworth stand in the Rietveld Pavillion. Henry Moore's *Three Standing Motifs* attract the eye at the Schaarsbergen gate. Don't miss the bronze tree by Giuseppe Penone standing in a row of beeches in the Sculpture Forest.

The park itself is the Netherland's largest nature reserve contained within 22 square miles. Inhabitants include deer, wild boar, and wild sheep. And visitors can ride white bikes around to each site. They are available free of charge from the Visitors' Center. Just be sure not to swipe someone else's bike in a remote area of the park—it could be a long walk back.

Apeldoorn

Het Loo Palace, 1 Park, was originally built (from 1685 to 1692) for Willem III, who was Prince of Orange-Nassau, Stadtholder of the Netherlands, and King of England, Scotland, and Ireland. When Queen Wilhelmina abdicated in 1948, she spent her retirement at Het Loo Palace until her death in 1962. Princess Margriet and her husband, Pieter van Vollenhoven, lived there with their children until 1975. After the state acquired the palace, it was restored to its 17th century appearance. Queen Beatrix commemorated Het Loo in 1984, following complete restoration.

The palace, now called *Rijksmuseum Paleis Het Loo,* displays memorabilia from 300 years of the House of Orange. The interior was planned by Daniel Marot, who left France after the revocation of the Edict of Nantes in 1685. He settled in the Netherlands along with a host of French Huguenots. Willem III was pleased to have him design Het Loo as well as the garden. Willem, a keen hunter, must have liked the hunting tapestries hanging in his reception room. More tapestries depicting Ovid's *Metamorphoses* hang in the Dining Room.

The ceiling in the chapel, divided into three sections, features ornate plaster decoration by Daniel Marot. Queen Wilhelmina lay in state there in 1962 with an 1862 "Bible of the Inundation" owned by King Willem III on her coffin.

In the state apartments, the bedroom of Mary II of England contains a ceiling featuring the four elements and the four virtues created by Gerard de Lairesse. Her portrait was painted in 1677, the year of her marriage to Willem III of Orange-Nassau. A traveling trunk, studded with brass nails in his monogram stands in Willem III's closet. Queen Wilhelmina's painting studio has now been restored as the Room of Sophie, Princess of Wurtemberg. Queen Sophie's Boudoir is furnished in Moorish style.

The gardens were designed in Dutch baroque style, with a series of fountains. Marot planned a geometric pattern similar to the gardens at Versailles. Restoration was possible from plans retained in the papers of the court physician during Willem III's time. The Royal Stables house carriages, coaches, sleighs and vintage cars. On one end there are stalls for horses retired from state service.

Arnhem

Netherlands Openlucht Museum, 89 Schelmseweg, is an open-air museum that offers visual examples of Dutch life over the centuries. Farmhouses, windmills, water-driven paper mill, brewery, wooden shoemaker's shop, smithy, fisherman's hut, school, and tollhouse were all collected from various spots in the Netherlands. A collection of regional costumes is also within the museum.

SOUTH OF AMSTERDAM
Utrecht

Utrecht is one of the oldest cities in the Netherlands, dating back to 695. In 1713, the Treaty of Utrecht, ending the War of Spanish Succession, was signed there.

Until modern building rose to staggering heights, the **Cathedral** (the *Dom*) on Domplein, was the tallest building in Utrecht, with its 365-foot-tall tower. Visitors can climb the 465 steps to the top or stop for a while in the bishop's chapel 40 feet up. The belfry houses 13 bells in its carillon. Cloisters next to the cathedral provide a quiet sanctuary for anyone who wants to listen to the carillon.

The **National Museum from Musical Clock to Street Organ** (*Rijksmuseum Van Speelklok Tot Pierement*) 10 Buurkerkhof, is housed in a medieval church. People walk through this unusual museum with smiles on their faces as they see one crazy musical instrument after another; some call it "Holland's Happiest Museum." Music boxes are wild, with birds hopping from one branch of a tree to the next, vessels pitching and rolling on the sea, and gurgling waterfalls. The *Phonoliszt-Violina,* created in 1939 has three violins with a moving bow. Street organs send their tunes outside the museum.

Museum Het Catharijneconvent, 63 Nieuwegracht, which opened in the late 1970s, houses one of the largest collections of medieval and ecclesiastical art in the Netherlands. Here's the place to see collections of manuscripts, vestments, carvings, paintings, religious relics, sculpture, and ornaments.

The **Central Museum,** 1 Agnietenstraat, has as its centerpiece a Viking ship dating to 1200. The antiquities section has artifacts from prehistoric days as well as the Dark Ages. A doll's house from 1680 is one of the favorite exhibits.

Railroad buffs will enjoy the **Dutch Railway Museum,** 6 Johan van Oldenbarneveltlaan, where original locomotives are on display. Cars are lined up at three stations.

SOUTHWEST OF AMSTERDAM

Delft

Who hasn't admired the blue and white Delft ware? Our color scheme at home was established with our first gifts of Blue Delft Porcelain. It was first made in the 17th century following the arrival of Chinese porcelain in the bags of Dutch sailors. Local potters began to design their own patterns based on Chinese designs.

Delft is also known as the City of Princes *(Prinsenstad),* dating back to the days of William the Silent of Orange, who is buried in the New Church. A statue of William's dog lies at his feet; unwilling to eat, the real dog starved to death. Visitors can climb the tower for a view of Delft and the countryside. The carillon of 48 bells peals out several days every week.

The **Prinsenhof** *(Het Prinsenhof),* 1 St. Agathaplein, was once a monastery, then the headquarters of William the Silent, and now the Municipal Museum. In 1584 William was murdered by an assassin sent by the Duke of Alva. Holes in the plaster still remain near the bottom of a winding stairway. The museum contains collections of silver, ceramics, paintings, and carpets. Exhibits trace the history of Delft from at least 989 A.D. The Liberation of the Netherlands from 1568 to 1648, when the Spaniards were in power, is explained through exhibits.

The Hague

The Hague *(Den Haag* or *S'Gravenhage)* is the seat of Parliament and the diplomatic center of the Netherlands, containing embassies and consulates of 60 nations. The International Court of Justice and the European Council of Human Rights are located here. Queen Beatrix lives with her family in Huis ten Bosch in the Haagse Bos woods; the house is not open to the public.

The **Inner Court** *(Binnenhof)* began life as a 16th-century hunting lodge for William II; some of these walls date to the 13th century. The Dutch parliament meets here, and the Queen arrives in a golden carriage drawn by eight horses to open the new session every September. The Binnenhof is a complex of medieval buildings complete with arches and passageways. The 13th century

Hall of Knights *(Ridderzaal)* is actually a banquet hall 118 feet long and 56 feet wide. The beamed-oak ceiling looks like the upside-down hull of a ship. Look for the larger ear on a painted head in the corner. Judges say that one must tell the truth with eavesdroppers up there. Stained-glass windows display a coat-of-arms for each major Dutch city.

The **Mauritshuis Royal Picture Gallery,** 8 Korte Vijverberg, was once the palace of Count Johann Maurits van Nassau-Siegen, who was also Governor-General of Brazil. One of the most famous works in the museum is Rembrandt's *The Anatomy Lesson of Dr. Tulip.*

The **Peace Palace** *(Vredespaleis),* 2 Carnegieplein, was built with a $1,500,000 gift from Andrew Carnegie between 1908 and 1913. Queen Wilhelmina and Andrew Carnegie were both there for the inauguration ceremony in 1913. Gifts were given by at least 30 countries.

The **Permanent Court of Arbitration** consists of experts in international law who are appointed by the government of member states. Seventy-four countries are members; many disputes have been settled since the conference of its founding in 1899.

The **Permanent Court of International Law** was organized as a court of law with members sitting for nine years. That practice ended after World War II, but the court has continued as the International Court of Justice by the United Nations. Also in the Peace Palace is the **Hague Academy of International Law,** set up in 1923. Lectures are given, and in 1957 a Center for Studies was added.

Madurodam is a miniature city measuring 1/25th scale. Buildings range from canal houses, a castle, public buildings such as the Binnenhof in The Hague, the Anne Frank House in Amsterdam, the town hall in Gouda, the Frans Hals Museum in Haarlem, Huis Ten Bosch Palace, the Peace Palace in The Hague, and a lighthouse.

To top it all, everything that should move, does. Ships navigate around the harbor, cars zip along four-lane highways, windmills twirl their sails, the lighthouse flashes its beacon, trains zoom along their tracks, merry-go-rounds and Ferris wheels encircle their centers, barges chug through the canals and music flows out from churches and barrel organs. The complex covers the size of a city block, and expansion is in the works.

If you're anxious to fill your lungs with salt air, head west to **Scheveningen,** a suburb of The Hague. Dating back to its early days as a fishing village in the 14th century, this village is now a resort as well as a fishing center. The herring fleet pulls into harbor on the southern end. Beach walkers enjoy the long beach all year round, although during the winter it can be cold and windswept.

We learned our first lesson about fine sand and cameras there many years ago: keep it covered! The pier, built in 1961, extends out to sea for 1200 feet. It is a popular place with a restaurant, observation tower and sun terrace.

Panorama Mesdag, 65B Zeestraat, is the largest circular painting in the world. Inside, *you* are on a sand dune looking at Schevingen in 1881, when it was a fishing village. The sand is there, refuse deposited during high water is scattered about, and the scene continues out to join the painting imperceptibly. Boats are pulled up on the beach, some have headed out to sea, a group of horsemen ride along the beach, and the town lies to one side.

Leiden

Leiden is a walking town full of the charm of gabled houses, canals, drawbridges, and cobbled streets. A special sense of belonging comes to Americans who, as children in school learned about the pilgrim fathers. The pilgrims left England because of religious persecution by Queen Elizabeth I and settled in Leiden because Calvinist "dissenters" had heard that religious toleration prevailed in the Netherlands. When they left Leiden to sail to America in 1620, their children were more Dutch than English.

The "Pilgrim Trail" begins in the **Leiden Pilgrim Documents Center,** Vliet 45. A room set up as a typical home includes a table, wooden plates, spoons, a cradle, and a chest. Displays set the stage for the walk. By the time the "Scrooby group" arrived from England in 1609, the University had been founded (1575). John Robinson, leader and pastor of the Pilgrims, had studied theology at Cambridge, was ordained in the Anglican Church in 1602, and arrived in Leiden where he became a member of the University in 1615. William Brewster began his life in Leiden by publishing the activity of the pilgrims.

The walk begins at the Pilgrim Center, along the Vliet Canal to the Begijnhof at 76 Rapenburg. Pilgrims held their services there after 1617, with permission given by Leiden University. **Jean Pesijnhofje** was built as an almshouse in 1683; earlier John Robinson had lived on the site from 1611 to 1625. Other pilgrims lived in houses behind Robinson's house, in a pleasant garden called "The English Close."

A plaque on the wall of Pieterskerk commemorates the date the pilgrims sailed on the *Mayflower*. Inside the church there is a plaque for John Robinson, who was buried there. Leiden's fortress, the Burcht, perches high on a hill. Don't miss the panoramic view from the top. Some of the pilgrims who stayed behind in Leiden are buried in the Hooglandsekerk.

If one walk in Leiden has just whetted your appetite, you can embark on another—the Rembrandt walk. Rembrandt was born on July 15, 1606, in the Weddesteeg in Leiden. His father was a miller. Although the house is no longer there, a plate marks his birthplace. This walk explores sites that Rembrandt must have enjoyed and perrhaps sketched. At 73 Rapenburg, records show that Rembrandt registered as a student on May 20, 1620. Now the Academy Building, it was once the chapel for the Convent of the White Nuns. Rembrandt's sister lived at 1 Muskadelsteeg. Rembrandt worked there from 1625 to 1631, using the room in front as his studio. Nearby, he attended the Latin School from 1614 to 1620. His tutor, Jacob Swanenburgh, lived in a house at 89 Langeburg; Rembrandt worked with him there from 1620 to 1624.

The **Municipal Museum of Lakenhal** *(Stedelijkmuseum de Lakenhal)*, 32

Oude Singel, is a museum housing paintings, an historical section with an old kitchen in characteristic blue and white, applied art with treasured city silver, and a modern art section.

The **National Museum of Antiquities** (Rijksmuseum Van Oudheden) 28 Rapenburg, features archaeological artifacts from Egypt, Greece, Etruria, Rome, and the Near East. Articles from the Stone Age are also on display. At the entrance, the Temple of Taffeh is hard to miss. Visitors can walk in and out of the temple. Mummies, coffins, tomb reliefs, terracotta vases and figurines, bronze pieces, and a display of cuneiform script are all there.

The **Botanical Garden of the University** *(Hortus Botanicus der Rijksuniversiteit)* 73 Rapenburg, contains a wealth of exotic plants in an attractive setting. Founded in 1590, it is one of the oldest gardens in the world.

The **Windmill Museum** (Stedelijk Molenmuseum de Valk) 2e Binnenvestgracht, is housed in an 18th-century windmill. Visitors can trace the development of windmill power and learn how the machinery operates.

Lisse

Keukenhof Gardens is the place to go for a visual treat of spring flowers. Tulips originally came from the Pamir Mountains, located in the corner where China, Russia, and Afghanistan meet. They were brought to Turkey and then to the Netherlands in 1650 by Carolus Clausius, a Leiden professor. Happily, the bulbs grew in sandy, humid soil in western Holland. Now tulips are seen in almost every window box, in bicycle baskets and briefcases and are for sale in buckets.

Keukenhof gardeners nurture over six million bulbs every year; beginning with the planning stage. About 100 Dutch bulb companies have a chance to showcase their blooms. The Keukenhof landscape architect begins planning during the summer for next spring's show at Keukenhof. And each year, one quarter of the gardens are changed so that at the end of four years every area is totally different. Planting is designed around trees, ponds, and paths. Swans glide over the waters, sometimes in silhouette against a sea of color. Perfect tulips, lilies, crocuses, dahlias, narcissi, and hyacinths raise their heads in their allotted spaces.

NORTH OF AMSTERDAM......................

Most of the following villages found around the old Zuider Zee, now turned lake, can be visited on a day trip from Amsterdam by being selective. However, one of our favorite excursions is encircling the IJsselmeer either clockwise or counter-clockwise in a couple of days. We will describe the villages in a clockwise fashion and let you select your choices.

Marken and Volendam

Both of these villages are sometimes labeled "costume villages," because the people who live there dress in traditional Dutch costume for the tourists. Marken, once an island, can be reached by car or by boat from Volendam. The **Marken Museum** displays typical fishermen's huts. The **Marken Dutch Reformed Church** has hung six locally made ship models from the ceiling.

Edam

Its famous cheese, encased in red wax, is known all over the world. Shipbuilding was a key industry in Edam, and during the 16th-century there were 33 wharves there. As land silted the reclaimed pastures bolstered their cheese industry. The **Cheese Weigh House** is still standing. The **Edam Museum,** once a sea captain's home, contains an amazing painting of Trijntje Kester, a local man who stood 13 feet tall when he was only seventeen. Edam sports a leaning tower—although it is not as spectacular as Pisa's. Its carillon dates from 1561.

Hoorn

It isn't hard to think of Hoorn in the old days when it was a major seaport—its elegant mansions are reminders of the prosperity of sea captains and merchants. Dutch traders set sail from Hoorn and eventually named Cape Horn after their village. As the Zuider Zee silted up and only flat barges could enter, English deep-keel vessels surged ahead of the Netherlands.

Noorderkirk contains a 17th-century model of a miniature Hoorn in the year 1650. The **West Frisian Museum** is located in the former "Statencollege," dating from 1632. Collections include archaeological findings, coins, weapons, ship models, regional costumes, tools, and furniture.

Traditional sailing vessels are moored in the harbor; some of them date to early 1900s. Visitors are invited to go for a sail with an experienced crew. And strolling by them for a peek is free!

Enkhuizen

Rijksmuseum Zuiderzee, 18 Wierdijk, is the place to go to see an extensive collection of old-time boats that used to sail the Zuider Zee. You'll see names like *botter, tjotter, aak,* and *kwak*—all familiar to the people who live there.

The open-air **Buitenmuseum Zuiderzee** opened in 1983. Original 17th-century houses, offices, shops, and a church have been moved from villages around the Zuiderzee and collected here.

CROSSING THE IJSSELMEER DIKE

Travelers who are planning on driving all the way around will cross on the 18-mile dike, which was finished in 1932. An observation tower stands in the middle of the dike where the opening was finally closed. The inscription on the monument reads, "A nation that lives is working on its future."

Urk

Urk, once an island, was home to people who did not worry about their isolation. In 1942 the Zuiderzee Project, which was working on its Noord-Oost polder, connected Urk with the mainland. Residents banned motor vehicles in 1951, but they relented in order to easily send their fish and eels to market.

On Sundays, many of the inhabitants wear traditional clothing as they go to church and observe the Sabbath. A **fisherman's choir,** *Urker Mannenkoor Hallelujah,* gives concerts from its collection of religious and fishing ballads. The Fishers Museum *(Visserijmuseum)* contains photographs, the remains of a sunken vessel, and displays of a variety of boats.

Ens

The church in Ens contains a jewel of a museum for those who want to find out more about the Zuiderzee reclamation project. Also on display are Bronze Age tools and a collection of bones including one from a mammoth.

Ketelhaven

Ketelhaven Museum *(Museum voor Scheepsarcheologie)* is one of those exciting places for many of us fascinated by maritime archaeology. Shipwrecks on the bottom of the Zuiderzee have divulged artifacts enough to keep scholars busy for years. Dutch ships, which went back and forth to foreign ports before sinking, contain complete household inventories including pots, pans, jugs, mugs, bowls, copper and pewter dinnerware, clothing, leather shoes, and coins. In addition, items used on board ships have been found, such as lines, sails, tools, paint, pitch, blocks, and nails.

This museum contains the wreck of a 17th-century merchant ship. It measures nearly 30 meters in length and is now being treated with polyethylene-glycol as a preservative.

Lelystad

Ancient Greeks believed in a lost "Atlantis," an ideal city that disappeared under the sea. The Dutch reversed the plan and constructed an ideal place out of the sea. Cornelis Lely, a civil engineer involved in the Zuiderzee Project, looked forward to the creation of four polders from reclaimed land. Three of those four polders have, since 1986, been called Flevoland, which is the 12th province of the Netherlands. Where water rippled, land is available for use. Lelystad, the new town, was named after Dr. Lely. Beginning in a swamp in 1965, the first residents arrived in 1967. People now live and work on top of the sea bed. A museum near the site of the *Batavia* (see below) displays the Zuiderzee Project. The story of dykes and the pumping out of water is fascinating.

Also in Lelystad a new museum grew out of the reconstruction of a 17th-century East-Indiaman vessel, the *Batavia*. The original *Batavia* was built in 1628; she foundered on the west coast of Australia on her maiden voyage. Although 276 men, women, and children survived the shipwreck, 125 of those died in the mutiny and massacre which followed. The wreck was discovered on "Morning Reef" during the 1960s, and excavation conducted during the 1970s. We were in Australia in 1987 when a large piece of her hull was dedicated in the Western Australia Maritime Museum.

In 1980, Willem Vos began to build another *Batavia* with the help of a work force of mostly young people. They learned skills necessary to construct a vessel in the traditional way. Her hull is strengthened by the use of the "sandwich" technique: the inner and outer hull contains oakwood planks placed lengthwise, and the inner sandwich consists of vertical oakwood ribs. She sails all over the world; when she is at home in Lelystad visitors may see her. The museum is open year-round and tells the tale of the *Batavia*.

NORWAY

Currency unit • Norwegian krone (NKR, written as NOK)
Language • Norwegian
Time difference from USA • six hours later (Eastern Standard Time)
Telephone access codes • to USA 095 or USA Direct 050–12–011; from USA: 47
National Tourist Offices • **USA:** Norwegian Tourist Board, 655 Third Ave., New York, NY 10017, tel. (212) 949–2333; **Norway:** Norway Tourist Information, Radhuset, Oslo 1, tel.: (2) 33–43–86
Britain • Norwegian Tourist Office, 5–11 Charles House, Lower Regent St., London SW1 4LR tel.: (01) 839–6255
Airlines • SAS (800) 221–2350; Britain: (071) 734–4020
Embassies • **American Embassy:** Drammensveien 18, Oslo, tel.: (2) 56–68–80; **British Embassy:** Thomas Heftyesgate 8, Oslo (2) 55–24–00

Travel through Norway is almost always both amphibious and mountainous, since the major roads must cross deep fjords and climb their precipitous walls. One example is the main road between Norway's two largest cities, Oslo and Bergen: after leaving Oslo, it climbs up to the Hardangervidda, a barren subarctic plateau, then plunges down through a series of tunnels to the ferries that cross the Hardangerfjord before continuing into Bergen. During the late fall, winter, and early spring, even this route may be blocked by snow, as we once discovered during an April crossing between the two cities; then one must make a big circle south around the Hardangervidda or another to the north that ends in a series of spectacular ferry crossings on the Sognefjord and its branches. On all routes, the motorist wins unmatchable views, and the train journey between the two cities is a miracle both of engineering and of scenic grandeur.

As if this were not enough, huge glaciers like the Jostesdahlbreen add icing to the cake. Our children could hardly believe that they were able to walk on ice in the middle of the summer. And connecting Stavanger, Bergen, Trondheim, and the North Cape beyond the Arctic Circle is what the Norwegians call Route 1: the coastal mail boat that winds through the fjords and islands of one of the world's longest stretches of stunning coastline. So, although this is a book focusing on major cities, they are only half the story in Norway; most travelers will want to imitate Norwegians and take to boats, skis, or their feet to experience the marvels of this land first hand.

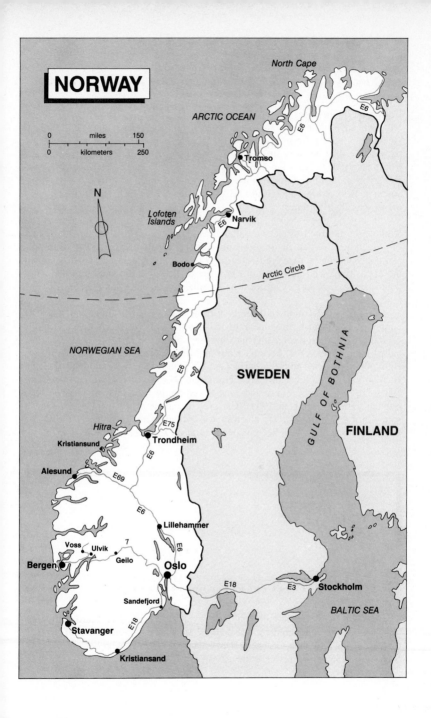

HISTORY.....................................

During the Stone Age, people lived in southern Norway, where they fished and left their shellfish refuse. Rock carvings of animals, boats, and mythological signs were left by Bronze Age folk in the area east of Trondheim. Germanic peoples lived in Norway up to the Arctic Circle during the Iron Age, and left Runic inscriptions from the 2nd century A.D. By 872 Harald Harfager the Fair-Haired, from a ruling family in the Oslofjord, had taken control and unified the country. Between 800 and 1000 the Vikings developed their longboat and went off to seek their fortunes.

The great-grandson of Harald Fairhair, Olav Tryggvason, was one of the Vikings; he returned to Norway after being baptized a Christian by the Bishop of Winchester. When he set foot on Norwegian soil in 995, Olav was proclaimed King of Norway. His efforts to convert people to Christianity rallied the opposition, who defeated him in a sea battle; Olav drowned himself rather than surrender. Nidaros Cathedral in Trondheim was built as a memorial to this martyred king.

In 1397, the Union of Kalmar forced Norway into subjugation, and she continued as a Danish province until 1814, when Sweden won Norway as spoils of war. In 1905 Norway came into her own when the Danish Prince Charles, called King Haakon VI, became King of Norway. The country became a constitutional monarchy with the Parliament *(Storting)*. During World War II, King Haakon lived in London in exile, returning to Norway in 1945 after liberation. When he died in 1957, the crown was placed on the head of King Olav V, who reigned until his death in 1991. The present monarch is King Harald, Olav's son. During World War II, Norway was occupied by Germany. During the 1970s, Norway increased her prosperity with oil from the North Sea.

OSLO

HISTORY.....................................

The city of Oslo was founded in 1050 by King Harald Hardraarda and then proceeded to be conquered by one country after another. Duke Erik of Sweden took over in 1310, then Christian II of Denmark in 1531, who became King of Sweden in 1537. Fire ravaged the city in 1624, demolishing most of the older

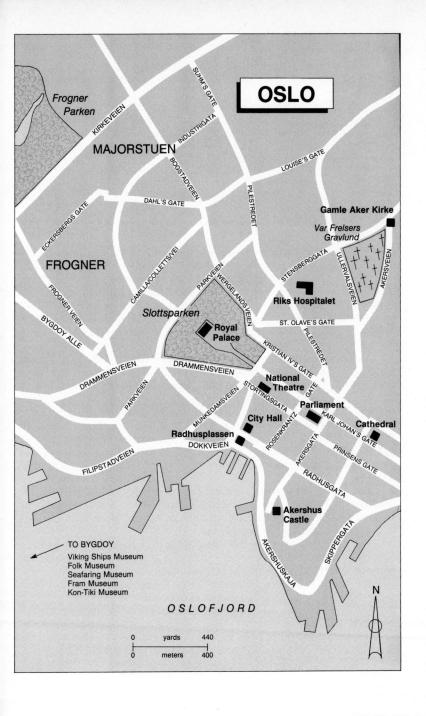

OSLO

Frogner Parken

KIRKEVEIEN

SUHM'S GATE

INDUSTRIGATA

MAJORSTUEN

LOUISE'S GATE

BOGSTADVEIEN

DAHL'S GATE

PILESTREDET

ECKERSBERGS GATE

Gamle Aker Kirke

FROGNER

Var Frelsers Gravlund

CAMILLA COLLETT'S VEI

STENSBERGGATA

ULLEVALSVEIEN

AKERSVEIEN

FROGNER VEIEN

PARKVEIEN

WERGELANDSVEIEN

Riks Hospitalet

BYGDOY ALLE

Slottsparken

ST. OLAVE'S GATE

Royal Palace

KRISTIAN IV'S GATE

PILESTREDET

DRAMMENSVEIEN

DRAMMENSVEIEN

PARKVEIEN

National Theatre

GATE

STORTINGSGATA

MUNKEDAMSVEIEN

Parliament

KARL JOHAN'S GATE

Cathedral

City Hall

ROSENKRANTZ

Radhusplassen

DOKKVEIEN

AKERSGATA

PRINSENS GATE

FILIPSTADVEIEN

RADHUSGATA

Akershus Castle

TO BYGDOY

Viking Ships Museum
Folk Museum
Seafaring Museum
Fram Museum
Kon-Tiki Museum

AKERSHUSKAJA

SKIPPERGATA

O S L O F J O R D

N

| 0 | yards | 440 |
| 0 | meters | 400 |

buildings. After 1624, Christian IV developed the new city closer to Akershus Fortress for protection. Two more fires, in 1686 and 1708, took their toll as well.

After the 1814 formation of a Norwegian constitution and crowning of a Norwegian king, Olso finally had a chance to grow. During the 19th century, building included the Palace, the Parliament and the University. Trade and prosperity increased and people poured into town to build wooden houses, which are prized today for their antiquity.

SIGHTSEEING.....................................

Oslo is situated in a spectacular location at the end of the 60-mile-long Oslo Fjord, with mountains rising on both sides. The natural beauty of Oslo and all of Norway never ceases to entice those who love mountains and the sea. Water is never far away, and people whose livelihood depends indirectly on the ships in the harbor can also enjoy the beauty of the fjord, swim in it, sail on it, and eat its delicacies. You can buy a bag of freshly cooked shrimp on the waterfront in Oslo or as you wait for ferries to cross the many fjords that make car travel through Norway slow but delightful.

Akershus Castle *(Akershus Slott)*, Festningsplassen, is the large fortress guarding the harbor. King Haakon V Magnusson built the castle and lived there from 1319 to 1380. Visitors can see the chapel where King Haakon is buried. Concerts are given on Sundays.

The **Resistance Museum** *(Norges Hjemmefrontmuseum)* displays memorabilia from World War II and emphasizes heroic resistance efforts. It gives an authentic portrait of the German occupation by means of documents, photos, and recordings. Outside, there is a memorial to the Norwegian patriots who were executed. Photographs document the defeated Germans giving up their weapons.

The **Norwegian Defense Museum** *(Forsvarsmuseet)* located in the old Arsenal depicts Norway's defense procedures during World War II. Outside, the statue of Peter Wessel Tordenskiold, who was an Admiral of the fleet from 1715 to 1720, stands pointing his finger to sea.

The **City Hall** *(Radhuset)*, Radhusplassen, is a large red brick building with two towers. Both modern and lavish, it is decorated with paintings and sculpture done by contemporary Norwegian artists.

The **Royal Palace** *(Det Kongelige Slott)*, Drammensvn, stands in a large park. Although the building is not open to the public the guard changes every day with a band playing when the King is in residence. The statue in front of the palace honors King Karl XIV Johan. The statue of Maud stands as a memorial to the former Queen, who was the wife of Haaken VII. Look across the street for a statue of Haakon VII, who reigned from 1905 to 1957. He is greatly revered for encouraging hope during World War II. His son Olav was also held in affection by his people, as is King Harald.

The **National Gallery** *(Nasjonalgalleriet),* Universitetsgate 13, contains works by Norwegian artists and old masters from all over Europe. Edvard Munch is featured in a room set aside for his work.

The Historical Museum *(Historisk Museet)* is next door to the National Gallery. This museum houses an extensive collection of Viking antiquities as well as artifacts and displays from the Stone Age, Bronze Age, Iron Age, and Middle Age. The numismatic collection includes coins from earlier days as well as medals and decorations. The ethnographical section houses African, Indian, Eskimo, and Siberian collections.

The **Oslo Museum of Applied Art** *(Kunstindustrimuseet),* St. Olavsgate 1, houses arts and crafts from Norway and abroad. Collections from the 7th century onward include furniture, glass, metal, ceramics, and textiles. Don't miss the 13th-century Baldishol tapestry and Crown Princess Sonja's gowns.

The National Museum of Contemporary Art *(Museet for Samtidskunst),* Bankplassen 4, opened in January, 1990. It contains a collection of Norwegian and international art, including pieces from the National Gallery's post-war collection.

The **National Theater** *(Nasjonalteatret),* Stortengsgaten 15, stands opposite the University. Statues in front honor Bjornstjerne Bjornson and Henrik Ibsen, two of Norway's most famous literary masters. A backstage fire in 1982 necessitated renovation, which has now been completed. The gold interior glitters against red seats and curtains.

The main street in town, Karl Johans Gate, runs from the palace to **Parliament** *(Stortinget).* Inside Parliament, modern Norwegian artists have created works of art.

Oslo Cathedral *(Domkirke),* Stortorvetl, was originally built in 1694 and restored during the last century. Bronze reliefs over the doors and tempera paintings on the ceiling are especially notable. The carved wooden pulpit dates from 1699. Emanule Vigeland, a brother of Gustav, created the stained-glass windows. The night watchman's room in the steeple has been restored for those who would like a view of Oslo.

The **Munch Museum** *(Munchmuseet),* Toyengate 53, is located on the south side of the Botanic Garden. Edvard Munch's collection of sketches, drawings, graphic plates, letters, sculptures, and paintings is there. Some consider his work in the 1890s as his best. After roaming Europe and having a nervous breakdown caused by overwork and alcohol, Munch returned to the Oslo Fjord where he lived until his death in 1944.

Bygdoy

Bygdoy, across the harbor from the city and easily reached by ferries, has a remarkable collection of museums. Those who enjoy the sea will want to spend a day there. In the **Viking Ship Museum** *(Vikingskipshuset),* Huk Aveny 35,

Bygdoy, there are three long ships that were apparently used as burial chambers. The 800 A.D. *Oseberg Ship,* 70 feet long, originally contained the remains of a Viking queen, horses, dogs, a bed, a loom, clothing, cooking equipment, and the skeletons of two women. This ship had been entered by thieves, who stole many objects, in the Middle Ages. A carved wooden cart, three sleighs, and a working sled are on display from the site.

The 850–900 A.D. *Gokstad Ship,* 76 feet long, was a seagoing ship. It is less ornate than the others. Warriors' shields were displayed over the gunwales as the ship was sailed or rowed on voyages in the Baltic, the North Sea, and the Atlantic. The skeleton of a man was found in the burial chamber. Artifacts on display include a gaming board with antler gaming piece, part of a leather purse, cups made of wood, three iron fishing hooks, three small boats, beds, oars, a sleigh, and a large keg. The *Tune Ship* consists of only a few pieces of the ship's bottom. Little grave furniture was found other than a carved piece of wood, some glass beads, and the blades of a few spades.

The **Kon-Tiki Museum,** Bygdoy, houses *Kon-Tiki,* the balsawood raft sailed by Thor Heyerdahl from Peru to Polynesia in 1947. It is on display with diaries and records of the trip. The ship's complement included five other men and one parrot. The *Kon-Tiki* sits on a blue-gray wavy plastic sea, moored to the ceiling with wires. The hut is lit from within; two chests and canvas buckets are nearby. A rope ladder climbs to the top of the mast and two stuffed birds hover overhead.

Stone statues from Heyerdahl's Easter Island work and sculptures from family caves are on display. It is thought they date from early centuries after Christ. His *Ra II,* which is a replica of an ancient Egyptian vessel used to cross the Atlantic in 1970, is also there. She sailed with eight men from eight nations from Morocco to Barbados in 57 days. Don't miss the aquarium-like display of sea creatures hovering under the *Kon-Tiki.* You'll see a whale shark, pilot fish, boneto, Dorado, flying fish, and more sharks.

The Framhuset, also on Bygdoy, houses the *Fram,* the ship that carried Nansen to the Arctic in 1893 and Amundsen to the South Pole in 1910. The *Fram* is preserved with equipment and rigging intact. Photos tell the story: the *Fram* was held for three years in the grip of the ice and was finally freed in August 1896. Fridtjof Nansen and F. Hjalmar Johansen must have had a lot of courage to leave their ship (in March 1895) with only three dog-drawn sledges. They didn't reach the pole, but instead spent the winter in a hut on Franz Josefs Land, then set out in two kayacks to Cape Flora in June. The rest of the crew drifted westward and eventually emerged from the ice and sailed to Oslo.

Roald Amundsen headed south in 1910, reaching the South Pole in 1911. He planted the Norwegian flag there in December—a month later Robert Falcon Scott arrived at the same spot. Unfortunately Scott and his four men died of cold and starvation on their return.

Visitors can climb up into the *Fram* and even climb down below. Nansen's cabin contains his polar bear rug, clothing made of skins, and a violin on his bed. A series of cabins display Dr. Svendsen's apothecary jars, the surgeon's tools, a metal brace for a broken leg, and momentoes of the men who sailed aboard her.

The **Norwegian Maritime Museum** *(Norsk Sjofartsmuseet)*, Bygdoynesveien 37, is the place to go to get an overview of Norway's maritime heritage. This modern structure was built with plenty of large windows overlooking the harbor. You can look through some exhibits out to sea, which seems to enter the museum. Displays link seafaring from early days to the present, with a variety of artifacts, models, photographs, memorabilia, and such. Walk up and down the three decks of a 1914 steamship, *Sandnoes,* from the cabins to the salon to the smokeroom above. The 100-foot-long 1916 *Svnan* is there when she isn't on a voyage.

The **Boat Hall** is housed in a separate building near the main entrance. We were intrigued by the display of boat building, complete with that wood-shaving fragrance. Many boats are on display with photos and explanations on their different origins in Norway.

The **Norwegian Folk Museum** *(Norsk Folkemuseet)*, Museumsveien 10, Bygdoy, includes an open-air collection of 150 wooden buildings arranged in courtyard groupings, which represent various provinces of Norway. The 12th-century stave church from Gol, beautifully carved, is there. Stave churches, unique in Norway, look like pagodas with dragon heads on the eaves. Henrik Ibsen's study is on exhibit, along with other Norwegian cultural collections. This museum is one to savor over several hours.

OUTSKIRTS OF OSLO

Frogner Park, located in the northwestern edge of Oslo, houses the **Vigeland Sculpture Park.** Gustav Vigeland contracted with the city of Oslo to create a sculpture garden in the park. In 40 years, he completed 1650 sculptures with the aid of assistants and workers. The results are very impressive, because he tried to create the cycle of human life in bronze and stone. Pathos, joy, agony, and other emotions are depicted in the nude figures. During the year of his death (1943), a gigantic monolith over 50 feet high and comprising 121 intertwined human figures was completed. The block of stone itself weighs 200 tons. The bridge is the place to stroll past 58 statues—try to pick your favorite to photograph. We like the bronze *Wheel of Life* at the end of the sculpture garden. The **Vigeland Museum,** Nobelsgate 32, houses sculpture, woodcuts, and sketches, all produced by Vigeland.

The **Henie-Onstad Art Center** is located west of Oslo at Hovikodden. Sonja Henie and Niels Onstad donated the painting collection. Concerts, theater, ballet, lectures, and films are available there.

There are several spots for a panoramic view of the Oslo Fjord and the city. One is Holmenkollen Tower, which was used in the 1952 Winter Olympic Games and is the most famous ski jump in Europe; the 1982 World Championships were held there as well. Be prepared for a long line of steps. In 1983, the **ski museum** was built in the rock to adjoin the ski jump; it contains the history of Norwegian skiing, plus equipment used by polar explorers Nansen and Amundsen. Their tents, skis, sleds, and cooking tools are guarded by stuffed huskies. Excavated skis from 600 A.D. were found in Abvdal, along with a 4000-year-old rock carving of a skiier from Rodoy. Skis from parts of Norway are there—some with seal or reindeer fur to help grip on uphill climbs. There are photos of the Royal Family on skis dating from 1907.

Up on the hill overlooking the ski jump bleachers stands a bronze statue of King Olav V on his skis with his dog. *The Joy of Skiing* was created by Annasif Dohlen in 1984.

Tryvannstarnet Tower has the highest elevation in Oslo and overlooks many square miles of fjords and towns. One may also enjoy the view looking up at the mountains by taking boat trips on the Oslo Fjord.

DAY TRIPS FROM OSLO ....

NORTH OF OSLO
Nordmarka

A local resident let us in on the secret retreat for Oslo natives. Nordmarka, or "north woods," is the most popular recreation area for Oslo. Three hundred and seventy-four square miles of beautiful woods are lovingly protected by the people living on its periphery, and by the ski club, which maintains paths. Our friend recommends taking the subway to Sognsvann and walking up to Ulleva-losater for "a cup of coffee and a warm waffle with goat cheese and raspberry jam, just to get the real Norwegian experience." The walk up will take 45 minutes to an hour and paths are clearly marked. Besides walking in the woods, people can cycle, pick berries, canoe, cross-country ski, and just get away from city life.

For those of you who have heard about Norwegian trolls, this may be the very place to ponder about them. Traditionally Norwegian trolls are old, dark, ponderous, and covered with tangled foliage. They look like they have taken root in the woods. People claim to have heard them calling to each other—although they say it takes a hundred years to receive an answer. Others have heard them talking during wild storms. Sometimes they have been spotted in the faraway mist, moving through the underbrush. Trolls in the forest can strike fear into anyone's heart. Norwegian folk tales will give any reader a picture of the true troll.

Lillehammer

Lillehammer is located on Lake Mjosa, which is the largest lake in Norway. Sports range from fishing, horseback riding, swimming and boating in the summer to ice skating, curling, and skiing in winter. The 1994 winter Olympic games will be held in Lillehammer. The paddle-wheeler *Skibladner* takes passengers from one end of Lake Mjosa to the other. It is also a gateway for Gudbrandsdalen, a picturesque valley and mountain retreat.

Aulestad was once the home of Bjornstjerne Bjornson, a famous Norwegian novelist, poet, and dramatist. He wrote the national anthem.

Maihaugen Open-Air Museum houses more than 100 buildings, which were collected from the country. Anders Sandvig began assembling them in 1862. The oldest building is the stave church from Garmo. A cottage that is said to have been the prototype of Henrik Ibsen's *Peer Gynt* dates from 1700. Sigrid Undset, who won a Nobel prize for her writing, lived in the area for many years.

BERGEN

HISTORY......................................

King Olaf Kyrre founded Bergen in 1070. By the Middle Ages, it had become the capital of Norway, which it remained until 1299. A Hanseatic League "counting-house" was established in 1343, and the city was under German control until 1760. Fishing made Bergen the major Norwegian fishing port until well into the 20th century. Artistic talent brought fame to Bergen through Ole Bull and Edvard Grieg in music and Bjornstjerne Bjornson and Henrik Ibsen in literature.

SIGHTSEEING...................................

The best place to begin a tour of Bergen is right on the **Bay (Vagen)**. Bryggen was once the site of German merchants' long, narrow wooden warehouses, gabled in restored splendor. Hand pulleys are still used to raise goods up into the lofts under the eaves.

The **Hanseatic Museum** *(Finnegard)* is located near the end of the quay. Inside, visitors can get an idea of the interior of most Hanseatic warehouses. The ground floor contained storage, the next floor housed the offices of the

Hanseatic merchant, as well as his living quarters. Apprentices lived on the top floor. Original furniture is dark and heavy—long wooden benches and tables, with a few high-backed chairs for the merchants. Women were not included in this life, and the men seldom mixed with local townsfolk. Don't miss the *two* sets of scales in the museum. One was used when goods were bought, the other when they were sold!

The new **Bryggen Museum** (Erling Dekke Naess Institute for Medieval Archeology) houses artifacts that were uncovered during excavation from 1955 to 1972. Artifacts from twelfth-century buildings are on display. Ruins of boathouses and warehouses are there, plus 13th-century ruins of the Guild Hall.

St. Mary's Church, just behind the warehouses, is the oldest church in Bergen, dating from 1130. Fires in 1198 and 1248 caused havoc. The altarpiece, in brilliant red, blue, and gold, came from Lubeck in the 15th century. The baroque pulpit, unusual with its tortoiseshell and lacquer work, was given by German merchants in 1676.

The **fish market** (*fisketorget*) is located at the end of the quay. It is busy with housewives shopping for fish, fruits, vegetables, and fresh flowers.

Bergenhus is a 12th-century fortress guarding Bergen's harbor. **Haakon's Hall** (*Haakonshallen*) was destroyed during a 1944 ammunition ship explosion but has now been restored and is used for formal functions. King Haakon IV was known for celebrating in his hall with friends for several days at a time. Tapestries, frescoes, and vaulted ceilings make this an elegant place. **Rosenkrantz Tower** dates from 1562. It was built by Erik Rosenkrantz as a defense as well as residential tower. High above Bergenhus fortress stand some of the walls of Sverresborg, which was constructed on top of the palace of King Sverre.

Sandviken is known for its **open-air museum** (*Gamle Bergen*) with its collection of old Bergen houses. More than 35 wooden houses from the 18th and 19th centuries are contained in the village. Fortunately, these houses were removed before fires destroyed part of Bergen.

The funicular leading almost straight up the mountain to Floyen will give you a marvelous view of the city and the waterfront. The panoramic view must be one of the most beautiful anywhere; it is a perfect spot for lunch. We remember wandering around up there with our little children almost 25 years ago savoring the view and then having a wonderful lunch of delectable open-faced sandwiches there. A cable car glides up to Mount Ulriken for a view of Bergen, the harbor, islands and the sea.

Edvard Grieg lived on the shores of Nordasvannet on the **Hill of Trolls** (*Troldhaugen*) for 22 years beginning in 1885. His Victorian gingerbread house has been preserved and is furnished with antiques. Concerts are held there. Visitors can retrace his steps beginning with his statue next to the chambermusic hall. Look down the hill beyond his statue to the red cottage where he did his composing. A thick volume of Beethoven scores sits on the piano stool—he needed the extra height Beethoven gave him. Grieg chose the site of his grave—15 or 20 feet up in a rock cliff near his favorite view.

Fantoft Stave Church, in Paradis, was built in the 12th century in the

Sognefjord area. Stave churches are built with four enormous beams set in a rectangle. The end of the beam goes out farther than the crossing point to provide stability. Huge pillars stand inside to support the roof, which looks like an upside-down ship. The outside of the church used to be coated with pitch to protect against the weather, now this one is retarred every four years—tar is less flammable than pitch. Dragon heads on the roof were there to keep away evil spirits.

DAY TRIPS FROM BERGEN ....

The fjords of western Norway are unbelievable. Hardangerfjord extends for 75 miles, and one can travel in and out of bays with pleasure. If you are there in the spring, you'll see the spectacular fruit trees.

Kinsarvik, Utne, and Ulvik are all pleasant destinations. **Kinsarvik** is at the mouth of the Sorfjord, breathtaking with mountains along its shores. **Utne** has a **cruciform church,** dating from 1858, and the **Hardanger Folkemuseet.** Furthermore, the Sorfjord arm reaches from Utne through a white and pink blossomed orchard vista in spring to Odda, near the Folgefonn glacier and Latefoss, a 540-foot-high waterfall. **Ulvik** is a popular vacation destination with a spectacular descent down into the village.

The town of **Voss** is located midway between Hardangerfjord and Sognefjord. This popular vacation resort area is located on a lake. The Gothic church has a wooden octagonal tower dating from 1270.

An **open-air museum** (*Molstertunet*) focuses on the rough life of farming families since the Middle Ages. **Tours** may be taken from Voss including one called "Norway in a Nutshell," which incorporates bus, boat, and rail transportation through the towns of Stalheim, Gudvangen, and Flam.

Sognefjord stretches its wobbly fingers into the Jotunheimen Mountains to the east and the Jostedalsbreen Glacier to the north. Ferries and roads link the entire system within this largest of Norwegian fjords. For a longer trip, we have driven our car up and down hairpin curves to a series of ferries, staying in one beautiful spot after another. This is one place to relax and enjoy nature to the fullest.

Balestrand has views of soaring snow-capped mountains that drop straight into the fjord. Viking mounds there date from 800 A.D. The **English Church of St. Olav** looks like a modern old-fashioned stave church.

Ferries ply the waters from Balestrand along the Fjaerlandsfjord to Fjaerland, which is popular with walkers and climbers who are heading for Jostedalsbreen Galcier. A new tunnel under the glacier opened in 1986, so the area is now easily accessible by road from Balestrand as well.

Two thirds of the way into the hinterland, Sognefjord branches off in four different directions. The southernmost arm winds its way from Sognefjord to

Gudvangen or along a further branch to **Flam.** The trip on the skinny Naeroyfjord to Gudvangen is one of the most popular in Norway Mountains soar to 3000 feet, with streaming waterfalls cascading straight down. During the winter the sun never reaches the water in the fjord past such tall vertical faces of rock. The trip to Flam, past Aurland is another wonderful trip. Visitors can choose to be whisked up to **Myrdal** on the Oslo-Bergen railway for a fine view.

Another finger of the fjord oozes to **Laerdal,** where **Borgund Stave Church** has stood since the 12th century. This medieval structure is alive with dragon decorations.

The third finger extends to **Ardal,** where there is a large aluminum factory; fortunately much of the works hide within the mountain. Climbers often take a three- to four-hour climb from Ovre Ardal up the Vettisgjel Gorge to the Vettisfoss, an 850-foot-high waterfall, now in a nature preserve.

The fourth finger of the Sognefjord stretches north between the Jostedal Glacier and the Jotunheim Mountains. We hiked around on the **Nigard Glacier,** which is part of Jostedal, with our small children years ago. It is mind boggling to see such an expanse of white and realize that is it still moving and changing.

EXCURSIONS FROM BERGEN...............

Stavanger

Stavanger is one of the oldest towns in Norway. Harald Fairhair was victorious in the Battle of Hafrsfjord in 872, and Norway became united for the first time. Stavanger was recognized as a town in 1125. By 1900, the town was thriving with fishing and shipping. The top industry was canned sardines, then oil in the 1960s. The old fishing village has grown, but the charm of the winding streets is still there. We remember wandering for several hours on a stop from England to Bergen over 30 years ago, wishing we had more time in Stavanger. Market Square is busy with fish sellers, and stalls are heaped with fruits, vegetables, and flowers. A statue of novelist and playwright Alexander Kielland stands in the square. Ledaal, the Kielland estate, now contains a museum.

The **12th-century cathedral** *(Stavanger Domkirke)* was begun by Bishop Reinald of Winchester, using British craftsmen. After the cathedral in Trondheim, the Stavanger Cathedral is the largest in Norway. Following a fire in 1272 the chancel was reconstructed in Gothic style. The carved pulpit dates from 1658.

Breidablikk, Eiganesv 40, is a 1881 manor house built by Lars Berentsen, a local shipowner. The garden is old-English style and the house looks like a Swiss villa.

The Canning Museum, Ovre Strand 88A, is in an old canning factory used from 1890 to 1920. Visitors can learn about sardine canning and fishcake production.

The Maritime Museum, N. Strand 17–19, shows shipbuilding, shipping, and harbor development from an environmental viewpoint. Life in the age of sail is traced through the oil business of recent years. Visitors will see a shipowner's office suite, sailmaker's loft from the last century, and a shopowner's home.

Stavanger Museum, Musegt 16, contains several buildings. It houses zoological exhibits including birds and fauna from the sea to the mountains in Rogaland. Fishing history is traced as an important part of Stavanger's growth. Arts and crafts from Rogaland are also there.

One of the most popular trips is a combined boat/bus tour to the **Pulpit** *(Prekestolen),* which is a dazzling 1800-foot-high rock cliff. The bus takes tourists through rolling hills on the coast to the top of the granite mountains; an exciting contrast. Then you'll head down to Lysbotn at the end of Lysfjord. The road down is new and built to service a hydroelectric power station. The road has an incline of 1:9, 27 hairpin turns, and several kilometers of tunnels. The view is awesome. A plus is driving into the tunnel leading to the hydraulic works and touring the facility. In Lysbotn, the tour transfers to a boat for the return trip to Stavanger. The best is yet to come—a view of Prekestolen from the fjord.

POLAND

Currency unit • zloty (ZL)
Language • Polsih
Time from USA • six hours later (Eastern Standard Time)
Telephone access codes • to USA, USADirect 010 480 0111 from Warsaw and from outside Warsaw add an initial 0 and wait for a second dial tone; from USA 48
National Tourist Offices • **USA:** Polish National Tourist Office, 333 N. Michigan Ave., Chicago, IL 60601, tel.: (312) 236–9013; ORBIS Polish Travel Bureau, 342 Madison Ave., Suite 1512, New York, NY 10173, tel.: (212) 867–5011; **Poland:** Orbis National Tourist Enterprise, ul. Bracka 1600–028 Warsaw, tel.: 26–02–71; **Britain:** POLORBIS Travel Ltd., 82 Mortimer St., London ViN 7DE, tel.: (071) 637–49–71/3
Airlines • **LOT Polish Airlines USA:** tel. (800) 223–0593 or (212) 869–1074; **Britain:** (071) 580–5037; **Poland:** 28–10–98; 28–75–80; 952 (Warsaw)
Embassies • **American Embassy,** Aleje Ujazdowskie 29/31, Warsaw, Poland, tel.: 283041–9; **US Consulate,** Ul. Stolarska 9, Cracow, tel.: 22–77–93 and Ul. Chopina, Poznan, tel.: 52–95–86; **British Embassy,** Aleja Roz No 1, 00 556 Warsaw, tel.: 281001–5; **Polish Consulate General USA:** 233 Madison Ave., New York, NY 10016 or **Polish Consulate General,** 1525 North Astor St., Chicago, IL 60610 or **Consular Division of Polish Embassy,** 2224 Wyoming Ave. NW, Washington D.C. 20006; **Consulate General of Polish People's Republic Britain:** 73 New Cavendish St., London W1, tel.: (071) 6364533

Before we visited Poland, a friend remarked that we would find it "gray," reflecting both the tone of the drab cement reconstruction following World War II and the spiritual residue of the horrendous suffering and destruction endured by its citizens for hundreds of years. So we were surprised to explore Renaissance castles overflowing with ornate tapestries, paintings, wall coverings, chandeliers, and furnishings that were anything but gray. Apart from these elegant remanants of the "magnates" who held vast landholdings, Poland's rural folk culture is full of vitality. It begins some 30 miles outside of the cities where the tools and customs of 19th-century peasant farmers remain—horses and carts,

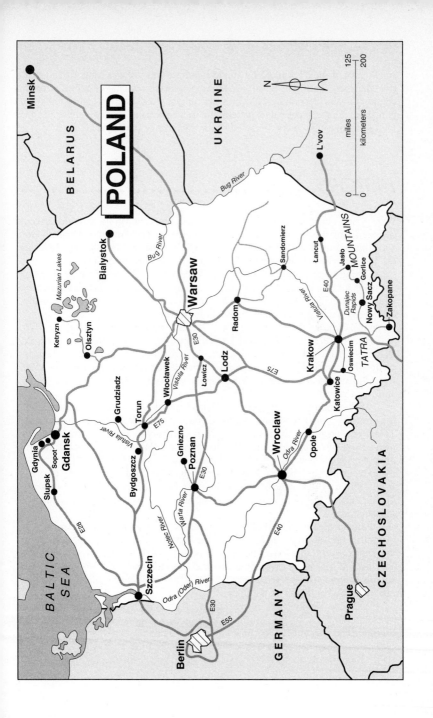

small, narrow fields worked by single families, and villages built around massive churches. There we found beautiful embroidered regional costumes in bright colors, flowers decorating balconies and doors, floral scarves, tablecloths and porcelain, unusual cut-paper patterns to frame or hang in a window, and the joyful dancing that visitors may enjoy as watchers or participants.

HISTORY......................................

West Slavs occupied Poland as early as the 6th century. In 966, Mieszko I accepted Christianity and Poland was christened. The Gniezno Archbishopric was founded in 1000 and Boleslav the Brave was the first Polish king. Boleslav the Bold succeeded him, consolidating the Piast dynasty in Poland.

During most of the years of Poland's existance, she has been besieged by her neighbors including Germany and Russia, as well as Tatars (Tartars), Swedes, and the Napoleonic Army. In 1226 the Teutonic Knights arrived from Germany, conquered warring tribes, and governed the northern part of the country from a castle in Malbork. Prince Wladyslaw Lokietek created a unified Poland in 1320. In 1410 Polish, Lithuanian, and Ukrainian troops defeated the knights in the Battle of Grunwald. Poland and Lithuania merged and the king, Ladislaus Jagiello, was the first in a new dynasty, which lasted for two centuries. In 1596, King Sigismund III, from the Vasa family in Sweden, ruled from Warsaw instead of Cracow.

At the end of the 18th century, Poland was divided between Russia, Austria-Hungary, and Prussia and did not achieve independence until 1918 with the Treaty of Versailles. The invasion by Nazi Germany in 1939 was the beginning of a period of occupation, until the liberation in 1945 when a socialist government was developed. In 1952 Poland became a People's Republic. The Solidarity movement, under Lech Walesa, began in 1980. Martial law was in effect from 1981 to 1983. June 1989 saw the first free elections in Poland in years. Today Poles have been asserting themselves on the way from communism to independence.

Famous people with Polish backgrounds include Mikolaj Kopernik (Copernicus) who asserted the theory that the earth revolves around the sun during the 16th century. Frederic Chopin was born in 1810 at Zelazowa Wola, near Warsaw. Marie and Pierre Curie discovered radium in the 19th century, and Joseph Conrad, son of a national patriot, wrote his voyage tales and political novels at the beginning of the 20th.

Poland is symbolized by the crown of the Virgin Mary, given to her in 1717 after prayers of the Polish soldiers brought success in battle against the Swedes. The Virgin Mary became known also as the Queen of Poland after that date; many churches place her in the center behind the altar with Jesus to her right. The cross is another strong symbol of Poland, as is the eagle.

WARSAW

If you'd like to stroll in a city with a beautiful past that was reconstructed from piles of rubble, Warsaw is the place to go. She now has her heritage of Renaissance and baroque buildings looking as if they have stood for many centuries. Bits and pieces of frescoes, facades, and door frames are original.

HISTORY..

It is said that a mermaid encouraged two fishermen named Wars and Sawa to build a city on the banks of the Vistula River. In any case, traders favored the site during the 13th century and the city was fortified by the 14th century. It served as the capital of the Duchy of Mazovia until 1526. In 1569, the Kingdom of Poland and the Duchy of Lithuania were united with a joint parliament in Warsaw. In 1596, King Sigismund III Vasa founded Warsaw as the capital of the Kingdom of Poland.

Sweden invaded Warsaw during the 17th century and took away treasures from the Royal Castle in 1657. The palace and park of Lazienki were created by King Stanislaw August Poniatowski from 1764 to 1794. On May 3, 1791, the Constitution was proclaimed in the Royal Castle. Jan Kilinski, a shoemaker, led the Kosciuszko Insurrection of the people who routed the Russian army. Seven months later, the Russians were back invading the city and killing citizens in Praga, the right bank district in Warsaw. Napoleon was in residence in the early 1800s, followed by the Russians again in 1813. The Vienna Congress of 1814 divided Poland into three parts and Warsaw came under Russian domination. Polish cadets invaded the home of the Grand Duke Konstanty, who was a brother of the Russian Tsar, during the November uprising in 1830. A year later Warsaw gave in after a siege by Russian troops.

Another uprising took place in January 1863, resulting in the formation of the Underground National Government. By 1864 the Kingdom of Poland was liquidated and Russia took over again. In 1920 the Polish army routed the Russians in the "miracle on the Vistula," when they were able to stand their ground by the river. Nazi Germany and Russia again were in control during the 20th century. Warsaw suffered unmercifully during the Nazi occupation beginning in 1939 with the first bombing of the city. In 1942, the Nazis started to extermi-

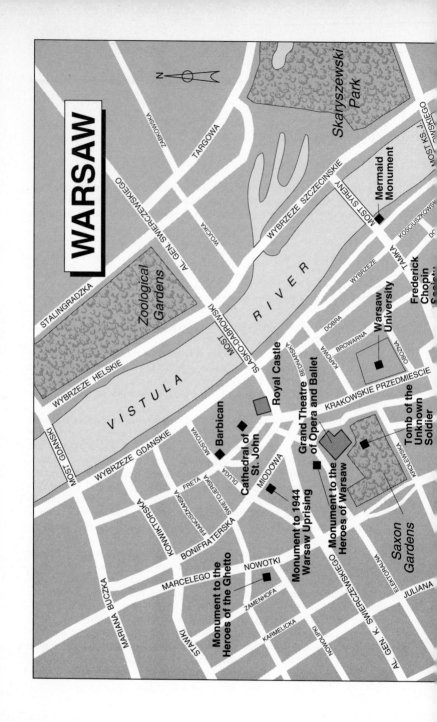

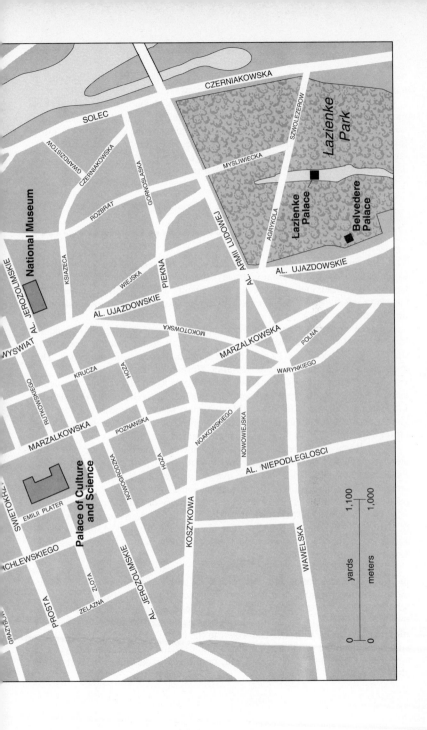

nate Jews in the ghetto. The desperate Ghetto Uprising in 1943 left a horrendous number of Jews dead and the district was razed.

In 1944 the Warsaw Uprising Jews and Polish partisans lasted for two months, resulting in the death of 180,000 citizens at the hands of S.S. troops. Later, the retreating Nazi Army methodically reduced the city to rubble just a few feet high. City planners used photographs, old prints, and drawings to re-create the city as it had stood before the seiges. By 1953 the Old Town Market and some of the adjoining streets had been reconstructed.

SIGHTSEEING.....................................

The Old Town *(Stare Miasto)* is located on the left bank of the Vistula River. Completely destroyed by Nazi Germany, the historic monuments and buildings have been painstakingly researched and rebuilt. Take a look at some of the Canaletto paintings in the National Museum to glimpse what it looked like before World War II.

Castle Square *(Plac Zamkowy)* marks the reign of King Sigismund III Vasa with a tall column to his memory. He wears his coronation cape over a suit of armor, holding a sword in one hand and a cross in the other. This monument was the first to be rebuilt after World War II.

The **Royal Castle** (4 Zamkowy Square) rose again after being completely leveled. Her treasures were plundered by the Swedes in 1656, the Prussians in 1795 and the Germans in 1939 (although most pieces had been removed and hidden before World War II). The clock stopped at 11:15 when the castle was hit on September 17, 1939; it was started again in July 1974.

The Royal Route begins at the castle and continues south for two miles along Krakowskie Przedmiescie, Nowy Swiat, and Ujazdowskie to Belvedere Palace and Lazienki Park. There are over 50 palaces along this route and in the area around the castle. Look for plaques on some of the walls of these restored palaces—usually dated 1939 or 1944 in the memory of Polish heroes.

The **Cathedral of St. John** *(Katedra Sw. Jana)*, on Swietojanska, is one of the oldest churches in Warsaw. The church dates from the 13th century. It was damaged in 1944 and rebuilt in 1956. The coronation of Poland's last king took place there.

At the intersection of Dluga and Miodowa stands a new memorial unveiled in 1989, commemorating the 63-day 1944 Warsaw Uprising. One section depicts a group of partisans with rifles. The second portrays a priest, a soldier with his helmet on, a woman with her child, and a young soldier with his gun just disappearing into the sewer through a manhole. The sewer was used by insurgents escaping from the Old Town to the center of the city. Black cobblestones surround the sculpture and the manhole where 5300 persons escaped.

The 15th-century **Barbican Gate,** on Nowomiejska Street, is part of the medieval wall of Warsaw. The walls have been partly restored. The Powder Turret is the only part of the Barbican to be completely reconstructed.

The **Monument to the Heroes of Warsaw** memorializing the many who died between 1939 and 1945 stands in a park near the Opera House. Called the *Warsaw Nike,* the statue of a woman leaps forward holding a sword with arms raised.

The **Tomb of the Unknown Soldier,** who died in 1920 at Lwow, stands in the Saxon Gardens; there is an eternal light with two guards on duty. Floral displays stand all around the tomb. Earth taken from World War II battlefields where Poles died was placed in urns in the cornerstones of the tomb. All diplomatic visitors come to this place to pay their respects.

The **Monument to the Heroes of the Ghetto** stands on ul. Zamenhofa, which was once the center of the ghetto. This is where the Nazis placed the Jews into vehicles for transportation to death at Auschwitz. The monument is made of gray basalt from Scandinavia; it was designed by the Nazis for a monument to Hitler. The figures seem to emerge from the stone, with strong faces and bold muscles standing out.

On Krakowskie Przedmiescie, Frederic Chopin lived at #5, which is now the **Academy of Fine Arts.** A reconstruction of the inside of his last home in Poland is also there. The Polish are partial to his polanaises, sonatas, and mazurkas. The **Chopin Museum** *(Muzeum Fryderyka Chopina)* in the Ostrogski Palace, 1 Okolnik Street, houses collections relating to Chopin. His heart lies in an urn in the Church of the Holy Cross.

The **National Museum** *(Muzeum Naraodowe),* 3 Jerozolimskie Alley, displays Polish art from the 14th to the 20th century. The *Battle of Grunwald* by Jan Matejko is also there. Although the painting was secretly removed and buried in Lublin, no one revealed its location to the Nazis, who offered 10 million Reichsmarks for the painting.

Next door stands the **Armed Forces Museum,** 3 Jerozolimskie Alley, which you can't miss with a variety of airplanes, guns, and tanks outside. There you will see an armored car made by the Polish insurgents for use during the Warsaw Uprising.

Lazienki Park contains the 18th-century Water Palace, which was the summer home for the last king of Poland, Stanislaus Augustus Poniatowski. The Orangerie contains a sculpture collection. Concerts are held there during the summer. The White House was the residence of Louis XVIII of France during his exile. Now it is the residence of the President of Poland. The Chopin Monument, also within the park, is the site of piano concerts on Sundays. The Warsaw University Botanical Garden was founded there in 1818. Around 6000 plant species and 1000 tree varieties are on display.

Wilanow Palace, 1 Wiertnicza Str, dating from 1677, is located six miles outside the city on the Royal Route. King Jan III Sobieski, who defeated Turkey in Vienna in 1683, bought the village of Wilanow and built a one-story manor house surrounded by a garden. He spent summers there in his miniature Versailles.

Visitors walking into the park will come first to the Neogothic mausoleum of Stanislaw Kostka Potocki and his wife Aleksandra, which is guarded by four lions at the corners. The Baroque gate to the palace is handsome with its "war and peace" motif.

Pavilion X of the Warsaw Citadel, on Zoliborz Hill on the northern part of Warsaw, is a 19th-century prison fortress. Used as a political prison, it was built from 1822 to 1828. Its inhabitants included those involved in the January Uprising following the bloody years 1863–1866, Russian revolutionaries, Polish workers' party members, and revolutionaries from 1905 to 1907. During World War I, the Germans imprisoned Warsaw strikers. Executions were conducted there. The last three Polish prisoners were executed in 1925. Prisoners were reminded by regulations: "Whoever got in here, should forget who he was and only have in mind, that he is a prisoner."

Inside, visitors today shiver with the cold, damp, gray, grim, dark atmosphere as they walk the corridors. Cells are identified with the name of some of the prisoners, including #42, which held Apollo Jozef Nalecz-Korzeniowski, Joseph Conrad's father, in 1861; Joseph was only 3½ years old when he waved goodbye as his father was imprisoned.

DAY TRIPS FROM WARSAW...............

Zelazowa Wola, 32 miles west of Warsaw, was the birthplace of Frederic Chopin. The house contains Chopin memorabilia and the gardens are very attractive. Concerts are given there on a Steinway grand piano during Sundays in the summer.

LUBLIN

HISTORY..................................

Lublin was the site of the 1569 agreement, which united Poland and Lithuania, forming the largest European state. In 1944, Lublin served as the occupation headquarters when the Allies tried to defeat the Nazis.

SIGHTSEEING......................................

One enters the **Old Town** *(Stare Miasto)* through a 14th-century Krakow Gate; there's a museum inside featuring regional displays. Visitors also have a view of the city from the museum.

The **Old Town Square** contains a collection of Renaissance houses. The **Town Hall** *(Tribunal)* dates from the 14th century.

The **Dominican Church and Monastery,** built by King Casimir the Great, is prized for its 17th and 18th-century frescoes. The painting *Lublin Fire of 1719* is there.

Lublin Castle, at ul. Zamkowa 9, dates from the 13th century but was renovated in 1826. It was originally built by King Casimir the Great.

Inside, the museum contains Polish painting and folk art. Displays include straw reindeer, baskets, metal andirons, candle holders, ceramics, stars made of cut paper, Easter eggs, and a Christmas creche. Coffin portraits were popular in a six-sided version.

A monument to one of the darkest moments in Polish and European history sits grimly at the outskirts of Lublin. The Polish Committee of National Liberation founded the State Museum in Majdanek, a Nazi extermination camp, in memory of those who died there. This camp was begun by the Third Reich in October 1941. More than 360,000 persons from 50 nations lost their lives there.

Visitors enter near a massive sculpture, the *Monument of Fight and Martyrdom,* with its rectangular stone sitting on two legs. The figures are indistinct, but the structure looks ominous and inescapable. Of the many concentration camps in Poland, Auschwitz was the largest. Majdanek was the second in size.

A film documenting the camp is shown in the information center; we were too late to see it but were not sorry. The immediate experience there was poignant enough. We were escorted by a guide whose grandmother, now in her early 80s, was one of the few survivors of the camp. It was a very solemn tour through the site of unthinkable mass murders. We walked through the bathroom/gas chamber and were told about the selection process and the Cyclone B used for extermination. Cyclone B took ten minutes to kill, whereas carbon monoxide took 40 minutes, while an SS man watched from an adjoining room.

The original barracks are there—some with the plank "beds" where hundreds slept. Displays in the barracks were graphic with photographs, descriptions of inhumane living conditions including sparse food and enforced labor. One barracks was filled with thousands of shoes—all black. Another displayed hats and caps taken from people as they entered, and the striped hats they wore from then on. A metal sculpture portrayed four grotesque figures in the center, staggering and falling on rubble.

DAY TRIPS FROM LUBLIN.....................

Sandomierz

We have discovered a jewel in Poland—a place few tourists know about. Our introduction was during an organ concert in the 1360 Sandomierz Cathedral one evening. We had plenty of time to let our eyes roam around the ornate interior and later to walk around for a closer look at the collection of paintings.

The **Sandomierz Museum,** on Sokolnickiego 3 in the Town Hall in the center of town, is the place to go for a plan of the old town and historical exhibits. Inside, we were able to find all of the places we wanted to visit in the large model in the center of the room. The Town Hall dates from the 14th century, and it has heavy wooden beams and an attractive blue and white tile stove. Warnings were given from the Belfry of attacking Tatars and Swedes.

The **Castle of Sandomierz** dates from the 14th century. Inside, the King's kitchen contains a wonderful collection of silver that had been hidden before World War II in a nobleman's cottage. It came to light in 1980 and includes 19th-century Polish silver, a French breakfast set, and large spoons from the 17th century made in Gdansk. Jewelry found in cellars in town is on display— probably much more will remain undiscovered forever. The town has a network of cellars that interconnect and lead under the river to the other side.

Visitors can tour the "Underground Tourist Route," which offers a chance to see some of the underground cellars that were so important during sieges.

Baranow Sandomierski

If you've read James Michener's *Poland,* you will already be familiar with this area. Castle Baranow is mentioned in his historical novel, and Bukowo, the fictitious place used as a focus in the book, is sited not far away along the Vistula River. Castle Gorka, again mentioned in detail, is just a bit farther along the river.

In the 12th century, Baranow was a small, wooden fortress with its village; by 1354, it had become a town. During the 15th century it belonged to the Baranowski family, who were involved with sheep and the woolen industry, then passed to the Kurozweckis and the Gorkas. Finally, in 1569, it was bought by Rafal Leszczynski. This was a golden age, as Leszczynski supported culture and the arts. King Stefan Batory stayed there several times during his reign.

Baranow is a three-storeyed castle with four round towers and a center quadrangle containing another tower in the facade. Because of frequent flooding from the Vistula River, the ground floor was placed three meters above the land.

Visitors can tour this beautiful castle, called a "small Wawel." It is handsome with parks and gardens including statues and spouting fountains. Arcaded galleries and grand staircases are decorated with rosettes, gargoyles, geometrical friezes, and heraldic emblems.

The ground floor contains the former chapel, which is now used for films of the castle as well as other Polish castles. The initials of the owner and the architect can be seen there.

Some say that a dragon lived in the cellar, devouring maidens until someone fed it sulfur. Several rooms illustrate the development and process of mining sulfur. Diagrams explain the layers in the earth and how they are extracted.

CRACOW

HISTORY......................................

Cracow was settled in the 9th century, the bishopric of Cracow founded in 1000, and the city established around the same time by Duke Krak. According to legend, Krak's daughter, Wanda, refused to marry a German and drowned herself in the Vistula River. Cracow was the capital of Poland between the 11th and 17th centuries. In 1364, King Casimir the Great founded Jagiellonian University where Nicolaus Copernicus was a student from 1491 to 1495. During Cracow's golden era, kings were crowned and buried in Wawel Cathedral, mansions were built by the wealthy, and victory parades were celebrated through the city.

Cracow was subjected to Tartar raids in 1241 and 1242, those of Swedes, Russians, Austrians, and Prussians during the 18th century, and a rash of uprisings and fires. After the Cracow Revolution of 1846, the city was stamped down and incorporated into Austria. By 1866, Cracow as given autonomous status and developed into a cultural center.

During World War II, the Nazis stole precious treasures during their occupation. Buildings are original there, as it was the only major city in Poland to escape the Nazi's destruction; they chose to live there instead.

SIGHTSEEING......................................

The Old Town *(Stare Miasto)* was a crossroads for trade from all parts of Europe. The **Market Square** *(Rynek Glowny)* is one of the largest medieval squares in Europe. Vendors set up shop for their fruits, vegetables and flowers under umbrellas all over the square. Pigeons wheel around; some say that these pigeons were once 13th-century knights who were cursed and turned into birds. A large 14th-century covered arcaded market called **Cloth Hall** *(Sukiennice)* is in the square; its museum contains 18th and 19th century paintings.

The only remaining tower of the Town Hall contains exhibits on the history of Cracow. Near the tower lies a stone, which marks the site where Tadeusz Kosciuszko rebelled against the Russians in 1794. A plaque marks the spot where Kosciuszko took his oath; flowers are placed there in his honor.

Along the east side, unmatched spires caught our attention. The **Church of the Visitation of the Blessed Virgin Mary** *(Kosciol Mariacki)* has two towers of uneven height and different design. According to legend, two brothers who were building the church became angry and fought each other; when one was killed, his tower grew larger all by itself. The murder weapon, a knife, hangs in Cloth Hall. The church contains a remarkable limewood winged triptych altarpiece that is opened every day at noon.

We didn't miss hearing the pensive **bugle call** *(Hejnal Mariacki)* from one of the church towers where the trumpeter plays through each of the four windows at the turn of the hour. Three buglers rotate through shifts of eight hours each; one watchman chose to play for 40 years. The call is cut short in memory of the trumpeter whose throat was pierced by an arrow as he was warning the people of a Tartar attack.

St. Florian's Gate *(Brama Florianska)* dates from the 13th-century, apart from its 17th-century cupola. The Barbican is a circular fortification that combined with towers and walls to make an impregnable bastion. Some of the fortifications have been replaced by a park called the **Planty.**

Czartoryski Museum, Sw. Jana 19, is a branch of the National Museum. This museum contains collections of Polish art from the 16th to the 20th centuries and European art from the 13th to the 18th centuries. There are also engravings, handicrafts, early weapons, and art from the Far East.

At the western edge of the Old Town, we visited the Jagiellonian University, which houses the **Museum of Nicolaus Copernicus** in the courtyard of the Collegium Maius. His instruments and equipment are on display.

The **Archeological Museum,** 3 Poselska Street, has a display of ethnographic development using ceramic dating of objects. The first floor contains a collection of mummies and bone X-rays of various animals including a cat and a bird. Climb up to the second floor to see collections of Roman gold jewelry, tools, and precious stones including amber, agate, lapis lazuli, and opals.

At the southern edge of the Old Town, on a bluff overlooking the Vistula stands **Wawel Hill** *(Wzgorze Wawelsky),* where you can see both a castle and a cathedral. **Wawel Castle** *(Zamek na Wawelu)* was the residence of Polish kings. During World War II, the Nazi governor general of Poland, Hans Frank, lived in the castle. Previously, many of the treasures were sent to Canada in 1939 for safe keeping. They were returned in 1961.

As in many Polish castles, visitors are expected to don felt slippers over their shoes to protect the floors; if you're lucky enough to snare a pair with elastic backs you can even walk carefully up the stairs. The royal chambers have been restored to the Jagiellon and Vasa period of time. The Throne Room contains a series of ''Noah'' tapestries beginning with building the ark, the deluge with water cascading down, the Ark in the Ararat Mountains, and Noah giving thanks to God. Concerts are held there every Wednesday. The architectural collection, called ''Wawel that is no more'' chronicles prehistoric findings dating back 50,000 years B.C.

If you like dragons, don't miss the large artificial monster standing below the castle—he spouts fire every few minutes as a reminder of the legend involving numerous maidens. A cave below the Wawel portrays the legend of dragons as they satisfied their appetites for eating maidens. Some say that a dragon ate a ram fortified with sulfur and salt and became so thirsty that he drank too much water from the river and finally exploded. Schoolchildren like to pose beside a replica of the dragon for photographs; we leaned over the wall to capture him from above after exploring the castle and cathedral on Wawel Hill.

Wawel Cathedral *(Katedra na Wawelu)* dates from the 14th century over two other cathedrals. In the nave, the coffin of St. Stanislas gleams with its ornately carved silver surface portraying events in his life. He was murdered in 1079 by those acting on behalf of the King. Angels hold the coffin on their shoulders.

Visitors can climb up to the tower for a view of the city as well as of the giant bell. The Zygmunt bell in the tower dates from 1520; it was placed there as a memorial to King Sigismund I and is rung on state occasions.

This is the see of the former Cardinal Wojtyla, Pope John Paul II. As the first Polish Pope in history, he was universally acclaimed on his return to his native land in 1979, 1983, and 1987. His birthplace was in Wadowice, 35 miles northwest of Cracow.

DAY TRIPS FROM CRACOW..................

Wieliczka Salt Mine lies 13 kilometers southeast of Cracow. Salt has been mined there since the 11th century; the mine now has nine levels. The museum displays mining tools and equipment from the Middle Ages up to the present. And the history of salt mining is described in detail. Don't miss the underground chapels, which have been created from salt.

The town of Czestochowa is famous for the **Black Madonna** in the Monastery of Jasna Gora. An icon of the Virgin Mary was darkened during artillery fire against the Swedes in 1655. She was taken up to the ramparts and it is said that her intervention forced the Swedes to leave Poland. Today, gifts are brought to her altar and she is uncovered two times during each day.

EXCURSIONS FROM CRACOW ••••••••••••••••••••••••••••••

In the south two mountain ranges rise: the Sudety and the Carpathians. The Carpathians include the Tatras massif, very much like the Alps.

Zakopane

This mountain resort community lies nestled in a bowl at the foot of the Western Tatra mountains, which rise in a wall of steep pinnacles. Visitors come to hike, ski, or restore themselves in pure mountain air.

The cable car ride to the Kasprowy Wierch took us to the top of the ridge that separates Poland from Czechoslovakia. We reached the height of 6510 feet through linked cable cars. When we were walking along the spine at the top, a couple with fluorescent gliders arrived and proceeded to arrange their gear. Almost within minutes, an officer arrived with gun and walkie-talkie to make sure they were not going to glide into Czechoslovakia and that they had permits. They took off easily from the spine and soared on wind currents across and down, wafting over the trees and fading out of sight.

Visitors can take a cart ride part way, then walk up to **Morskie Oko** (called eye of the sea), which is a large glacial lake surrounded by starkly vertical peaks that daunt climbers. Photographers were entranced by the many different reflections they could capture of the peaks in the clear water.

Zakopane is a small town, easily walkable, but it can also be enjoyed on a horse-and-cart trip. We were fascinated with the very unusual architecture found on wooden houses in town and the surrounding countryside. Very steep roofs make sense in a region known for heavy snow—they are made of narrow wooden slats or metal. Dormerlike v-shaped sections stick out on all sides and many of them have intricate wooden carved facades. Also, smooth, round stones from the river are used in foundations.

The **oldest church,** from 1848, is located on Koscieliska Street. It is wooden with a matching wooden fence covered with a slat roof in front. The same steep roof and v-shaped porch lead the eye up to the cross on top. Inside there are benches on each side, a number of biblical paintings, and folk art. Walk through the gates in the stone wall into the cemetery, which has beautiful tombs and decoration.

The **Tatra Museum** *(Muzeum Tatrzanskie)* is the oldest regional museum in Poland, founded in 1888. When we were there a bevy of energetic girl scouts were chasing each other up and down the steps and behind trees. Inside there is a large statue of a mountaineer sitting as if welcoming visitors. The room to the right contains a history of the settlement in the area dating back to the 14th century.

PORTUGAL

INFORMATION
Currency unit • escudos (the $ symbol is placed after the amount)
Language • Portuguese
Time difference from USA • five hours later (Eastern Standard Time)
Telephone access codes • to USA 097 1; from USA 351
National Tourist Offices • **USA:** Portuguese National Tourist Office, 590
Fifth Ave., New York, NY 10036-4704, tel.: (212) 354–4403; **Portugal:**
Praca dos Restauradores (Palacio Foz) Lisbon, tel.: 346–33–14; **Britain:**
New Bond St., London W10DB, tel.: 071–493–3873
Airlines • **TAP Air Portugal USA:** (800) 221–7370; **Britain:** (071) 828–
0262
Embassies • **American Embassy:** Avenida das Forcas Armadas (a Sete
Rios) 1600 Lisbon, tel.: 726–6600 or 726–8880; **British Embassy** 35/
37 Rua de Santa Domingos, a Lapa Lisbon 1296, tel.: 661191 or 661122

As aficionados of anything maritime, we felt almost like the ancient mariner himself when we stood on the rocks at Cabo da Roca. The sign there says it all: "The Land Ends and the Sea Begins." One can imagine explorers heading off westward into the unknown, taking a last glimpse of Portugal as it receded out of sight. Their accomplishments, particularly in the last two decades of the 15th century, made the first voyage of Columbus possible, as well as reaching the East Indies, Japan, and China by rounding the Cape of Good Hope and sailing eastward. To accomplish this, Portuguese navigators first had to ride down tradewinds from Africa to South America, then pick up prevailing westerlies farther south to run back to the tip of Africa. Without Prince Henry's famed school of navigation near Cape Vincent, the westernmost promontory of Europe, none of these world-transforming voyages would have been possible; many of them will be commemorated 500 years later throughout the 1990s.

HISTORY •

The coasts of Portugal were settled by people during the Palaeolithic period. Skeletons unearthed in cemeteries date from the Mesolithic period. Both the

311

Greeks and the Phoenicians had set up trading centers along the coasts as early as 1000 B.C. By 700 B.C., Celts arrived and Lusitanians inhabited hilltops in southern Portugal. Romans gained power and Lusitania became a Roman province by 179 A.D. By 418, the Visigoths had arrived and united several kingdoms under their rule. The Moors invaded in 711 and took over the entire Iberian peninsula. In 1094, King Alfonso VI was defeated by the Moors at Lisbon. Afonso Henriques vanquished the Moors in 1139 and became King Afonso I. He also gained Lisbon from the Moors in 1147 during the Second Crusade.

In 1418, Henry the Navigator founded the School of Navigation at Sagres that began a remarkable series of voyages of discovery. By 1498, Vasco da Gama had discovered how to reach India by sea, securing Portugal's role as a leading European sea power. In 1668, Spain recognized the independence of Portugal. An earthquake destroyed Lisbon in 1755; the Marques de Pombal planned the rebuilding of the city. Portugal was proclaimed a Republic in 1910 after the monarchy fell. Portugal was neutral during both World War I and II, although the country gave support to the Allies. Portugal became a member of the North Atlantic Treaty Organization as a founder in 1949 and in 1955 joined the United Nations.

LISBON

HISTORY......................................

Lisbon is a city oriented toward the sea. Portuguese voyages of discovery originated here; the navigators returned with details of their findings, as well as riches. Sailing and the sea are intertwined in the motifs on medieval buildings in the city. Lisbon is justly proud of her famous sons, who went out and discovered the world. They brought back gold and diamonds from Brazil, ivory from Africa, pearls, rubies, silks, and spices from the orient.

On November 1, 1755 an earthquake destroyed over two-thirds of the city. Many of the people were attending mass on All Saints' Day, with wax candles glowing in churches. The resulting fires from the candles spread to woodwork, vestments, and furnishings. Buildings collapsed, and people ran to the river only to find a gigantic tidal wave cascading upstream and over the town. Fortunately, the towering aqueduct that brought water into the city was left standing; it still stands today.

The Prime Minister, the Marquis of Pombal lived in his coach for the first

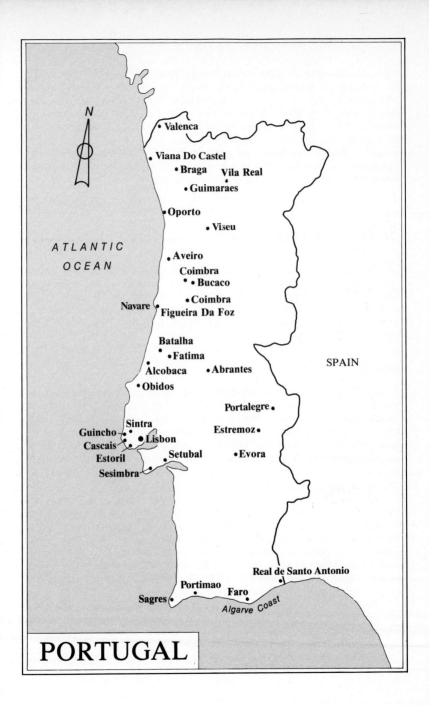

N

ATLANTIC
OCEAN

• Valenca

• Viana Do Castel
• Braga   Vila Real
• Guimaraes

• Oporto
• Viseu

• Aveiro
Coimbra
• • Bucaco
• Coimbra
Navare • Figueira Da Foz

Batalha
• • Fatima
Alcobaca • Abrantes
• Obidos

SPAIN

Portalegre •
Sintra
Guincho • • Estremoz •
Cascais • Lisbon
Estoril • Setubal
Sesimbra • • Evora

Real de Santo Antonio
Portimao •   •
Sagres • • Faro
Algarve Coast

PORTUGAL

week after the disaster, directing the cleanup and planning reconstruction. For the first time in its history, Lisbon's streets were straight and wide. Mosaic pavements are still in use today. **Black Horse Square** *(Praca do Comercio)* was designed by Pombal to honor his king at the time of the quake, Dom Jose, who sits on his bronze horse looking out on the river. Read Voltaire's *Candide* for a graphic account of the earthquake.

The "flower" revolution took place on April 25, 1974 when soldiers stuck carnations into their guns in a bloodless coup. Prime Minister Salazar and his successor Marcelo Caetano were quietly overthrown.

SIGHTSEEING...................................

Lisbon is a city of distinctly different districts. The central business area is called Baixa. Bairro Alto contains art galleries, restaurants, and night spots. Alfama is the oldest section of Lisbon, between the river and the castle. Belem is to the west and is the site that focuses on the history of the voyages of discovery. We suggest beginning in the Belem section of Lisbon. All of the sights are within walking distance along the river.

Belem

A statue of Prince Henry the Navigator, father of the age of Portuguese discovery, stands at the prow of a sailing ship, carved in stone on the River Tagus. The **Monument to the Discoveries** *(Padrao dos Descobrimentos)* is a tall, white, limestone monument built in 1960 to commemorate the 5th Centenary of the death of Prince Henry (Infante Dom Henrique). Following him are 33 figures, including navigators Vasco da Gama, Dioga Cao, and Fernao de Magalhaes, the poet Luis de Camoes, the scientist Pedro Nunes, the painter Nuno Goncalves, and a host of others.

His ship looks as if it is about to lurch forward with a gust of wind and take off for another voyage. The Portuguese coat-of-arms and the Cross of Aviz are sculpted above the sails of this classic caravel. A large compass rose lies at the foot of the monument, its marble mosaic stones picture a chart of the world inside the compass. One can stand on the oceans and chart the first voyages made to the Azores in 1427, the Congo River in 1482, the Cape of Good Hope in 1488, India in 1498, Brazil in 1500. One can also chart Magellan's first circumnavigation of the globe from 1519 to 1522.

Behind the monument stands the **Maritime Museum** *(Museu da Marinha)*, which brings the age of discovery alive with examples of many galleons, fishing, trading, and pleasure boats displayed in one room after another. Models of Egyptian and Greek warships from 3000 years B.C. are in the collection.

The **Calouste Gulbenkian Planetarium** stands next door to the Maritime

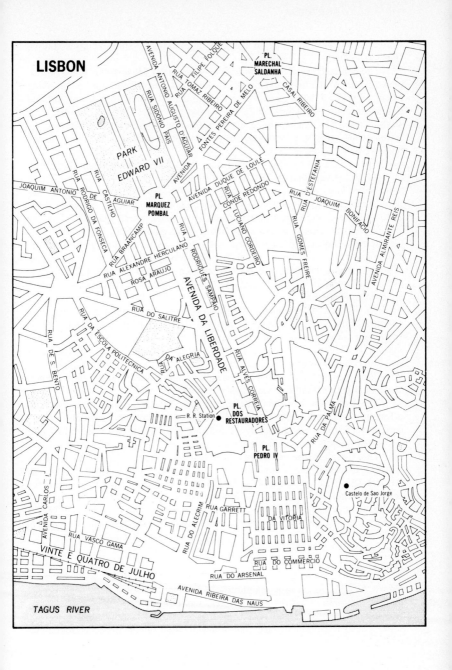

Museum. It offers information displays of the solar system, eclipses, falling stars, and comets.

The **Monastery of St. Jeronimo** *(Hieronymites Monastery)*, Praca do Imperio, is one of the finest examples of Manuelistic architecture in Lisbon. King Manuel I took an oath before Vasco da Gama left for India, promising to build a monastery after the navigator returned from his successful voyage to India. In 1498, Vasco da Gama returned and construction began in 1502. The site selected is the same spot where departing navigators prayed in the small chapel before embarking on a voyage.

At the west door, King Manuel with St. Jeronimo and Queen Maria with St. John the Divine live on in sculpture. In addition, the sculptor enjoyed a free hand with motifs of the sea in his work—shells, seaweed, and ropes are incorporated. Inside there are tombs of Camoes and Vasco da Gama as well as those of King Manuel and Queen Maria—both on the backs of elephants.

We looked closely at the walls where sketches had been left by the architect as he designed the arches. It's not often one sees working drawings on finished walls. If one looks up at the rib-vaulting and then down at the six central columns, the image of palm trees comes to mind, again following the use of natural motifs. The cloister will find photographers clicking away, using the arches as frames.

The **Tower of Bethlehem** *(Torre de Belem)*, Avenue Marginal, was constructed in the water as a mate to the Sao Sebastiao fortress across the river. Both were supposed to guard the entrance into Lisbon. This five-story tower was the last sight of Lisbon for departing sailors. Dating from 1521, the tower was used as a prison during the next two centuries, then rebuilt in 1845. The view from the terrace at the top includes the Tagus estuary, Belem, and the port area. Changing exhibitions are displayed inside.

The **Folk Art Museum** *(Museu de Arte Popular)*, Avenue de Brasilia, offers folklore and crafts from each Portuguese province. Costumes, tools, earthenware, rugs, and a variety of folk art objects are on display. In 1948, allegorical murals were painted inside.

The **Coach Museum** *(Museu dos Coches)*, Praca Alfonso de Alburquerque, is housed in the former riding school building of Belem palace. One can see coaches used by kings, as well as carriages and sedans of the last three centuries. There are collections of hunting horns, spurs, saddles, costumes, and uniforms. Look for the straw doll used to train lancers during the Middle Ages— it looks like a scarecrow. A gallery of paintings showing each king of Portugal is also on view.

Alfama

Here's the place to get lost—on purpose. Climb up and down steps, walk deeper into the labyrinth of narrow passageways, and look up at wrought-iron balconies festooned with flowers and plants, green shutters and laundry fanning the air. This is also the place to hear *fado* sung at night. *Fado* music is sometimes melancholy, reminiscent of lost love, sliding in and out of minor modes with ease. It can also portray great happiness and love. Not only the tourists enjoy listening to *fado*—local inhabitants are just as likely to spend an evening in a *fado* restaurant.

The **Museum of Decorative Art** *(Fundacao Ricardo Espirito Santo Silva)*, Largo das Portas do Sol 2, is located in the Alfama. Inside this 17th-century palace, visitors are treated to a collection of Portuguese and European furniture, china, silver, tapestries, musical instruments, and carpets. This museum is well known in the restorative art world, as its professional staff restore pieces for Versailles, Fontainbleau, the Library of Paris, and collectors all over the world.

The **Cathedral** *(Se or Patriarcal)* of Lisbon is located just below the castle. Dating from the 12th century, it was restored after each earthquake, especially that of 1755. It still retains its Romanesque architecture. The relics (bones and a hand) of St. Vincent are kept in an oriental mother-of-pearl casket. The casket is opened once a year on St. Vincent's Day, January 22nd. According to legend, his body was taken in a ship from Africa to Portugal by two black ravens. The baptistry contains panels of glazed tiles, which depict St. Anthony's sermon to the fishes. Tombs include that of Lopo Fernandes Pacheco, who was a man-at-arms of King Afonso IV, and his wife, Maria Vilalobos. There are rose windows, one over the central nave and one in the North transept.

Ten towers linked by extensive battlements make **St. George's Castle** *(Castelo San Jorge)*, Largo do Chao da Feira, a massive sight from below; one can sense the shrouded legends of such a place. Situated high on a hill above the Alfama, the castle is indeed impressive. Dating back to the Visigoths in the 5th century, the castle was rebuilt by the Moors in the 9th century and has undergone some changes since then. Gardens and pools with peacocks roaming around provide a quiet and pleasant place to wander. From the terrace, one can see the curve of the Tagus, ships in the harbor, the Ponte 25 de Abril bridge, and a large statue on the opposite shore called *Christ in Majesty (Cristo-Rei)*. This statue is a replica of one in Rio de Janeiro; it is 279 feet high.

Central Lisbon

From Pombaline Lisbon on the water, head north to **Rossio Square,** which contains two fountains and a bronze statue of King Pedro IV. Cafes, shops, and flower stalls make this a place for people to congregate. Santa Justa Lift, which was designed by Gustave Eiffel, the creator of the Eiffel Tower, begins its journey on Rua do Ouro and heads almost straight up to Carmo Square on top. This lift, looking like a lacy iron birdcage, is wedged in between buildings. Inside, the wooden cabin has brass accents and is enclosed in glass. The bird's-eye view from the top is of the Alfama crowned with St. George's Castle, Rossio Square, Avenida da Liberdade, and shopping streets in the Chiado. The Rossio Station is also here, with a neo-Manueline facade.

Speaking of transportation, the "Electrico" is one way to get around town. Once English trolleys, now orange cars zip up and down steep inclines on a narrow-gauge track. Care must be taken not to collide with another car; sometimes Electrico employees stand with large "ping-pong" paddles, one with green for "go" and the other stating "no entrance." The rules are meant to be flexible—depending on which car gets there first, or on the whim of the man with the paddles! Sometimes passengers have to help move a small car that has parked too close to the tracks. It's an experience!

The next square to the north is called **Praca dos Restaurandores;** the obelisk in the center honors the people who led a revolt against the Spanish in 1640. Walk along the Avenida da Liberdade north to the Praca Marques de Pombal where there is a monument for the Marquis of Pombal. King Edward VII Park is next; it was named after the King of England who visited in 1902 to cement the Anglo-Portuguese Alliance. Ponds, waterfalls, and grottoes add beauty to the floral displays.

Near the north end of King Edward VII Park is the **Calouste Gulbenkian Foundation,** Avenida de Berna, named for the Armenian oil magnate who donated his art collection to Portugal, which contains the Gulbenkian Museum, an auditorium for concerts and other performances, temporary exhibition areas, and a library on the art, history, literature, and culture of Portugal. The museum houses the founder's extensive art collection. A highlight of the museum world is the Lalique jewelry collection from the Art Nouveau and Art Deco periods.

Gulbenkian's European paintings range from primitive masters to the Impressionists. In 1930, he bought the marble sculpture *Diana* by Houdon, which had belonged to Catherine the Great of Russia. Gulbenkian also collected French furniture, tapestries, Greek coins, Egyptian sculpture, oriental ceramics, Syrian glass, and more. The entire collection is now housed in a building constructed in 1969.

In your exploration, you are sure to come upon one of the *Miradouros,* which are plateaus located somewhere high with a view. Sometimes they are cement platforms with benches, trees, a place for children to ride bikes and for people to congregate to look at the view or play cards. Also while wandering, you will see lots of *azulejos,* which are decorative tiles found on the outside and inside of many buildings. Although they come in all colors, blue and white seem to be predominant.

DAY TRIPS FROM LISBON ....

WEST AND NORTH

This circular route can be done by car with a lunch stop along the way. Bus tours include a number of the sites on their schedules; most of them can also be reached by train from Lisbon.

Heading toward the west from Lisbon, one passes through Carcavelos, which is a favorite with surfers. A 17th-century castle is located above the town.

Estoril is known for its casino, horse racing, and regattas. Carbonic acid found in radioactive hot springs is sought by those who have bone and joint diseases, rheumatism, and other ailments; a small beach next to the hospital is a favorite for soaking in the restorative elements. Surfers and swimmers enjoy the sandy beaches of Estoril. Palm trees and tropical plants grow in the park as well as along the avenues. Luxury villas in town have been home to deposed European kings and expatriates. During World War II, both allied and axis spies played in Estoril; Portugal was neutral and at the time a location for international intrigue. Monte Estoril, an area of lovely homes high above the town, also has expansive sea views.

Cascais is still a fishing village where fishermen pull their colorful wooden boats up on the shore, then spend time mending their nets and talking with friends. We watched several meticulously finding all of the holes and reweaving them. Early morning is the time to watch the daily fish auction.

From 1870, Cascais was the summer residence for kings of Portugal, and now the President of the Republic lives in the Citadel on the southwest side of Cascais Bay. The **Palace of the Condes de Castro Guimaraes,** located near the park, contains a museum displaying 17th-century Portuguese and Indo-Portuguese azulejos tiles and furniture, 18th-century silver and gold, bronzes, and carpets. A church built in Manueline style, **Nossa Senhora da Assuncao,** is rich with 18th-century *azulejos* tiles.

Boca do Inferno, which is a mile farther west, is the place to go to watch a wild sea pound the rocks. Called the "mouth of hell," the 65-foot-high cliff contains a number of sea caves, which have been scooped out by the violent water over the years. Waves crash boomingly into the caves and spray dramatically in all directions.

Guincho is a wild place, where the Atlantic roars in with a shrieking bellow. The word *guincho* means "scream" in Portuguese, which is what the wind sounds like after turning the corner of the coastline and facing nothing but a long stretch of Atlantic. Currents and a strong undertow make swimming here extremely dangerous.

Cape of the Rock *(Cabo da Roca),* the most westerly point of Europe, is marked by a lighthouse and a sign that says, "The Land Ends and the Sea Begins." Visitors can purchase a certificate that proves they reached the spot.

Sintra has long been a favorite respite for kings, writers and other travelers. Lord Byron called Sintra a "glorious eden" and the town was featured in his *Childe Harold's Pilgrimage.* There are three palaces to visit in Sintra: a Moorish castle dating from the 7th century, the Royal or National Palace, once Moorish with Portuguese additions, and Pena Palace, which was built by King Fernando II in the middle of the 19th century.

Castle of the Moors *(Castelo dos Mouros)* was built on a summit at 450 meters beginning in the 8th or 9th century and rebuilt several times since then. Some of the walls still stand along the hill in gray stone splendor. Stairways lead to the frames of arches, and stone towers still look out over the mountains, the sea, Sintra, and Pena Castle. One has an eerie feeling when exploring this extensive ruin. The Romanesque Chapel of Sao Pedro lies in ruins as well. Two Romanesque doorways, tombs, and traces of fresco paintings remain.

The **National Palace** *(Palacio Nacional de Sintra or Palacio Real)* dates from the 14th century, and its style ranges from Moorish to late Gothic. One can't miss it when coming into town, as its two, tall, cone-like chimneys tower over the rest of the building. Additions were made at different times over the years, following the initial building erected by Joao I. The wings and windows are definitely Manueline.

Mad King Afonso VI was confined for six years by his brother Pedro II in one room in the palace. The floor is worn due to his constant pacing. Pedro took not only his freedom, but his throne and his queen.

The Magpie Room is so called because the ceiling consists of rows of magpies holding a rose in each beak. According to legend, Queen Philippa caught her husband King Joao I kissing a lady-in-waiting, but he replied there was "no harm in it." He had the room painted with a magpie for each of the women in court—to allay their gossip.

Pena Palace perches at the highest point in the Sintra range of mountains. Built by King Fernando II in the middle of the 19th century around the remains of a 16th-century Hieronymite monastery, this castle looks medieval. Entering by drawbridge is only the beginning. The castle contains the King's collection of china, furniture, oriental rugs, stag antlers, and weapons. Pena Park is lush with flowering shrubs, trees and flowers in among grottoes, lakes with black swans and ducks, and an island in one of the lakes complete with a small replica of a castle. The architect, Baron von Eschwege, planted a statue of himself dressed as a knight on an adjoining crag.

Quinta de Monserrate, about two miles out of town, was built in 1856 for Sir Francis Cook, a London merchant. The park contains extensive gardens, now maintained by the State. Subtropical plants, ferns, and exotic trees blend into an attractive landscape enhanced by fountains, pergolas, and stone bridges. In the 1850s, the head gardener at Kew Gardens in London offered his expertise on the landscaping.

The **Palace of Queluz,** a baroque palace with rococo decoration in pink and white, stretches its wings around a series of gardens. They were laid out by the French architect Jean-Baptiste Robillon and include sculpture, fountains, and grottoes. The *Ribeira de Jamor* is an ornate *azulejo* tile fountain, located in the lower garden. The ghost of the Infante Dom Francisco may wander in the gardens at night.

The main building in the palace was built in 1758 and finished after the marriage of Dom Pedro to Dona Maria Francisca. In 1792 Queen Maria imagined herself burning in "Hell's own fires" and went mad in her bedroom there.

EAST AND SOUTH

To the southeast, **Palmela Castle** is in a bucolic setting amid deep green pines, thriving vineyards, and the scent of eucalyptus. The 12th-century castle, which is 238 meters tall, located in the foothills of the Arrabida Mountains. The view from the castle encompasses the vineyard-covered countryside, the mountains of the Arrabida, the Troia Peninsula, and the sea beyond. The hill town, dating back to neolithic times, huddles under the castle, now the Pousada do Castelo Palmela. Dating back to the 8th century B.C., the first inhabitants were the Moors. In 1147, Dom Afonso Henriques, first King of Portugal, captured the castle. In 1172 he rebuilt the castle and founded a monastery for the Order of Santiago. By 1423, construction was begun on the monastery; the headquarters of the Order were established there in 1443. In 1484, the Bishop of Evora, who was thought to have conspired against Dom Joao II, was imprisoned in the dungeon of the castle, where he died. The monks of Palmela were also knights of the castle; their emblem carries a cross in the shape of a sword.

The 15th-century Convent of Santiago is part Romanesque and part Gothic. It is adorned with 16th-century *azulejo* tiles. King Joao II's son, Jorge de Lencastre, reclines in his tomb there. Visitors can walk around the rampart and into the tower for expansive views. The ruins of a church built around a mosque and destroyed in the earthquake of 1755 are situated below the keep.

Setubal's roots date back to Roman times during the first to the 4th centuries. The salting of fish was started on the banks of the Sado River; Sado salt-pans produce high quality salt. This fishing industry thrives there today.

The **Church of Jesus** *(Igreja de Jesus)* has unusual Manuelino pillars supporting the vault inside—similar to giant twisted ropes. *Azulejo* tiles provide contrast to the granite columns. The cloister built of Arrabida marble of the Convento de Jesus now contains the **Municipal Museum.** Archaeological artifacts are on display as are paintings by Portuguese, Flemish, and Catalan artists.

The castle, built in 1590, has been turned into a *pousada,* Castelo de Sao Filipe. A chapel contains 18th-century *azulejos,* which depict the life of St. Philip.

The **Arrabida coast,** with its sand beaches, lies below the Arrabida Mountains, which rise and fall from Palmela to Cape Espichel. Each side of the mountain range has different topography: the northern is fairly dry with vineyards and olive groves, and the southern slides down to the ocean in a mass of cypress and pine. The shore road leads to a number of sand beaches at Figuernina, Galopos, and Creiro. A side excursion to Portinho da Arrabida brings one to another beach and a pleasant cove. Craggy cliffs rise abruptly from Portinho.

Lapa de Santa Margarida is a cave that is the site of a religious festival held every July 20th. Hans Christian Andersen wrote "it is a vast cave ornamented with stalactites and opening out to the clear sea water; its grandeur is beyond description. . . . It is a veritable church hewn out of the living rock, with a fantastic vault, organ pipes, columns, and altars." Then the road turns inland, passing a castle at Santana, before heading down the mountain to Sesimbra.

Sesimbra, has been and is still a fishing village. When we were there, fishermen were straightening their nylon fishing lines by pulling them around a pole set some distance away. Hooks were attached to short strings, in turn fastened to the long lines. Fish are spread out on the sandy beach ready for auction. Sesimbra is world-famous for its sea angling. Record swordfish catches have been taken from the area.

Sesimbra Castle, once dominated by the Moors, was taken by King Henry I of Portugal in 1165. Crenellated walls make this castle unmistakeable from a distance.

Cabo Espichel is the most westerly point of the peninsula. A lighthouse and a pilgrimage chapel, **Our Lady of the Cape** *(Nossa Senhora do Cabo)* provide a perfect setting for a fishermen's festival in October. And the cliffs drop away into the Atlantic just beyond.

The **Caparica coast** is one of long sandy beaches. Private coves have formed naturally in between craggy outcroppings. Major roads have not been built along this coast; all the better for peace and solitude.

EXCURSIONS FROM LISBON................

Algarve

The Algarve might be thought of as a ninety-six-mile-long Mediterranean garden. Flowers bloom year-round; orchards and fields produce one harvest after another. Visitors enjoy the warm weather—sometimes warmer than the Mediterranean in winter—and the little fishing villages and sandy beaches interspersed with craggy outcroppings. Many of the beaches can be considered private, with secluding rocks on each side.

Variety in terrain includes the coast east of Faro, which is sandy with long offshore spits and the west, which is rugged with craggy, monstrously high cliffs. We once watched some local people sitting on the edge of a very high cliff at Cabo San Vicente having lunch, hanging their legs over the side. It was all we could do to sit near enough to see the waves crashing below.

Cabo San Vicente is one of our favorite places anywhere. Photographers will appreciate the exhilaration engendered by leaning over a little to catch just one more wave crashing down below. Views from the lighthouse terrace usually include one of the 200 or so ships that cruise around the cape into the Mediterranean every day.

Prince Henry the Navigator, the son of King Joao I, received the title of Duke of Viseu after crushing the Moors in North Africa in 1415. Intensely interested in navigation, Prince Henry settled in Sagres so that he could be near the "end of the world." Now he sits here for all time, in statue form, with a sextant in his hand.

Prince Henry developed the School of Navigation, located across the bay from Cabo de Sao Vicente, in 1421 and gathered around him enough expert scholars, geographers, astronomers, and cartographers to work on new navigational theory. Among other things, they improved the sextant and astrolabe in order to determine latitude by celestial navigation. Young Portuguese students, who came to him to be turned into seamen, became among the best and bravest in the world. Magellan, Costa Cabral, and Vasco da Gama were in that group. The paving in the parade ground, uncovered under a church in 1921, contains a large compass rose, perhaps used in their instruction. Prince Henry's trained crews later sailed off into the blue from nearby Lagos.

Francis Drake, a swashbuckling Devonshire privateer and world circumnavigator, used this corner of the world as his own private lair. He would lurk in hiding until he spotted a ship coming from the South Atlantic and Mediterranean on its way to Lisbon. Once he captured a precious cargo of seasoned barrel hoops and staves, precious because it took such a long time to season. All water, food, and gunpowder supplies were transported in barrels, so this was a real catastrophe. But as he built a bonfire with glee he chortled, "they burned right merrilie."

SCOTLAND

Currency • Scottish pound, equal to British pound (L)
Language • English and Gaelic
Time difference from USA • five hours later (Eastern Standard Time)
Telephone access codes • to USA 010 or USADirect 0800 89 0011; from USA: 44
National Tourist Offices • **USA:** British Tourist Authority, 40 W. 57th St., New York, NY 10019, tel.: (212) 581–4700;
Scotland: • Scottish Tourist Board, Ravelston Terrace, Edinburgh, Scotland, tel.: (031) 332–2433
Airlines • **British Airways USA:** (800) 247–9297; **Britain** (081) 897–4000 **Virgin Atlantic USA** • (800) 862–8621
Embassies • **American Consulate,** 3 Regent Terrace, Edinburgh, Scotland EH 75BW, tel.: (031) 556–8315

One of my favorite memories is of the time I sat by myself in a field of heather, deeply inhaling the wonderful fragrance and feeling very peaceful and happy. Just that morning I had seen Queen Elizabeth in person for the first and only time. I had stood by the road leading up to Crathie Church near Balmoral waiting for her to drive by. Afterward I walked into the church where she had been minutes before.

My husband's recollections of Scotland are quite different. He sees a remarkable interpenetration of mountains and sea in a land that might have been a series of islands with a little more geological prompting. He remembers most vividly the bleak fascination of the Isle of Skye and the wonder of the Outer Hebrides seen at first light from the air.

HISTORY......................................

Scotland, first called Caledonia, was independent for many years, constantly warring with England. When James VI of Scotland was crowned James I of England, the two countries were joined, although the Scots to this day maintain their traditions and heritage. Parliament decreed that Scots could not wear their

SCOTLAND

• Nairn
• Inverness
• Grantown-on-Spey

Loch Ness

Aberdeen •
• Braemar

• Fort William

• Pitlochry

Dunkeld • • Dundee

Iona • Oban

Perth •

NORTH SEA

Dunblane • St. Andrews

ATLANTIC OCEAN

Stirling •

• Glasgow

Edinburgh

• Peebles

• Prestwick

N

N. IRELAND

ENGLAND

kilts after Bonnie Prince Charles was defeated at Culloden in 1746. Today Scotland's legal system is independent of England from its base in Edinburgh; the country is represented in Parliament as a part of the British Isles.

EDINBURGH

HISTORY......................................

Archaeologists who have been doing tunnel excavation under Edinburgh Castle feel that early civilization began there during the Iron Age in the late first or early 2nd century. The Picts probably built their huts on the windy, volcanic lump where the castle now stands. The site provided greater security from invaders than anything else around. The Romans built a fort nearby at Cramond, but after they left, the King of Northumbria, Edwin, built Dun Eadain (fortress on a hill) on Castle Rock. King Malcolm and Queen Margaret moved from Dunfermline to Edinburgh Castle during the 11th century; their son David I founded the Abbey of Holy Rood and built a chapel to honor his mother. In 1329 Robert Bruce granted a charter to the town. By 1450 the town walls had been started and the medieval golden age had begun, ending with the disaster at Flodden in 1513 when the king and many others were killed. During the Reformation, Catholics and Protestants fought and continued to fight into the 17th century.

SIGHTSEEING...................................

The Old Town

There are several ways to enjoy Edinburgh Castle. The image that has remained in our minds for almost 40 years is that of a magical, crispy-cool evening when we were entranced by the Edinburgh Tattoo. The sound of romantic bagpipes brings back a vision of handsome Scots marching in their kilts under the stars with the castle ramparts in silhouette.

The **Esplanade,** where the tattoo is held, was once the site of the volcanic ridge on the now extinct volcano, which gurgled up Castle Rock. To the right is the **Witches' Well,** where more than 300 "witches" were burned between

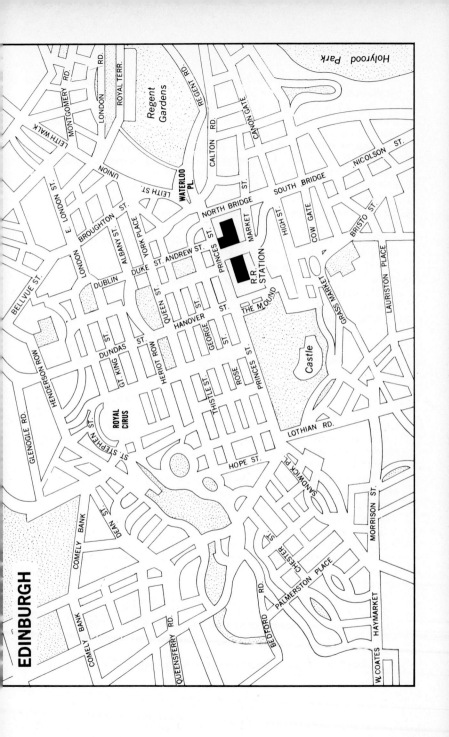

EDINBURGH

1479 and 1722. Look for the serpent as well as a good witch and a bad witch on the memorial.

As visitors pass through the **gatehouse,** the Royal Arms of Scotland are poised above, guarded by statues of Robert Bruce and William Wallace. Be prepared to walk up a fair amount inside the castle as every road is on a slant. The **Battery** is seen on the left as a high series of stone half-circles built above the natural craggy rock. The **Portcullis Gate** is next, resplendent with the red lion on a gilt background, arms of the Earl of Morton. You'll wind up the hill past the **Argyle Battery,** the **Mill's Mount Battery,** where the one o'clock gun is fired each day, an 18th-century cart-shed, the **Governor's House,** and on to the vaults to see **Mons Meg.** This siege-gun was made in the 1440s for the Duke of Burgundy; it served in the Scottish service for many years until it exploded in 1680. It has now been returned to the Castle and is on display in the vaults as weather was damaging its metal.

The **Scottish National War Memorial** sits on the site of the medieval church of St. Mary. The long **Gallery of Honor** leads to a steel casket containing the names of the dead. Stained-glass windows were created by Douglas Strachan.

Across the road stands **Saint Margaret's Chapel,** which is the earliest surviving building in the castle. David I, who became King in 1124, probably built this chapel for his mother. Inside, the vaulting contains an ornate white-on-white decoration; one stained-glass window portrays St. Margaret in a purple robe.

The **Crown Room** in the Old Palace contains the Scottish crown, scepter, and sword, which were once forgotten in a chest and discovered by Sir Walter Scott in 1818. **Queen Mary's Apartments** contain the tiny room where Mary Queen of Scots gave birth to her son James VI of Scotland. Mystery still surrounds this room, where workmen in 1830 found a small coffin behind the paneling. The remains of a tiny infant were found, dressed in silk embroidered with a "J."

The **Great Hall,** with its open-timber, hammer-beam ceiling not unlike the unfinished hull of a ship, was the scene of the Black Dinner of 1440. When a black bull's head was brought into the room everyone knew that a violent death was about to occur—the boy Earl of Douglas and his young brother had been invited to the dinner by Chancellor Chrichton. The brothers were executed in front of the eight-year-old king, James II. Armor and weapons now festoon the hall. Next door, **Queen Anne Barracks** now houses a collection of the Scottish United Service Museum. Visitors can see the changes and features of military uniforms and kit for the last 200 years.

The **Royal Mile** stretches from Castle Rock to Holyrood Palace. Once a squalid place where people lived and worked, the Royal Mile is today restored and pleasant to walk. Heading down Castlehill visitors will pass **Tolbooth Church** with an octagonal Gothic spire rising to 73 metres. This church has services in Gaelic.

Gladstone's Land, dating from 1617, is the only example left of the old high-rise tenement of the period. Only its arcaded front remains but restoration revealed original painted ceilings. The house has been furnished with period pieces, including Dutch chests and a carved Scottish bed. **Lady Stair's House,** Lawnmarket, contains a collection of Robert Burns, Sir Walter Scott, and Robert Lewis Stevenson memorabilia.

Brodie's Close was made famous by Deacon Brodie who was the Town Councillor and an upstanding citizen by day, and a burglar by night; Robert Lewis Stevenson used his image in **Dr. Jeykll and Mr. Hyde.** Brodie was found stealing from the Excise Office in Chessel's Court in the Canongate, fled to Holland, and was brought back to be hanged near St. Giles. Ironically, he had designed the gallows and when he asked to use a steel collar so he could survive—it didn't work.

St. Giles' Cathedral, now the High Kirk of Edinburgh, has not been a cathedral since 1688 when the Church of Scotland got rid of the bishops. Although there has been a church on the site since 854, the present building is a 15th-century Gothic structure. The **Thistle Chapel,** designed by Robert Lorimer in 1911, contains ornate canopies over the carved oak stalls.

Parliament House is located behind St. Giles. The statue of John Knox marks the spot of his burial when the cemetery of St. Giles occupied the place.

John Knox's House, 45 High St., was his home from 1561 to 1572. The house has been restored to show the original fireplaces, walls, and painted ceilings. Behind this house is **Moubray House,** where Daniel Defoe edited the *Edinburgh Courant* in 1710.

Canongate Tolbooth, earlier a council chamber, courthouse and jail, now contains a museum containing a tartan collection. **Huntley House,** the city museum of local history, contains a fine collection of Edinburgh silver. **Canongate Church** was built in 1688 for those who were removed from Holyrood's Chapel Royal by James VII of Scotland (James II of England).

The **Palace of Holyrood House** stands at the end of the Royal Mile. It has been a royal residence since the reign of James IV; Queen Elizabeth lives there when in Edinburgh, and the palace is closed when she is in residence.

The **Abbey of Holyrood** is an earlier structure that is now in ruin. Only the roofless nave remains. The burial vault holds the remains of David II, James II, James V, and Lord Darnley. Its mythical origins stem from David I who was out hunting when he was tossed from his horse and wounded, by a stag. As he reached for the animal's horns the stag bounded into the woods and he was left holding a cross, which saved his life. In gratitude, David founded the Abbey of Holy Rood in 1128. In all likelihood the name Holyrood may have come from the relic of a part of Christ's cross, which his mother, St. Margaret, had in her possession.

Built in 1500 by James IV, burnt in 1544 and rebuilt, the palace was the site of a series of incidents in Mary Queen of Scots's life. She arrived as the young widow of Francis II of France in 1561, was subjected to the tirades of John Knox because of her Catholic beliefs, married Lord Darnley in the Abbey, was forced to watch the murder of David Rizzio while six months' pregnant, found Darnley strangled in Kirk o'Field, and married James Hepburn, the Earl of Bothwell in 1567. Her son, James VI, continued to live in the palace until he took the English crown and spent his time in London.

The New Town

Princes Street, named after Prince George, who became King George IV, was designed with buildings on only one side and a wide garden running down the entire one-mile length. Here is the focal point for inhabitants and visitors alike, to stroll and to relax in a peaceful setting away from the bustling city.

The **Floral Clock,** near the base of The Mound, is the oldest floral clock in the world, dating from 1903. In bloom during warm months, the clock is kept in meticulous order all year round. Its face is laid out in a new pattern every year; the 38-foot circumference can hold anywhere from 14,000 to 20,000 plants.

Sir Walter Scott's Monument, soaring upward 200 feet in Gothic splendor, forms a canopy over his statue with that of his dog, Maida. Sixty-four statuettes of Scott characters stand around him. Visitors can climb the 287 steps to the top for a view of the city.

Calton Hill contains a 102-foot-high monument to Admiral Nelson, in memory of Trafalgar. The climb to the top produces a citywide view including Holyrood, Arthur's Seat, Leith, and the Forth River. In 1861 a "time ball" was installed at the top of Nelson's monument by the Edinburgh Royal Observatory. The ball drops simultaneously with the firing of the cannon from the castle at one p.m. Even though the Royal Observatory has moved to Blackford Hill, the master-clock keeps the ball on schedule on Calton Hill.

An extinct volcano can be found in Queen's Park—its name is Arthur's Seat. The legendary King Arthur of the Round Table and his knights are supposed to have been buried there. The view from the top includes the city, and across the Lowlands up into the Highland hills.

The **Royal Museum of Scotland,** Chambers St., is housed in a Victorian building designed by Captain Francis Fowke. It was placed near the University so that its resources could be used by students. In 1855 the Natural History collection of the University was transferred to the museum.

The **Scottish National Portrait Gallery** houses portraits of famous Scots from the 16th century to the present. Collections include those of Mary Queen of Scots in an early portrait dressed in mourning for Francis II, her son James VI, Charles I, Charles II, James VII, and George IV. Flora Macdonald, who saved the life of Bonnie Prince Charlie by taking him "over the sea to Skye" is pictured there.

The **Royal Museum of Scotland,** called the national Museum of Antiquities until 1985, contains artifacts from the Stone Age to the present. The Dark Age Sculpture Collection dates from 650 to 900 A.D. The Traprain Treasure dates from the 5th century and includes silver bowls, goblets, and jewelry.

Scholars speculate that this treasure may have been buried by pirates. Also on display is "the Maiden," the guillotine that lopped off many Scottish heads.

The **National Gallery of Scotland,** The Mound, contains Scottish paintings as well as European old masters and impressionist works.

DAY TRIPS FROM EDINBURGH ....

WEST OF EDINBURGH
Hopetoun House

Hopetoun House, located on the Firth of Forth, is the home of the third Marquess of Linlithgow, who is also the 9th Earl of Hopetoun. Sir William Bruce began the building in 1699 and it was enlarged by William Adam in 1721; it is now known as Scotland's greatest Adam mansion. The Hope family continues to live in part of the house. There is a view of the Firth of Forth from the rooftop terrace. The deer park houses both fallow and red deer as well as St. Kilda sheep, which are black with four horns. A nature trail and sea walk are on the grounds.

Linlithgow Palace

Linlithgow Palace, which was the birthplace of James V in 1513 and of Mary Queen of Scots in 1542, is now a ruin. Although the top is open to the sky, the walls still stand and one can imagine life there in ages past. Mary of Guise, the mother of Mary Queen of Scots, said that Linlithgow was the most princely home she had ever seen. The royal family stayed in Linlithgow every year and at one time parliament met there. In 1746, the Duke of Cumberland's army stayed in the palace overnight, then left fires burning as they departed—it was soon in flames. The chapel contains five large windows that once contained stained-glass panels. James IV received a ghostly apparition there, warning him not to fight the English at Flodden—the prophecy of disaster came true.

One of the best views of the palace can be seen during a walk around Linlithgow Loch. In less than an hour, visitors can walk through the home of a variety of wildlife, birds, and plants.

NORTHWEST OF EDINBURGH
Stirling Castle

Stirling Castle sits on a pile of volcanic rock just as Edinburgh Castle does. Some say that the first inhabitants were ancient Welsh, and that King Arthur took over from the Saxons. The first King to have definitely lived in Stirling Castle was Alexander I, who died there in 1124. The castle exchanged hands between the English and the Scots during the next several hundred years.

Although there may have been a number of skeletons found around the castle, one was attributed to James II, who in 1452 invited the eighth Earl of Douglas, whom he did not trust, to the castle, stabbed him, and threw his body out the window. James II, when only eight years old, had been present when the previous Earl of Douglas was murdered during the Black Dinner in Edinburgh Castle.

Nearby, **Cambuskenneth Abbey,** found in 1147 by David as an Augustinian monastery, was used by the Scottish Parliament in 1326. The 13th-century belfry tower soars to 79 feet. Inside, there is a monument to James III and his Queen Margaret.

The **Wallace Monument** stands eight miles to the northeast on Abbey Craig. Here, Wallace's two-handed sword is on display. Sir William Wallace rounded up Scottish forces against the English in 1297; they were successful at the Battle of Stirling Bridge.

The **Bannockburn Heritage Center,** two miles south of Stirling, is the place to go to learn about the Battle of Bannockburn in 1314. This battle was a turning point in the War of Independence. An equestrian statue of Robert the Bruce is in the rotunda.

Culross

Culross, a village reminiscent of the 16th- to 18th-century Scotland, has been carefully restored by the National Trust for Scotland. The palace, built between 1597 and 1611 by George Bruce, is really the home of a wealthy merchant who made his money by salt panning, coal mining, and trade. He was a clever man who avoided paying too much tax for windows by creating half-shuttered and half-glazed windows in his house.

The parish church contains a large group of alabaster effigies—Sir George, his wife, and eight children.

The Tolbooth, or Town House, is now headquarters for the National Trust of Scotland; an audio-visual presentation sets the stage for the village.

Dunfermline

Dunfermline was the birthplace of Andrew Carnegie, who was born into a poor family that emigrated to Pennsylvania. Carnegie became wealthy through the iron and steel industries, bestowing endowments in America and in Britain. His story is told in the local museum adjacent to his birthplace cottage. Pittencrieff Glen, the site of a park Carnegie was not allowed to enter as a child, was purchased by him so "no wee child should ever feel locked out." It was given to the town complete with beautiful gardens.

Dunfermline's Abbey Church dates from 1072, when Malcolm Canmore and Queen Margaret dedicated the Church of the Holy Trinity; in 1128, David I gave it the status of an abbey. The grave of Robert the Bruce is beneath the pulpit. His stone coffin was excavated in 1818 to reveal a shroud woven with threads of gold. His breastbone had been split so that his heart could be taken for burial in Jerusalem; Sir James Douglas was killed while on his way, and the heart was returned to Scotland and placed in Melrose Abbey.

NORTH OF EDINBURGH

Glamis Castle

Glamis Castle, where Queen Elizabeth the Queen Mother spent much of her childhood, is also the place where Princess Margaret was born. Little chairs, one for the then Princesses Elizabeth and Margaret, stand ready for other royal children. The castle is the home of the Earl and Countess of Strathmore and Kinghorne; it has been in their family since 1372 when Sir John Lyon was so honored by King Robert II. Sir John married Princess Joanna, the daughter of the king, in 1376.

The castle is the legendary setting of Shakespeare's *Macbeth*. Besides that, it *looks* like a castle should, with towers and turrets rising up to seek the flag on top. When we were there, the long drive was a billow of yellow daffodils interspersed with frolicking lambs.

SOUTH OF EDINBURGH

Floors Castle

The largest inhabited house in Scotland, Floors Castle is the home of the Duke and Duchess of Roxburghe. William Adam designed the house for the first Duke of Roxburghe in 1721. This castle has a myriad of rounded towers on the corner of each of its sections—it seems to be one square building after another, but the rounded tops soften the whole effect.

Abbotsford

In 1812 Sir Walter Scott bought the Cartley Hall house located on the banks of the River Tweed. In 1822 he pulled down the house and built another, which stands today. His friends came to visit—Wordsworth, Thomas Moore, and Washington Irving. In later years, Queen Victoria came to tea with the family in 1867, King George V and Queen Mary with the Duke and Duchess of York in 1923 and the Duke and Duchess of Gloucester in 1964.

His study is as he left it—with his writing desk containing two secret drawers. In 1935 the drawers were discovered, and 57 letters between Scott and his beloved wife were found. Sir Herbert Grierson published them in *The Letters of Sir Walter Scott* in 1937. Scott died in his dining room in 1832. His bed had been placed near the window so he could see his favorite River Tweed.

EXCURSIONS FROM EDINBURGH ••••••••••••••••••••••••••••••••

It is not easy to select excursions from Edinburgh, as there are so many ways travelers can go—from more exploration of the Border Country, to Aberdeen and the northeastern corner of Scotland, to Glasgow and points west, to the upper northwestern corner with its Orkneys, Hebrides, and points in between. We suggest a tour of the Great Glen up to Inverness, leaving the return trip up to you.

The main road from Edinburgh goes through Glencoe, a place with a bloody history. In August 1691 a proclamation was issued offering to pardon those who had been fighting against King William III—if they took the oath of allegiance before a sheriff by January 1, 1692. MacIan of Glencoe delayed until December 31, when he appeared before the Governor in Fort William. The Governor did not have the authority to administer the oath and sent MacIan up to Inveraray. Due to a snowstorm and also detention by a government garrison, MacIan did not reach Inveraray until January 2. The sheriff was not at home, but when he arrived on January 6 he administered the oath. However, this case never came before the Privy Council in Edinburgh, as some members felt it was not fair to accept a tardy oath. On February 1, 120 men of Argyll's regiment arrived in Glencoe under the command of Captain Robert Campbell. They settled into local homes, were entertained royally, and then—in a surprise move on February 13—killed all of the men, women, and children in Glencoe. Some escaped but died of exposure in the hills.

Now the Glen is popular for mountaineering, skiing, and hiking. The landscape is barren, with waterfalls, sheep grazing, white water on the rivers, and often a fierce wind blowing. Visitors are often relieved to drive down into civilization in Ballachulish.

Fort William, named for William III, became less important as a stronghold and more involved in trade as an economic center of Lochaber. The **Caledonian Canal** opened in 1822 and Fort William was then the principal port for the shipping trade. Steamship lines were successful and stagecoaches operated between Fort William and Inverness to the north and Glasgow to the south. By 1889 the railway line began service and steamship excursions were inaugurated for tourists.

The **West Highland Museum** originated with the private collection of Victor Hodgson. Exhibits range from artifacts of the Stone Age all the way to the present day.

Fort William is a touring center for the western Highlands. Britain's tallest mountain, Ben Nevis, is very popular with hikers and mountain climbers. Hikers can enjoy walks of varying lengths into Lower Glen Nevis and along the gorge as well all the way up the mountain. With limited time available, we chose to walk for a few hours along a path Prince Charles had taken a few weeks earlier. Our cameras had all they could do to keep up with the scenic beauty we wanted to capture. Water rushed beside a well-maintained trail as we waded through or jumped over streams and waterfalls.

The **Great Glen** proceeds northeast past Loch Ness where visitors can look for the monster. The Loch Ness Monster has been reported many times, and was even observed by Saint Columba around 565 A.D. Legendary or not, Columba received sainthood for this phenomenon. In 1933 more sightings were recorded by local inhabitants of Drumnadrochit. In 1960 the BBC aired a film of *something* crossing the loch. During the 1970s sonar was used in collaboration with underwater cameras. Patrols scoured the loch in 1982. However, the riddle still remains—hoax or a real live plesiosaur gliding through the water—this mystery has brought attention to Loch Ness.

Castle Urquhart, once one of the largest castles in Scotland, stands in ruin on the west shore of the lake. Ruins with the lake in the background provide photographers with opportunity. The castle was given by James IV to John Grant of Freuchie in 1509; his family held it for four centuries.

Inverness may have been the site occupied by the Picts, then a fort during the Dark Ages. Shakespeare placed MacBeth in his fortified castle there; Duncan was murdered in the castle. Castles were destroyed and rebuilt until Mary Queen of Scots was turned away at the door by Alexander Gordon, son of the Earl of Huntly. Cromwell built an even more strongly fortified fort called "The Sconce," which disappeared during the Restoration.

A few miles to the southeast lies **Culloden,** scene of the last important battle on British soil, in 1746. Bonnie Prince Charlie led his 5000 men onto Drumossie Moor against the Duke of Cumberland's 9000. The Culloden Visitor Center has an audio-visual presentation that explains the history of the rebellion in detail. Old Leanach Cottage, which was the only farmhouse to survive the battle, has been restored and furnished as it would have been then. Graves of the clans lie on either side of the road; the Mackintosh Clan has the longest trench of 54 yards. A 20-foot-high Memorial Cairn stands on the battlefield.

SPAIN

> **Currency unit** • Spanish peseta (PTS)
> **Language** • Spanish
> **Time difference from USA** • six hours (Eastern Standard Time)
> **Telephone access codes** • to USA 07; from USA: 34
> **National Tourist Offices** • **USA:** National Tourist Office of Spain, 666
> Fifth Ave., New York, NY 10022, Tel.: (212) 759–8822; **Madrid:** Madrid Tourist Office, Torre de Madrid, Plaza de Espana, tel.: 91/241–
> 2325; **Britain:** 57/58 St. James's St., London Sw1A lLO, tel. (071) 499–
> 0901
> **Airline** • Iberia USA (800) 772–4642; **Britain** (071) 437–5622
> **Embassies** • **American Embassy:** Serrano 75, Madrid, Spain, tel.: 276–
> 3400 or 3600; **British Embassy:** Calle de Fernando el Santo 16, Madrid
> 4

Are there really "castles in Spain?" On our first trip to the Iberian Peninsula, we tested the truth of the old phrase by just looking up. Apart from castles, looking up is a useful habit in Spain. The upward glance may reveal a hillscape spread with white houses and red tile roofs and church spires, or, in closer focus, cathedral gargoyles, flowers hanging from balconies, and people leaning their elbows on the iron grillwork of balconies to watch the world go by below.

Spain is sometimes referred to as a miniature continent because its terrain includes everything from rugged mountains (*sierra* means "sawtoothed"), forests, vast plains, and fertile valleys to sandy beaches and raised coastal headlands. You can exchange one topography for another within a matter of hours, ski and sunbathe all in the same day. The variety of contour provides an infinitely changing landscape full of striking contrasts.

HISTORY......................................

The record of life in Spain dates back 25,000 years; paintings in the Altimira caves near Santander belong to this period. Phoenicians and Greeks arrived to

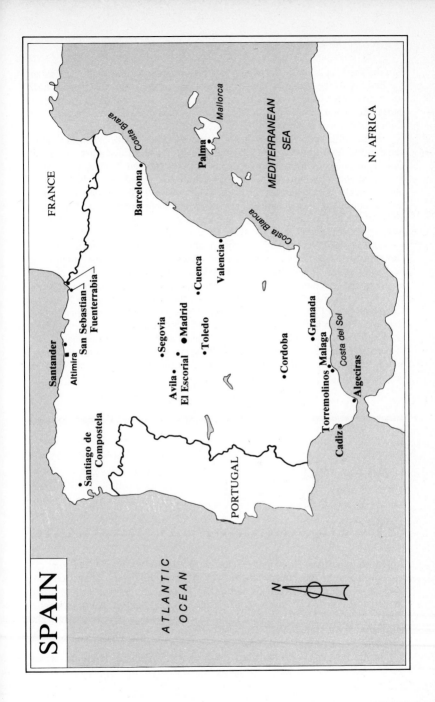

join the Iberians in the 11th century B.C. Their culture blended with the Iberian; the *Lady of Elche* is one of the sculptures that survives from this period. Each successive wave of newcomers from the north, east and south profoundly influenced the character of Spanish life. Celts invaded from central Europe, then Carthaginians and Romans arrived in the second and third centuries B.C.

In the fifth and sixth centuries A.D. the Visigoths ruled. When the Moors came in the eighth century, the Christians fled to the north; not surprisingly, the delicate nuances of Moorish architecture are concentrated in Andalusia with a few more northerly outposts of Moorish culture like Toledo. In 1492 the Catholic monarchs, Ferdinand and Isabella, finally drove the Moors out of Granada just as Columbus was stumbling onto a new continent to the west. The year is a true watershed in Spanish history because it marks two events that led to the peak of Spanish power in the world.

During the 19th century, Spanish unity and power began to disintegrate due to repeated disputes surrounding the Carlist succession to the throne. The beginning of the War of Independence began in 1808 when Spaniards revolted as the queen and her children were trying to escape. Spain became a republic in 1931. In 1936 Franco led a rebellion from the military garrison in Morocco. Civil war from 1936 to 1939 consisted of mass slaughters and other violent reprisals. Franco took over, establishing order by execution. Spain was devastated politically and economically. After Franco died in 1975, King Juan Carlos disbanded Franco's government. In 1978 Spain became a constitutional monarchy. Recently Spain has been concentrating on modernizing and unifying their now peaceful and prosperous country.

MADRID

HISTORY ....

Prehistoric man lived in a small village on the site of Madrid, but the area did not develop until the Phoenicians arrived in about 1000 B.C. They were followed by Greeks, Carthaginians and finally Moors, who built a fortress in the 8th century. Alfonso VI, the King of Castile, invaded the fort in 1083. Spanish monarchs enjoyed Madrid, and by 1477 the Catholic kings were in control. The Monastery of San Jeronimo el Real was built, and Emperor Charles V renovated the Muslim fortress now called the Alcazar.

In 1561 Madrid was ordained the capital of Spain by Philip II. It has

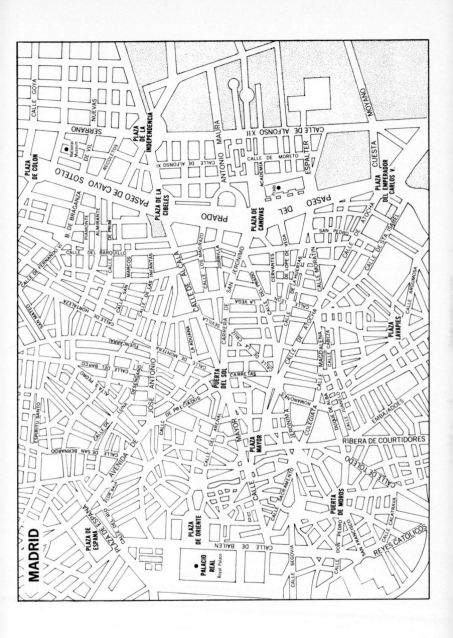

remained the center of governmental authority ever since, apart from interruptions during the Carlist Wars in the 19th century and the Civil War in the 20th.

SIGHTSEEING......................................

Madrid looks the part of a capital city, with broad, tree-lined avenues, many statues, circles built around elaborate fountains, and a generous supply of massive buildings that visually remind one of the role of central governments in European history. Madrid is like Paris in these respects. But there is another, less ponderous side to the city: take time to wander through the old town, La Ciudad Antigua, with its alleys, steps, and narrow streets. The Plaza Mayor was once the center of Old Madrid. This arcaded square has been the setting for religious observances, dramas, bullfights, festivals, and a tournament held in 1623 to honor King Charles I of England. Balconies line one side of the square; royalty and nobility watched events there, above the crowds. Giovanni da Bologna created the equestrian statue of Philip III, which stands in the middle of the square. Look for the Royal House of Bread *(Real Casa de Panaderia)* in 17th century Mandrilenian style. Some of the city archives are kept there.

The **Town Hall** *(Casa de la Villa), Ayuntamiento),* dates from the 17th century. Receptions for visiting dignitaries are held inside and visitors may tour these elegant rooms at specified times. Portraits include those of Elizabeth II at age 8, Maria Christina and her son, Alfonse XIII as a boy, and Alfonse XIII as king. Look for the symbol of Madrid, a bear standing on its hind legs beside a madrilene tree, in the reception room; seven stars stand for the bear constellation, and the crown of Charles V is there too. A Sevres vase with pink flowers dates from 1909. Don't miss the elaborate monstronce from 1573, still used in processions, which glistens in a glass case.

The **Royal Palace** *(Palacio Real),* Plaza de Oriente, begun in 1737, was the residence of the royal family for two centuries. Charles III was the first to live in the Palace and Alfonse XIII the last until he moved to Rome in exile in 1934, where he died. King Juan Carlos does not reside there now, but it is still used for state ceremonies and banquets, so there is a lot to see in the ornately furnished apartments.

The **Throne Room** is resplendent in red velvet and ornate gold mirrors. Silver and crystal chandeliers lead the eye up to the colorful frescoed ceiling. The **Gasparini Room** has unusual floral ceiling decoration in Chinese style, and the French chandelier gleams in gold and crystal. The **Porcelain Room,** ordered by Charles III has green and gold raised decoration on ivory. The **Dining Room** is lit by 1000 lights to enhance the 16th century Flemish tapestries. The Body of St. Felix lies in a tomb with a glass front in the Chapel. Statues of Isabella and Ferdinand stand just outside the chapel door.

The **Royal Armory** *(Real Armeria),* contains one of the most extensive collections of medieval armor and arms anywhere. Don't miss the steel cuirass of the famed pirate Barbarossa. The **Royal Carriage Museum** in the nearby Campo del Moro, houses the wedding carriage of Alfonso XIII and Victoria Eugenia, who was the granddaughter of Queen Victoria. Someone threw a bomb at the carriage during the 1906 wedding procession, causing some damage.

The extraordinary **Museo Lazaro Galdiano,** 122 Calle Serrano, is housed in the home of Jose Lazaro Galdiano. Here are five floors of treasures, including a portrait by Leonardo da Vinci on the ground floor. Other masters include Murillo, Velazquez, Rembrandt, Reynolds, and Goya.

Museo Arqueologico displays a replica of the Altamira caves; because they are often closed this is a chance to see the prehistoric paintings. The renowned ancient sculpture, *La Dama de Elche,* from the south of Spain is there. Artifacts from burial sites such as the 6th-century B.C. alabaster figures from Granada are also on display. Mosaic floors range from an astrological theme to Hercules and also a Medusa. A skeleton from Segovia still wears earrings, necklace, metal decoration on footwear, and some sort of armor. Moorish jewelry from the Alhambra includes silver bracelets in the shape of a snake plus a sword and dagger.

The **Naval Museum** (Museum Navale) houses extensive collections of ship models, charts, portraits, figureheads, uniforms, and more. The **Carta de Juan de la Casa** from 1500 chronicles the first voyage of Columbus; it is the earliest extant map of the Atlantic and America. Although no one really knows what Columbus looked like, this museum displays a number of portraits—you can take your pick. Surprisingly, an original letter to his son has not crumbled. Other sections of the museum chronicle two crucial naval battles important to Spain and all of Europe, Lord Nelson's victory at Trafalgar, and Don John of Austria's defeat of the Turks at Lepanto.

Museo del Ejercito displays armor, arms, trophies, and a sword that once belonged to El Cid. This museum is on the site of a Norman castle built for Philip II and his queen, Mary Tudor. Mary did not live there, and it was eventually turned into the Royal Palace of the Buen Retiro, of which one building stands to house the museum.

Museo Taurino, which details the history of bullfighting, is located next to the Las Ventas Bullring, the largest one in Spain.

We've been saving the most famous museum for last—the **Prado** *(Paseo del Prado),* one of the finest in the entire world. Most of the works hung here were originally in private collections—notably that of the monarchy, from the 16th through the 19th centuries. The museum contains whole sections devoted to major Spanish artists such as El Greco, Velazaquez, and Goya, Flemish paintings collected by the monarchy, and Italian and Dutch works commissioned by Charles V and Philip II.

DAY TRIPS FROM MADRID ··················

El Escorial

El Escorial is a monastery, a palace, and a mausoleum. Philip II, like the pharaohs who built pyramids to memorialize themselves, created this immense building as a residence and as the tomb for his burial. The gray granite looks forbidding and cold from the outside; in fact, it is cold inside as well, at least in winter. Philip's bedroom was located right next to the church so that he could go in whenever he wished; when he was very ill and dying he could watch the mass from his bed.

There are paintings and intricate tapestries throughout the palace. Some of them were designed from Goya's work, as well as from the work of other Spanish artists; others are Flemish tapestries. Brussels tapestries are hung in the throne room.

Valle de los Caidos (The Valley of the Fallen)

The huge cross memorializing the agony of Spain in the thirties is visible from a great distance, and a church has been built into the mountain there. Franco built the monument to commemorate the dead from both sides during the Civil War, but there is still bitter feeling about it among those who were alive during those dreadful times.

Segovia

Segovia reminds us of a ship, with the shape of the Alcazar forming the bow. The Alcazar itself looks like a Disney castle with its many slender spires and turrets. Walk on the ramparts for a view of the narrow, curving streets of the old town. Don't miss the Roman aqueduct, which is 800 meters long and rises 100 feet above the Plaza de Azoguejo at its highest point.

Avila

As we approached Avila we noticed an unusual collection of enormous rocks, with three or four piled on top of each other. Although a natural phenomenon in the hills surrounding the city, the rocks are so strangely flattened that one speculates whether prehistoric man had anything to do with these striking formations.

Avila itself, surrounded on three sides by hills and mountains, is completely walled. The walls, built from 1090 to 1099, are thought to be the best preserved in all of Europe. They average 12 meters in height and three meters in thickness, and their shape is hexagonal. There are 90 towers spaced along the walls, giving them a scalloped effect. Of the nine entrance gates, those of San Vincente and the Alcazar are among the oldest and most interesting.

Avila is noted as the birthplace of Saint Teresa, who worked for reform all her life. She founded 17 convents and gained many converts for the church. As one of the most influential figures in the Counter Reformation, her letters, autobiography, and other mystical writings have been handed down through the centuries.

EXCURSIONS FROM MADRID...............

Toledo

One of the remarkable sights of Toledo is the **cathedral,** especially from an adjoining hilltop. It is lighted several nights a week, depending upon the season. The building is massive, and the 300-foot spire dominates the town, but you cannot see much of the outside of the cathedral from the street because it is surrounded by other buildings.

The **Treasure** is located at the foot of the great tower, in the Tower Chapel. The collection includes the monstrance, a masterpiece of gold and silver work by Enrique de Arfe in the 16th century. It is 1½ meters high, weighs 200 kilos, and has 5000 parts. During the feast of Corpus Christi, in late May or early June, the monstrance is carried through the streets. The town is decorated with tapestries and bunting; flowers and thyme in the decorations perfume the air. You will also see a hat dangling near the main altar. At one time cardinals were buried in a spot of their choosing, with their hats hanging above them.

El Greco, Domenico Teltocopulos, was born in Crete but lived in Toledo for much of his life until his death in 1614. His paintings are full of rich color and violet movement, often with supernatural emphasis. You can visit the house he lived in, which contains a museum of his paintings.

The church of San Tome has an annex in which you will find another of El Greco's masterpieces, *The Burial of the Count of Orgaz.* This painting is based on the life of the Conde de Orgaz, a man who protected the needy and the poor. During his funeral in San Tome, Saint Augustine and Saint Stephen miraculously appeared, lifted up his body, and laid it in the tomb. El Greco took two years to paint this work; each of the faces in the group surrounding the count is a portrait of a well known figure from the 16th century. The person who is fifth from the left end of the group is supposed to be El Greco himself, and the little boy in the bottom left is his son, Jorge Manuel. The signature of the artist and the date of the completed work can be found in a handkerchief in the little boy's pocket.

Near the church of San Tome lived the architect who built the bridge of San Martin. According to legend, Juan, the builder, realized that he had made a serious mistake in construction and that the bridge would collapse when the scaffolding was removed. He knew that his prestige and respect would vanish if that happened. As he became more despondent, his wife planned to solve this problem. One night she left the house, went to the foot of the bridge, and set fire to the framework supporting it. Her husband was able to rebuild the bridge into the solid structure you see today. In gratitude to his wife, he carved her portrait on the main arch of the bridge.

Salamanca

Salamanca was conquered in the third century B.C. by Hannibal. At the end of the siege, Hannibal's troops ransacked the city after forcing all of the inhabitants to leave. The men were not allowed to wear cloaks or to take their swords, but the crafty women hid their husband's swords under their clothing.

In the 8th century the Moors arrived, staying for 300 years. In the 14th and 15th centuries, Salamanca was divided by the wars between two prominent local families. During an argument over a game of *pelota,* the Manzano brothers killed two Monroy brothers. Their mother, Dona Maria, arranged to have the killers decapitated and the Manzano heads were placed on the Monroy tomb. As in any blood feud, such as that between the Capulets and Montagues in Verona, these retributions continued interminably, in this case until 1476.

Salamanca is home of one of the oldest and most illustrious universities in Spain. Take a look at the facade from the Patio de Escuelas. Built at the beginning of the 16th century, it was designed and sculpted by gold and silver smiths. The ornate carving was done on three levels, with heads in scallop shells, impressive medallions, and pinnacles on top. On the lower end of the right-hand pilaster, the frog on one of the three skulls is famous among students, who rub him for good luck on examinations.

There are two cathedrals to visit in Salamanca. The **Old Cathedral,** built in Romanesque style, was constructed in the 12th century. Look at the 53 tablets by Nicolas Florentino on the reredos of the main altar. In the center you will see the image of the Virgen de la Vega in copper, with Limoges enamels around the throne. The cupola, Torre de Gallo, shows Moorish influence.

The **New Cathedral,** begun in 1513, is in Gothic style. There is a legend that the Cristo de las Batallas, now located in the Sagrario Chapel, was carried by El Cid during his campaigns. It is also said that he later gave it to Bishop Don Jeronimo de Perigueux.

There is a particularly interesting house in Salamanca built by a knight of Santiago. As a memento of his homeland, Galicia, he had scallop shells sculpted into the walls; the Casa de las Conchas also has Isabeline windows and wrought-iron grillwork.

Valladolid

Once the capital of Spain, Valladolid was the home of the monarchy in Castile in the 15th century. Ferdinand and Isabella were married there in 1469, joining

Castile and Aragon and thereby setting the stage for centuries of Spanish world power. In 1809 Napoleon also set up his headquarters in Valladolid, leading to the long and difficult Peninsular War.

San Gregorio College now houses the **National Sculpture Museum.** This fine collection includes three rooms containing the work of Alonso Berruguete, considered to be the most outstanding 16th-century Spanish sculptor. Many other artists are represented there as well. In Calle Miguel Iscar you can see the house in which Cervantes lived. It contains furnishings of the period, some of which belonged to him; he spent the last years of his life there.

Burgos

You may have seen the 1951 film, *El Cid,* with Charlton Heston as the legendary knight. Although Rodrigo Dias, ''El Cid,'' was born nine kilometers away in Vivar, Burgos claims this hero, and his body is buried in the cathedral with that of his wife, Ximena.

El Cid, a loyal supporter of Ferdinand the Great, was equally prepared to support his son, Sancho II. However, Sancho was mysteriously killed; there was some suspicion that Alfonso VI, his brother, was not entirely innocent. At that point, El Cid demanded an oath from Alfonso stating that he had not killed his brother. Annoyed at this suspicion, Alfonso banished El Cid from court. Later, following a reconciliation, El Cid supported the king and on his orders conquered Valencia in 1094. Although El Cid died in 1099, Ximena managed to hang onto Valencia for three more years. When defeat came she placed her husband's body in the saddle and rode through the lines to Burgos.

The cathedral in Burgos, begun in 1221, is the third largest in Spain. The **Capilla Del Santo Cristo** contains an image of Christ that is said to have human hair and nails; it is covered with either the hide of a water buffalo or human skin. Look for the Flycatcher Clock *(Papamoscas),* which opens its mouth when the clock chimes the hour, and take time to visit the Cloisters, where you will see large figures sculpted from stone, clay, and wood. Besides Ferdinand and Isabella, the figures include representatives from each of the continents.

SEVILLE

HISTORY......................................

Seville has been enriched by all of the many civilizations it has nurtured during the past 2000 years. After the city was founded by Iberians or Phoenicians, the Romans conquered it in 205 B.C. The Visigoths settled and controlled the city until the Moors arrived in 712. King Fernando III reconquered Seville from the Moors; King Pedro the Cruel continued the monarchy, and the son of Ferdinand and Isabella, Juan, was born there. With the discovery of America in 1492, Seville became prosperous as the mercantile center of the New World. Many explorers set out from Seville, including Amerigo Vespucci and Magellan.

SIGHTSEEING...................................

The massive **Gothic cathedral** in Seville is the third largest in the world. Near the entrance to the cathedral, the coffin of Christopher Columbus is carried by four giant figures who represent Aragon, Castile, Navarre, and Leon. Originally his coffin rested in the cathedral in Havana, but it was sent to Seville after Cuba became independent of Spain. Don't forget to climb the 34 ramps and 17 steps up the **Giralda,** a 322-foot-high tower next to the cathedral. Tote your camera up with you for some fine shots of the city.

Guides hover between the cathedral and **the Jewish Quarter** *(Juderia)*, hoping to lure you into a tour. It is not always a bad idea to snap at this bait if you don't mind getting hooked for an hour and can tolerate the guide's idea of what will interest you, but don't forget to set the price first unless you want a full-scale squabble later.

Pilate's House *(La Casa de Pilatos)*, Calle de Aguilas, was said to be copied from that of the Roman praetor in Jerusalem. It is also called "San Andres Palace" from the family's patron saint. The Carrara marble in the courtyard was brought over from Italy as ballast. Statues include Pallas Athena, Minerva, Ceres and a Muse. Twenty-four busts of Roman emperors from Italy were installed by the first Duke of Alcala. Inside, there are titles with 63 different designs and an Arabian dome with gold leaf and stalagmites.

Cultural tradition in Seville is rich and fascinating. Miguel de Cervantes spent his early years in Seville; he was imprisoned in the **Royal Prison** *(Carcel Real)* in the late 16th century because of arrears during his period as tax collector. (At that time, any official in arrears was flung in jail.) The episode was fortunate for Spanish literature, because Cervantes began to write *Don Quixote* while he was incarcerated.

Music—particularly opera—has always flourished in Seville, just as it has in southern Italy. A number of the world's best-loved operas are set in Seville, featuring such protagonists as the wild and passionate Carmen, Don Juan, archetype of lovers, and Figaro, barber, guitar player, and master schemer, a character type inherited from Greek and Roman comedy.

If you fancy a vision of Carmen lounging by the door of the tobacco factory, you can visit the 18th-century factory, now a building owned by the university. In the 19th century 10,000 female cigarerras were employed there.

If you can be in Seville for Holy Week, by all means do so. The religious significance of the week is taken seriously, with 50,000 people involved in processions that may last for hours; fifty-two brotherhoods carry more than a hundred floats; they wear heavy robes and carry the penetential cross or candles, and some go barefoot. Two weeks later the **Spring Fair** *(Feria)* brings another festive week of song and dance.

The landscape of Seville has been enhanced by two grand expositions. The first, the Ibero-American in 1929, left a huge crescent-shaped building in the Plaza de Espana as well as other buildings in the beautiful Parque de Maria Luisa. The second, in 1992, developed a futuristic complex of pavilions on the island of Cartuja, across the Guadalquivir River from the old city, as well as a river walk and dramatic new bridges.

DAY TRIPS FROM SEVILLE ·················

Huelva

Columbus aficionados will want to visit this area just an hour from Seville. Moguer is the town where Columbus came to give thanks following a storm at sea on March 16, 1493. He vowed that if they returned safely he would make a visit to the Convent of Santa Clara. The cloister has just been renovated and there is an unusual tomb with sculptures of five members of the Portocarrero family lying in a row on its cover looking up at the altar.

Juan Ramon Jiminez, a Nobel Prize-winner in literature in 1956, and his wife Zenobia lived in Moguer in a house that has been turned into a museum. His first famous book, *Platero y yo,* was completed in 1914 and it is on display with many translations. Books with dedications to him include those from Oscar Wilde, Jean Cocteau, and Auguste Rodin. His table and typewriter are there, also Xenobia's scrapbook with postcards, letters, a bit of lace and embroidery floss, a telegram announcing the Nobel prize, and their marriage certificate from 1958.

Farther down the river, Palos de la Frontera is rich in Columbus associations. Here Columbus filled his ships with water from the ''fontanilla,'' had his ships blessed in St. George's Church and walked down the hill to the harbor to begin the voyage. The Mudejar-style church has three round stained-glass windows honoring the *Nina, Pinta,* and *Santa Maria.* A new museum has opened in the house of Martin Alonzo Pinzon, with collections of caravel models, paintings, sculpture, and Columbus stamps. Walk up the street to see the statue of Martin Pinzon in the plaza.

During the years he sought support for his voyages, Columbus spent many months living with the monks in the nearby Franciscan monastery in La Rabida, now beautifully restored. Inside visitors see frescoes of the Columbus episodes, including a serious scene where Columbus looks solemnly out to sea. Models of his ships, maps of his voyages, portraits of the Catholic kings, and period furniture are on display. A series of wooden and metal boxes are filled with the earth of the American countries; each country's flag is also displayed.

Across the river at the edge of Huelva stands an immense statue of Columbus, who is gazing out to sea with his hood over part of his face. The 1929 monument was placed there by Gertrude Whitney with support from the Columbus Memorial Fund.

Cordoba

Cordoba is one of the oldest of Spanish cities, dating back to 152 B.C. when it was a Roman municipality. From the 8th to the 11th century, Cordoba was the capital of Moslem Spain. Ferdinand the Holy conquered the city in 1236; 200 years later Isabella had two interviews with Columbus there and decided during the second to support his voyage of discovery.

The courtyard of the mosque is filled with orange trees. Head for the tower in the outer wall for a view of the city; the steps have risers that are about 12 inches high, so wear comfortable shoes. When you enter the mosque your eyes will need time to adjust to the darkness inside. This amazing building is composed of red and white supporting columns, pillaged from a variety of buildings as far away as France and Carthage. There were originally 1096 pillars; after the Cathedral was built inside the mosque, only 860 were left. That is a story in itself—nowhere else has a cathedral been built inside a mosque. Charles V sadly observed that Christian churchmen had built what could have been built anywhere else, but had destroyed something that was unique in the world.

Part of the charm of Cordoba can be discovered by wandering in the narrow streets around the mosque. Be sure to peek into any open courtyard gates; the interior patios have been decorated with flowering plants, ceramic tiles, and fountains. On our way through this section we came upon an organ grinder merrily playing as his sad-eyed donkey stood by patiently. And visit the Alcazar de los Reyes Christianos, built by Alfonso XI in the 14th century. It is located around the corner from the entrance to the mosque, and contains a concert hall with Roman mosaics embedded in the walls. A large Roman marble sarcophagus sits in the hall, with a relief of an open door, perhaps symbolic of life everlasting.

Cordoba was the birthplace of a number of famous citizens. Lucius Annaeus Seneca, who lived from 4 B.C. to 65 A.D. is considered by some scholars to have been the most influential of all Spaniards. He was not only a philosopher, but also a poet, playwright, and orator; his political stature led him to serve as consul of Rome. Seneca taught Nero as a child and later became his counselor, but ironically, was commanded to commit suicide by the same Nero. Many Spaniards, as well as people around the world, live by the principles of Seneca's philosophy of Stoicism.

If you can arrange to be in Cordoba in late May you can enjoy the fair of Our Lady of Salvation. Bullfights, plays, flamenco dancing and singing, competitions, and exhibitions take place, the most notable of the latter being the parade of horses and riders. Cervantes wrote that Cordoba was "the mother city of the best horses in the world." Men ride wearing dark, tightly fitting suits, boots, short jackets trimmed with braid, ruffled shirts, sashes, and the typical flat Cordoban hat. Women ride sidesaddle, wearing brightly colored dresses with flounced skirts and silk shawls gracefully wrapped around them.

Granada

Like most visitors, you are likely to find yourself caught in the almost inescapable spell of Granada. The poet Francisco de Icaza wrote of a blind beggar to capture this feeling: "Give him alms, woman, for there is nothing in life, nothing, so sad as to be blind in Granada." The visual beauty of the **Moorish Palace** in the Alhambra is magnificent in itself. You may find it overwhelming when your ears pick up the sounds of fountains and waterfalls interspersed with the sound of bells. And, as you walk through Alhambra's many gardens, you will become aware of the aromatic scents of jasmine, rose, myrtle, eucalyptus, and orange. Granada is a city for walking, listening, looking, and inhaling sweet and spicy scents.

We spent several hours taking photographs inside the Moorish palaces. The rooms contain exquisite, fragile-looking walls, arches, ceilings and decoration. Avid photographers look for series of arches, ornate window-frames to shoot through, and one ceiling after another to capture. On subsequent visits we discovered new perspectives such as the reflection of the opposite wall in a pool of water in the Hall of the Abencerrajes.

Another section of the Alhambra, the **Generalife,** was a retreat for the Moorish kings, a palace built overlooking the city. Walls and terraces were constructed in definite patterns, with flat, gray stones standing on edge to form fluting, and round, white stones placed in the middle. Gardens were developed on several levels; they are lush with flowers, shrubs, and hedges of cypress trimmed in various shapes. The sound of fountains splashing and water flowing into pools is everywhere. Water cascades down three flights of steps along the handrails, sending up spray where it bounces forcefully. And there are views of the city from every angle as you walk through the apartments in the Generalife.

BARCELONA

HISTORY.....................................

Barcelona was founded by Hamilcar Barca of Carthage in the 3rd century, and named after Barca, who was Hannibal's father. It became a colony under the Romans, who ruled for six centuries, followed by Visigoths, the Moors, and finally the Franks in 800. During the Middle Ages the city prospered as a center for commerce and as a seaport. As the capital of Catalonia, Barcelona was the most powerful port on the Mediterranean and maintained this status until the discovery of America. The city is also the center of a strong Catalan tradition, including their own Catalan tongue, which was outlawed for many years after Barcelona revolted against the Spanish government.

SIGHTSEEING..............................

The **Gothic Quarter** *(Barrio Gotico)* contains many buildings from the 13th to 15th century, constructed on a site dating back to Roman times. Two Roman towers, which were once part of the city walls, still stand. Walk into the doorway and partway up the stairs of the Centro Excursionista de Cataluna to see the Corinthian columns dating from the 2nd-century temple dedicated to Augustus.

The remains of the Roman city are now on display in the lowest floor of the **City Museum** *(Museu d'Historia de la Ciutat),* Plaza del Rei. Walls, pools, hot baths, the sewage system, a mosaic floor depicting the "Three Graces," and storerooms containing large amphoras are indicated as visitors push marked red buttons to light them. Upstairs the city museum displays copper pots, a collection of tiles, paintings, wood blocks and prints, coins, and a fine collection of maps.

The **Cathedral** was begun in the 13th century; its spire and west face are reconstructions using the plans developed in 1408 by a mason from Rouen. It was dedicated to Saint Eulalia, a young girl who was martyred at age 13 for professing Christianity; her body lies in the crypt in an alabaster sarcophagus. The carved and painted chancel stalls date from the 14th century, handsomely decorated with the gilded coats-of-arms of the Knights of the Order of the Golden Fleece. The King of Spain is President of the Order and offers a necklace of the Golden Fleece to distinguished guests, who have included Queen Elizabeth II in 1989.

Christopher Columbus brought five Native Americans to the cathedral in 1493 for baptism. Walk in the attractive cloister to see the fountain of St. George. On Corpus Christi Day, an eggshell is placed on the fountain to "dance" on the water. A gaggle of geese live there to guard the treasures.

The **Chapel of the Most Holy Sacrament** contains the figure of Christ of Lepanto, once the figurehead of John of Austria's flagship during the battle of Lepanto.

Placa del Rei is a medieval square usually inhabited by students sitting on the stairway leading up to the Palace of the Kings. Inside, visitors can see the **Hall of the Throne,** where Columbus met the Catholic Kings. The room is unusual in that it is very large and supported only by a low arched ceiling with no pillars in the center.

Pablo Picasso came to Barcelona when he was 14 years old. His "blue period," from 1901 to 1904, coincided with some of his years in Barcelona. The **Picasso Museum,** 15 Calle de Moncada, includes works from every phase of his life but concentrates on his pre-surrealist period. In 1968 Picasso donated 44 paintings on the theme of Las Mininas. The museum, housed in two 15th-century palaces, contains one of the world's most complete collections of Picasso's work.

La Rambla is a wide promenade on one boundary of the Gothic Quarter lined with flower stalls, cafes, restaurants, stores, and bird sellers. Joan Miro designed a kaleidoscope of paving stones in the Placa de la Boqueria, and Art Nouveau street lamps enliven the scene.

The **Maritime Museum** (*Museu Maratim*) is located in the old Royal Dockyards in the 13th-century structure, the *Atarazanas Reales*. A replica of the royal galley of Admiral Don John of Austria is resplendent in red and gold in the center of the museum; it was his flagship during the Battle of Lepanto. Visitors can walk up steps to peer into the vessel and see its elaborate decorative paintings and sculpture more closely. A series of enlarged photos traces maritime evolution from ancient triremes in stone at Lindos, mosaics from Ostia, and funeraria dating from 1570 B.C. Models include the **Kyrenia** from the 4th century B.C. as well as Columbus' caravels. The museum also displays the oldest chart found in Europe, made in 1439 by Gabriel de Valseca. You can't miss the gigantic monument in Placa Portal de la Pau topped by Christopher Columbus. It was erected for the Universal Exhibition of 1888.

Take time to enjoy **Montjuich,** the hill just south of the Gothic Quarter, where you will find **Pueblo Espanol,** a Spanish village containing buildings selected to portray the architecture and daily life in 19th-century Spain. Regional artisans work on their crafts there. Visiting this village before touring Spain can be useful, because typical buildings from every region are laid out before you.

The **Joan Miro Museum,** also on Montjuich, fills a contemporary white building designed by Josep Lluis Sert to provide daylight in abundance. The collection includes Miro's tapestries, a group of eight umbrellas on a woven rope background, sculpture, and drawings. As a foundation supporting experimental concepts and materials, it displays works by other artists in acrylic plexiglass, papier mache, screening, cut paper and wood.

Montjuic is also the site of the Olympic complex for the 1992 summer games. New in 1992, the Olympic Ring includes an enlarged Olympic Stadium, which increased the capacity from 35,000 to 70,000. All types of sports events and open-air pop concerts are held there every week.

The **Sports Palace,** the largest geodesic dome in the world, resembles a Japanese temple. Inside, activities range from ice skating and concerts to wind surfing and ball sports. Nearby the indoor Olympic Pool provides more space for training and recreation, and the Sports University offers varied courts and gymnastic facilities for training future teachers.

Barcelona expanded beyond the old walls during the 19th century, leaving a heritage of wide, tree-lined boulevards reminiscent of the right bank in Paris. The newer sections of the city have some exciting modern architecture, including the structures of Antonio Gaudi, a Catalan native who lived and worked in the city from 1852 to 1926. His **Templo de la Sagrada Familia,** a cathedral, Calle Mallorca and Calle Provenza, was started in 1882 by public gifts but was never completed because he did not leave completed plans before his untimely death. (He was killed by a trolley as he was crossing the street.) The finished part includes eight spires rising to over 300 feet; four more were to have been built so the spires could stand as symbols of the twelve apostles. His style is marked by curves, asymmetrical lines, representation of nature, fantasy, and a touch of surrealism.

Gaudi became so obsessed with the Sagrada that he moved into a room in the yard. Photographs in the **Cathedral Museum** show a small room with his bed piled with pillows as if he slept almost sitting up—perhaps to relieve his rheumatism. Walk inside the uncompleted nave to see a beehive of construction and one lovely stained-glass window in blue, turqoise, and green. Take an elevator partway up the spires, and then walk out onto a bridge between two towers for the view. The museum underneath displays his models for sculpture (taken from neighbors), models of the Sagrada as a whole, photos of other Gaudi buildings, of his furniture, of his lamps, and of his funeral procession.

On one of the high hills overlooking the city, Gaudi designed **Parc Guell** for his patron Eusebio Guell, who tried to develop a fashionable residential area of 60 homes. Because people thought the site too far out, only two plots were sold, one to a lawyer and one to Gaudi. Gaudi's house is now a museum containing some of his furniture and personal belongings. The main square of this extraordinary park is decorated with an undulating wall of colored tile, constructed from old plates and discarded ceramics. **The Hall of One Hundred Columns** provides enough angles for any photographer to enjoy, and the carriage and walking ramps are supported by angled columns that distort one's sense of vertical and horizontal.

DAY TRIPS FROM BARCELONA...................................

Monserrat

One of Spain's most impressive natural sites and shrines is Monserrat. The mountain itself is part of a sawtoothed range that you see from miles away along the motorway (*autopista*). There is a monastery and a basilica up there amid enormous spires of jagged rock. The atmosphere on top is almost more than eye or mind can comprehend—the gigantic masses of rock, some shaped like fingers stretching upward, some appearing to be overbalanced and hovering, tower above the solid, somewhat ponderous basilica itself. This is truly a wild and beautiful place for a shrine.

In such a place one would expect many legends, such as the one that says St. Peter placed a carving of the Virgin in an inaccessible cave. According to the legend, a strange light hovered over the cave and drew shepherds to it. The bishop was summoned to remove the Black Virgin, and as his procession moved along, a mysterious force caused it to stop on the site of the present monastery. Although that monastery was destroyed by the French in 1811, the Black Virgin survived.

When you arrive at the top, walk through the basilica after entering from the courtyard, where there are fine angles for viewing the facade. You will pass a number of chapels before you climb the stairs to see the Black Virgin, placed on a throne high above the altar. She is in a niche domed by beautiful Venetian mosaic work. Nine silver lamps stand for Monserrat and the eight Catalonian dioceses. Many pilgrims have made their way to this spot, and their pilgrimages are reflected in gifts like the two alabaster candlesticks. Ancient paintings do not show the Madonna as black originally; some art historians believe that she has gradually become black over the centuries. She is enclosed in glass and holds a wooden ball in her hand for pilgrims to kiss. Her child is on her lap. There are also stained-glass windows, murals, paintings, and sculpture to admire inside the basilica.

Outside, the mountain is framed by many arches, all with different perspectives. Don't forget your camera on this trip. There are a number of hikes to even higher caves and hermitages for the active and curious visitor, each with its own magnificent set of views; the more sedentary can reach some of these by aerial tramway. You may feel as Goethe did: "nowhere but in his own Monserrat will a man find happiness and peace."

SWEDEN

Currency unit • Swedish krona (SKR)
Language • Swedish
Time difference from USA • six hours later (Eastern Standard Time)
Telephone access codes • to USA 009 (or 020) 795–611 for USADirect); from USA: 46
National Tourist Offices • **USA:** Swedish Tourist Board, 655 Third Ave., New York, NY 10017, tel.: (212) 949–2333; **Sweden:** Sveriges Turistrad, Box 7473, S-103 92 Stockholm, Sweden, tel.: (08) 789–20–00; **Britain:** 29–31 Oxford St., London WIX 1RE, tel.: (071) 437–5816
Airlines • SAS USA (800) 221–2350; **Britain:** (071) 734–4020
Embassies • **American Embassy,** Strandvagen 101, S-115 27 Stockholm, Sweden, tel.: (08) 7835300; **British Embassy,** Skarpogatan 6–8, S11527 Stockholm, tel.: (08) 6670140

Have you ever walked into a room in a foreign country for the first time and found photographs of yourself, your family and your past life spread out on a table? In such circumstances shock and emotion well to the surface in a flash, but the residue is a pleasure of recognition. Both my husband and I are half Swedish, and we met his cousins during an earlier trip. Then, in 1984, we asked them to telephone and translate for us so we could meet my side of the family, leading to the moment of recognition. Since then we have visited both sets of relatives again, and some of them have traveled to our home in the U.S. It is wonderful to share our common past and to realize how much we are alike. Thus we recommend digging up old records and following through for a family reunion if you have any relatives in Europe.

HISTORY . . . .

A number of people settled in Sweden during ancient times—the Danes, Finns, Svears, and Goths. Rune stones remain as a record of the past in Sweden. In 830 the first Christian church was founded by Ansgar, a Frankish monk. During the 9th through 12th centuries, Scandinavian Vikings actively sought to win trade routes by invasion. They had become skilled at shipbuilding, navigating, and sailing on long voyages. Vikings set off to explore and conquer Greenland, England, Ireland, Iceland, the Faroes, Normandy, Russia, the Mediterranean, and Asia.

In 1397 the Nordic Union was formed under Danish leadership to fight the Hanseatic League. A Swedish rebellion under Gustav Vasa was victorious in 1521; he was crowned in 1523. Gustav Vasa built up the Swedish economy by confiscating Catholic Church property. His grandson, Gustavus Adolphus, became king in 1611. By 1648, the end of the Thirty Years' War, Sweden had received a large portion of northern Germany from the Treaty of Westphalia. The end of the Swedish empire came in 1721 when Denmark, Saxony-Poland, and Russia united in the Great Nordic War to defeat Sweden.

During the 1700s a strong constitutional government with a parliament strengthened Sweden. By 1818 neutrality had become the mainstay of Swedish foreign policy. She remained neutral during World Wars I and II.

STOCKHOLM

HISTORY..

Stockholm was founded during the 13th century by a powerful ruler, Birger Jarl, who built a fortress on the island of Strommen in 1252. The main tower was put up on a 500-yard-long heart-shaped island. He used gigantic stones, which kept invaders out; these stones still support the present royal castle, which was built on the site in the early 1700s. Pieces of walls and fortresses are still standing within some of the houses in the Old Town. And sometimes real treasures are still found where the monks hid ecclesiastical riches after the king ordered Catholic property appropriated in the 1500s.

In 1520 a terrible massacre took place in the Royal Palace. Kristian the Tyrant of Denmark invaded Stockholm and was finally given the right to rule both Sweden and Denmark. During his coronation festivities, all of Sweden's officials attended a dance in the Palace. Without warning, the King's men entered and beheaded 90 persons, including bishops, councillors, noblemen, mayors, aldermen and any other citizen who was on the scene. The heads of the victims were piled pyramid-style in the center of the square.

In 1697 the castle, called Three Crowns after the emblems on the Swedish coat-of-arms, was destroyed by fire. A new castle, the Stockholm Castle, was

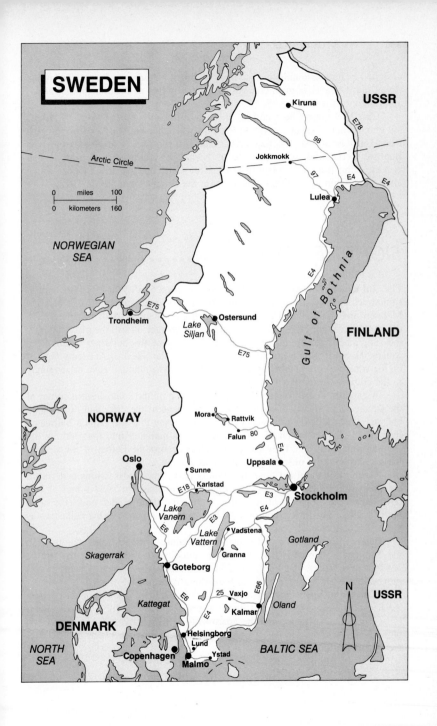

designed in Italian-Renaissance style by architect Nikodemus Tessin. Today the Royal family have rooms there, but they actually live at Drottningholm Palace, amid nature instead of a city.

Carl XVI Gustaf became king in 1973 at the age of 27. Gustav VI Adolf, his grandfather, died at the age of 90; his own father had died in a plane crash when Carl Gustaf was less than a year old. The King's line descends from Jean Baptiste Bernadotte, who was one of Napoleon's marshalls. Bernadotte had become King Karl XIV Johan in 1818. King Carl Gustaf married Queen Silvia after a courtship of four years; they met at the Winter Olympics in 1972.

SIGHTSEEING......................

The **Old Town** (*Gamla Stan*) is the place to begin a tour of the city. Stockholm, sometimes called the "Venice of the North," is built on 14 islands in Lake Malaren and the Baltic. Gamla Stan is perched on three small islands, which are connected by bridges. The main square, Stortorget, is still the place to enjoy the sun, meet friends, and enjoy the architecture of the buildings framing the square. Nobel Prizes in literature are awarded in the Swedish Academy located on the square. Alfred Nobel made his fortune in dynamite and gave prize money to the country during the 19th century.

A cannonball still remains in a yellow house on the southwestern corner of the square. The Danish King Kristian II laid siege to the city, and this cannon ball may be a leftover reminder of him. Others say that the cannon ball came from 1743 when a bunch of 4500 livid farmers marched into town during the "Great Dala Dance." They came to protest against the defeat of Sweden by Russia and hold the officials in charge accountable.

During this unsettled time, one family buried their possessions underneath the floor of their house at 5 Lilla Nygatan. Renovators in 1937 found 18,000 silver coins and 85 pieces of decorative and dining silver hidden under the stone floor. Visitors can look down into the hole at a photo showing the collection as it laid for hundreds of years.

Many visitors head first for the **Royal Palace of Stockholm,** dating from the 12th-century fortress into the elegant building of today. After the fire of 1697, a new palace was built; in 1754 King Adolf Fredrik and Queen Lovisa moved into what is now called the Bernadotte Apartments.

The **State Apartments** include Karl XI's Gallery, the White Sea where the King entertains, the Cabinet Room where each new Swedish administration is sworn in by the King, and the apartments of King Oskar II and Queen Sophie. Today visitors see the apartments as they were when Oskar and Sophie, the last inhabitants, lived there.

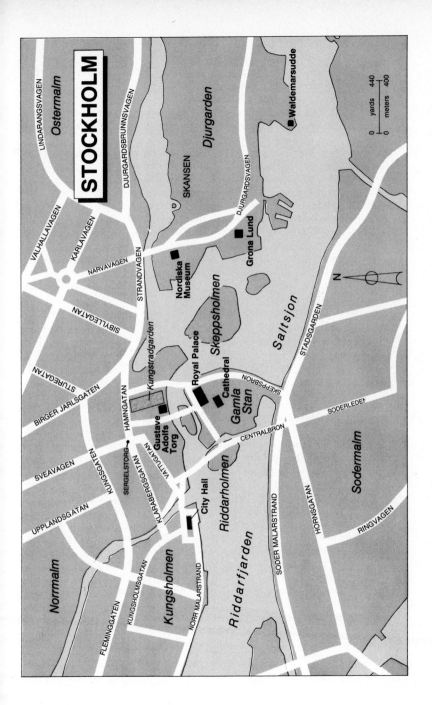

Oskar II's writing room is just as he left it upon his death in 1907. We were touched by the family photographs and memorabilia. Don't miss the portraits of the present royal family in the Outer Dining Room.

The Royal Palace Guard marches every day in the garden between the two wings of the palace. A gray drum horse leads the procession of mounted guard on the days when the Dragoon Lifeguards march.

The **Crown Jewels** are housed in the **Royal Treasury** (Skattkammaren), in the cellar. Gustav Vasa's swords, Erik XIV's coronation regalia from 1561, crowns, scepters, and orbs are on display. Maria Eleonora's crown from 1620 is covered with gold over rose fabric. Lovisa Ulrika's funeral crown from 1782 is somber in gold on black; her regal crown is dated 1751. Erik XIV's coronation robe with mantle and cloak is still intact from 1561. Don't miss Charles XI's large chest-high silver baptismal font, which was created by Cousinet. Three silver figures hold the bowl on their heads.

The **Armory** *(Livrustkammaren)* houses a collection of armor, weapons, and uniforms. Gustav III's suit dating from the night he was murdered is on display. The assassin, Jakob Anckarstrom, was armed with two guns, two knives, and daggers—all on display.

Gustavus II Adolphus's clothing worn in Poland is on display. He was shot in the elbow and neck on Nov. 6, 1632. The clothing in another case shows a bullethole in the chest. Because it took so long to return his body, it is said that his wife carried his heart in a bloody handkerchief. Karl XII was shot in Norway in 1718. There is a bullethole in his hat, and his coat is still stained with clay.

The **Stockholm Cathedral** *(Storkyrkan)*, dates from 1250. Swedish kings were crowned there until Gustav V discontinued the practice in 1907. Bernt Notke created a carved wooden statue of St. George and the Dragon, which was given to the church in 1489. It symbolizes the rescue Stockholm from Denmark with the Princess as of Stockholm and the dragon as Denmark.

The **House of the Nobility** *(Riddarhuset)*, Riddarhustorget, was built in the Dutch-Classic style in the mid-17th century. Crests of Swedish nobility are displayed. Today the building is used as an assembly hall.

Riddarholm Church has been the burial spot for Swedish kings for many centuries. The oldest kings to be entombed in the Church were Magnus Ladulas, who has lain there since 1290, and Karl Knutsson Bonde a couple of hundred years less in 1470. They lie side by side in front of the high altar. The Bernadotte chapel contains Karl XIV Johan, 1844, in a red porphry tomb and Queen Desirce, 1860, in a sarcophagus of green Swedish Kolmarden marble.

Coats of arms from the Knights of the Seraphim Order hang on the walls in between chapels. When a knight dies the Riddarholm bells, called the Seraphim chimes ring.

On the left, the **Carolean Chapel** contains King Karl XII's black marble sarcophagus. Don't miss the skull and crossbones on the tomb of Lennart Torstenson from 1651. King Gustavus Adolphus, of Thirty Years' War fame, and

Gustav V, who died in 1950, are interred there. Outside, the black, delicate Riggarholm Church tower looks almost like a silhouette.

Workmen digging a garage for the Parliament in the late 1970s struck ruins from the town wall of 1530. Walk down the steps from Norrbro Bridge to the **Museum of Medieval Stockholm** (*Medeltids Museum*), Stromparterren, where you'll walk through a tunnel into an underground sample of old Stockholm. The spiritual life is expressed, as visitors walk under arches with mirrored walls on each side, giving the feel of a cloister. Gregorian chants play in that area. Next, look through a slit in the round tower to glimpse the light of a fire flashing over buildings. The wall from 1530 is straight ahead with a 15th-century oak, clinker-built sailing vessel in front.

A display of 14th-century skulls and bones, with X-ray photos to show injuries, shows how the lack of Vitamin D contributes to soft and deformed bones. Cobbled streets abut houses of the 1470s, complete with workshops, including a model of a shoemaker at work. The harbor scene comes alive with the sound of seagulls and waves. More models of masons, bricklayers, carpenters, and woodsmen round out the picture.

The **City Museum** (*Stadsmuseet*), on Sodermalm near the Slussen, dates from the former city hall of the 17th century. Artifacts reach back to the founding of the city over seven hundred years ago.

City Hall (*Stadshuset*), Kungsholmen, is a stunning modern building containing lovely interior gold mosaic walls. Nineteen-million gold pieces were set into the building. The Golden Room, the Council Chamber, the Prince's Gallery, and the Blue Hall are open to visitors. The annual Nobel Dinner is held in Stadshuset; a restaurant is housed in the building for special dinners. There is an elevator built into the tower for a panoramic view. The carillon plays a Swedish medieval war song twice a day.

The **Museum of Mediterranean and Near Eastern Antiquities** (*Medelhavsmuseet*), on Fredsgatan 2, is the place to see Greek, Roman, and Egyptian artifacts. The Swedish Cyprus Expedition has been excavating in Cyprus since the turn of the century—the largest collection of artifacts is there. Walk into a darkened room with spotlights, and you'll see an amazing group of 6th-century B.C. terracotta sculptures. They range in size from almost six feet to a few inches. These stylized images look like gnomes with pointed hats. About 2000 of them are grouped around the low altar.

The **National Museum**, on Blasieholmen, is another waterside museum. It began in 1529 with King Gustav Vasa's collection of 13 works, mostly German and Dutch art. At the end of the Thirty Years' War, Rudolf II's collection from the Kleinseite in Prague was taken to Stockholm. The 1697 fire in the Royal Palace of Three Crowns destroyed many works. During the 1740s, Carl Gustaf Tessin, the Swedish ambassador in Paris, bought French art; Dutch and Italian art followed. Carl Larsson created murals in the museum.

Deer Park, *Djurgarden,* is the place to spend a day doing many things. This large island lies east of the Old Town and can be reached either by ferry or bridge. The park contains dirt paths through the woods, gardens, a village of restored houses, the Nordic Museum, Waldemarsudde, Thiel Gallery, Liljevalch Art Hall, Grona Lund, Kaknas Tower, and the *Wasa*. One hardly knows where to begin.

Personally, we can hardly wait to revisit the *Wasa*, which we have seen four times since she was raised. In 1625 King Gustavus II Adolphus, grandson of Gustavus I Vasa who founded the Vasa dynasty, commissioned a Dutch shipwright named Henrik Hybertsson to build him this warship. She was to be 190 feet long and 36 feet wide. Of her three masts the mainmast measured 150 feet above the keel. She was elegant with tall masts, a sculptured stern and lion figurehead.

As the *Wasa* glided out into the harbor on her maiden trip in 1628, several of the wives of crewmembers were on board for the short voyage. No one knows how many persons were on board but it has been thought around 250. Her sails were unfurled and raised just as the wind came up. She fired the national Swedish salute, called "Svensk losen," and sailed 1500 yards when a sudden gust of wind caught her and she heeled over. (Experts feel that theory is incorrect. There is evidence that her instability due to the topheaviness of another deck, heavy guns, masts, and rigging was known as she was launched. Eyewitnesses do not mention a strong wind, and the assumption now is that the southwest wind was eight knots. It may be that as the lee sheets were let off, the wind was not strong enough to pull the sheets through the new blocks.) Water rushed in the open gun-ports, people fell into the water, and she lay on her side, sinking rapidly.

In 1961 she was raised from the depths by the use of lifting cables and two pontoons. She was placed in her drydock and conservation procedures were begun. Sprinklers sprayed water over her constantly, then polyglycol was used and humidity was maintained in her pontoon house. As the years went by, less spraying was needed and finally her sculptured pieces were regilded and placed in their original positions.

A new building with a copper roof provides room for representation of her tall masts and her long bowsprit. Visitors can walk up seven levels for views of her. She was moved into the Wasa Museum in 1989, and the inauguration took place in 1990 with King Carl XVI Gustaf in attendance.

Of course all of the artifacts that were brought up have also been preserved and placed in the Wasa Museum. We were touched to see the contents of a sea chest including a hat, mittens, shoes, wooden spoon, 66 copper coins, a box with the owners' mark, thread, sewing ring, wax, and a bone comb. The skeleton of a 35-year-old man was found pinned under a gun carriage on the lower gun deck, still with coins in his pocket.

Children were hard at work on computers in a center entitled "Sail the *Wasa*." They worked with a mouse to change the wind velocity, sail area, ballast, armament and hull shape. A printer ground out sheets saying "The King is pleased. You may keep your job" or "You're fired!"

Two other vessels are moored near the *Wasa*. A 1915 icebreaker, *Sankt*

Erik, and a 1903 lightship, *Finngrundet,* are open to view. Visitors can peek into the galley and cabins to imagine what life was like for seamen in the early 20th century.

Skansen, on Djurgarden, is an open-air museum containing 150 houses and other buildings that date from the last century. The museum opened in 1891 with craftsmen working on their trades, and guides dressed in period costumes. Concerts and folk dancing are featured in summer. A zoo houses Nordic animals including wolves, lynx, wolverine, bears, elk, otters, and seals. **Moonlight Hall** contains nocturnal animals who are awake so that visitors can see them.

The Nordic Museum contains folk art, peasant dress, and displays of Swedish life since the 16th century. There is a collection of bridal gowns, including delicate gold coronets worn by brides. Artur Hazelius, who founded Skansen in 1891, left much of his collection to the Nordic Museum. Four floors of exhibits tell the story of Swedish life from the Middle Ages.

The Biological Museum was founded by Gustaf Kolthoff in 1893. The building itself reminds one of a Norwegian wooden stave church with lots of carving on top of brown wood. It contains two 360° dioramas featuring wildlife standing in front of painted backdrops.

Waldemarsudde House, on Djurgarden, was the home of a well-known Swedish painter, Prince Eugen, who was King Gustav V's brother. The mansion contains many of his own paintings as well as his private collection of Swedish art. The setting is dramatic, on the end of a wooded promontory with the sea all around.

Rosendal Palace (*Rosendals Slott*), Djurgarden, is a French chateau built by King Karl Johan, a formal marshal of France. Completed in 1827, the estate is set in the middle of the woods. Its 24 rooms are open to visitors.

Grona Lund is an amusement park with the usual rides as well as a harlequin theater. Rock concerts are sometimes given at night.

Kaknas Tower, Kahnastornet, is a 508-foot-high television tower with observation levels and a restaurant on top. A glassed-in observation area contains panoramic photographs, which are labeled to help visitors orient themselves.

As in many Venice-like cities, a **city boat trip** can provide orientation and relaxation from hours of walking. On our recent trip we chose one called "Under the Bridges of Stockholm." We cruised from Norrstrom south along Gamla Stan, through the lock, past Riddarholmen, the Stadshuset on Kungsholmen, under Vesterbron leading from Marieberg to Langholmen, past the rocky shore of Fredhall, around Sodermalm, and back to the dock.

DAY TRIPS FROM
STOCKHOLM NEAR THE CITY.............

Millesgarden

Carl Milles' home is on the island of Lidingo just outside of Stockholm. His statues stand inside as well as out in the terraced garden amid fountains next to the harbor. Some of our favorites include *The Wings, The Little Naiad, God's Hand, Pegasus,* and *Poseidon.* His private collection of Greek and Roman sculpture and paintings is also in his home. Milles was still working at age 80 when he died at Millesgarden.

Drottningholm Castle

Drottningholm Castle, sometimes called the "Versailles of the North," is located on a small island in Lake Malaren. Nicodemus Tessin created the 17th-century palace and his son, Tessin the Younger, designed the gardens. Today the palace is the residence of the royal family. Some of the elegantly decorated rooms are open to the public. The **China Palace,** also on the grounds, is the place where King Gustav III and his court could retreat from the world.

Drottningholm Court Theater was built in 1765 for King Gustavus III; it has now been fully restored and is open for productions. Costumes are replicas of 18th-century originals. The stage machinery was created by an Italian shipbuilding engineer, Donato Stopani. Gustav commissioned a French painter, Jean-Louis Desprez, to paint a number of stage sets; the originals have survived and are being preserved. Replicas are in use in the theater today. This collection is the only major group of 18th-century sets still preserved in Europe.

Gustav was murdered during a masquerade ball in the opera house in 1792. Giuseppe Verdi used this incident in one of his operas, *Un Ballo in Maschera.*

THE STOCKHOLM ARCHIPELAGO

One of the treats of Stockholm is to take a boat trip out into the islands. Ferries and pleasure boats ply the waters between stops among the inner islands as well as among the outer islands. Here's a way to get the cobwebs of gravel out of one's head. We have found that it pays to bring lots of film to capture the attractive red cottages, green foliage, gray rocks called skerries and deep blue water.

Vaxholm

Vaxholm is sometimes called the "Pearl of the Archipelago" and it is only an hour away by boat from Stockholm. Houses decorated with gingerbread line the streets. A Folk Art Museum explains the life of local fishermen in days past. Vaxholm fortress stands guard over the entrance into Stockholm harbor. In 1612 it halted a Danish attack and in 1719 one from Russia. The museum inside displays uniforms, weapons, and military regalia.

Sandhamn

Sandhamn is a popular yachting center during the summer. The Royal Swedish Yacht Club is based in Sandhamn and international regattas are held during the summer.

DAY TRIPS FROM STOCKHOLM ....

SOUTHWEST OF STOCKHOLM
Gripsholm Castle

Gripsholm Castle, dating from 1537, is located on an island near the town of Mariefred at the southern end of Lake Malaren. The **Swedish National Portrait Gallery** is located there, with kings, queens, and noblemen represented. Up in the top floor, the Mirror Theater waits for a performance with its five rows of benches and a trompe l'oeil-coffered ceiling. Mirrors make the room seem larger and reflect action all over the stage. Gustav III built this theater and also acted upon its stage. Today the castle offers music, theater, and Shakespearean plays.

Also in Mariefred, a steam locomotive pulls turn-of-the-century carriages between the town for four kilometers to Laggesta. The **railway museum** is one of the oldest in Sweden.

NORTHWEST OF STOCKHOLM
Uppsala

Uppsala University houses the illuminated manuscript **Codex Argentus** or the Silver Bible. This stunning book has gold and silver letters on purple parchment; it is the earliest known work in ancient Gothic. Besides the university, Uppsala has a 16th-century castle where several kings lived while in power. Uppsala Slottet now serves as the residence of the governor.

The **Cathedral** (*Uppsala Domkyrka*) dates back to the 13th century. Twin spires soar upward almost 400 feet. Swedish kings were once crowned there and King Gustavus Vasa is buried there. A trapdoor leads down into the ruins of the pagan temple of Odin, or so they say.

Karl von Linne, known in the botanical world as Carolus Linnaeus, created a garden at the university while he was a professor there from 1741 onward. He laid out his garden in an orderly fashion, with rectangles and semicircles, so that he could use it for classification and research. Today an orangery forms a backdrop behind his garden.

OLD UPPSALA

The original site was a political and religious center for the Sveas by 500 A.D. The burial ground holds several thousand burial mounds. Swedish kings from the 6th century, Aun, Egil, and Adils, are probably lying in the three largest mounds, called the "pyramids" of Scandinavia. The 12th-century cathedral houses an old bishop's throne and a wooden clock.

EXCURSIONS FROM STOCKHOLM ....

NORTHWEST OF STOCKHOLM
Dalarna

The "Heart of Sweden" is the area where folklore still thrives—Dalarna, old Sweden in miniature. Our Swedish relatives vacation there and especially enjoy the Midsummer Day festivities held in late June. This festival includes processions of decorated boats from various parishes sailing on Lake Siljan; they are sometimes called church boats and that is where they are headed. Long and slender, with many oars paddling in rhythm, they look like miniature Viking ships.

Wildflowers and slender birch branches are gathered from the fields and woven into traditional Dalarna garland patterns. The Maypole is raised with much merriment, handsome with its floral garlands. Fiddlers tune up for folk dancing, with each dancer dressed in regional dress from home. Young girls often pick seven wildflowers and pop the bouquet under their pillows to encourage a dream of future husbands.

The famous painted **wooden Dalarna horses** (called *dalahast*) are made there; we have a collection of orange, black, white, and blue horses, with their foals beside them. Furniture and walls are decorated in the same bright colors. Many of the houses are red, which contrasts with green foliage, white birches, and blue lakes. Dalarna is a cheery place to visit.

Folk crafts are very popular in Dalarna. Besides carving horses, bowls, spoons, and plates inhabitants enjoy a semi-primitive painting, which includes pictures of biblical persons wearing Dalarna regional costumes. Weaving schools are also well attended in the area.

Leksand is also involved in the church boat parade on Lake Siljan. An open-air allegorical play, *The Road to Heaven,* which involves God, the devil, prophets, and saints, is performed every July. Carl Hansson, of the Leksand school of painters, lived in town.

Mora is known for Lake Silva and skiing. It is also the starting point for the 53-mile Vasaloppet long-distance skiing race, which is held in early March between Mora and Salen. We had a friend who began training for the famed race months before the start.

The race had an earlier beginning in 1521, when Gustavus Vasa tried in vain to get the inhabitants of Mora to band together against the king of Norway and Denmark, Christian II, who had massacred a large group of Swedish noblemen in Stockholm as he proclaimed himself king of Sweden. Because Vasa was not able to convince his neighbors to join with him, he began skiing toward the Norwegian border, where he planned to gain support for a rebellion. The two fastest skiers from Mora caught up with him near Salen, calling his name in his local dialect to identify themselves. The people of Mora had reconsidered and wanted him back as their leader, so he returned and eventually became the first king of Sweden. The story is told in detail in the Vasalopp Museum in Mora.

Anders Zorn, a famous modern painter, was born in Mora. His house is open and the **Zion Museum** contains his etchings and paintings. Also a Zorn holding, is an open-air museum, **Gammelgarden,** which contains a number of buildings as much as 600 years old.

Rattvik is the home of another painter, Malar Erik Eliasson, who created biblical wall paintings. Church boats are also seen in town, as well as all of the other midsummer festivities of Mora and Leksand. A homestead open-air museum is the place to find local crafts—textiles, wood carving, hand-wrought iron, and baskets.

Falun is the capital city of Dalarna. Since medieval days it has been a copper mining center. The original mine and the Stora Kopparbergs Museum illustrate the history and development of mining. The Dalecarlia Museum contains colorful regional costumes and a host of other regional items.

Carl Larsson, once a poor struggling artist from Falun, paints in the style of Norman Rockwell, but with a lighter touch so that scenes look as romantic as one could wish. He uses a lot of red, white, and blue and his people look happy. His home, Sunborn, located just outside of Falun, is open.

MALMO

HISTORY......................................

Malmo dates back to the 12th century and was a member of the Hanseatic League with an important harbor location. At one time, the city was the second biggest in Denmark—until Karl X conquered the Danes. The Treaty of Roskilde, signed in 1658, returned Skane, Blekings, and Bohuslan to Sweden. Malmo is now the third largest city in Sweden.

SIGHTSEEING...............................

St. Peter's Church, in red brick Gothic style, dates from the early 14th century. It has a delicate clock, baroque altar, and ceiling paintings. The 1546 Radhuset stands on the market square, Stortorget, and Karl V rides his horse in the center of the square. Lilla Torget is alive with half-timbered houses and 19th century warehouses housing the Form Design Center.

   Malmo Castle (*Malmohus Slottet*), on Malmohusvagen, is a large 15th-century Renaissance-style castle. Inside there are four museums: the **City Museum, Art Museum, Museum of Natural History** and **Aquarium.** It is located within a park encircled by a canal and was built between 1536 and 1542 on the ruins of a castle from 1434. Danish kings used to visit there. When Skane became Swedish in 1658, fortifications around the castle were expanded and strengthened, including an outer moat, bastions, and defense additions. Between 1828 and 1914, the castle was used as a prison; its fortifications walls were torn down. In 1937, three new buildings in the courtyard housed museum collections. Don't miss the Hall of Knights.

   Across the road stands the **Governor's House** (*Kommendanthuset*) containing military history exhibits. The Technical/Maritime Museum shares the building. Upstairs there's a ferry to walk through complete with original saloon. Children can climb aboard pirate and Viking ships. A submarine waits outside for visitors. Aircraft are housed in the technical side, along with displays on aviation history. A horse-drawn tram, a 1908 locomotive, cars from the past, and motorbikes are there.

DAY TRIPS FROM MALMO ·················

Lund

Lund was founded by King Knut the Great in 1020 and flourished as a major cultural, religious, and political center in Scandinavia during the Middle Ages. The **Cathedral** (Domkyrka) dates from 1080; it has a 14th-century astronomic clock, which emits knights and the Three Wise Men every day at noon and at three p.m. The crypt contains a stone giant who clutches one of the pillars. Reportedly, he was annoyed to be awakened by the church bells, raced to crush them, and was turned into stone as he grabbed a pillar. The church also contains a mosaic of Christ in the apse, and beautifully carved choir stalls. The **Archaeological Museum** (*Drotten*) lies underground.

The **University of Lund** was founded in 1668; adjacent to the church is a 16th-century red brick royal residence that was the original university center. You will enjoy walking the winding old streets of Lund, especially with a stop in the market at **Martenstorget.**

The **Museum of Cultural History** (*Kulturen*) is an open-air museum containing collections from nine centuries. Take a couple of hours to stroll through its 30 buildings standing within an idyllic village scene complete with a pond, trees, formal garden, and pens of domestic animals. The museum was founded by Georg Karlin 100 years ago; buildings were brought in from the local area and other places in southern Sweden. Houses represent four levels of life—nobility, burghers, clergy, and peasants.

When we were there a wedding party entered the red shake 1652 church. Models sit for all time in some houses—a man at work making wooden shoes, a woman churning, a cat on the bed, and chickens poised to take a step.

Castle aficionados may want to visit any number of castles in Skane. **Trollenas Castle,** near Eslov, is called the "dolls castle" because it contains a wonderful collection of dolls dressed in regional costume. The portrait gallery is available by guided tour. The church on the grounds dates from the 12th century.

Bosjokloster, called the white castle of Lake Ringsjon, stands in a lovely green landscape beside a lake. A Benedictine convent was built there in 1080. Letters written from 1255 onward indicated that "he who showed charity towards nuns should have his sins forgiven." Therefore, as more wealthy persons made donations to the nunnery, it became richer. Further, girls who wished to enter were expected to bring generous gifts. Bjorn Svensson, a knight in the fourteenth century had to pawn 7½ farms to send his two daughters to Bosjokloster.

Svaneholm is located near Skurup. Dating from 1530, this Renaissance castle with museum is in a park near Lake Svaneholmssjo. Fishing is available there, as are rowboats.

Christinehof, the "Pink Castle" two kilometers north of Andrarum, was built in 1740 by Christina Piper. She started an alum factory in Andrarum, which became the most productive industry in Scania. The estate is now a center providing theater and concerts. Boars and stags live on the grounds in a protected wildlife park.

Glimmingehus, ten kilometers southwest of Simrishamur, was built between 1499 and 1505. It is considered to be Scandinavia's best preserved medieval stronghold. Its 2.5-meter-thick walls contributed to its strength. Although it was built as a fortress, it was never tested. The walls are so thick that the Swedish Crown was unable to blow it up for demolition. The castle museum houses objects found in the moats in the 1930s. Pictures of past owners are on the walls.

Kivik

The **Kivik Royal Grave** (*Kungagraven*) is located on the east coast of Sweden not far from Simrishamn. The large rounded lump contains stones covering a bronze age tomb. Stone carvings can be seen in the crypt.

Oland

The longest bridge in Europe stretches from Kalmar to the island of Oland. This skinny island is a mecca for sailors, windsurfers, swimmers, and beachwalkers, with its 300 kilometers of coastline. Eketorp is the site of a pre-Viking ringfort, which has been restored. Bronze and Iron Age burial mounds are everywhere. Graborg Fortress probably dates from 500; its stone walls range up to 25 feet high and 25 feet thick. Viking rune stones are found in Gettlinge to the southwest.

Borgholm Castle (*Borgholm Slotte*), was once a medieval fortress, which was rebuilt during the 16th and 17th centuries, then ruined by a fire in 1806. It still is large and impressive, especially by moonlight.

Solliden is the summer residence of the royal family. The gardens may be toured.

Oland has over 400 windmills, and some of them are lined up for wonderful photo opportunities.

Migratory birds appreciate Oland during spring and fall. Much of the island is made up of a limestone plateau without trees so the birds are easily visible to quiet watchers. A bird station stands on the southern part of the island at Ottenby.

Kalmar, at the other end of the bridge from Oland, is famous for its proximity to a number of **glass works.** Visitors can watch the glass blowers and/or buy glassware to take home.

Kalmar Castle houses the **Kalmar Museum** collections. Its towers soar upward and reflect in the surrounding moat. There is a chapel and the dungeons to visit.

Those who have enjoyed Vilhelm Moberg's novels, *The Emigrants* or *Unto a Good Land* will also enjoy this area. Some of our relatives left Sweden and moved to Minnesota; we can empathize with their feelings as they left their homeland never to return.

Ystad

Medieval Ystad features at least 300 half-timbered houses from the 16th century. The oldest preserved schoolhouse in Scandinavia, **Latinskolan,** is there.

St. Mary's Church dates from the 13th century. The baroque altarpiece was carved by Johan Jerling between 1718 and 1733. The altar painting portrays the Last Supper and the baptism of Jesus, painted by Carl Mort. He also painted himself into the picture. A tower watchman blows his horn every quarter of an hour from nine in the evening to three in the morning to let the people know all is well.

The **Latin School** next door dates from 1500; it is the oldest preserved school in Scandinavia. Also on the same square, the **Krook House** is handsome with half-timbering. The clergy's tithe was once stored in the **Gussing House** which dates from the 16th century.

On Mattorget Square, the **Ystad Theater,** built in 1894, is known for the Ingemar Bergman films shot there. The National Theater and the Ystad Opera use the building.

Grabrodraklostret Monastery is one of the two best preserved monasteries in Sweden. **St. Peter's Church** dates from 1267. It contains the Frojel baptismal font, which dates from the 14th century. Nearby stands the **Ekberg Homestead,** which is really two connected half-timbered houses and a stucco house. August Korling, a Swedish composer, lived there until he died in 1919.

Ale's Stones (*Ales Stenar*), the "Swedish Stonehenge," stands on the Kaseberga Ridge. Its stones are thought to be an astronomical construction from the Bronze Age. We walked up the hill to see a large ship-shaped stone oval; it is sometimes called the Kaseberga Ship. Some say that it is a Viking age burial tumulus encircled by the upright stone slabs.

Dag Hammarskjold's farm (*Backakra*) stands several miles to the east. The museum contains objects that he received on his peace trips. Concerts are given there in the summer.

SWITZERLAND

Currency unit • Swiss franc
Languages • German, French, Italian, and Romansch
Time difference from USA • six hours later (Eastern Standard Time)
Telephone access codes • to USA 001 or USA Direct 046–05–0011; from USA: 001 41
National Tourist Offices • **USA:** Swiss National Tourist Office, 608 Fifth Ave., New York, NY 10020, tel.: (212) 757–5944;
Britain • Swiss Centre, New Coventry St., London WIV 8EE, tel.: (071) 734–1921
Airline • Swissair USA (800) 221–4750, (718) 995–8400, or (312) 641–8830; **Britain** (071) 439–4144
Embassies • **American Embassy,** Jubilaeumstrasse 93, 3005 Bern, Switzerland, tel.: (031) 437011; **British Embassy,** Thunstrasse 50 3005 Berne 15, tel.: (031) 44 50 211/6

Most young girls have been enthralled with Johanna Spyri's *Heidi.* Her romantic life in beautiful mountains aroused my longing to be transported to the Alm Uncle's cottage. Believe it or not, some of that feeling returns each time I have visited the Swiss Alps; the impact of a childhood dream won't soon be forgotten. But subsequent visits to the high country of Switzerland, with and and without children, have been equally satisfying for me and my husband. Often we have been on skis, as we were at Zermatt and Verbier, but below those altitudes we have walked, driven the passes, cruised the lakes, and explored the old sections of venerable cities. New images have been grafted onto old ones, and the romantic dream has become a partial reality.

HISTORY.....................................

Paleolithic caves, such as Wildkirchli in the Appenzell region, date settlements of hunters in Switzerland during the glacial periods. By 8000 B.C. after the glaciers had run their course hunter-fisherfolk settled in Wauwiler Moos in Lucerne and Mooseedorf in Berne. Celts and Romans clashed; Julius Caesar obli-

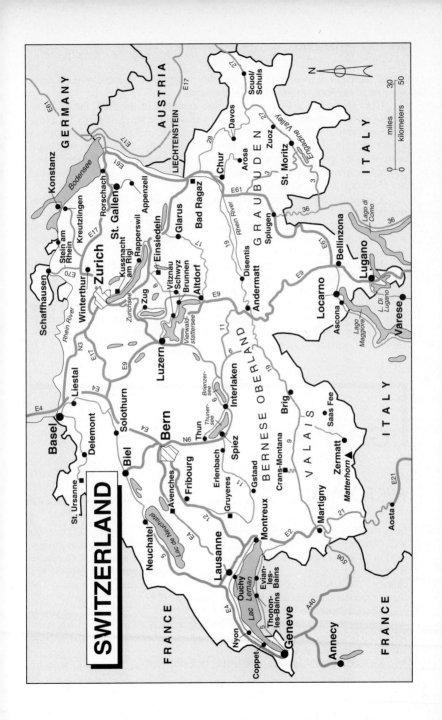

terated the Helvetii tribe in 58 B.C., and they were forced to move west. Romans were in power then, followed by the Barbarians.

Germanic tribes moved in by the fifth century A.D. In 1200, the St. Gotthard route was opened, and this provided a trade route into Lombardy for Swiss sheep and cattle. In 1291 the towns of Uri, Schwyz, and Unterwalden joined in a pact to help each other against the Habsburgs. By 1353 there were eight cantons in the group. Mercenaries in some of the cantons tried to extend Swiss power but, after losing at Marignano, signed an alliance with France, which did not encourage further exploration.

During the Reformation, Switzerland became involved in the conflict between Protestants and Catholics. Zwingli arrived in 1506 and got rid of processions, sacraments, and monasteries in the Zurich Canton. Calvin settled in Geneva and proceeded to preach like a dictator; his statue stands in the Reformation Monument in the Old Town.

By 1648 the Treaty of Westphalia assured Switzerland of its preference for neutrality. Although the Swiss preferred to remain neutral, their land was a battlefield as the French fought the Austrians, Prussians, and Russians.

Today, Switzerland has a mixture of languages. The German-speaking group is the largest in the country. As might be expected, the French-speaking area is next to France, and the Italian, north of Italy. The Romansh section is in southeastern Switzerland.

GENEVA

HISTORY......................................

Lake dwellers chose the site of Geneva for their home as early as 4000 to 5000 B.C. Celts were followed by Romans; Julius Caesar defended his Roman stronghold in 58 B.C. Geneva became a bishopric during the 5th century. A Germanic Burgundian tribe arrived in 443 A.D., and the Franks arrived during the 6th century. The left bank of the River Rhone became the center of the town. The Swiss Declaration of Independence was signed in 1291.

The **Cathedral of St. Pierre** was built between the 10th and 13th centuries. During the Middle Ages, Geneva became a center with its large trade fairs. John Calvin arrived in 1536, turning the city away from entertainment to rigid austerity during the Reformation.

In 1602 French soldiers, under the Duke of Savoie, attacked Geneva by

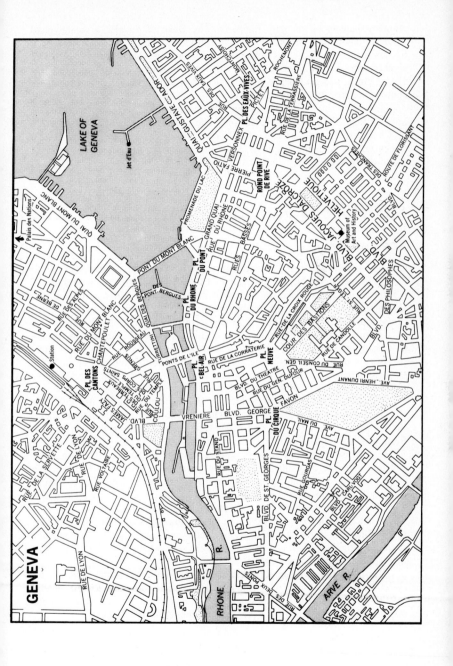

climbing ladders up the city ramparts. The Duke of Savoie, a wealthy and powerful landowner who had lost control of Geneva earlier, tried to get it back by this maneuver. Geneva celebrates this victory, Escalade, every year in December with a torch-light parade in costume. Napoleon invaded in 1798. By 1815 Geneva had established itself as a canton in the Swiss Confederation. A confederation of 26 cantons exists today.

Geneva is now the home of the International Red Cross, the International Labor Office, the UN Conference for Trade and Development, World Council of Churches, European Center for Nuclear Research, and the World Health Organization—to name a few. It is a cosmopolitan and international center of world renown.

SIGHTSEEING.....................................

The Left Bank

One of our favorite ''first'' activities in a city is to head up a spiral staircase to the top of a church tower for orientation. **Cathedrale Saint-Pierre's** north tower (157 steps up) is the place for a view of the old quarter, with Lac Leman, the Jura mountains, and the Alps in the distance. The cathedral houses the Chapel of the Maccabees with angelic musicians seemingly floating on the vaults.

John Calvin's chair, left over from his 16th-century thunderings of austerity has a narrow, carved wooden back and triangular base. An archaeological site is now open on the grounds; during cathedral restoration, begun in 1976, excavation penetrated under the cathedral as well as in surrounding areas. Ruins are coded so visitors can identify layers of time.

Calvin Auditorium was restored in 1959 to commemorate the 450th anniversary of Calvin's era. Calvin and Theodore de Beze gave sermons. There, John Knox, Thomas Bodley, and Miles Coverdale worked on the first English Bible (the Geneva Bible).

The **Museum of Old Geneva,** (*Tavel House*) located next to Calvin's Auditorium at 6 rue du Puits-St. Pierre, is in the oldest house in Geneva. We started our tour by climbing up to the attic to see a large model relief map of Geneva as it was in 1850. Created by August Magnin, it took 18 years to finish. Each floor of the house displays collections of daily life in Geneva.

The **City Hall** (*Hotel de Ville*), on Grand Rue, dates from the 16th century. In 1864 the Geneva Convention determined safety and neutrality for medical stations on the battlefield and the papers were signed there. The Red Cross was founded by Henri Dunant in 1863.

The **Monument de la Reformation,** in the Parc des Bastions, is not far away. This 330-foot-long wall contains statues of Reformation leaders: Knox, Calvin, Beze, and Farel, among other Protestant men. It was started on the 400th anniversary of Calvin's birth and inaugurated in 1917.

The **University of Geneva,** Rue de Candolle, was begun in 1873 by Calvin. Museums inside include the Jean-Jacques Rousseau collection of manuscripts, his death mask, and the Reformation Museum. The library also contains papers from the Reformation. The 6th-century sermons of St. Augustine were inscribed on papyrus and housed in the library.

The **Musee d'Art et d'Histoire,** 2 Rue Charles-Galland, houses archaeological treasures as well as a fine arts area. Henry Moore's *Reclining Figure with Arched Leg* greets visitors outside. Antique clocks, watches, coins, and sculpture are on display. Medieval armor and furniture have been collected there, as well as a guillotine.

The **Musee d'Arte Moderne,** 2 Terrasse Saint-Victor, is located in the Petit Palais. An elegant townhouse, the Petit Palais is an appropriate setting for paintings in a homelike atmosphere. The owner, now in his 80s, lived in Washington D.C. until after World War II.

The **Museum of Old Musical Instruments** (*Musee d'Instruments Anciens de Musique*), 23 Rue Francois Lefort, was originally collected by the present curator. There 16th to 19th-century instruments are sometimes played by professional musicians.

The **Musee de L'Horlogie et de L'Emaillerie,** 15 Route de Malagnou, has collected watches, clocks and music boxes from the last three hundred years. The history of watch making can be traced in this museum.

The River and LakeLeman

Tour de L'Ile is an ancient tower standing on the bridge in the middle of the river. The original castle was built in 1219 by Bishop Aymon de Grandson. A plaque confirms the fact that Julius Caesar came to Geneva in 58 B.C.

Below the bridge, a statue of Jean-Jacques Rousseau stands on an island of the same name. He was born in Geneva at 40 Grand Rue in 1712 and unhappily lived to see his books burned in a public square.

Also in the water, out in the lake, the Jet d'eaux shoots up a steady spray 145 meters into the air. It is located in front of the Quai Gustave Ador.

The Right Bank

The **International Museum of the Red Cross and Red Crescent,** 17 Avenue de la Paix, is the newest museum in Geneva. A visit there can be a profoundly moving experience. Outside, this ultra-modern glass and stone structure casts reflections and creates images of a cross—by design. Visitors walk through a narrow passageway toward a group of barefoot shrouded and blindfolded statues who seem to approach with hands tied. Inside, its subterranean cavern offers a stark gray and white atmosphere within a variety of angles and textures. Visitors are exposed to battlefields, symbolic white shades set at an angle over rocks to illustrate Confucius's condemnation of war and violence, the writing of a Hindu Emperor, and words of the prophets and others. Slides and audio-visual presentations draw the viewer into reacting to the Good Samaritan. Florence Nightingale, and Clara Barton, among others. Seven million POW and refugee cards beginning with World War I are filed in tall cases almost to the ceiling, row after row. John Lennon's *Imagine* wafts through the air. A timeline wraps around the room detailing conflicts, epidemics, and conferences devoted to peace. White statues sitting on a bench represent waiting for judgment.

Based on the Geneva Convention, delegates must be allowed to see all prisoners and talk with them in private. They are to examine the physical and psychological conditions of detention. Confidential reports are written after each visit. The Red Cross and Red Crescent provide medical assistance and relief to those in need.

The message of this museum is to convince visitors that although war can be vicious, human beings can also give of themselves generously to aid both friend and foe.

The Institut et Musee Voltaire, 25 Rue des Delices, was Voltaire's home from 1755 to 1756. The building now houses a library and a museum. A model wearing his suit is seated at Voltaire's desk.

The Palais des Nations, Avenue de la Paix, now contains the European office of the United Nations. It was originally constructed for the League of Nations in 1929. The original building was built in the shape of a double horseshoe; one faces the lake, the other the Jura. A new wing was added in 1968. Visitors may see the building on a guided tour.

Many UN bodies and offices have their headquarters in the Palais des Nations. About 7000 meetings are held there each year. The UN was developed after World War I to maintain international peace and security. It strives to bring about the settlement of international disputes by peaceful means. Four big "Ds" include Disarmament, Development, Defence of Human Rights, and Decolonization. On the lawn, the armillary sphere stands as a symbol of peace.

DAY TRIPS FROM GENEVA ....

CERN

CERN is a European scientific lab for particle physics, which brings together people from 14 member states in Europe. The aim is to "probe the innermost constituents of matter to find out how our world and the whole of the Universe works." An LEP electron-positron collider whirls beams of electrons and their antimatter counterparts in a 27-kilometer-long ring underground. Huge detectors intercept, record, and analyze the results. Over 3000 persons are involved in running the operation. Scientists from all over the world come to study and work there.

Visitors may come on Saturdays for a three-hour visit. An appointment must be made a least two weeks in advance. Write CERN, Organization des Visites/AG 1211 Geneve 23, Suisse.

Lausanne

Lausanne is the second largest city on the lake, growing upward on a series of hills as high as 120 meters. The 12th-century cathedral in the center of town contains a 13th-century figure of Christ and a magnificent rose window, also from the same period.

Musee des Beaux-Arts, Place de la Ripponne, displays art from the 18th to the 20th centuries. French, Italian, and Dutch masters are included.

Musee Olympique, 18 Avenue Ruchonnet, houses a collection of the history of the Olympics. Lausanne is the headquarters of the International Olympic Committee.

Montreux

The Chateau de Chillon is the place where Francois Bonivard, who displeased the Duke of Savoy, was cast into the dungeons and lived chained to a pillar for four years. Byron visited the castle in 1816 and wrote the lyrical poem about Bonivard, ''The Prisoner of Chillon,'' that made the castle famous. This medieval castle is one that's well preserved.

Chamonix

Chamonix has been popular since the first Winter Olympic Games held there in 1924. Skiers flock to the many lifts departing from several locations in town. Twenty-nine cable railways move skiers up to try 160 kilometers of marked trails. The cross-country network spreads out along 40 kilometers of trails. The ice skating rink attracts aficionados to curling, figure skating, and ice hockey.

The Valley of Chamonix rises up to Mont-Blanc on one side and the Aiguilles Rouges chain on the other. During spring, summer, and fall visitors can take the Aiguille du Midi two-stage cablecar up to the summit for a view of Chamonix Valley and the mountains in the French, Swiss and Italian Alps. From April to September, the Vallee Blanche cablecar links Aiguille with Helbronner Point of the Franco-Italian frontier. This 5½-kilometer run was once only available to alpinists. The rack-railway Mer de Glace chugs from Chamonix to Montenvers to see a seven kilometer long glacier (only in summer). To reach Brevent, one takes cablecars to reach the 2,525 mile high observatory.

ZURICH

HISTORY..

By 15 B.C., Zurich was a Roman customs post known as Turicum, located on the Limmat. During the 10th century the town became fortified to protect its citizens. The Holy Roman Empire established Zurich as a free city in 1218. Rudolf von Brun inaugurated a guild constitution in 1336 and in 1351 Zurich became part of the Swiss Confederation. Mayor Hans Waldmann developed the city into a cultural and intellectual center by the end of the 15th century. Huldrych Zwingli was responsible for bringing the Reformation into Zurich. By the 19th century Alfred Escher continued to develop Zurich into the international business and industrial center it is today.

SIGHTSEEING...................................

Come along with us to the Lindenhof, the highest part of the old city on the west bank of the Limmat. The view includes river activity—boats, ducks, a group of divers, and several racing shells. The University medical facilities, hospital, and technical schools stand across the river. Also, the twin towers of Charlemagne's Grossmunster rise above the old town. Above the steep streets of the residential area, miles of wooded hiking paths intertwine.

Linden trees emit fragrance when first blooming. In early days, the Roman Custom station stood there. Underneath the park rest walls from the 10th century. Over the years, kings slept in the building called the Free Mason's Lodge.

We were intrigued with the fountain containing a woman in armor as a reminder of the 1292 war. When Dietrick von Habsburg thought it would be easy to take Zurich because the men were off fighting, the women of the town put on men's armor and made such a clatter that he thought the area full of soldiers. Zurich was saved.

Farther south on the west bank of the Limmat, you will find St. Peter's Kirche, which is the parish church of Zurich. The nine-meter dial on the gold clock is one of the largest in Europe. Until 1912 St. Peter's had a watchman living in a room at the top of the tower.

Turn down *Little Bread Street* (*Weggengasse*) to see ruins of the Roman

Baths, Turicum, dating from 70 to 80 A.D. A glass display case holds items found there including a leather sole, hairpins, a perfume bottle, and clay pieces.

The **Munsterhof** is famous for a collection of Zurich, Meissen, and Strasbourg, porcelain in the 18th-century guildhall. The porcelain is owned by the National Museum.

The **Fraumunster** was originally founded by Ludvig in 853 as a convent. His daughter Hildegard was its first director. Marc Chagall, who was born in Russia in 1887, created a number of stained-glass windows for this church. The green ones offer a scene of Christ without the Cross; the yellow, of King David, Bathsheba, and an angel announcing eternity; the blue features Jacob dreaming; the red, the prophet Isaia; and in the last blue window, Chagall himself is pictured. A rose window in the church was also created by Chagall.

The **Swiss National Museum** (*Schweizerisches Landesmuseum*), Museumstrasse 2, contains over 100 rooms tracing the history of Switzerland from prehistoric days. Collections include simple artifacts, ceramics, stained glass, tapestries, frescoes, altarpieces, furniture, and a display of Swiss costumes. Entire rooms patterned after 16th- and 17th-century life have been developed, complete with stained-glass windows, paneled ceilings, tapestries, and painted walls.

On the east bank of the Limmat, Grossmunster was begun in 1100 over an earlier church. Its two Romanesque towers are visible all over Zurich. It was here that Zwingli preached during the Reformation. He was able to abolish religious processions and closed the monasteries in the Zurich area. Charlemagne's statue dominates the south tower.

Kunsthaus (*Fine Arts Museum*), 1 Heimplatz, houses German, Swiss, and French paintings from the 13th to the 20th centuries. Don't miss the Edvard Munch paintings, the largest group outside of Scandinavia.

The **Zurich Spring Festival**, (*Sechselauten*) is held the third Monday in April, when we had the good luck to be there. Guild members appeared in their traditional costumes as they paraded through the city. Although the procession started out with sedate bands and marchers, it soon took on a gaiety, and rapport with the crowd as fish were tossed, candies cascaded into waiting hands, cannons popped, and wine flowed into cups. Women with baskets of flowers jumped up to greet friends marching by with a bouquet and a kiss. A beautiful blond girl in front of us was in constant motion kissing handsome fellows and giving each a pretzel tied with blue and white ribbon. So much for the image of Zurich as the habitat of dour bankers!

Most of those bankers are now members of ancient guilds unrelated to modern professions. Each of the 26 guilds was represented by members on horseback, marchers, and a float containing their theme—from wine barrels, boat, castle, palm tree, anvil, water wheel, to giant scissors and baking equipment. Guild costumes are elaborate indeed, ranging from waistcoats and tricornered hats, ladies in velvet long-skirted riding habits, men wearing chain mail, and woodsmen wearing raccoon tails on their caps.

After two hours, the crowd oozed to a huge pile of straw topped by the

Boogg, a cotton-wool snowman symbolizing winter. Fire crept up to him as spring overpowered winter. Guild horsemen roared around and around as if to fan the flames.

Those who enjoy hiking and walking will want to find a way up into the hills and mountains around Zurich. Dolderbahn is a cog railway departing every 10 or 15 minutes from Romerhofplatz. **The Dolder Recreational Area** contains a swimming pool with waves. Get out at the last stop for nature trails and a path to the zoo.

The Polybahn Funicular takes off every three minutes from the square near the Main Station Bridge for the Poly Terrace, which overlooks the city. The Polybahn has been running since 1899.

An adhesion rail line chugs up to Uetliberg from Zurich main station and Selnau station every 30 minutes. From the 2867 summit you can see the Limmat Valley, Lake Zurich, and the Alps from the Jungfrau to the Santis. Climb 167 steps up the Belvedere Tower for a view. An aerial cableway departs from the main station and Selnau to a cableway terminal at Adliswil for Felsenegg.

James Joyce and his wife lie in a joint grave in the Fluntern cemetery. Joyce was writing *Ulysses* in Zurich in 1920. A bronze statue stands beside their graves.

Rietberg Museu, Gablerstrasse 15, is located in Wesendonck Villa, overlooking Lake Zurich, Exhibits range from the 1500 B.C. Shang dynasty in China to artifacts from South and Central America, Japan, India, and Africa.

DAY TRIPS FROM ZURICH ··················

Lake of Konstanz

The Lake of Konstanz, *Bodensee,* is 64 kilometers long and 13 across at its widest point. It is bordered by three German-speaking countries: Switzerland, Germany, and Austria. Lunch along the promenade beside the lake in Konstanz is pleasant. Originally a fishing hamlet, it became a fortress in Roman times, and then a center for the Holy Roman Empire.

The Rosgartenmuseum, on Rosgartenstrasse, was built by the butcher's guild in the 15th century. The building itself is interesting, with paneling and leaded glass windows, and the art collection includes pewter, silver, wooden carvings, engravings, and pottery. **The Munster** has a single spire with a baroque pulpit inside.

The **Isle of Mainau** (*Insel Mainau*) is a tropical garden containing a baroque palace and church, owned and operated by the Swedish Bernadotte family. The botanical garden contains an array of flowering shrubs, exotic trees and flowers.

Luzern

The old town charms us with its many painted buildings, squares, and ancient walking bridges, including two with painted triangular panels under the roof. Since the city center is on a small scale, park your car in Bahnhofparking, where there is a large underground lot, and enjoy the day on foot.

The Jesuits' Church can be identified by two towers with domed belfries. Inside, the effect of red marble pillars and painted frescoes on walls and ceiling against a white background is quite dramatic. The church was completed in 1663 and renovated in 1980.

Cross the river on **Mills Bridge** (*Spreuerbruck*), a covered bridge. Panels that represent the Dance of Death line the bridge in the V of the roof. These skeletal figures interact with citizens of the city in each panel. As you wander around the old town, you will spot the **Muhlenplatz,** dating from the 16th century, which was the site of markets. **The Weinmarkt,** with a Gothic fountain in the center, features St. Maurice, the patron saint of soldiers. Buildings around the square are decorated with paintings representing the guilds they once housed.

After wandering around into the old town you can cross the river again on the **Chapel Bridge** (*Kapellbrucke*), another covered bridge built in 1800; it is supposed to be the oldest covered bridge in the world still in daily use. The paintings depict scenes from Swiss history and the life of St. Leodegar, who is the patron saint of Luzern. There is a 13th-century octagonal water tower beside this bridge (*Wasserturm*) to lend the perfect touch for photographic composition. As you enjoy the views, you will catch glimpses of the **Musegg Wall,** built in the 12th century, and the **Town Hall,** (*Altes Rathaus*), built around 1600; the latter overlooks the Kornmarkt.

Mark Twain wrote of the Lowendenkmal, ''the Dying Lion of Lucerne,'' as ''the saddest and most poignant piece of rock in the world.'' It was erected in 1819 to honor the Swiss guardsmen who died in Paris during the French Revolution. The inscription above the nine-meter-high lion, poignantly simple, reads: ''Dedicated to Swiss loyalty and courage.''

The Garden of Glaciers (*Gletschergarten*), on Denkmalstrasse, was discovered in 1872; it represents 20 million years of geological history from the time when Luzern was covered by a layer of ice. Under a large, white, conical tent there are 32 ''giants' potholes'' hollowed out and polished by water falling through the ages. One of them is 29 feet deep. A pamphlet received at the ticket window describes each of 43 numbered stations. Fossil shapes imbedded in the rock include oyster shells and a palm leaf. Ripple marks in the sandstone were shaped by waves and current action on the bottom of the shallow seabed; we wondered how the water became still enough to allow the sand to petrify. The museum contains prehistoric artifacts, including the skeleton of an Ice Age bear standing upright, and skulls of prehistoric men.

The oldest relief map of central Switzerland was completed in 1785 by

Franz Ludwig Pfyffer de Wyher. The museum considers this cultural-historical exhibit the most prized.

We were taken with a display of models of Swiss houses organized in two glass cases by regional styles. A rock and mineral collection includes colorful yellow, green, pink, and beige examples. Antique furniture and furnishings include one room with the puffiest puff on a bed, a cradle, and dolls. The dining room contains lovely carved furniture, china on the buffet and a spinning wheel.

The Swiss Transport Museum (*Verkehrshaus der Schweiz*), Lido Strausse 5, contains many original vehicles, models, dioramas, and exhibits, including early railway locomotives, carriages, motorcycles, bicycles, vintage airplanes, and boats. The "Air and Space" hall displays the space suit worn by Astronaut Mitchell and travel is presented in the Cosmorama area. And the Longines Planetarium offers an interesting program of astronomical demonstrations. In the light of infinity with space, the sun, planets, constellations, and galaxies to consider, man's space explorations seem modest indeed.

The **Richard Wagner Museum,** Wagnerweg 27, is in a country house he called home from 1866 to 1872. Some of his original manuscripts are on display. He composed *Siegfried Idyll* there. The collection of old musical instruments is priceless.

Mount Pilatus overlooks Luzern; you can take a cog railway (the steepest cog wheel in the world with a gradient of 48%) or an aerial lift to the top of the 7000-foot-high summit. The panoramic view is lovely, whether or not you believe the local proverb: "When Pilate hides his head, sunshine below will spread; when Pilate's head is bare, of rain beware."

Mount Rigi can be reached by cog-wheel railways from Vitznau or Arth-Goldau. Called the Queen of the Mountains, this one provides views of central Switzerland. People have traditionally planned to be up there to watch the sun rise over the Alps. Victor Hugo was one who wrote about that "incredible horizon—a chaos of absurd exaggerations and frightening diminutions."

TURKEY

Currency unit • Turkish lira (TL)
Language • Turkish
Time difference from USA • seven hours later (Eastern standard time)
Telephone access codes • to USA 091; from USA 90
National Tourist Office • **USA:** Turkish General Consulate Information Office, 821 United Nations Plaza, New York, NY 10017, tel.: (212) 687–2194; **Turkey:** Gazi Mustafa Kemal Bul, 33 Demirtepe, Ankara, tel.: 2317380/95 or free-phone: 9–00–44–70–90; 12 Eylul Meydani, Bodrum, tel.: 1091; Lskele Mey 67, Canakkale, tel.: 1187; Ataturk Mah, Focaa Girisi, 1, tel.: 1222; Taksim, Tilton Oteli Girisi, Istanbul, tel.: 133 05 92; Ataturk Cad. 418, Izmir, tel.: 220207/8 or 224409; Cumhuriyet Meydani, Kas, tel.: 1238; Ataturk Mah. Agora Carsisi, 35, Selcuk, tel.: 1945–1328; **Britain:** British Turkish Tourist and Information Centre, 170/173 Piccadilly, London W1V 9DD, tel.: (071) 734–8681
Airline, • **Turkish Airlines USA** (800) 874–8875 (212) 986–5050; **Britain:** (071) 499–9240/47/48
Embassies • American Embassy, Ataturk Bulv. 11, Cankaya, Ankara, tel.: 126–54–70 American Consulate, Mesrutiyet Cad. 34, Tepebasi, Istanbul, tel.: 143–62–00 or 143–62–09; Ataturk Cad. 92, Izmir, tel.: 131369 or 149426
British Embassy • Sehit Ersan Caddesi 46/A Cankaya 27 4310/14 (Ankara)

Our first glimpse of Turkey was from the sea, as we cruised through the Dardanelles and the Sea of Marmara until we finally glided into the Strait of Bosphorus to view the exotic skyline of Istanbul. It was every bit as extravagant as we had dreamed it might be. The towers and turrets beckoned, both literally and figuratively, encouraging us to learn a little more about the tumultuous history they have seen. Every morning before dawn, minarets sounded the haunting call of the Muzzeim to remind the faithful of obligations that seem far removed from the modern center of Istanbul but fully appropriate to its mosques and back streets, which we visited and walked as much as we could. Once Lord Byron swam the Bosphoros from continent to continent as a lark; now a modern suspension bridge unites Asia and Europe, suggesting the two faces of Istanbul itself.

HISTORY••

Turkey can be said to straddle the fence in between west and east. Images include the mysteries and flavor of the Orient along with the ruins of very early civilization. During the prehistoric period beginning around 7000 B.C. people lived in Anatolia. Excavations have produced signs of life in the Antalya as well as caves which date back to the Upper Palaeolithic period. Bones of cattle, sheep, and goats, and food including lentils, wheat and barley date to 7040 B.C. In 6500 B.C., people created wall paintings, which have been preserved in museums.

During the Bronze Age, the Hatti people created bronze, silver, and gold works of art, which were uncovered in royal tombs. The Hittite Empire's art can compare with the treasures of ancient Egypt. Ancient Greeks settled in Ephesus, Troy, Pergamum, Miletus, and Halicarnassus, and those Hellenistic ruins can be seen today. During the Roman period, the Greek influence continued along with new building methods developed by the Romans. In 129 B.C., Rome founded the Province of Asia, using Ephesus as the capital. St. Paul traveled throughout Turkey spreading the gospel; in Ephesus, silversmiths objected to his philosophy curtailing their sales of silver effigies.

The Ottoman Empire dates from 1288, and by 1453 had captured Constantinople. The reign of Sultan Suleyman the Magnificent began in 1520. World War I brought the defeat of Germany and the Central Powers with whom Turkey had joined forces. Their country was taken over, but by 1919 a Turkish resistance movement had begun; the Turkish War of Independence lasted until 1922 when the Greeks were forced back. In 1923 Turkey was declared a republic and changes were made in legal codes. Kemal Ataturk is a national hero; he protected the democratic system in Turkey until he died in 1938.

⌐ ISTANBUL

HISTORY•••••••••••••••••••••••••••••••••••••

In 1930 the name Constantinople was changed to Istanbul along with other changes in the new republic. Once a fishing village in 1000 B.C. the city was named Byzantium by the Greeks in 657 B.C. The founder, Byzas, had asked the oracle at Delphi for a suggestion as they looked for a new site. He followed

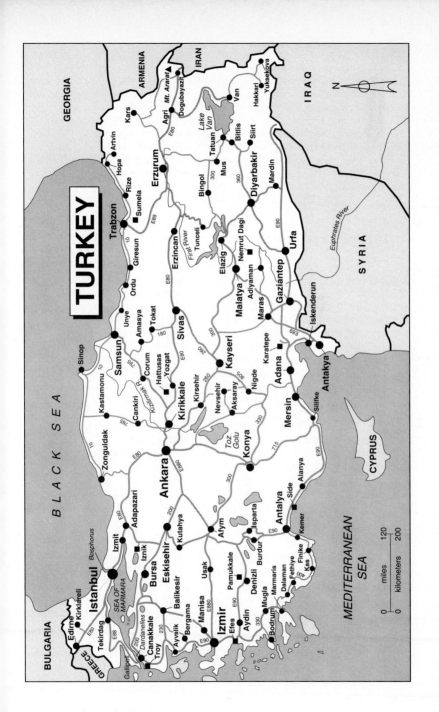

the words, "opposite the blind" and found a perfect place in what is now Golden Horn harbor, thinking the settlers on the opposite shore to be blind not to have taken the land first. The oracle was right, as this site is located on the Bosphorus, which provides access to the Black Sea and the Sea of Marmara.

A Roman, Septimium Severus, named it Augusta Antonina in 196, then Constantine invaded and renamed this city Constantinople. It became powerful in the 1100s, then blossomed further during the era of the Ottoman Turkish Empire in the 1500s. Today, Istanbul is the largest city in Turkey and contains the largest port.

SIGHTSEEING..

Istanbul is divided into north and south by the Bosphorus, and connected by the Bosphorus Bridge, a long suspension bridge which is the only one like it connecting two continents. The European side of the city contains most of the sightseeing attractions. This section is further divided by the Golden Horn, which separates the Old City of ancient Byzantium in the south from Beyoglu, earlier called Galata, in the north. Galata Bridge connects the two areas and also provides views of the Golden Horn, the Bosphorus, the Old City, and Beyoglu.

Topkapi Palace was built by Mehmet the Conqueror in 1453, and sultans lived there for the next three centuries. Mozart, among others, called the palace "Seraglio" in his *Abduction from the Seraglio;* his opera is performed there during the Istanbul International Festival.

This palace is large; it has been said that by 1640, 40,000 persons lived inside the palace grounds. The headquarters of the government, including the cabinet rooms, archives, and mint, were housed in the palace. The name Topkapi comes from the words "cannon gate"; as cannons guarded the palace from the sea portals.

There are three main courtyards in the palace, each with a different function. The fountain in the first court was once important to the executioner who washed the head of a victim who had displeased the sultan in the fountain, then displayed it on the "warning stone," which was meant to warn any future transgressions.

The entrance to the **museum** leads into the second courtyard which contains the Harem, Imperial Council Chambers, Royal Stables, Halberdiers Dormitory, Internal Treasury, and the Imperial Kitchens.

The Topkapi Chinese and Japanese Porcelain Collection is on display in the former kitchens. Pieces are placed in the order of the dynasty in which they were used. Celadon ware, from the 10th and 13th centuries, was popular with the sultans as the green color of the dish showed any poison in the food. Suleyman the Law-giver especially enjoyed the blue and white Ming dynasty pieces.

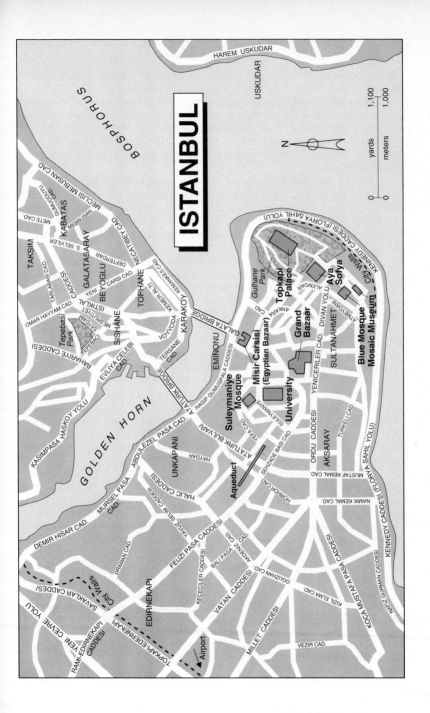

ISTANBUL

HAREM USKUDAR

USKUDAR

BOSPHORUS

N

yards   0   1,100
meters   0   1,000

TAKSIM
KABATAS
GALATASARAY
BEYOGLU
TOPHANE
SISHANE
KARAKOY
EMINONU

MECLISI MEBUSAN CAD.
METE CAD.
GUMUSSUYU CAD.
S. SELVILER
MEBBUSAN CAD.
DEFTERDAR
NECATIBEY CAD.
KEMER ALTI
KEMANKES CAD.

TARLABASI CAD.
OMAR HAYYAM CAD.
ISTIKLAL CADDESI
MESRUTIYET CAD.
SAYDAM
TEPEBACI
EVLIYA CELEBI CAD.

Tepebasi
Park

BAHARIYE CADDESI

GOLDEN HORN

KASIMPASA HASKOY YOLU

DEMIR HISAR CAD.

MURSEL PASA
HALIC CADDESI
ABDULEZEL PASA CAD.
UNKAPANI
HAYDAR

A.ATATURK BRIDGE
TERSANE CAD.
YAVUZ SELIM CADDESI
AKDENIZ CAD.

GALATA BRIDGE

RAGIP GUMUSPALA CADDESI

Misir Carsisi
(Egyptian Bazaar)

Suleymaniye
Mosque

Aqueduct

ATATURK BULVARI

YEFA CAD.
SULEYMANIYE
SELIZADE BASI CAD.
HORHOR CAD.

University

Grand
Bazaar

YENICERILER CAD.

ORDU CADDESI

AKSARAY

Gulhane
Park

Topkapi
Palace

ANKARA YOLU

DIVAN YOLU

ALEMDAR

Aya
Sofya

ATMEYDANI

Blue Mosque
Mosaic Museum

SULTANAHMET

TURKELI CAD.

MUSTAF KEMAL CAD.

NAMIK KEMAL CAD.

MILLET CADDESI

VEZIR CAD.

VATAN CADDESI

KECECILER CADDESI
BALI PASA CADDESI
OGUZHAN CAD.
KIZIL ELMA CAD.

FEUZI PASA CADDESI

EDIRNEKAPI

City Walls

TOPKAPI-EDIRNEKAPI CADDESI

RAMI-EDIRNEKAPI CADDESI

SAVAKLAR CADDESI

YENI CEVRE YOLU

Airport

KENNEDY CADDESI (FLORYA SAHIL YOLU)

KOCA MUSTAFA PASA CADDESI

NEVZ GURMAN CADDESI

KENNEDY CADDESI (FLORYA SAHIL YOLU)
City Walls

Polychrome ware of the Ch'ing dynasty dates from the 17th century. A collection of Turkish kitchenware used in the palace is also there.

The Gate of Felicity was the place where the sultans conducted important ceremonies, such as giving pay to the Janissaries once every three months, presenting the imperial banner to the commander of the forces as they left on a campaign, and accepting felicitations on religious holidays. This gate was also known as the gate of the white eunuchs because they were stationed there to guard the harem.

The Throne Room contains a decorated wooden canopy perched on four posts over the throne, which is covered with golden pillows embroidered and set with precious stones. Sometimes officials and ambassadors would be frisked for weapons and led into the throne room by a white eunuch on each side. Gifts were expected to be presented to the sultan and the visitor addressed him through an interpreter.

The Hall of the Royal Costumes contains articles of clothing that date from the period of the Conqueror. Robes of the sultans were kept in the treasury after each sultan died. They range from velvet and gilt brocade to taffeta. The robe of Osman II, who was executed in 1622 by the Janissaries, still contains blood spots. Silk prayer rugs are also on display.

The Treasury contains gifts given to the sultans as well as personal items collected in a variety of ways. The suit of armor, which was worn by Mustafa III, is encrusted with gold and precious stones. Koran cases are decorated with diamonds, pearls, and other jewels. Murad IV's throne is made of ebony inlaid with ivory and mother-of-pearl. A hookah used by Mustafa Pasha, who was one of the governors, is on display. Daggers, swords, and pistols were made with jewels and decoration. Flasks, also decorated, were used for ceremonial purposes. The throne of Ahmet I is a mass of precious stones set into tortoiseshell and mother-of-pearl. The ''spoon maker's'' diamond is an 86-carat stone set in a silver frame set with 49 brilliants. Some say that a fisherman found the gem and sold it for three spoons.

The **Mosque of Sultan Ahmet,** or the Blue Mosque, is the only mosque created with six minarets. Built by Ahmet I between 1609 and 1616, the young sultan actually worked on his mosque to speed its completion. Inside, the hand-painted ceramic tiles and stained-glass windows contain, predominantly, shades of blue, hence the nickname. Natural light streams in through the 260 windows. The pulpit is carved in marble; in 1826, the Janissary corp was disbanded from Topkapi Palace. A grandfather clock to encourage people to attend prayers, a Black Stone from the Kaaba in Mecca, and marble latticework on the imperial loge are all in the mosque.

The Mosque Museum houses mosaic floors dating from 500. Scenes include mythology, hunting, and portraits of the emperors. Excavations in 1935 brought out pieces of sarcophagi, capitals, columns, and walls from the great palaces once standing on the site of the Blue Mosque.

The dome of the Haghia Sophia presented an architectural problem, as it was to be a large circular cupola set on top of a rectangle. The plan worked, and this large basilica has been standing since the 6th century, with little earth-quake damage. Inside, there are green medallions with gold letters inscribing the names of Allah, Mohammed, the first four caliphs, and grandsons of the prophet, Hasan and Huseyin. Mosaics include one in the apse of the Virgin holding her child and one of the Archangel Michael. Above the main entrance, Jesus is on a throne with his right hand gesturing the Greek Orthodox Benediction. Over the door to the museum, the Virgin is portrayed as a protectress of St. Sophia and Constantinople.

The 16th-century **Suleymaniye Mosque,** the largest in the city, was built when the Ottoman Empire was in its prime. Sultan Suleyman the Magnificent commissioned a Turkish architect named Sinan to design and build his mosque. The gigantic dome did not move, even during several earthquakes. Stained-glass windows bearing Turkish motifs are set into the wall of the prayer niche (mih-rab). Ceramic tiles decorate the walls around the pulpit. The tombs of Sultan Suleyman and his favorite wife, Roksana, stand in the forecourt. The architect, Sinan, is also buried in the mosque.

DAY TRIPS FROM ISTANBUL.................

Troy

For contrast with bustling Istanbul, we visited Troy, which was almost deserted except for the aura of many layers of civilization, clearly marked for visitors to ponder. To get there we drove across rolling hills to Homer's "windy plain," and sure enough a brisk breeze was blowing as we poked around in this piece of legend and history. Heinrich Schliemann first discovered it in the late 19th century with a copy of Homer's *Iliad* in his hand, and successive generations of archaeologists have established many layers of civilization at a site with extraordinary military and commercial importance in the ancient world. Whether there was a real Trojan War to rescue Helen and punish her captors, Greeks would have had good reason to capture a city that controlled the entrance to the Dardanelles.

The Early Bronze Age folk were the first to live there and leave a bit of their past. Heinrich Schliemann received permission from the Ottoman government to begin excavating in 1871. He dug ten meters down and created a "north-south" trench, which later archaeologists realized destroyed some of the evidence. Wilhelm Dorpfeld and Carl Blegen totted the score up to nine different civilizations. **Troy I** (3000–2500 B.C.) can be seen in a tower beside the city gate and House # 102, which has walls made in a herring-bone pattern. Two skeletons of infants were found in a grave under the paving of the largest room. **Troy II** (2500–2200 B.C.) is unique, in that a city plan was developed for the first time. Megarons were built side by side in orderly fashion. Structures from **Troy III** are located to the northwest of the ramp.

Troy VI, 1800–1275 B.C., saw new life, and the town doubled in size with the arrival of the Mycenaeans. A watchtower with a well in a cistern was used when the city was under seige. The "pillar house" stood two stories high, and one of the pillars still stands. The Trojan War and an earthquake wreaked havoc on the city. Some archaeologists feel that Homer's Troy was VIIa from 1275–1240 B.C. rather than Troy VI. Troy VII saw the beginning of a decline; Troy VIII came to life as a Greek city, and Troy IX as a Roman one.

EXCURSIONS FROM ISTANBUL ·····································

Ephesus

Ephesus, located 18 kilometers from Kusadasi, was dedicated to Artemis (Diana), and the temple is one of the seven wonders of the ancient world. Selcuk is the place to see the ruins of the **Temple of Artemis.** Although when we were there, pieces of the columns were lying around in a field inhabited by one cow, goats, sheep and a group of ducks in an adjoining pond, one column had been raised and reassembled. The top of the column was a busy place, with three storks nesting and flapping.

Up on the hill stands the **Basilica of St. John.** Legend reports that St. John lived on the site and was buried there. In the 6th century Emperor Justinian built what are now ruins. During the Middle Ages the Basilica was destroyed by an earthquake.

The road leading from Selcuk to Ephesus passes by the Grotto of the Seven Sleepers, on the eastern slope of Mount Panayir. The Emperor Decius, who ruled from 249 to 251 and was an enemy of Christians, had seven Christian disciples imprisoned and walled up in the grotto. After 150 years they awoke, as if from a deep sleep, and went into town to discover that their friends were all dead. This was taken by the Christian Emperor Theodosius, who reigned from 408 to 450, as a sign from heaven of the resurrection of the body. When these men died, their bodies were wrapped in shrouds of gold thread; a church was built over their tomb.

The Ephesus site, located about two kilometers from Selcuk, is one of the major archaeological sites of the ancient world. The area to visit is large; comfortable shoes and several hours are recommended. Dating back to the 10th century B.C., Ephesus had a population of 300,000 during its golden age in the second century. It was one of the most important ports in the Mediterranean, combining financial and commercial power with a popular cultural center.

The entrance ramp leads to the **Arcadian Way,** paved in marble, which then leads from the theater to the old port. Columns stand, and other chunks of marble are tilted and scattered. Notice the game boards, which are engraved in the pavement; most of them are circles with spokes. Arcades once covered walkways on either side of the Arcadian Way. Four columns topped with statues of four Evangelists added grandeur to the road. At the end of the Way, you will reach the harbor, which was silted up, but the Harbor Gate bases and parts of columns are still there. The **Roman Baths** are accessible by a thorny path at the end of the Way.

Retrace your steps back on the Arcadian Way to the **theater,** which is the best preserved building in Ephesus. Seating 25,000 persons, the theater has been restored and is used today for the International Ephesus Festival in May. St. Paul once preached in the theater. Demetrius, a local jeweler, who thought his stock of Artemis statues would be worthless if the people listened to St. Paul, stirred up a demonstration shouting ''Great is Diana of the Ephesians'' until the head of the city calmed him down.

The Marble Road is a sacred road leading up the hill as the main thoroughfare of the city. Soon after passing the theater, look to the right for a little iron fence enclosing a section of pavement once intended as an advertisement for the brothel. The sketch of the head of a woman, her footprint, and a heart, pointed the way to sailors newly arrived in port.

The Celsus Library, on the right, is also very well preserved; although the reading room was destroyed by fire, the facade of the building remains. The library was built in 110 by Consul Gaius Julius Aquila over the tomb of his father, Gaius Julius Celsus Polemaeanus, whose skeleton still resides there in a lead casket in a marble sarcophagus.

INNS, HOTELS, CASTLES, AND CHATEAUX

AUSTRIA
Innsbruck

Goldener Adler • *Herzog-Friedrich-Strasse 6, A-6020 Innsbruck, tel.: (0512) 586334; fax: 584409* • An inn since 1390.

Schwarzer Adler • *Kaiserjagerstrasse 2, A-6020 Innsbruck, tel.: (0512) 587109; fax: (0512) 561697* • 16th-century guesthouse.

Weisses Kreuz • *Herzog-Friedrich Strasse 31, tel.: 59479; telex: 533110* • Mozart stayed there when he played for Maria Theresia.

Salzberg

Goldener Hirsch • *Getreidegasse 37, A 5020 Salzburg, tel.: (800) 792–7637; (0662) 848511; fax: (0662) 848517* • Dates from 1407, located in the center of the city near Mozart's house.

Schloss Monchstein • *Monchsberg Park 26, A-5020 Salzburg, tel.: (0662) 848555; fax: (0662) 848559* • A 14th-century castle with chapel on a hillside above Salzburg.

Vienna

Hotel Im Palais Schwarzenberg • *Schwarzenbergplatz 9, A-1030, Wien, tel.: (0222) 784515; fax: (0222) 784714* • A 300-year-old baroque palace in a park.

Parkhotel Schonbrunn • *Hietzinger Haupstr. 10–20, 1130 Vienna, tel.: (0222) 87–8040, fax: (0222) 828–4282* • Former emperor's guesthouse, located near Palace.

Sacher • *Philarmonikerstr. 4, tel.: (0222) 514560; fax: (0222) 51 4 57 810* • An 1876 hotel, famous for the original sachertorte.

BELGIUM
Brussels

Hotel Metropole • *31 Place De Brouckere, Brussels, tel.: (0) 2/217 23 00; fax: (0) 2/218 0220* • A grand old turn-of-the-century hotel.

Brugge

Hotel Oud Huis Amsterdam • *Brugge, Spiegelrei 2, 8000 Brugge, tel.: (050) 34 18 10; fax: (050) 33 88 91* • Located in two combined 17th century homes, garden, antique bar and terrace.

Gent

Cour St. Georges • *Botermarkt 2, Gent, tel.: (091) 24 24 24 fax: (091) 24 26 40* • 1228 hotel complete with Gothic hall.

CZECHOSLOVAKIA
Prague

Hotel Pariz • *U Obecniho Domu 1, 111 00 Praha, tel.: 232 20 51, telex: 12 10 82* • Art-Nouveau style, near Wenceslas Square.

U Tri Pstrosu (Three Ostriches) • *Drazickeho Namesti 12* • 11800 Prague 1, tel.: 53 61 51. 17th-century atmosphere.

DENMARK
Copenhagen

D'Angleterre • *Kongens Nytorv 34, tel.: (33) 12 00 95; fax: (33) 121 118* • A 1755 majestic palace, with Old World charm.

Nyhavn 71 • *Nyhavn 71, tel.: (33) 11 85 85; fax: (33) 93 15 85* • An 1804 harbor warehouse decorated with nautical motif.

Kong Frederik • *Vester Voldgade 25, DK 1552, tel.: (45) 33 12 59 02; fax: (45) 33 93 59 01* • 19th-century building near Town Hall.

ENGLAND
Arundel (Near Brighton)

Amberley Castle • *Arundel, W. Sussex BN18, 9ND, tel.: 0798 831992; fax: 0798 831998* • Dates from medieval times when it began life as a fortress.

Bath

Homewood Park • *Hinton Charterhouse, Bath, Avon BA3 6BB, tel.: (0225) 723731; fax: (0225) 723820* • An 18th-century country house.

Royal Crescent Hotel • *16 Royal Crescent, Bath BA1 2LS, tel.: (0225) 319 090; fax 339 401* • 18th-century hotel is a semi-circle.

Brighton

Old Ship Hotel • *Kings Rd., Brighton BN1 1NR, tel.: (0273) 29001; fax: (0273) 820718* • Original owner Nicholas Tettersell saved the life of King Charles II on board his ship in 1651.

Cambridge

Arundel House Hotel • *53 Chesterton Rd., Cambridge, CB4 3AN, tel.: (0223) 67701* • Overlooks the River Cam and Jesus Green.

University Arms Hotel • *Regent St., CB2 1AD, tel.: (0223) 351241* • Original building an 1834 coach inn.

Cotswolds Area

The Cotswold House • *Chipping Campden, Gloucestershire GL55 6AN, tel.: (0386) 840330; fax: (0386) 840310* • 17th-century hotel located on Market Square in a pleasant village.

Lords of the Manor • *Upper Slaughter, Cheltenham, Gloucestershire, GL54 2JD, tel.: (0451) 20243; fax: (0451) 20696* • The original section of the house dates to 1650.

Lower Slaughter Manor • *Lower Slaughter, Gloucestershire,GL54 2HP, tel.: (0451) 20456; fax: (0451) 22150* • 17th-century Manor lies on a pleasant road next to a running brook.

Stow Lodge Hotel • *Stow-on-the-Wold, Cheltenham, Gloucestershire GL54 1AB, tel.: (0451) 30485* • Secret passageways include a "priest's hole" in the lounge.

Lake District

Field Head House • *Outgate, Hawkshead, Cumbria LA22 OPY, tel.: (09666) 240* • 17th-century house is set on six acres of gardens and rolling landscape.

The Old England • *Bowness-on-Windermere, Cumbria LA23 3DF, tel.: (09662) 3432* • Georgian mansion stretches along Lake Windermere.

The Swan • *Grasmere, Ambleside, Cumbria LA22 9RF, tel.: (09665) 551* • William Wordsworth met his friends there.

London

Brown's Hotel • *Albermarle & Dover sts., London W1A 4SW, tel.: (071) 493 6020; telex: 28686* • 1837 country-house hotel.

The Gore • *189 Queen's Gate, London SW7 5EX, tel.: (071) 584 6601; fax: (071) 589 8127* • An 1851 town house built by the marquess of Queensberry.

The Goring Hotel • *Beeston Place, Grosvenor Gardens, London SW1W OJW, tel.: (071) 8348211* • 1910 family-run hotel near Buckingham Palace.

22 Jermyn Street • *22 Jermyn St., St. James's, London SW1Y 6HL, tel.: (071) 734 2353, fax: (071) 734 0750* • Once "residential chambers" dating from turn of the century.

Montague Park Hotel • *12–20 Montague St., London WC1B 5BJ, tel.: (071) 637 1001, fax: (071) 637 2506* • Located behind the facades of nine Georgian townhouses.

The Portland Bloomsbury Hotel • *7 Montague St. WC1B 5BP, tel.: (071) 323 1717, fax: (071) 636 6498* • Regency building, the garden backs onto the British Museum.

Hotel Russell • *Russell Square, London WC1B 5BE, tel.: (071) 837 6470, fax: (071) 837 2857* • A Victorian hotel with traditional English decor.

St. James Court • *Buckingham Gate, SW1E 6AF, tel.: (071) 834 6655; fax: (071) 6307587, U.S.: (800) 44–Utell or (212) 245–7130* • Formerly a 1900 apartment block, near Buckingham Palace.

Norfolk

Felmingham Hall • *Felmingham, North Walsham, Norfolk, NR28 OLP, tel.: (0692) 69631, fax: (0692) 69320* • An Elizabethan manor house on 15 acres, dates from 1569.

Norfolk Mead Hotel • *Cottishall, Norwich, NR12 7DN, tel.: 0603 737531* • A Georgian manor house on 12 acres of gardens and parkland, near the River Bure.

Oxford

The Randolph Hotel • *Beaumont St., Oxford OX1 2LN, tel.: 0865/ 247481* • An 1864 hotel in the center of town.

Rutland (Near Nottingham)

Hambleton Hall • *Oakham, Rutland, LE15 8TH, tel.: (0572) 56991* • An 1881 hunting lodge overlooking Rutland Water.

Rye

Mermaid House • *Rye, Sussex, tel.: (0797) 223065, telex: 957141. Thirty rooms* • A half-timbered building rebuilt in 1420, ripe with tales of smugglers and French invasions.

Stratford-Upon-Avon

The Falcon Hotel • *Chapel St., Stratford-Upon-Avon, Warwickshire, CV37 6HA, tel.: (0789) 205777; fax: (0789) 414260* • A half-timbered hotel dating from 1640.

The Shakespeare • *Chapel St., Stratford-Upon-Avon, Warwickshire, CV37 6ER, tel.: (0789) 294771* • Dates from 1637, also half-timbered.

Weston-on-the-Green

Weston Manor • *Weston-on-the-Green, Oxfordshire, OX6 8QL, tel.: (0869) 50621; fax: (0869) 50901* • 400-year-old country house, which was once a Priory.

Winchester

Lainston House • *Sparsholt, Winchester, Hampshire SO21 2LT, tel.: (0962) 63588, from U.S. (800) 223–5581; fax: (0962) 72672* • Dating from the 17th century with a 12th-century chapel.

York

Middlethorpe Hall ● *Bishopthorpe Rd., York YO2 1QP, tel.: (0904) 641241, fax: (0904) 620176* ● Dates from 1699 and is located in 26 acres of parkland.

Wales

Royal Victoria Hotel ● *Llanberis, Gwynedd, North Wales LL5 4TY, tel.: LLanberis (0286) 870253; fax: (0286) 870149* ● At the foot of Llanberis Pass over Mount Snowdon.

Ruthin Castle ● *Ruthin, Clwyd LL15 2NU, Wales, tel.: (08242) 2664; fax: (08242) 5978* ● 13th-century castle once the scene of intrigue and historical activity, castle ghost.

FINLAND
Helsinki

Klaus Kurki ● *Bulevardi 2, tel.: 90618911; fax: 90 608 538* ● Turn-of-the-century Finnish atmosphere.

Turku

Hotel Seurahuone ● *Humalistonkau 2, 20100 Turku, tel.: (921) 637-301; fax: (0) 664 170* ● Located in the center of town, dates from 1928.

Aland

Hotel Arkipelago ● *Strandgatan 31, Mariehamn, tel.: 928–24020* ● Located on the water.

FRANCE
Fontainebleau (near Paris)

Napoleon ● *9 rue Grande, 77300 Fontainebleau, tel.: 64222039; fax: 64222087* ● Located one block from the entrance to the Chateau.

Loire Valley

Chateau du Gue-Pean ● *Monthou sur Cher, 41400 Montrichard, France, tel.: 3354714301* ● Castle with a history, museum collected by the owner, Marquis de Keguelin de Rozieres de Sorans.

Paris (also see St. Symphorien, Versailles, Fontainbleau)

Hotel d'Angleterre • *44 rue Jacob, 6e, tel.: 42603472; fax: 42 601693* • 18th-century building once the British ambassador's residence.

Crillon • *10 place de la Concorde, 8e, tel.: 42652424; fax: 4742 72 10* • Originally two adjoining town houses dating back to the time of Louis XV.

Moliere • *41 Rue Moliere, ler, tel.: 42962201; fax: 42606868* • Voltaire once gave a preview of his plays here, said to be the oldest hotel in Paris. Located in the Palais Royal area.

Raphael • *17, Av. Kleber, 16e, tel.: 45021600; fax: (1) 45012150* • Dates from 1920, furnished with oriental carpets, a Turner painting, carved wooden panelling.

Saint Symphorien (near Paris)

Le Chateau d'Esclimont • *28700 Saint Symphorien-le-Chateau, France, tel.: 37311515; fax 37315791* • Castle built in 1543 by the Archbishop of Tours, later owners included Francois de la Rochefoucauld, godfather of Francoise I.

Courchevel

Hotel Le Lana • *73120 Courchevel 1850, tel.: 79080110; fax: 79083670* • Floral painted outside walls under a peaked roof.

Meribel

Hotel La Chaudanne • *73550 Meribel-les-Allues, tel.: 79086176; fax: 79085775* • Alpine decor with large stone fireplaces.

Val Thorens

Hotel le Val Thorens • *73440 Val Thorens, tel.: 79000433; fax: 79000940* • Located right on the main ski slopes.

Versailles (near Paris)

Hotel de France • *5 rue Richaud, 78000 Versailles, tel.: (1) 39500250* • Built in the 17th century, owned by Prince Roland Bonaparte, grandnephew of Napoleon I, in 1880.

Hotel Pullman Place d'Armes • *2 bis Avenue de Paris, 78000 Versailles, tel.: (1) 39533031; fax: (1) 39538720* • Facade blends with old Versailles; the Chateau is one block away.

Trianon Palace Hotel • *1 boulevard de la Reine, Versailles, tel.: 33 139503412* • Treaty of Versailles negotiations in 1919 were held there, located near the gardens of the palace.

GERMANY
Berlin (also see Potsdam)

Bristol-Hotel Kempinski • *27 Kurfurstendamm, 1000 Berlin 15, Germany, tel.: (030) 881091; fax: (030) 8836075* • Dates from the 1920s.

Hotel Grand • *Friedrichstrasse 158–164, 1080 Berlin, tel.: (0372) 20920; fax: (0372) 2294095* • Recently built in 1900 grand style, in former East Berlin.

Hogel Stuttgarter Hof • *Anhalter Strasse 9, 1000 Berlin 61, tel.: (030) 264830; fax: (030) 2139066* • Near Anhalter Bahnhof, dates from 1907, renovated in 1991.

Cologen (also see Essen)

Dom-Hotel Koln • *Domkloster 2A, Koln 1, tel.: (0221) 2024–0; fax (0221) 2024260* • Located adjacent to the cathedral.

Essen

Hotel Schloss Hugenpoet • *August-Thyssen-Strasse 51, D-4300 Essen 18 Kettwig, tel.: (02054) 12040; fax (02054) 120450* • 17th-century chateau in private park between Dusseldorf and Essen.

Frankfurt (also see Kronberg)

Hotel Frankfurter Hof • *Am Kaiserplatz, D 6000 Frankfurt 16, tel.: (069) 20251; fax: (069) 215900, from U.S. (800) 223–5632* • Hotel dates from 1876, located near the railway station.

Friedrichsruhe (near Heilbronn & Heidelberg)

Wald-und Schlosshotel Friedrichsruhe • *7111 Friedrichsruhe, tel.: (079) 4160870; fax: (079) 461468* • Built as a hunting lodge for Prince Johann Friedrich of Hohenlohe-Oehringen in 1712.

Garmisch-Partenkirchen

Post Hotel • *Marienplatz 12, D-8100, tel.: (08821) 7090, fax: (08821) 709205* • Bavarian kings stayed there from 1542.

Grand Hotel Sonnenbichl • *Burgstrasse 97, tel.: (08821) 7020, fax: (08821) 702131* • Grand old hotel located in the center of Partenkirchen, overlooks a garden and mountains.

Heidelberg (Also see Friedrichsruhe)

Zum Ritter St. Georg • *Hauptstrasse 178, D 6900 Heidelberg, tel.: (06221) 20203; fax: (06221) 12683* • Built in 1592, the hotel is the oldest Renaissance building in Heidelberg.

Kronberg (near Frankfurt)

Schloss Hotel Kronberg • *Hainstr. 25, D 6242 Kronberg, tel.: (06173) 70101; fax: (06173) 701267* • Built by Empress Friedrich in a park.

Munich

Bayerischer Hof-Palais Montgelas • *Promenadeplatz 6 Munchen 2, tel.: (089) 2 12 00; fax: (089) 2 12 09 06* • Built by 19th-century architect, Friedrich von Gartner.

Hotel Rafael • *Neuturmstr. 1, D 8000 Munchen 2, tel.: (089) 29 09 80; U.S.: (800) 233–1588; fax: (089) 22 25 39* • A neo-renaissance building, paintings by Raphael.

Potsdam (near Berlin)

Hotel Schloss Cecilienhof • *Neuer Garten, Potsdam 1561, tel.: (23141) 42 43 44; telex: (23141) 15571* • Built for the family of the Crown Prince in 1913, the Potsdam Agreement was signed there in 1945.

Rothenburg

Markusturm • *Rodergasse 1 D 8803 Rothenburg; tel.: (098) 612370; fax: (098) 61 26 91* • It's the 1264 hotel next to the clock tower.

Weimar

Hotel Elephant • *Am Markt, 5300 Weimar, tel.: (0037) 61471; fax: (0037) 5310* • Dates from 1696, 100 rooms.

Hotel Russischer Hof ● *0 5300 Wiemar, Goetheplatz 2, tel.: (0037) 62162331; fax: (0037) 621 62337* ● Located near the National Theater, dates from 1805.

GREECE
Athens

Astir Palace Vouliagmeni Complex ● *Vouliagmeni, tel.: (01) 8960211/ 20; fax: (01) 215013* ● Three hotels in the complex, Arion, Nafsika, and Aphrodite, located 16 miles south of Athens.

Grande Bretagne ● *Syntagma Square, tel.: (01) 323 02519* ● 394 rooms. The Grand Dame of Athens, on Syntagma Square.

St. George Lycabettos Hotel ● *Kleomenous 2, tel.: (01) 729 0710; fax: (01) 90 439* ● Located on Mount Lycabettos.

HUNGARY
Budapest (also see Balaton)

Duna-Intercontinental ● *Apaczai Csere Janos Utca 4, Budapest V, tel.: (361) 1175122; fax: (361) 1184973* ● Located on the Danube Quay, balconies.

Gellert ● *Szent Gellert Ter 1, Budapest XI, tel.: (361) 852200, fax: (361) 666631* ● Grand hotel named after Bishop Saint Gellert.

Hilton ● *Hess Andras Ter 1-3, Budapest I, tel.: (361) 1751000; fax: (361) 1560285* ● On Castle Hill, with the tower and part of a 13th-century Dominican monastery.

Ramada Grand Hotel ● *Margitsziget, H 1138 Budapest, tel.: (361) 132 1100; fax: (361) 153 3029* ● Located on Margaret Island, over 100 years old.

Lake Balaton (near Budapest)

Neptun Hotel ● *H-8623 Balatonfoldvar, tel.: (3684) 40 388 or 40 392; fax: (3684) 40 212* ● Located in a park on the south shore of Balaton Lake.

Hotel Tihany ● *Tihany, 8327 Tihany, tel.: (3686) 48 088; fax: (3686) 48110* ● A holiday complex of hotel rooms with balconies and Danish-built bungalows on the north shore.

IRELAND
County Clare

Gregan's Castle Hotel • *Ballyvaughan, County Clare, tel.: (065) 77005; U.S: (800) 223–6510; fax: (065) 77111* • The home of 17th-century Princes of Burren, castle ruins nearby.

County Cork

Ballylickey Manor House • *Ballylickey, Bantry Bay, County Cork, tel.: (353) 2750071; fax: (353) 27 50124* • Once the shooting lodge of Lord Kenmare, now the home of the Graves family.

Country Kerry

Park Hotel Kenmare • *Kenmare, County Kerry, tel.: (064) 41200; fax: (064) 41402* • Chateau-style country house.

Dublin

The Gresham Hotel • *O'Connell St., Dublin, tel.: (01) 746881; fax: 787175* • Oldest Dublin hotel.

Country Mayo

Newport House • *Newport, County Mayo, tel.: (098) 41222; telex 53740* • This country estate was home of the O'Donels for 200 years.

County Waterford

Waterford Castle • *The Island, Ballinakill, Waterford, tel.: (051) 78203, fax: (051) 79316* • Pampers guests with modern conveniences within a castle setting.

County Wexford

Marlfield House • *Gorey, tel.: (055) 21572; fax: 21572* • Once the residence of the Earl of Courtown, this regency mansion contains woodland and gardens.

ITALY
Amalfi

Hotel Santa Caterina • *84011 Amalfi, tel.: (089) 871012 or 871387; fax: 871351* • Patio 150 feet above the sea, balconies.

Assisi (near Florence)

Hotel Subiaso • *2 Via Frate Elia, tel.: 075/812-206* • Located in a converted monastery.

Bellagio (near Milan)

Grand Hotel Villa Serbelloni • *Lungolago Bellagio, tel.: (031) 950216* • Dating from 1872, located within a park.

Capri (near Naples)

Quisisana • *Via Camerelle 2, tel.: 081/837 0788; fax: (081) 837 6080* • 19th-century health resort, garden, balconies, swimming pool, located near the Piazza.

Cernobbio (near Milan)

Villa d'Este • *Via Regina 40, Lake Como, 22012 Cernobbio, tel.: (031) 511–471; fax: (031) 5121027* • Lakeside villa in a park, built in 1568 for Cardinal Tolomeo Gallio.

Florence (also see Assisi)

Excelsior • *3 Piazza Ognissanti, tel.: (055) 29 43 01; fax: (055) 210278* • An elegant palace on the bank of the Arno.

Villa San Michele • *4 Via Doccia, Fiesole, tel.: (055) 59 4 51 or 59 99 23; fax: (055) 598734* • Converted 15th-century monastery designed by Michelangelo; garden with waterfall and pool.

Genoa

Bristol Palace • *Via XX Settembre 35, tel.: 010 592541* • 130 rooms. Dating back to the last century.

Savoia Majestic • *V. Arsenale di Terra 5, tel.: 261641* • 19th-century hotel near the Principe station.

Ischia (near Naples)

Hotel Regina Isabella • *Piazza Umberto 1, 80076 Lacco Ameno, Ischia, tel.: (081) 994 322* • Two swimming pools, private beach, balconies overlooking the sea.

Milan

Grand Hotel et de Milan • *Via Manzoni 29, tel.: (02) 870757* • Located near La Scala, 19th-century hotel, antiques.

Mira Porte (near Venice)

Hotel Villa Margherita • *Via Nazionale 416/417, Mira Porte, tel.: (041) 4265800; fax: (041) 4265838* • On Brenta Riviera in a garden, villas on both sides of the river.

Naples (see also Amalfi, Positano, Ravello, Sorrento, Ischia, Capri)

Excelsior • *Via Partenope 48, tel.: 081/417111; fax: (081) 411743* • Turn-of-century neo-classicial building.

Portofino (near Genoa)

Splendido • *16034 Portofino, tel.: (0185) 269551; fax: (0185) 269614* • A 16th-century Benedictine monastery converted into a villa on a hillside overlooking the sea, 35 km from Genoa.

Positano (near Naples)

San Pietro • *Via Laurito 2, 84017 Salerno (Amalfi Coast Rd.), tel.: (089) 875454; fax: (089) 811449* • Outside of town with lush garden terraces stepped down to the sea, overlooking the Amalfi Coast and Positano.

Rapallo (near Genoa)

Grand Hotel Bristol • *Via Aurelia 369, Rapallo, tel.: (0185) 273313* • 19th-century villa with balconies overlooking the sea and Rapallo.

Ravello (near Naples)

Palumbo • *Palazzo Confalone, tel.: 089/857244* • 12th-century palace, antiques, garden terraces.

Rome

Atlante Star Hotel • *Via Vitelleschi 34, 00193 Roma, tel.: (06) 6879558; fax: (06) 6872300* • Located near St. Peter's Cathedral, view of Michelangelo's Cupola.

Hassler-Villa Medici • *Piazza Tinita dei Monti 6, Tel.: (06) 678–2651; fax: (06) 679 9278* • 19th-century hotel at the top of the Spanish Steps.

Forum • *Via Tor dei Conti 25, tel.: (06) 678–2446; fax: (06) 678479* • View of Forum, located in an old restored apalazzo.

Hotel Lord Byron • *Via Giuseppe De Notaris 5, 1-00197 Roma, tel.: (06) 3224541; fax: (06) 332 0405* • Originally a private patrician villa within a park, located near the Borghese Gardens.

Santa Margherita Ligure

Imperial Palace • *Via Pagana, tel.: 0185/288991* • Old-World hotel in a park.

Sorrento (near Naples)

Excelsior Vittoria • *Piazza Tasso 34, tel.: (081) 878–1900 or 8071044* • Caruso stayed six months in 1921.

Stresa (near Milan)

Grand Hotel Des Iles Borromees • *Corso Umberto I, 67 28049 Stresa (Novara) tel.: (0323) 30431; fax: (0323) 32405* • In a park on Lake Maggiore with view of the Borromean Islands.

Venice (see also Mira Porte)

Hotel Cipriani • *Giudecca 10, 1-30133 Venezia, tel.: (041) 5207744, fax: (041) 5203930* • Old villa located on the island of Giudecca with a view of the lagoon.

Gritti Palace • *Campo Santa Maria del Giglio 2467 Venezia, tel.: (041) 794611; fax: (041) 5200942* • 15th-century palace of Doge Gritti.

Danieli • *Riva degli Schiavoni 4196, 30122 Venezia, tel.: (041) 522-6480; fax (041) 5200208* • Located in a 15th-century palazzo.

Venice Lido

Hotel Des Bains • *Lungomare Marconi, 17, 30126 Venezio Lido, tel.: (041) 5265921; fax: (041) 5260113* • Turn-of-the-century hotel attracted literary figures to its peaceful seclusion.

Hotel Excelsior • *30126 Venezio Lido, tel.: (041) 5260201; fax: (041) 5267276* • 1907 Neo-Byzantine hotel.

Verona

Colomba d'Oro • *Via Cattaneo 10, tel.: (045) 595300* • 47 rooms. Located in a 14th century building near the Arena.

LUXEMBOURG
Echternach

Hotel Bel-Air • *1, route de Berdorf, 6409 Echternach, Luxembourg, tel.: 72 93 83; fax: 72 86 94* • In its own park, with large reflecting pool and fountains.

Esch-Sur-Sure

Hotel Beau-Site • *2, rue de Kaundorf, L 9650 Esch-Sur-Sure, tel.: 89134* • Located in a town surrounded by craggy mountains, with a castle ruin on top.

Luxembourg City (see also Echternach, Esch-sur-sure)

Hotel Cravat • *29 Boulevard Roosevelt, L-2450 Luxembourg, tel.: 2 19 75; fax: 2 67 11* • A city hotel convenient to the old town, family run for three generations.

NETHERLANDS
Amsterdam

American Hotel • *Leidsekade 97 1017 PN Amsterdam, tel.: (020) 245322; fax: (020) 25 32 36* • Over 100 years old, located near the Rijksmuseum.

Die Port van Cleve • *Nieuwezijds Voorburgwal 178–180, 1012 SJ Amsterdam, tel.: (020) 244860; fax: (020) 220240* • Has a collection of old Blue Delft tiles, Heineken took over in 1863.

Pulizer ● *Prinsengracht 315–331, 1016GZ Amsterdam, tel.: (020) 228333, (020) 276753* ● Constructed from 17th-century merchants' houses with restored facades.

Grand Hotel Krasnapolsky ● *Dam 9, 1012JS Amsterdam, tel.: (020) 5549111; fax: (020) 228607* ● An Old-World hotel with Winter Gardens, one featuring music recitals on Sundays.

Sonesta. ● *Kattengat 1, 1012SZ Amsterdam, tel.: (020) 21223, fax: (020) 275245.* ● A circular Luthern church plus 13 17th century houses are found within the hotel.

NORWAY
Bergen

Hotel Admiral ● *C. Sundtsgate. 9, N 5004 Bergen, tel.: (05) 32 47 30; fax: (05) 23 30 92* ● Located in an old warehouse on the waterfront, the hotel has its own pier.

Augustin Hotel ● *C. Sundtsgate 24, 5000 Bergen, tel.: (475) 23 00 25; fax: (05) 23 31 30* ● Newly renovated, family run hotel, centrally located near shopping.

Hotel Norge ● *3-star, Ole Bulls Plass 4, N 5001 Bergen, tel.: (05) 210 100; fax: (05) 210 299* ● Located beside a rushing fountain in the City park, roofed in atrium.

SAS Royal Hotel ● *Bryggen, 5000 Bergen, tel.: (05) 318 000, fax: (05) 32 48 08* ● On the wharf, facade of old wooden buildings.

Oslo

Continental ● *Stortinsgate 24/26, O161 Oslo, tel.: (02) 419060; fax: (02) 334520* ● 19th-century hotel opposite the National Theater with view of the Royal Palace.

Grand ● *Karl Johans Gate 31, N 0159 Oslo, tel.: (02) 429390; fax: (02) 42 12 25* ● Opposite Parliament and city park, frequented by Ibsen.

Holmenkollen Park ● *Kongeveien 26, Oslo 3, tel.: (02) 146090; fax: (02) 146192* ● 1894 Norse-style building near ski jump.

POLAND
Cracow

Grand Hotel • *ul Slawkowska 5/7, 31-014 Cracow, tel.: 21 72 55; fax: 21 83 60* • Built as a mansion for the Czartoryski ducal family.

Lublin

Unia • *Al. Raclawickie 12, 20-037 Lublin, tel.: 320 61; telex: 0642346* • On a quiet street near the University.

Warsaw

Europejski • *Krakowskie Przedmiescie 13, 00 071 Warsaw, tel.: 265 051; telex: 813615* • Built in 1856, located in the city center by the Royal Tract.

Zakopane

Giewont • *ul. Kosciuszki 1, 34 500 Zakopane, tel.: 20 11; telex: 0322 270* • Located in the center of town.

PORTUGAL
Lisbon (see Palmela)

Hotel Eduardo VII • *Av. Fontes Pereira de Melo, P 1000 Lisboa, tel.: (1) 530141; fax: (1) 53 38 79* • Old hotel located on Parque Eduardo VII.

Ritz Lisboa Hotel • *Rua Rodrigo da Fonseca, 88, tel.: (1) 692020; fax: (351) (1) 69 17 83* • All rooms have terraces, some overlook Parque Eduardo VII.

York House Rua das Janelas Verdes 32, tel.: (01) 662544; fax: (01) 67 27 93 • *A former convent dating from the 16th century, set in a garden.*

Palmela (near Lisbon)

Pousada de Palmela • *2950 Palmela, tel.: (01) 235 04 10 or 2335 12 26* • A 15th-century monastery became a pousada in 1979.

SCOTLAND
Edinburgh

Caledonian Hotel • *Princes St., Edinburgh EH1 2AB, tel.: (031) 225 2433* • "The Caley," in the heart of Edinburgh, has been the grand dame of the city since it opened in 1903.

Fort William

Inverlochy Castle • *Torlundy, Fort William, Ph33 6SN, tel.: (0397) 2177/ 8; fax: (0397) 702953* • The castle was host to Queen Victoria.

The Lodge on the Loch • *Onich near Fort William, Invernessshire Ph33 6RY, tel.: (08553) 237 or 8; fax: (08553) 463* • This family-run hotel has views of the Loch and the mountains.

Inverness

Culloden House • *Inverness IV1 2NZ, tel.: (0463) 790461; fax: (0463) 792181* • Once a Jacobean Castle, Bonnie Prince Charlie visited this Georgian mansion.

Kelso (Near Peebles)

Sunlaws House Hotel • *Kelso, Roxburghshire TD5 8JZ, tel.: (0573) 5331; fax: (0573) 6511* • Owned by the Duke and Duchess of Roxburghe, hosted Bonnie Prince Charlie in 1745.

SPAIN
Barcelona (see also Cardona)

Colon • *Avda Catedral 7, tel.: (93) 301 1404; fax: (93) 317 2915* • In Gothic Quarter, overlooks cathedral.

Condes de Barcelona • *P. de Gracia, 75, tel.: 487 3737, fax: 487 1442* • Near the Museu d'Historia de la Medicina, art nouveau style.

Gran Hotel Havana Palace • *Gran Via de les Corts Catalanes, 647, tel.: (93) 412 1115; fax: 412 2611* • A modern hotel behind an historic facade, renovated in 1991.

Cardona

Parador de Cardona • *08261 Cardona (Barcelona), tel.: (93) 869 12 75; fax: (93) 869 16 36* • A sprawling castle perched on a hill, dates from 798.

Carmona (near Seville)

Parador de Carmona • *41410 Carmona (Sevilla), tel.: (954) 14 10 10; fax: (954) 14 17 12* • Also known as Alcazar Del Rey Don Pedro.

Chinchon (near Madrid)

Parador de Chinchon • *Avda. Generalisimo, 1 28470 Chinchon (Madrid), tel.: (91) 894 08 36; fax: (91) 894 09 08* • Set in an ancient convent with a pleasant cloister.

Granada

Parador de Granada • *Alhambra 18009 Granada, tel.: (958) 22 14 40; fax: (958) 22 22 64* • Also known as San Francisco, dates from 1302, the grounds contain the Generalife gardens.

Madrid (also see Chinchon)

Palace • *Plaza de las Cortes 7, tel.: (91) 429 7551; fax: (91) 420 0056* • Turn-of-the-century hotel opposite Neptune fountain and the Prado, stained glass dome over lounge.

Ritz • *Plaza Lealtad 5, tel.: (91) 521 2857; fax: (91) 532 8776* • Garden terrace. Overlooks the Prado, built so guests of King Alfonso XIII could be sumptuously entertained.

Seville

Hotel Alfonso XIII • *San Fernando, 2, 41004 Sevilla, tel.: (954) 222850; fax: (954) 216033* • Grand old hotel in Mudejar style, inner courtyard with fountain.

Hotel Dona Maria • *Don Remondo n. 19, tel.: 4224990; fax: 4229765* • Palace of Contessa de Albalat, near Giralda in the Old Town.

SWEDEN
Malmo

Savoy Hotel • *Norra Vallgatan 62, tel.: 040 702 30* • Old world hotel near railway station.

Stockholm

Diplomat • *Strandvagen 7C, tel.: (08) 663–5800; fax: (08) 783–6634* • Turn-of-the-century townhouse, known as the Bostrom Palace, later became an embassy.

Lady Hamilton ● *Storkyrkobrinken 5, tel.: (08) 23 46 80; telex: 10434* ●
Built as home in 1470 in Old Town beside the Royal Palace.

Lord Nelson ● *Vasterlanggatan 22, tel.: (08) 232390* ● Located on pedestrian street in Old Town, nautical atmosphere.

Reisen ● *Skeppsbron 12–14, tel.: (08) 223260; fax: (08) 20 15 59* ● 18th-century building housed a coffee house, then became a popular watering-hole for seafaring men.

Victory ● *Lilla Nygatan 5, 11128 Stockholm, tel.: (08) 14 30 90; fax: (08) 21 77* ● Nautical theme with a collection of ship models, paintings, 18th century buried treasure.

Malardrottningen Hotel ● *Riddarholmen, 11128 Stockholm, tel.: (08) 24 36 00; fax: (08) 24 36 76* ● 58 cabins. Once Barbara Hutton's yacht, built in 1924 and reconstructed in 1980–82.

Ystad

Continental Hotel ● *Hamngatan 13, Bodx 88, S27122 Ystad, tel.: (411) 137 00* ● Built in 1829, renovated in 1984.

SWITZERLAND
Geneva (Geneve)

Les Armures ● *1, rue du Puits-St. Pierre, CH 1204 Geneve, tel.: (022) 28 91 72, fax: (022) 28 98 46* ● Center of Geneva near St. Peter's Cathedral 17th century setting.

President ● *47, Quai Wilson, CH 1211 Geneve 21, tel.: (022) 731 10 00; fax: (022) 731 22 06* ● On Lake Geneva next door to the old Woodrow Wilson Hotel soon to be a conference center.

Luzerne

Carlton Hotel Tivoli ● *Haldenstrasse 57, CH 6002, tel.: 041 51 30 51; fax: 041 51 19 29* ● Located on the shore of the lake, opened in 1820.

Hotel Zum Rebstock ● *St. Leodegar-Strasse 36006 Luzern, tel.: (041) 51 35 81; fax: (041) 51 39 17* ● The Rebstock was the vintners' meeting place beginning in 1443.

Zurich

Dolder Grand • *Kurhhausstr. 65, 8032, 8000 Zurich ZH, tel.: (251) 62 31; fax: (251) 88 29* • Victorian grand hotel on the mountain, 10 minutes by car from the city or ride the funicular, panoramic view.

Zum Strochen • *Am Weinplatz, 8001 Zurich, tel.: 211 55 10; fax: 211 64 51* • 14th-century hotel between St. Peter and Fraumunster on the bank of the River Limmat.

TURKEY
Istanbul

Pera Palas • *Mesrutiyet Caddesi 98 100 Tepebasi, tel.: 151 45 60* • 145 rooms. Constructed in 1892 especially for Orient-Express passengers.

INDEX